HAWKE

HAWKE
THE PRIME MINISTER

BLANCHE D'ALPUGET

MELBOURNE UNIVERSITY PRESS

A note on Cambodia/Kampuchea: I have consistently kept to Cambodia to avoid confusion from the name changes that occurred during the scope of the narrative.

MELBOURNE UNIVERSITY PRESS
An imprint of Melbourne University Publishing Limited
187 Grattan Street, Carlton, Victoria 3053, Australia
mup-info@unimelb.edu.au
www.mup.com.au

Text © Blanche d'Alpuget, 2010
Design and typography © Melbourne University Publishing Limited, 2010

This book is copyright. Apart from any use permitted under the *Copyright Act 1968* and subsequent amendments, no part may be reproduced, stored in a retrieval system or transmitted by any means or process whatsoever without the prior written permission of the publishers.

Every attempt has been made to locate the copyright holders for material quoted in this book. Any person or organisation that may have been overlooked or misattributed may contact the publisher.

Text design by Phil Campbell
Cover design by Phil Campbell
Typeset by TypeSkill
Printed by Griffin Press, South Australia

National Library of Australia Cataloguing-in-Publication entry

d'Alpuget, Blanche, 1944–
Hawke: The Prime Minister/by Blanche d'Alpuget.
9780522856705 (hbk.)
Hawke, Bob, 1929–
Prime ministers—Australia—Biography.
994.0630924

For my dear friend, Maria Finlay

Contents

Preface	ix
Acknowledgements	xii
Chapter 1	1
Chapter 2	54
Chapter 3	99
Chapter 4	122
Chapter 5	153
Chapter 6	174
Chapter 7	208
Chapter 8	234
Chapter 9	259
Chapter 10	307
Chapter 11	357
Appendix: The Powell Plan for Palestine	372
Notes	376
Bibliography	380
Index	382

Preface

Bob Hawke's political career began in 1929 when his pregnant mother, Ellie, a woman who was both religious and spiritual, found her Bible opening as if of its own volition at the verse in Isaiah that says, 'and the government shall be upon his shoulder'. Ellie Hawke took this as a sign that, disappointingly, the baby she was carrying would be a son and not the daughter she longed for, but that God had destined this son for leadership.

By the early 1980s Hawke was an Australian political phenomenon.

Before he had achieved the destiny foreseen for him more than thirty years earlier, I wrote a biography that explored the tensions in his life, attempting to answer the question people were constantly asking, 'What's he really like?' That book is now a first volume. This is the second volume. It appears at a time when Hawke's brilliant political career is over but the long tail of its comet still shines.

Many books have been written about his period in office, including by Hawke himself. Members of his government have been the subjects of biographies; they have written autobiographies and memoirs; there are academic and other assessments of Hawke's prime ministership; there are books devoted to single issues, like the Combe–Ivanov affair. I have drawn information from all these works, but am most indebted to Paul Kelly's

The End of Certainty, a magnum opus on the economics and politics of the 1980s.

In this biography I have not attempted a full account of Hawke's prime ministership and have not even touched some important areas—the creation of the Aboriginal and Torres Strait Islander Commission (ATSIC), for example. Instead I have tried to answer the question, 'What sort of leader was he?'

For answers I turned to the prime minister's personal staff and senior public servants. They are people whom other writers have ignored, often from necessity, since an unofficial—and, in some cases, an official—vow of silence was cast upon them while Hawke was in office. I was fortunate that Hawke's office family are now at liberty to speak and that their memories of those days are clear and sharp. Only one professed scant recall. But constrained by time and distance—some were living abroad—I was unable to interview them all. I did speak to at least two from each period of Hawke's four terms as prime minister. Unless otherwise indicated, all quoted statements, direct and indirect, are from interviews or remarks made to me. Except with the famously anonymous and invisible Peter Barron, with two journalists and two Chinese, whom I had to interview by telephone (one with the help of an interpreter), I tape recorded all interviews. These tapes are archived in the Bob Hawke Prime Ministerial Centre in Adelaide as a resource for future researchers. Many of the interviews happened in noisy venues—in hotel lobbies and bars, with the sound of ice makers, espresso machines and exuberant patrons creating colour and inaudibility. My badly spelt and typed transcriptions are also archived and, in most cases, fill in the audio gaps. There are also properly spelt and typed transcriptions of some later interviews by Elizabeth Dale, who came to my assistance when I was very pressed for time.

Since he had already published his memoirs, the person I avoided as an interviewee was the subject himself. Only when

I had the manuscript almost finished did I ask him to give comments. There are no taped interviews with Hawke.

The account of his 2003 trip to Ramallah to see Yasser Arafat is drawn from notes that I, being present, made at the time. The descriptions of meetings of Education International and the lunch at which the Boao Forum for Asia was planned are also from my own memory. I hope readers will enjoy discovering these and other aspects of Hawke's life that have been, so far, unrecorded or unknown in Australia.

Blanche d'Alpuget
Sydney, April 2010

Acknowledgements

This book owes its existence to Louise Adler of Melbourne University Publishing. Over lunch in April 2008, Ms Adler so exercised the mesmeric persuasion for which she is famous that I agreed to her urgings to update my 1982 biography of R. J. Hawke. When the coffee arrived we were discussing an addition to the original book—perhaps 20 000 words, perhaps more—to be launched just before Hawke's eightieth birthday on 9 December 2009. It was this milestone birthday that persuaded me to undertake the effort I knew would be in store. But, despite setting aside nearly all my other commitments, a civilised life and the company of my friends, I missed the deadline.

The original concept of an add-on turned out to be lucky, however, because it forced me to bring into focus what I thought would be the most important thing I could say about Hawke as prime minister. I would leave to others a full account of his prime ministership, which will perhaps have to wait another ten years, until Cabinet and other classified documents are released. I decided to address the question of his leadership.

By the time I had the manuscript finished, Ms Adler and I realised we had a problem: the expanded book would be a brick, almost 1000 pages long, so we decided to publish my new work as a separate volume.

Many people have helped me. I would like to thank first Hawke's current office staff, Jill Saunders and Francie Grew, who assisted with digging out speeches and providing me with space in his office to read Hansards from the period 1983 to 1991. Hawke's personal advisers and public service staff from his prime ministership have been extraordinarily helpful in finding time for interviews, some of them several times. I thank Peter Barron, John Bowan, Craig Emerson, Graham Freudenberg, Ross Garnaut, Bob Hogg, Sandy Hollway and Hugh White. Former politicians Kim Beazley, John Dawkins, Michael Duffy, Nick Greiner, the Hon. John Howard, Graham Richardson, Warwick Smith and Ralph Willis were also gracious, as were public servants Mike Codd, Michael Costello, Helen Williams and Richard Woolcott. David Combe, Michael McHugh and Neil Young were very helpful in explaining aspects of the Combe–Ivanov affair. I sought to interview the Hon. Paul Keating, through direct and indirect approaches, but he declined. He was, however, gracious in refusal and spent almost an hour on the telephone explaining his reasons.

MUP provided press cuttings for me, but in addition I sought interviews with three political journalists: Paul Kelly, Brian Toohey and Marian Wilkinson. All three were generous in sharing their insights. Josh Klenbort, a colleague from Shanghai, provided fascinating insights into the early years of Hawke's association with China.

Chapter 11 deals with Hawke's time after leaving parliament, and for this period I want to thank the contributions of President Fidel Ramos of the Philippines, Jiang Xiaosong and Long Yongtu, respectively founder and former secretary general of the Boao Forum for Asia. Liz Ho, director of the Bob Hawke Prime Ministerial Centre, gave me a long and fascinating interview of which, alas, I have been able to use very little. I am confident it will be of use and interest to future researchers. Fred van Leeuwen, secretary general of Education International, found time for an interview in Brussels in the midst of a schedule of international meetings.

My close friend and confidant, John Lonie, read early drafts and discussed the structure of the narrative with me, sometimes over my kitchen table in Sydney, sometimes on long walks beside the Brisbane River. The finished work owes much of its dramatic pace to him.

At MUP, executive publisher Foong Ling Kong gave calm, lucid support. Susan Keogh, whom MUP assigned to edit the book, was a pleasure to work with: we developed a certain intimacy and affectionate feeling for each other although we have never met, and I found her excellent as an editor.

Finally, I would like to acknowledge the help of Bob Hawke himself, who provided quotes on request, corrected errors, read the page proofs and made many useful suggestions. I also thank his daughters, Sue and Rosslyn, for their quoted comments, and my son, Louis, for bringing my computer skills up to date.

Blanche d'Alpuget
Sydney, April 2010

1

NOTHING IS AS ENIGMATIC as the wheel of history: some it favours, some it will crush—but who, and why, is a guessing game. Aware of that yet ignoring it, every political leader embraces an irresistible urge to try to take hold of history. Gough Whitlam, brilliant, imperious, an inspiration to a generation, was the greatest leader of the Opposition Australia had ever known. He laid his hand on the wheel and it flung him, chariot and all, over a cliff. The Prime Minister and the government he led were politically destroyed, but history favoured Whitlam with the radiant legacy of a social and cultural reformer.

Malcolm Fraser, a giant with a mirthless laugh, snatched the steering from Whitlam, only to shrink. His achievements were minor, and he ended walking from the stage of public life in tears. It was a surreal moment, as if a boulder had sobbed and, in a man of Fraser's temperament, an unforgivable weakness.

Now there was Hawke, whose entry into parliament caused Bill Hayden to declare, 'The disaster of my life'.

Hayden, who had lost one election to Fraser, had been leader of the Australian Labor Party for six years and had rebuilt it from the Whitlam wreck of 1977, which had been a political catastrophe for Labor even worse than that of 1975. Hayden constructed a fighting force with a chance of winning the 1983 election. Hawke, from the moment he decided to overcome his weakness for alcohol, control his social behaviour and stand for preselection for the seat of Wills, was determined to seize the leadership for himself. He would not wait for another election to pass before he did so. But always impatient, optimistic and boundless in self-confidence, he made his grab too soon and lost a Caucus challenge to Hayden in 1982.

Hawke's solution to his setback was ingenious. He changed tack, setting out on a chess game in the upper echelons of the party, allowing him to bypass the Caucus, for he had realised, a little too late, that Caucus' mind was set in parliamentary traditions. As a new member, Hawke did not fit them. He had not served his time. Two decades of fighting for Labor ideals, first as the advocate, then as the president of the ACTU, did not count for much in parliament, where nobody became leader of a party without first serving a good five to ten years in the House. Hawke's only virtue, and questionable at that as far as Caucus was concerned for it was a nest of envies, was that the Australian people loved him and would vote for him if given the chance.

The pieces Hawke set up on the chessboard were his national popularity, the political force of the trade union movement inside the Labor Party and sections of the news media. With these he plotted to capture not only all of Hayden's pieces, but to trap his king. The pragmatic New South Wales Right swung behind Hawke but the Victorian Right, less pragmatic, more idealistic, was still for Hayden. The game dragged on through the torpid Christmas–January holiday of 1982–83. Hayden's friends and advisers were away. Nobody could find the key man, Senator John Button of Victoria, nor know that he was on an island in the South Pacific with his colleague, Michael Duffy. Both were Hayden men. Away from the hectic emotions of parliament and in the balm of the tropics, they discussed the future of their party and its leader. Button had known Hawke for years, did not like him much and never would. But he returned from Fiji convinced that Hawke, not Hayden, must lead Labor at the next election. He wrote Hayden a letter urging him to step aside for the good of the party. It was a devastating blow for the leader. Hayden had difficulty in trusting others, but he had considered Button a friend.

Hawke now had Hayden in check. The only move through which Hayden could succeed needed total self-confidence that *he* would win the 1983 election. But Hayden, a thoughtful, honourable, gentle though deeply angry man, was easily assailed by self-doubt. While he was convinced that Hawke could win the 1983 election, he was not sure he could.

On 3 February 1983, behind closed doors, in the secrecy of an ALP executive meeting in the Commonwealth Offices in Ann Street, Brisbane, Hayden resigned as leader of the Labor Party. Away to the south in Canberra, just hours earlier Malcolm Fraser sensed danger and rushed to Government House for permission to call an election. As Fraser had snatched the prime ministership from Whitlam by a well-timed dash to Government House in 1975, he was to repay his debt to history by an ill-timed one. When he arrived at Yarralumla unannounced, the Queen's representative declined to receive him: the Prime Minister needed an appointment.

By the time Fraser returned several hours later at a time convenient to the Governor-General, he was too late. A few hours earlier he would have been fighting Hayden, whom he felt confident of defeating once more. Now he was matched against Hawke. When a messenger entered the executive meeting in Ann Street with urgent news, the room, until that moment filled with passionate acrimony, exploded with laughter. 'We've tricked the bastard!' someone shouted.

Hawke had usurped without a Caucus vote, without a drop of blood spilt in public. Behind the scenes, where the struggle had been conducted, Graham Richardson noted that Hawke had been ruthless and 'there was a smell of blood ... more blood ... than the entire stage at the end of *Hamlet*'. He said, 'There are many people who want to be the leader—there were eight or ten of them in the Caucus at the time—but very few have the courage to challenge.' Richardson was the New South Wales Right's numbers man, busy for months putting to the sword enemies of his hero. 'I worshiped Hawkey,' he recalled wistfully. 'I would have killed for him.'

With the nostalgia of a love cherished now only in memory, he added, 'And I did. I did.'

For his part, Hawke already subscribed to the political axiom: 'A statesman never stoops into the gutter, but makes sure he has around him those whose loins are suppler.'

That night, a live television interview took place that made Hawke's supporters wonder if they had just made an egregious mistake. The old Hawke, the wild man who would shout down a crowd when sober and when drunk shout obscenities in a bar, the man they believed was dead and buried—or if not dead, at least prisoner in some dungeon far from the light of television cameras—suddenly seemed to have escaped. Hawke was teetotal now: how long, they wondered, would that last under pressure? ALP polling, never publicly released, had revealed that the electorate, who in large swathes adored him, thought him brilliant, brave, handsome, touched by some magic—a rolled-gold Aussie larrikin, but a super-sized one, a hero—was at the same time apprehensive that his behaviour could embarrass the nation. They confided to pollsters their concern that a Prime Minister Hawke may not deport himself appropriately with the Queen. Mr Fraser, unlikeable as he was, nevertheless knew how to behave as a gentleman; Hawke's larrikinism could be sufficient reason not to vote Labor. Hawke did not know any of this, but he well understood that his demeanour from the moment he became leader was of critical importance.

The dramatic events of 3 February—Fraser's double dash to the Governor-General, Hayden's sudden resignation, the charismatic new Labor leader, a federal election just weeks away—seemed to have sprung out of the air. That night the public thronged to their television sets. There was a huge audience for Hawke's first in-depth interview as leader, to be shown live on ABC. Hawke was tense; the day, although victorious, had been emotionally draining: there had been hard bargaining over the division of spoils before Hayden would give way. It had required Lionel Bowen, who had converted to Hawke's side only recently, to give up his dream of being Foreign minister. Hayden insisted on that, and he insisted that his closest allies, John Dawkins, Peter Walsh and Neal Blewett, be given the ministries they wanted. For a while in the Ann Street meeting there was a stalemate as Hayden and Bowen shouted abuse at each other. Then Bowen gave way. The deal was done, the doors were opened, and a group of smiling men presented a united front to the waiting media.

Richard Carleton, a star television journalist, was the interviewer that night. Carleton was tall and dark-haired with a smugly condescending manner. His long teeth, long nose and small chin gave him the appearance of a very handsome rat. Carleton prided himself on his skill in provoking interviewees. After a few desultory questions, he leaned forward, lowered his voice to a suggestively insinuating tone and asked, 'Mr Hawke, do you have blood on your hands tonight?'

Around the nation hundreds of thousands of viewers were transfixed by Carleton's effrontery, and on tenterhooks for Hawke's response.

Hawke seemed momentarily stunned. His eyes narrowed and became hooded. He sat perfectly still, focusing his gaze on

Carleton's face. Then there was a flash of such fury from Hawke that Carleton appeared to have been hit in the solar plexus. It was not what Hawke said—'You haven't improved, have you?'—that was shocking, it was how deadly in aggression he appeared. His close supporters were appalled. Bob Hogg, then the secretary of the Victorian ALP, recalled,

> There was a campaign committee meeting that night—the first for Bob and the last for Bill. They were both there, so it was awkward. But what had just happened had to be addressed. I said to Bob, 'If you go on like that, you can kiss your arse goodbye.' And he copped it. It would have been better to say it in private, but there was no opportunity. We were straight into the campaign.

Apart from one interview in Brisbane with John Barton during which Hawke became testy, the rest of the campaign went without a hitch. As his press officer, Geoff Walsh, said, 'The thing about Bob is he's obviously very intelligent and he's incredibly disciplined, and once he was convinced that what had been put to him made absolute sense, he acted on it.'

Hawke had a vision for Australia that he captured in the slogan: 'Reconciliation, Recovery, Reconstruction'. The party under Hayden had built a platform of policies to take to the electorate, but it was Hawke's vision that fired the campaign. 'Reconciliation' gave it a churchy ring, evoking Jesus reuniting God and man, but it was authentic Hawke. He promised that, if elected, he would hold an economic summit of employers and employees, state governments, social security groups and churches, to work out some new co-operative arrangement to help the country out of the hole it was in. It all sounded to the hardheads in the party kind of fluffy, but they were not willing to argue. Their leader was fighting an election in the midst of a national crisis—and if he won he would have to fix the country any way he could. The economy was stalled and New South Wales, Queensland, Victoria, Tasmania and South Australia were in the grip of the worst drought on record. It lasted 334 days, affected 4 million people and destroyed and damaged $3 billion (in 1983 terms) worth of property. Dust storms caused the loss of millions of dollars of topsoil; a total of 86 million sheep and 14 million cattle were without adequate food and water and many had to be destroyed. Wheat production fell by 37 per cent, with similar falls in barley, oats, rice, cotton and sugar. Unemployment in some rural areas was 40 per cent. An unknown number of destitute farmers died 'by accident', in sheds, under the wheels of tractors, in the brown shallow water left in their dams. On the midafternoon of 8 February, a dust storm covered Melbourne in choking darkness, and eight days later, on Ash Wednesday, a conflagration destroyed more buildings and property—including some of Australia's most beautiful paintings—than any other bushfire. It also claimed seventy-five lives. Hundreds of thousands more lives were being slowly destroyed by unemployment and inflation, both just under 11 per cent. For eighty years Australia, once one of the two richest counties on earth—the other was Argentina—had been sliding slowly down the economic ladder. By 1983 it was feeble. The nation was full of social cracks and fissures, without common purpose, adrift, and with no new ideas about how to rescue itself. If Hawke wanted a summit, it was worth a try.

On a hot night in a suite at the Lakeside Hotel in Canberra, surrounded by his wife, Hazel, his father, the Reverend Mr Clem Hawke (now retired as a Congregational minister), a few close friends and staff, Hawke learned from watching television that he was officially Australia's twenty-third prime minister. The atmosphere was happy, relieved and subdued: everyone was conscious of the wild euphoria of the Whitlam victory a decade earlier, and the disasters that had followed. 'Our win was tempered by a good deal more realism than the Whitlam victory,' Hawke said. By odd coincidence his election was fifty years to the day (adjusted for international time), since Franklin D. Roosevelt had offered the frightened and wretched people of the United States a 'New Deal'. Hawke, similarly, wanted and needed to rebuild Australia, and recognised his task would be difficult. Already his mind was tinged with the knowledge of tragedy with which, Max Weber wrote, 'all action, but especially political action, is interwoven'. For the new Australian leader the moment was also tinged with sadness as he reflected aloud several times what a pity it was that his mother, Ellie, whose photograph he carried in his wallet, had missed seeing the fulfilment of her dreams. But it was a personal comfort that his father, whose eighty-fifth birthday it was, was with him, and brimming with joy.

Bill Hayden, according to his friend, John Dawkins, who was 'as close as anyone could be with Bill', had sulked during the campaign and was sulky for some months after it. Asked on television what he thought about Hawke's seizing of the leadership from him, Hayden remarked that a drover's dog could win the election. It was hard to know if his scorn was directed at himself, at Hawke, or at his colleagues who had pressed him to step aside. For many, perhaps a majority, of professional politicians the unspoken apprehension was: Hawke's an election winner, he has the ruthless courage of a leader, but does he have good political judgment?

John Button, whose letter to Hayden had ended the chess game, had also written in it,

> I must say that even some of Bob's closest supporters have doubts about his capacities to lead the party successfully, in that they do not share his own estimate of

his ability. The Labor Party is, however, desperate to win the coming election.

Button was a droplet of a man, a thimble of wit, vitality, charm and scepticism. He was a very attractive character who, as a university student, was wildly popular for his knowledge of scores of dirty songs, and, according to Hawke, the most consummate liar he ever met in politics. In the same letter to Hayden, Button dismissed Hawke as 'a media performer and winner of popularity polls'.

Hawke's political judgment—in every successful political leader an intuitive quality, observable but unteachable, apparently inborn—would determine if his government would survive and prosper or crash and burn. The magnificent Whitlam's political judgment turned out to be so inept that, from his starting point as an ALP Moses leading the Children of Labor out of the wilderness, his ending was as a kind of political Bhagwan Shree Rajneesh, the guru whose cult of freedom degenerated into orgy and criminality, as the Whitlam government was to degenerate into desperation and a folly that resembled madness. Hayden, who admired Whitlam's capacious intellect and oratory, said of him, 'He should have handed over to someone else to run the government, because he couldn't. He just couldn't. He had no idea.'

The omens for Hawke were mixed: he was possessed of an abundance of courage, the cardinal political virtue, since the first job of a political leader is to *fight*. But Whitlam was courageous too. Political leaders have to inspire confidence and they must not only possess courage but also the flair to display it theatrically. Like justice, courage in politics must be seen to be done and the leader must be a good actor. Hawke was—but so was Whitlam. And Fraser, through his sheer physical dominance—his giant's body, brass forehead, iron jaw, deep-set eyes—achieved the same effect: he embodied the patriarch come to restore order to a chaotic family. Another essential of leadership is a steely will, a true intransigence—perhaps the most dangerous of a leader's qualities for, if combined with poor judgment, intransigence can lead not just to political defeat but to national catastrophe (as citizens were to learn, all over again in the twenty-first century, from the case of George W. Bush). Whitlam, Fraser and Hawke had steely wills, but Hawke's had only recently been tested by giving up alcohol, and usurping Hayden. His philandering, though potentially dangerous, had not been a cause for censure in the Men's Union of the Labor Party—or any Australian political party, since by mutual consent such matters were either forgivable, unexceptional or taboo. Parliament House was and always had been a place of intrigues and *liaisons dangereux*.

By Hawke's own estimation, one of his strongest attributes as a leader was the one John Button had scorned: his popularity. Hayden recalled campaigning in a shopping centre with Hawke:

> a dumpy little woman held up her baby—it was no more than six months old—held her baby over the head of the crowd so it could see the Great Man. She seemed to be telling the baby, 'Look at the Great Man! His feet don't touch the ground when he walks.'

Already tokens of love were arriving in Hawke's office, as they had been for years: cards and letters, portraits done in oils, in pencil, in watercolours, his face embroidered on cushions, even woven into a rug. His pottery head served as beer mugs. In plastic, he became a wine cask.

Hawke had a clear, simple-sounding, ambition: to improve the lives of ordinary Australians by reforming the economy and the social security system. His motivation sprang from his deepest feelings of what he believed in and what was sacred to him. After his childhood and youth in the Congregational church, in his early years at university, Hawke had been a Sunday school teacher and had preached sermons at Young Christian Movement camps. His brand of Christianity had been dull, worthy and teetotal. It was untouched by ecstasy. By his late twenties he had abandoned the church, did not know whether he believed in God or not, and had rejected all Christian dogma. But Christian principles were in Hawke's bones and he found their expression not in lifeless Sunday ritual but in the vibrant, communal, morally cohesive and uplifting labour movement. As for many others, this was his new and true religion. And it was ecstatic: the ecstasy of drinking together in bonded fellowship with men who shared broad ideals for society and would fight as a band of brothers to achieve them.

The Australian Labor Party of Hawke's childhood and youth was the glorious union-based party of John Curtin and Ben Chifley. Curtin, a man with a serious drinking problem, like Hawke, and a West Australian, steered the nation to safety through World War II. Chifley, calm, simple and wise, prepared Australia for prosperity in peace. The ALP of Hawke's childhood and youth was the party of national pride, led by honourable, compassionate men—among them his uncle, Bert, who was Premier of Western Australia. There had been Labor governments in almost every state.

As Hawke turned twenty, it all collapsed. For most of the next thirty-four years Labor was the party of Opposition: impotent, angry, scarred with the wounds of disappointment, a party of energetic pathology. Hawke wanted to regain Labor's honour, and restore Australia's prestige among the nations. But what he wanted to do would run headlong into cherished popular attitudes and the money and muscle of vested interests. Only with the Australian people behind him could he hope to succeed.

On 5 March, when Hawke's television would confirm that Labor had won that day's election and he was now prime minister, the national mood became hopeful, but apprehensive. The Liberals had run a fear campaign, saying that if Labor won people would be better off hiding their money under their beds than entrusting it to banks. Fraser had screamed into a megaphone at a Melbourne rally that Labor would 'rob' the Australian people 'to pay for their mad schemes' and repeated this threat in other venues. Andrew Peacock, who was to become Liberal leader after Fraser, predicted a 15 per cent devaluation of the dollar. Promptly, $2.7 billion in capital fled the country and on Monday, 7 March, another $200 million left.

The intellectual elite, of which Hawke was a member, knew that the economic system under which Australia had operated since its birth as a nation was dying, and was dragging the country with it towards the grave. But they were a tiny few. The mass of Australians did not realise that the entire system, bit by bit, would have to change. They knew that something was wrong, that a ten-year cycle of boom and bust, of inflation, wage hikes, then unemployment, had beset national life. In the 1960s middle-class Australians could afford a holiday in Europe, returning with prêt-à-porter designer clothes and other luxuries. No more. The nation lurched from crisis to crisis, each wave of wage rises and unemployment growing higher. In 1980 Lee Kuan Yew, the Prime Minister of Singapore, remarked, 'If it goes on in the same way, Australia will become the poor white trash of Asia.' To be berated by Singapore, a nation the size of Sydney, dependent for its water supply on Malaysia, was indicative of the scant respect Australia commanded abroad.

At this remove it's difficult to recall how divided, uncertain of themselves and insecure Australians felt at the beginning of 1983. Although Malcolm Fraser was an ardent anti-racist, an upholder of human rights and the creator of national multiculturalism, tragically for him his method of seizing power poisoned his image in the electorate. What's more, he seemed to have more compassion for an impoverished black African than he did for an impoverished white Australian. He became a divisive leader, setting group against group. His government pilloried the unemployed as 'dole bludgers'; women demanding equal rights were dismissed as 'lesbians'. There was constant industrial strife. It was a harsh, uncivil time.

Hawke's solution was the 'Economic Summit', at which he would fully unveil an 'Accord' with the trade union movement. Through a summit, he believed he could put into effect the slogan of the campaign: 'Reconciliation, Recovery, Reconstruction'. He wanted to end the dog-eat-dog temper of the Fraser years and restore the Christian ethos of tolerance and respect for human brotherhood in which he had been raised. In those days secularism was virtually a religion in itself. No Australian political leader could afford to talk openly in churchy language without being labelled wet. Hawke himself now thought in a different terminology, but those with sharp noses got a whiff of the theology behind it. Neville Wran, Labor Premier of New South Wales, summed up what the hardheads thought when he said of the summit, 'If the greedy bastards want spirituality they should join the fucking Hare Krishnas.' The conservative side of politics, and the public service, considered the idea simply odd. 'They were all sceptical,' Hawke recalled. 'They went along with it just to humour me.' He was, for the moment, Mr Charisma, so exceptional that he was almost a fetish object. He was a multimillionaire in political capital, and while it lasted he could spend it as he wished. The Summit, he decreed, would be held in Parliament House before the first sitting of the new government.

Before any action could be taken, on the Sunday morning after the election, the secretary of the Treasury, John Stone, called on the new Prime Minister. The message he brought was hair-raising: the projected budget deficit for 1983/84 was $9.6 billion dollars (in 2010 terms about $43 billion). It was the largest budget deficit in history and, in its percentage of GDP 'almost without precedent among the major OECD countries in the post-war period', Stone's official note said. Someone in Treasury had leaked this news of a huge deficit to Hawke during the campaign, but he had decided to keep it secret until he had been officially informed. He commented, 'I was painfully aware of the implications of the figure for our program, and for our economic management of the country.'

While painful for Hawke's election promises, the deficit was political gold. Hawke had a huge economic headache but also a huge stick with which to beat the Opposition, and a huge lever for reform. Australia was one of the world's oldest and at the time feistiest and most argumentative democracies. All democracies demand explanation of policy. In Australia no leader could hope to persuade the people to accept something they did not like without explaining the very good reason for it. With the drama of a national economic crisis to announce because of the deficit, Hawke could begin the economic education of the electorate. On that foundation, he could successfully reform.

The same day that Stone visited, the weather changed. It began to rain. In a country town during the campaign Hawke had joked to some locals, 'Elect me, and I'll fix the drought!' By the end of the first week the whole of the parched east coast of Australia was awash with life-restoring water. The nation rejoiced. Hawke, laughing, said, '*I* did it!' The press began calling him 'The Messiah'.

But unknown to the new Prime Minister, on the night before the election something had happened that could smother all his hopes for national rebirth.

In 1983 the Cold War was being fought in deadly earnest, but it was almost invisible in Australia and analogous to a greenhouse gas—undetectable unless one was aware of it, and went looking. George Orwell had coined the term 'Cold War' in late

1945, when he warned of a 'peace that is not peace'. Since then the Cold War had become the toxic air the planet breathed and to which it had become accustomed. Hawke's entire adult life and almost all his enmities within the trade union movement and the Labor Party, stretching from the 1960s into the 1980s, were infected with the unseen poison of a peace that is not peace. After the bitterness of the Vietnam War, disillusion with international military adventures took hold of Australia, so much so that foreign policy played almost no part in the election campaign and almost no part in politics. During the Fraser years, little had been done in foreign policy terms: there were no major military deployments and hardly any minor ones—except a small force sent to Afghanistan, which the Soviet Union had invaded on Christmas Eve, 1979. Paul Keating, the physically beautiful, sharp-as-a-whip bovver boy from the New South Wales Right, spoke for most people when he interjected in parliament 'Who cares about Afghanistan? Anyway, where is Afghanistan?' Indonesia's invasion of East Timor and America's bases in Australia were left-wing issues, boring for the rest of the electorate. But in January 1981 the idiosyncratic and strangely gifted Ronald Reagan took office as President of the United States, and almost immediately announced his goal of confronting the Soviet Union. His aggressive stance, combined with his amiable manner, mellifluous voice and previous career as a movie actor, made him in Australia a figure of incredulity and fun. His obsession with the Soviet Union, which he dubbed the 'Evil Empire', seemed to opinion-makers in the media and academia both inscrutable and dangerous.

Until Reagan, there was virtually no national recognition that, if the policy of mutually assured destruction (MAD) between the United States and the Soviet Union broke down and a nuclear war ensued, the bases in Australia would be targets. Nuclear-armed Soviet submarines standing off the north and west coasts would attack them, and probably sooner rather than later.

Australia, as a United States ally and a central cog in America's military intelligence machine, was both a Cold War and a hot war target and as such the Soviet Union since the 1950s was spying on it. Unfortunately—or fortunately—not only did Australians not realise the country would be attacked in a nuclear war, they did not believe in the reality of the world of espionage. Australia had an internal counter-espionage service, ASIO, and a little-known external one, ASIS. Labor had established ASIO but the party had grown fervently hostile to it, thanks to the Petrov Affair in 1954. Petrov was a Soviet spy whom ASIO persuaded to defect, but Labor, in an unbelievable act of folly, managed to turn what was a political plus for Menzies into a total disaster for itself. The Petrov Affair was the fine crack that opened a chasm in the Labor Party, the split that would keep it out of office for almost two decades and sear the words 'ASIO' and 'Russian spy' through Labor foreheads into its tribal consciousness as symbols of danger, defeat and humiliation. Members of the Labor Party's Left and, especially, clandestine members of the Communist Party who had succeeded in infiltrating the ALP felt personally threatened by ASIO. During the Whitlam years Labor hostility and paranoia about ASIO had been so severe that the Attorney-General, Lionel Murphy, had in person 'raided' its offices in Melbourne, searching for information that, supposedly, it was withholding from him. Labor's platform for many elections had been to abolish ASIO completely and in the last mad days of his government, Whitlam summarily dismissed the head of ASIS over a trifle that had been beaten up in the press. There was institutionalised contempt and distrust on both sides.

On Friday, 4 March 1983, the night before Hawke and his inner circle gathered to watch the election result in the Lakeside Hotel, David Combe, the former secretary of the ALP, had dinner with the first secretary of the Soviet embassy, Valeriy Ivanov, at Ivanov's house in Canberra. Dinner began rather early and ended late and David Combe had a lot to drink. He also had a lot to say. He disparaged Hawke's 1979 visit to Moscow, 'at the height of his drinking', he recalled to Ivanov, during which Hawke had asked for, and had believed he had achieved, the release of Soviet Jews. As prime minister, Combe asserted, Hawke might restrict Australian–Soviet trade were he to attempt once more to have Jews released, and to fail. Combe was certain that Labor would win the election scheduled for the next day—the same day, by the time he left Ivanov's house—and his excitement for his party was mingled with a certain resentment that he had put in eight years as national secretary, years of struggle and grinding disappointment, only to be relegated to bystander status for the victory parade. Eighteen months earlier he had resigned as national secretary to set himself up as a lobbyist and business consultant. It was a career move that a half-dozen smart young-men-about-town, former political staffers from both sides of politics, had already made. They were considered trendy, but not quite respectable.

Combe's wife, Meena Blesing, was a partner in the company and mother of his four sons. (In 1981 Caroline Combe, as she then was, had become a follower of Rajneesh and changed both her names.) Combe was eager to foster trade with the USSR, which, until recently, had been one of Australia's largest trading partners, the balance being heavily in Australia's favour. He was a member of the Australia–USSR Friendship Society, and in 1982 had visited the country as its guest. While in Moscow Paul Dibb, an Australian defence and intelligence analyst, had warned Combe that a senior official of the umbrella organisation, the Union of Friendship Societies, Andrey Parasteyev, was 'a bad bastard'—by which Dibb meant he was from the KGB. Both Combe and his wife suspected that Ivanov was a KGB officer. Why they did not take the next step of imagination and consider that, if this were the case, there was a chance that Ivanov was under surveillance is explicable only in the context of the contempt in which Labor people held ASIO. A nightmare for the Combes and their children was taking form.

David Combe was a tall, gangling man with a mop of black curly hair and a personality so open, so hearty, so expansive, so obviously good-natured, so essentially innocent, he put one in mind of a huge puppy. There was something of the soft sweetness of a child in his nature, as if he had carried into adulthood the Anglican chorister and altar boy he once was. He had grown up in a conservative Adelaide family with staunch Liberal-voting parents. 'My mother,' he recalled, 'used to take the Labor "How to Vote" card on polling day and very ostentatiously tear it up.' The family was socially respectable, his cousin on his father's side being a former archbishop, but they were not well off and David could only attend a private school, Prince Alfred's, thanks to winning a scholarship. The school was associated with the Methodist church and unlike St Peter's, the Anglican college, had no record of notable left-wing alumni, but boasted a long menu of Liberal parliamentarians. At university, Combe joined the Liberal Club. His study of politics, and the 1961 election campaign, began his rebellion. He was working part-time in a service station to help the family finances. During 1961, he said,

> guys whom I'd been serving for years would come in asking if they could have ten bob's worth of petrol on the slate, so they could go looking for work. Then I'd go home and see Menzies on the television say, 'The only people who are not working are those who will not work.' This was terribly wrong, to me. It upset me greatly.

Soon afterwards he met the state Labor MP, Don Dunstan,

> and I was totally captivated by him. He invited me to lunch in Parliament House ... [and this started]

> a long association. Most Sundays I would go to his home in Norwood, sit down and learn at the feet of the master.

In those days Dunstan was married and he and his wife were both superb cooks. Combe never suspected that Dunstan was bisexual, although his sister did, referring to Dunstan as her brother's 'boyfriend'. In August 1962 Dunstan persuaded Combe to join the Labor Party. 'So I went home and told my parents that I'd joined the Labor Party and my mother took to her sickbed. Neither of them would speak to me for several days.' Finally one night when Combe and his father were washing the dishes after dinner, they had a man-to-man talk. Combe senior said, 'This has come as a great shock to your mother and me, but I suppose we have to accept it.' Then he added, 'But promise me one thing: promise me you'll never come home and tell us you've decided to become a Catholic.'

Around 1964 Combe met Hawke when the star trade union advocate was scheduled to come to South Australia to address a Young Labor seminar, and Combe was designated his chauffeur. He knew that Hawke was the son of a Congregationalist minister and assumed he would be teetotal.

> It was a stinking hot Adelaide day, and I had been playing tennis for the ALP tennis club, and I was determined to say to him, 'Look, Mr Hawke—I don't know about you, but I've got to have a beer.' We met at the TAA counter and the first thing he said to me was, 'Jesus Christ! Where can we get a beer?

A friendship began immediately. From the start their relationship was familial—Combe took Hawke home to meet his parents that very afternoon—and accepting. Bill Hayden recalled 'going to Combe's home one day and Bob was there, coming out of a bender, and he was in a terrible state. Combe had been that kind of friend to him.' In the Labor movement, through a century of hard times and disappointments, 'mateship' and 'sticking by your mates' had developed the status of a blood bond.

But by 1983 Hawke had already on two occasions been angry with Combe, once justly, once not. The first was over the Iraqi Loans Affair, perhaps the worst folly of the dying Whitlam government when Combe, as secretary, and Whitlam, as leader, had agreed to borrow money for the ALP from the Ba'ath Socialist Party of Iraq, already then a heinous organisation given to torture, murder and public executions. Hawke, as president of the party, was beside himself with rage when he learned of the plan, but his handling of an ALP national executive meeting in 1976 that was held to decide how Combe and others be punished—expulsion from the party was a strongly suggested option—was deft and generous, leaving Combe deeply grateful to him. Then in early 1980, when Hawke (who had not yet become teetotal) was already set upon overthrowing Hayden, he berated Combe in a bar in front of others, including Stuart Hornery, the chairman of the building and development conglomerate Lend Lease, over his support for Hayden. It was an ugly scene but they got over it. It would be fair to say that Hawke doubted Combe's judgment.

Despite believing the Soviet First Secretary was a KGB agent, the Combes were confident it was nothing to worry about, although his very name may have given them pause to reflect. Meena was particularly well read and most certainly familiar with the classic novel of Soviet oppression *Darkness at Noon*, in which the unfortunate character under suspicion is entangled by a man called Ivanov. In a book she wrote about the affair when it was over she noted, 'we both knew that Ivanov was not dangerous'.

Sadly, they knew no such thing.

One

Not without reason is espionage known as the second-oldest profession: its lineage stretches to the fall of Troy and further back in the mists of prehistory. Over millennia the world's intelligence services have developed an assembly of sophisticated skills, but spy movies and books presented espionage as so whacky that nobody outside the loop took it seriously. In the early 1980s, there was little understanding of how a spy could, by patient cunning, turn an honest but humanly flawed citizen into a type of slave. It happens through grooming or 'cultivating' as it was termed. Combe was a superb target to cultivate: he knew everyone in the new government, knew their quirks and weaknesses, knew their staff members and their oddities, he was keen to make money, he loved to eat and drink. He was the perfect Trojan horse to penetrate the fortress of government. He needed no access to secret documents—that might or might not come later and almost certainly not from him. All he had to do was *talk*. Over dinner on the night before the election, he boasted of the access he enjoyed to the men who were about to become Labor ministers. He suggested that at their next meal together, Bill Hayden, the soon-to-be Foreign minister, and his wife, Dallas, should be invited along. He also revealed he thought the party owed him something substantial for his years of service, telling Ivanov, 'I'm entitled to something. I want my job for the boys: Ambassador, Moscow, will suit me—thank you very much.' He also mused on being appointed chairman of Qantas. And in what must have been Tchaikovsky to Russian ears, he spoke bitterly against the United States, saying he believed the CIA had destabilised the Whitlam government, and had gone unpunished for it. He wanted, he said, to 'really nail the Americans'.

Unconsidered by Combe but not, it seems, by Ivanov, there was a nest of scorpions in the house; ASIO, whose name in cable traffic for many years was SCORPION, had bugged the residence (as it had a number of other diplomatic buildings in

Canberra, to the astonished, sometimes sour, approval of the new Labor ministers when they found out). It already knew Ivanov was from the KGB. Its job was to catch him seducing someone. On reading the transcript of Combe's conversation that night, the case officer monitoring Ivanov realised that ASIO had an exquisite dilemma: the organisation was about to trap a Soviet spy, its first since 1963 (a man named Skripov), but how would the new Labor government react to the news that a favoured son was being cultivated? Harvey Barnett, who had been an ASIS officer, now ran ASIO. He decided to keep listening and see what developed. Neither Hawke nor the Attorney-General, Gareth Evans, was to be told anything—yet.

Hawke and his staff were flat out planning the Summit, scheduled for the following month. 'I had been aghast at the way Fraser was setting Australian against Australian,' Hawke recalled.

> In the period after my first challenge to Hayden I started thinking deeply about what I could do to really change the country. I believed in the goodness of the Australian people, I believed they did not want to be attacking each other, and from those thoughts I got the idea of 'Reconciliation' in the campaign slogan and of turning this into something practical by calling a summit to bring representatives of all sections of society together, from the wealthiest to the poor.

In this he was following in the footsteps of Curtin, whose first great achievement was to reconcile a frightened, divided nation to the single purpose of fighting the war and saving the homeland from Japanese invasion.

Although the drought had broken, the misery of unemployment continued. Hawke's grand plan was that the Summit, besides giving practical effect to 'Reconciliation', would deal with the problem of unemployment *without* causing a new round of wage rises and inflation. His instrument for this was an 'Accord' with the trade union movement. In his chess game for the leadership, the Accord had been a winning gambit. The ACTU had refused to sign off on it until Hawke replaced Hayden as leader. Hawke then announced it during the election campaign.

While the Summit was Hawke's idea, the Accord was the brainchild of his former ACTU assistant, Ralph Willis, a quietly spoken, gentle, self-deprecating man of strong intelligence. Willis had entered parliament in 1972, experienced the rise and the crash of the Whitlam government and, as an economist, understood that the whole Australian industrial and tariff system was collapsing: from the end of World War II until 1973, with only a couple of ripples, there had been full employment, low inflation and steady economic growth, an environment that could, with relative ease, accommodate the uncoordinated and adversarial pursuit of wage claims and price rises. Those comfortable days were gone. When Hayden became leader, he had promoted Willis to shadow Treasurer and in that role Willis visited the UK, where the Callaghan Labor government had managed for two years to control wage rises through an arrangement with the Trades Union Council. But in the third year the government tried to keep wage rises down to 7 per cent and, as Willis described it,

> the TUC just walked away, went out in the field and got an increase of about 15 per cent which basically blew the Callaghan government out of office and ushered in Thatcher in 1979. I was there in '78 when this had all blown up and I had long talks to people like [Denis] Healey and others who had been involved in it, and it seemed to me that we could learn from their mistakes, because for a couple of years it had served them pretty

well ... At home Labor's credibility on inflation was not good, we were tagged with the Big Spender line from the Whitlam days so we had to develop some sort of credibility that we could keep inflation down whilst growing the economy at a rapid rate ... I could talk easily with Bill Kelty [secretary of the ACTU] and Jan Marsh [the advocate] and Bob [still president], so we started doing some formal work then, but Bill Hayden was always uncomfortable and didn't trust the unions, didn't really have a rapport with unions ...

Hayden observed,

Unionists have a narrower agenda than politicians. At Labor conferences the trade union people weren't much interested in anything other than industrial issues—but on those they would fight like bloody tigers ... They're like a big family, they're looking after their members and they've got a whole lot of things to look after: industrial battles, medical problems, housing—they're expected to be half-baked priests in some ways.

Indeed, trade unionism performed the functions of social cohesion and defence of the group that are fundamental to religion.

Willis recalled, 'Bill never really wanted to push the Accord along. At the 1980 election we had a very generalised expression of some sort of agreement to co-operate, but nothing more than that.'

After the 1980 election when Hawke entered parliament, he moved into an office next to Willis, and they 'talked about the Accord all the time'. Gradually, its acorn started sprouting into the mighty oak it was to become: one of the grandest pieces of social and economic reform in Australian history.

The key negotiating team was Kelty, Marsh and Willis, with input from many sections of the union movement, especially the Left. Laurie Carmichael, the highly respected, wiry, fierce and fiercely intelligent Communist leader of the Metal Workers' Union, was a major influence. Carmichael, Willis said,

> [insisted on] a decent industry policy. The unions were saying if it's okay for us to accept conditions on incomes, we want to talk about the *social* wage. We want to make sure a Labor government delivers on other areas that are in our interests—we want to see Medicare [a Whitlam initiative castrated by Fraser] reformed, we want educational reforms and social security changes. It became bigger than *Ben Hur* ... The context seems almost foreign now. Our economy at that time was replete with anti-competitive behaviour. We had high tariffs, which meant there was no competition from imported goods in lots of areas so people could charge what they liked. We had lots of anti-competitive arrangements internally in Australia, we had regulations and controls everywhere ... In that situation it was very easy for employers to cave in to wage demands, push wages up and push prices up, creating inflationary take-off which would then be crunched by monetary and fiscal policy, leading to unemployment ... It was a hopeless situation. I thought if we got into office we didn't want to be blown out of it by inflationary take-off, crunch then unemployment.

Willis, as shadow Treasurer, believed he would be Treasurer in a Labor government led by Hawke. But, in what were to be the final days of his leadership, Hayden decided to punish Willis for his open support of Hawke by demoting him. In an effort to shore up his support in Caucus, Hayden promoted Paul Keating into Willis' place. Willis was deeply upset. Keating knew almost nothing about economics and not much about trade unions, but he was the brilliant young leader of the New South Wales Right and had the might of the machine behind him. It was as putative Treasurer, therefore, that Keating went to the polls, against the experienced Liberal Treasurer, John Howard. Hawke was confident that after the election he could re-promote Willis and give Keating some other portfolio. This confidence was misplaced: before his government was sworn in, Hawke was to have a personal demonstration that the New South Wales machine was a big family, too, and had its own religion, and would fight like a bloody tiger for its co-believers. With a prime minister from Victoria, the second most prestigious job, Treasury, had to go to New South Wales. Keating was to stay Treasurer.

For his part, Keating was sceptical about the Summit, the Accord, and his new job. 'I've been handed the poisoned chalice, mate,' he remarked.[1]

While Hawke had made some speeches about an accord with the trade unions during the election campaign, just how expansive it would be was too complex to explain. Hawke was certain the only way to gain understanding of its potential and to win wide acceptance by rank-and-file unionists and employers (many of whom found the existing arrangements to their taste) was to inform them how dire the situation really was. He proposed to give to the Summit participants (representatives of government, business large and small, unions, the welfare sector and churches) all the relevant information the government had about Australia's economy. These were statistics that until that time had been state secrets.

The public service was appalled.

Public servants did not like the sound of the Accord. Willis said,

It was impure policy, an arrangement that went outside Treasury control, Finance control, the control of the Prime Minister and Cabinet department. The public service likes to control things and this was something they didn't understand, had no control over, no involvement in and no say in, and never really came to grips with. But they learned to live with it.

It was scandalous for many—public servants, politicians and journalists—that the Prime Minister had insisted the Summit be held in Parliament House, in the Chamber of the Representatives. Their reason for disdain? *It had never been done before.*

'There were,' Hawke recalled, 'many humorists, sceptics, agnostics and doomsayers—but few true believers.' Clyde Cameron, the former Whitlam Minister for Industrial Relations, wrote to him,

> Your economic conference will fail; the participants won't be able to deliver and will be addressing the record. If you can succeed in making a worthwhile compact with the unions, you'll go down in history as the greatest Australian Prime Minister ever.

The final flourish aside, Cameron's assessment was the general view: what was planned would turn into a vapid talk-fest.

The Summit opened on 11 April, ten days before the newly elected government and its equally new Opposition would take their seats in parliament. In his opening address, Hawke said that the minimum measure of the Summit's success should be,

> first, a heightened appreciation of the need to work constructively together to meet the great challenges now confronting our country; and second, an increased

> likelihood of all participants tailoring their expectations and claims upon the community's resources to the capacity of the economy ...

He continued,

> Australia can no longer afford to go down the path of confrontation and fragmentation which has embittered and disfigured so many aspects of the national life ... It is not only a question of the need for national reconciliation in this current economic crisis ... It is a question of the shape of the future of Australia.

The hand Hawke laid upon the wheel of history was pleasing to it: his Summit was a stunning success.

As Curtin in 1941 had set out to forge a national consensus to save the nation, so Hawke, after a decade of bitterness and eighty years of economic mediocrity, was re-civilising public life and founding a modern Australia.

In his opening speech to the Summit, the Prime Minister said that the participants needed to recognise they had a common goal, and therefore a common interest: an improvement of their standard of living due to real economic growth.

He had wondered to himself before the Summit how traditional foes, captains of industry and trade union leaders, would comport themselves when brought face to face, taking morning and afternoon teas together, lunches and dinners under the same roof. He recalled,

> It was fascinating to observe the 98 delegates ... time and again leading industrialists would take me aside and say, 'You know, Bob, this is the first time I've really talked to a trade union leader; they're not bad blokes.'

Trade unionists made the same discovery about captains of industry: they were not, after all, ogres, but responsible citizens. Hawke said, 'Those simple observations excited me because, after all, that was what the whole thing was about.' (Not every trade unionist was a convert: 'Stormy Normy' Gallagher, the burly thug who led the Builders Labourers' Federation, when asked by a reporter, 'Mr Gallagher, what did you think of the Summit?' replied, "I'm still tinkin'".' Ralph Willis, as Industrial Relations minister, was later to deregister Gallagher's union for illegal behaviour.)

On the Summit tide, a sea change in national life swept in. The managing director of BHP, John Prescott, in thanking Hawke some years later for the new approach he had brought to the steel industry in particular and to the economy generally said, 'In BHP we preferred it if our workers left their brains at the gate. Now, in this new atmosphere of industrial relations we realise that is absurd. They are, in a sense, our best resource.' The Summit cemented the Accord into place, the unions agreeing to wage restraint. 'This took the employers somewhat by surprise ... but they also rose to the occasion,' Hawke wrote. It sounds preposterous now, but this was the first time that employers publicly accepted that government policy could simultaneously pursue reducing unemployment and reducing inflation.

There were many practical spin-offs from the Summit, one of them being the shock of employers on recognising how disorganised, compared with the unions, they were. In response they formed the Business Council of Australia, to this day an important wheel in economic policy formation. Out of the Summit too, the Economic Planning and Advisory Council (EPAC) was established. This body, unprecedented in Australia, created a forum for co-operation between federal and state governments, business, unions, the rural sector and community groups. Its main role was to analyse medium- and long-term economic performance, and the factors that influence it. EPAC's secretariat proved so skilful in analysis that in 1985 it also became the secretariat for the Cabinet committee on long-term growth; it was later named the Structural Adjustment Committee.

Thanks to the Summit, for the first time since World War II the state premiers agreed to a joint communiqué on national economic policy. And from the time of the Summit onwards, the number of industrial disputes began to fall. It kept falling—to the point where Australia's international reputation of the 1960s and 1970s as an unreliable supplier and a poor bet for investment turned 180 degrees.

The ripple effect of the Summit's success was further demonstrated when other nations began copying it. First was New Zealand, in 1984. In March 1985 the new Canadian Prime Minister, Brian Mulroney, held a national economic conference, modelled on the Australian Summit, to which he invited Hawke as keynote speaker. In 1989 the new government of the Republic of Korea asked Australia to brief it on the Accord and in December 1992, President-elect Bill Clinton held an Australian-style summit in Washington. In Zurich, even gnomes clapped their manicured hands. Bryan Kelman, the general manager of CSR, was a summiteer who travelled to Europe immediately afterwards for meetings with bankers in Frankfurt, Basel, Zurich, Brussels, Paris and London. 'The interest expressed was quite extraordinary,' he told Hawke. 'Many of the Swiss bankers volunteered the opinion that a strong and unified Labor government would be better placed than a Coalition government to guide Australia through the economic difficulties ahead.'

At international conferences into the twenty-first century, government and business leaders were still approaching Hawke for informal discussions about the Summit and the Accord.

Another positive outcome was that the young, green Treasurer, Paul Keating, abandoned his Accord scepticism and 'embraced it with the fervour of a convert'. If Keating loved something, he loved it madly. Hawke was delighted that his Treasurer, whose lack of economic education he found alarming, had begun forming a close association with the ACTU and its secretary, Bill Kelty. Kelty was a well-trained economist and would help balance the views that the Department of Treasury, under a flint-faced conservative, John Stone, were hammering into their young minister's head.

The Summit's final communiqué was unanimous but for the abstention of Sir Joh Bjelke-Petersen, Premier of Queensland, a personally charming redneck who, like his state in those days, waltzed a couple of beats behind the music.

Within months the Accord bore its first fruit: the Conciliation and Arbitration Commission granted a wage rise that was only the size of the increase in the CPI, and the vast majority of unions made a written undertaking to forgo additional claims. In years to come—first in 1986, when the dollar collapsed, then during the boom of the late 1980s—wages stayed steady. Inflationary expectations had been swept away on the tide of change.[2] The new leader of the Opposition, Andrew Peacock, felt obliged to acknowledge the Summit's success (before launching into criticism of things he did not like about it), telling the House at the beginning of May,

> I think that all Australians have recognised that the National Economic Summit Conference was a valuable opportunity for Government Ministers, trade union leaders and the leaders of industry to exchange views, and I am certain that all participants found that that aspect of the Summit was of great value. I also acknowledge the many thoughtful, pertinent and useful contributions made at the Summit by a number of participants; in particular, some of the employers ...[3]

Hawke had time to savour his Summit triumph for just twenty-four hours. Unknown to the Labor Caucus, the news media and the public, the government had a crisis on its hands.

On the afternoon of 20 April the head of ASIO, Harvey Barnett, was granted his request for an urgent meeting with the Prime Minister 'on a matter of national security'. Barnett considered it so important he wanted to tell Hawke before he told his own minister, Gareth Evans (an action many in the Caucus deemed sinister when they heard of it). The Prime Minister and the head of ASIO had never met before but Hawke had little or none of the ALP's paranoia about ASIO and liked Barnett on first meeting. Barnett was a slim, well-bred, conservative man in his late fifties, his manner of upper-middle-class restraint offset by an open, velvety smile. He appeared, and was, a person deeply at peace within himself. Hawke was unaware of Barnett's spiritual life but recognised something about him that recalled his father's peacefulness. There was nothing tricky about Barnett, to Hawke's eye. A number of his ministers, large sections of the Caucus and, of course, the news media, thought otherwise. Barnett was a *spook*. To them this meant he was not a patriot but treacherous. Such was the temper of the times.

The only other person in the room that afternoon was the Prime Minister's principal private secretary, Graham Evans, permitted to be in attendance because he had a top-secret security clearance. Barnett told them about Combe and Ivanov. 'I was very surprised,' Hawke said. A couple of weeks earlier Combe had annoyed the Prime Minister when he had walked uninvited into his office behind the Chief Minister of the Northern Territory, a man with whom Combe had a business association. Hawke had considered Combe bumptious on that occasion. Barnett explained that since Combe's dinner with Ivanov there had been further contacts, and that Ivanov was showing skittish signs—as if he thought his house was bugged and he wanted

Combe to shut up. The head of ASIO pointed out that Ivanov's next step with Combe would be to suggest they stop meeting in public and in his house—that is, to begin a clandestine relationship. If Combe were to agree he would be a lost man, literally and metaphorically. As Prime Minister, Hawke had two paramount responsibilities: first, to defend the nation; second, to defend the government. He found it distasteful that Combe was assuming entitlements thanks to his mates in government, and alarming that Combe felt so friendly towards the USSR, a country whose political system Hawke detested.

Combe, Hawke decided, was toxic. 'Here was a clear security risk,' he said. 'And I immediately thought of what it meant for the government.'

His government had not yet sat a single day in parliament—that would happen the next afternoon—but already a time bomb was ticking. There were two electoral death traps Labor had to avoid. One was mismanaging the economy, which Hawke believed his team would avoid despite his misgivings about the Treasurer. The other was security. Graham Evans said, 'It's probably impossible to think of anything that could have been more challenging early in the period of a Labor government.'

As Barnett talked, Hawke thought, 'If this blows, we'll only last one term.'

He would say later, 'The Tories have been the myth-makers of Australian politics: they created the myth that Labor was a bad economic manager, and weak on security.' Unfortunately, at that time there was a truckload of historical grist to the mythological mill. There was the insane reaction of the ALP's leader, Dr Evatt, to the Petrov Affair: in 1954 Evatt wrote to the Soviet Foreign minister, Vyacheslav Mikhailovich Molotov, asking Comrade Molotov if it were true there were Soviet spies in Australia. Molotov had, in his long career as an acolyte of Stalin, claimed the bombs he was dropping on Finland in World War II were actually 'food baskets for the starving Finns'. (The starving Finns promptly invented 'a drink to go with the food' that they named the Molotov cocktail, and threw at Soviet tanks.) Comrade Molotov wrote back to Dr Evatt, assuring him there were no Soviet spies in Australia. Evatt announced this news from Moscow to the Australian nation. Had he done so a few years later people would have asked each other what he was smoking. After Petrov, there were the party's anti-Vietnam War campaigns, which conservative governments used to assert Labor was an unreliable ally for the US and to suggest it was 'soft on Communism'. The Whitlam government follies of the 1970s and the widely believed and later confirmed fact that the party had been infiltrated by Communists added to the charge sheet. Being anti-war had been Labor's signature through the 1960s and 1970s and was still in the 1980s—although Australia, like the rest of the West, was in the midst of an undeclared but violent war, in which espionage and counter-espionage were on the front line.

As Barnett talked, what Hawke immediately understood was that the Opposition would have a weapon in parliament and through the press to beat his newborn government to pulp. He could imagine the headlines already: 'ALP Official Russian Spy!'

In 'Politics as a Vocation', Max Weber noted that a successful politician must have passion, a feeling of responsibility and a sense of proportion. He described 'the decisive psychological quality of the politician: his ability to let realities work upon him with inner concentration and calmness. Hence, his *distance* to things and men.' Within Hawke's warm and passionate nature, *his distance to things and men* had already formed. He asked Barnett what his options were. There were three: to counsel Combe quietly; to expel Ivanov quietly; or to expel Ivanov publicly. Hawke rejected the first out of hand, as he believed Combe, a member of the anti-ASIO wing of the party, would not respond positively and, anyway, to do so would be a security breach. The second he also rejected 'because it would leak'. They settled on the third option, plus bugging Combe's phone to monitor further contacts with Ivanov or other Russians, as there was the chance that Ivanov was not the only KGB officer in town, and he could hand over Combe's grooming to a colleague. Barnett assured Hawke before he left that nobody but ASIO, Hawke and Graham Evans knew of the situation.

In any circumstance, a prime minister's staff is important to the smooth functioning of government; in a crisis, it is critical. Hawke's principal private secretary, Graham Evans, ran the Prime Minister's office.

Evans had been a diplomat who had taken time out while in Washington to do postgraduate economic studies, later working in the Treasury. He was a calm, good-humoured, highly organised man of the finest type of public servant. He gave polite, thoughtful, frank advice. He and Hawke had sounded each other out in Washington and Canberra in 1982; when Hawke offered him the job, other senior men in the public service—Stone from Treasury, Sir Geoffrey Yeend from the Department of Prime Minister and Cabinet and Michael Cook, also a former diplomat and intelligence analyst who had been Fraser's principal private secretary, encouraged Evans to take it.

> All three said they thought there were significant advantages having a public servant running the office, because it made the liaison a lot better. But in fact, Bob had already thought about that. It was clear that he had in mind the Whitlam experience: he said, 'You know, a lot of the issues the Whitlam government encountered were a consequence of not having as good a relationship with the public service as they could have had without compromising on their policies.' He welcomed the fact that I had a background in both economics and foreign policy.

Of Barnett's briefing, Evans recalled, 'My first reaction was great surprise, but my next was "Oh, my God. The buck stops with Bob and, to some degree what I say to him about whom he should talk to next."' 'Loose lips sink ships', as the saying goes. The problem was to decide on whom to bring into the loop.

Hawke called a meeting of the National and International Security Committee for that evening at which he laid out what had been discovered and called Barnett back in to brief the ministers and discuss expelling Ivanov. 'Hayden was apprehensive,' Hawke said. 'He wanted Ivanov out of the country, but quieter than quiet, without so much as a word to the Soviets. To Mick Young, this was a nonsensical idea.' Hayden recalled,

> Bob was always a dramatist, he was in a great drama. He told us what had happened, and we were all shocked. And when we walked out I said to Mick Young, 'Why would Combe do that?' and he said, 'Just bloody greedy.' And I remember going home and sitting on the edge of the bed and telling Dallas. I was really upset.

But by the next morning, after another briefing from Barnett in the Prime Minister's office, Hayden came to the conclusion that Combe was 'just big-noting himself. He comes on so strongly—and he has nothing to offer.' Gareth Evans, too, was becoming doubtful. Evans was a long-time ASIO critic; now he was its minister but he had been snubbed by Barnett. When the Attorney-General asked Barnett for the transcripts of Combe's dinner with Ivanov, Barnett refused to hand them over. His refusal was correct in terms of 'trade craft', since raw intelligence is notoriously difficult to interpret. Politically, his refusal was of questionable judgment. Barnett's agenda was security and the prestige of his organisation. He did not yet grasp the government's political agenda. And Combe, third leg of what had turned into a triangle, had his own pecuniary agenda backed by his network of mates in the party, the press and the Canberra lobbying business. From these three forces, a thunderhead of suspicion would explode.

The Australian Capital Territory, which consists of Canberra and some paddocks, in those days was a pampered enclave, living comfortably on federal largesse, a showpiece for national pride. Its roads were as smooth and as charcoal grey as a diplomat's suit. Its lawns were neatly clipped; its civic buildings, although lamentably unimaginative, were immaculately maintained. It was the best paid and most highly educated city in Australia and small enough for the citizens to be forever running into someone they knew at the shops or in a restaurant or cinema. Socially liberal, Canberra residents were allowed to possess for personal use small quantities of marijuana, and to consume it in private. The national capital was also the Australian distribution hub for the pornography industry. It had the amenities of a quiet, high-minded university and foreign embassy city, which it was, and the mentality of a colonial outpost, with its expatriate pukka sahibs and memsahibs, its cliques, intrigues, storms in teacups, rules of behaviour, parties, clubs and affairs so numerous that Canberra hostesses were plagued with indecision when compiling dinner-party guest lists. Gossip ran from tongue to tongue as in a village. Parliament House was Gossip Central, for this was the place of work not only of politicians and their staffs, but also of the press gallery. Senior members of the gallery were the sahibs and memsahibs of Australian journalism and the most expatriate; as standard bearers of free speech they saluted a higher civilisation than the one they observed, that of the natives: the members of parliament. It was the role of the sahibs to keep the natives in line—and especially the wily new sultan, who had snatched the throne without any of them being tipped off in advance.

As the Combe–Ivanov Affair was to reveal, those making the transition from Opposition to government traverse a minefield.

Unknown to any of his colleagues, a member of the National and International Security Committee had leaked. On the night of 21 April, in a car park outside the 19th Hole Restaurant, he had confided to Eric Walsh, a former Whitlam press secretary, now a lobbyist, 'We're going to kick out a Russian.' The minister had gone on to warn that David Combe was involved with the Russian and that Walsh should be wary of doing business with Combe. He also disclosed that the deputy Prime Minister, Lionel Bowen, had expressed hatred for a third man, X, another person involved in the Russian trade.

The friend confided in X. But X, as it happened, was an informant. The minister's indiscretion would in due course find its way back to the ears of the Scorpion. And there, as the raw intelligence of a 'report of conversation', it would lie for months: a second time bomb for the Hawke government.

The next day, at lunch, the same minister told Rod Cameron, the ALP pollster, that the government was about to expel a Russian. Two hours later Bill Hayden announced Ivanov was *persona non grata* and would be leaving the country within days. This was an exciting event for the media and the prestigious win for ASIO that Barnett wanted. He returned to his headquarters in Melbourne a happy man. His organisation, which 'in fact was *good*', according to Bill Hayden and others who had top-secret security clearances, was about to enjoy one of its very few public successes.

The most realistic of espionage writers, John le Carré, had one of his characters remark of political journalists 'they put out their tongues and fart and think they've invented democracy'.[4] On news of Ivanov's expulsion and rumours about Labor figures being involved, hot gusts of wind began blowing from both ends of the press gallery.

Meanwhile, following accepted precedent, the government gave Andrew Peacock a two-hour background briefing on the expulsion and Ivanov's relationship with Combe. Peacock gave his word that he would tell nobody about Combe's association with the spy.

On the evening Ivanov was publicly revealed as an enemy agent, David Combe had discovered from Rod Cameron, the ALP pollster, who heard it at lunch from the minister that day, 'that Ivanov was expelled because he was too close to people who had influence with the government'. Meena Blesing exclaimed to her husband, 'But that's you!'[5]

At that moment the Combes realised that their business, which depended upon David being *persona gratissima* with government, was in great danger.

A formal decision to blackball Combe was only days away but already Parliament House, the bars around town and the Journalists' Club were hives of rumour and paranoia. There was bitter division in Hawke's own office, between those who thought the Prime Minister had acted correctly and those who hated ASIO as something both impure and bumbling, and who felt Combe was being badly treated. Bob Hogg, Hawke's political adviser from the Victorian Left, was accused by ASIO of having breakfast with Combe after the Prime Minister had expressly told him not to. Hogg vehemently denied the accusation when he discovered what ASIO had reported, but until then he recalled, 'It was as if I had plague. I walked into the office and people wouldn't speak to me. I didn't know why.'

A problem confronting the Prime Minister's office, as Graham Evans explained,

> [was that] there was no recognised process to follow ... at the time we had to move forward step by step in how people were brought in, and how [giving secret information] was managed. There was no precedent, no standing process that we could turn to. Bob and I had been having conversations about 'How on earth do we

manage this issue? We can't let David Combe go on talking to ministers because down the line someone will say, "Why did you let him do that, knowing what we'd been told by ASIO?"' On the other hand, Bob couldn't go in and say to the ministers, 'You're not to have anything to do with Combe, because of this.' That would have been a breach of national security. So he had to stop one without doing the other. Bob had been thinking about the risks of having heaps of lobbyists dealing with the government and how to get around it, and there had been some general discussions, but nothing had been done.

John Dawkins, the new Minister for Finance, had also been pondering what to do about lobbyists, and may have discussed the problem with Hawke. Certainly, he had a constructive suggestion.

The night before the Cabinet meeting in Adelaide at which Hawke was scheduled to inform the rest of Cabinet about Combe, Graham Evans was getting ready for bed when the Prime Minister, dressed in pyjamas, knocked on his door and said, 'We need to resolve this issue.' Evans, also pyjama-clad, recalled,

> And it was at that point that we came up with the idea of a register of lobbyists and that ministers were not to engage in the use of lobbyists until the rules of engagement had been worked out, and a register had been established.

It was one in the morning by the time they said good night. Exactly how events unfolded is not clear, but later that day in the Cabinet, Dawkins proposed a register of lobbyists, which his colleagues endorsed. Everyone was henceforth constrained from dealing with *any* lobbyist.

Evans added, 'It would have happened at some point anyway, but I was the only person who knew it was because of Combe.' The Cabinet meeting was on 26 April.

Combe recalled,

> By 29 April I knew I was under surveillance, because Richard Farmer [a former journalist and ALP press officer] and the other guy who was coming into partnership with me [David Butler] came round to tell me [they would not be joining the business]. It was pissing with rain and they wouldn't come inside the house. So they obviously believed it was bugged ... they didn't say that, but I just knew.

The Prime Minister, in a fish restaurant in Adelaide, had himself told both Farmer and Butler to avoid Combe—later gleefully reported in the press as a breach of national security by the Prime Minister.

Soon after the visit from Farmer and Butler, a letter arrived from Combe's old friend, John Button, now Minister for Industry, which said:

> Dear Mr Combe
>
> As you will undoubtedly appreciate my ministerial duties make it impossible for me to discuss with you the business of your client.
>
> Yours sincerely
> John M. Button[6]

By now Caucus was full of rumours. Hayden supporters, who would never forgive the Prime Minister for overthrowing their leader, were lining up against Hawke. In the Prime Minister's office, and the Cabinet, there were suspicions that Combe had been tipped off by an insider. Distrust was pervasive.

On the day he received Button's letter, David Combe, 'in a highly emotional state' according to his wife, had dinner with his friend, Brian Toohey, for many years an anti-ASIO crusader and also editor of the *National Times*. Combe poured out his heart to Toohey, begging him, Toohey said, to write his story. It was, as Combe saw it, one of betrayal of himself and dark right-wing forces taking over the government. A number of teasing, Delphic stories appeared in the *National Times*, whetting the appetite of its leftish intelligentsia readership for more.

On 10 May the first bomb exploded. In the House of Representatives, Ian Sinclair, deputy leader of the National Party, asked if Hawke had instructed members of the government 'to dissociate themselves from the former secretary to the Federal Australian Labor Party. Mr David Combe? If so, why?' Hawke answered 'that in respect of any lobbying activity there is to be no association', and immediately asked that further questions be put on notice. He was furious and had a strong suspicion about who had given Sinclair his information.

'RUSSIAN SPY! LABOR OFFICIAL NAMED' was the front page of the *Daily Mirror* that afternoon. The subheading read 'ASIO Briefs Hawke'.

From the tenor of Sinclair's question and two other questions in parliament that day, the government was convinced that *Peacock* was Sinclair's informant and that the Opposition was bent on a strategy of attacking Labor's 'weak spot', just as Hawke had feared.

In politics and in certain sections of the news media, bad faith is a given: attacks are made in full knowledge they are baseless. It was suggested to Hawke that Mick Young, his closest friend on the National and International Security Committee and one of his closest friends in the party, had leaked. Hawke called Young in, asked him if he had been indiscreet, and Young assured the Prime Minister that all he had done was mention to Rod Cameron that a Russian would be expelled in a couple of hours. Hawke took him at his word, and in parliament vigorously defended Young, noting

> that from the moment he made that comment at about 12.30 to the point at which the Minister of Foreign Affairs announced, about two hours later, the expulsion of Mr Ivanov, Mr Cameron had been with him [Young] at all times.

He went on to add that Young had 'in all other respects acted ... with honour and propriety'.

But Young had lied to Hawke; as a result, the Prime Minister had just misled the parliament. Why did Young lie? Presumably from fear. It was the first indication that the most popular man in the party, the jester whose wit had buoyed up Caucus spirits during the long, grim years of Opposition, would be out of his depth in government.

On 11 May, the day after the first public explosion, Gareth Evans called in David Combe, read his remarks to Ivanov to him, asked him to acknowledge that he had blotted his copybook so badly he would just have to realise he was no longer acceptable as a lobbyist, to put up and to shut up. The government would make no more comments; Combe was to make no more comments.

Combe agreed.

But within hours he changed his mind, urged to do so by journalists. They persuaded him he had been betrayed and abandoned by his erstwhile mates, and he should resist. 'PM faces backbench revolt over Combe', the *Australian* reported on its front page next morning; there was a 'Flood of support from

ALP' to Combe. The electronic media was running hot with the Combe story. As Bob Hogg, a close friend of Combe's, remarked, 'They were willing to fight to the last drop of David's blood.' Combe's case was that the Cabinet, and the Prime Minister in particular, had trampled his civil liberties. The sahibs and memsahibs of the gallery seethed with indignation on his behalf and with the excitement of a great story. They could see themselves giving that sultan a good flogging.

On the same day as Combe was asked, and agreed, to remain silent, Hawke tried to calm the situation with a statement to the House setting out the reasons for the government's decisions and defending it against the charge already being made, that individual civil liberties—Combe's—had been trampled. He concluded,

> It is perhaps inevitable that there will always be elements of doubt and suspicion in the minds of all Australians in circumstances where there can be less than full disclosure of information. This is a responsibility a government must accept, and for my part I accept it. But I trust this statement will put to rest the uncertainty of the last few days. A climate of innuendo and deceit is not one which my government will be guilty of creating or permitting to flourish. Finally ... in no way will my government be compromised when matters of our national security are at stake.

But the storm gathered force.

Combe was winning the battle for public sympathy. Less than a week after Hawke made his statement to the House, hoping to bring calm, the atmosphere grew so hostile that the Prime Minister announced a Royal Commission. Michael McHugh of the Sydney bar, husband of a Labor backbencher,

Jeanette McHugh, would represent the government, with Neil Young, from Melbourne, as his junior.

McHugh recalled,

> Combe was very clever. He was running his case in the press. He was obviously in daily contact with the press, probably at the Journalists' Club. Richard Carleton was very pro-Combe, the press generally were very supportive of Combe. And that persisted for a long period of time... I was sort of running the case as just an ordinary, straight legal proceeding. But one day Jeanette said to me, 'You think this is just another court case. This is really an extension of a parliamentary debate.' And that really woke me up.

The barrister suddenly understood the politics. McHugh now realised the government's life depended on Mr Justice Hope, the Royal Commissioner, finding that Hawke and the National and International Security Committee had acted correctly in expelling Ivanov and in blackballing Combe as a lobbyist.

McHugh said, 'The government had not been shown the transcript of the tapes [of Combe's conversation with Ivanov] until weeks after Harvey Barnett first called on Hawke. Barnett had only given them a summary.' When McHugh and Neil Young read the transcripts they were taken aback: they had a very weak case to argue.

Such was the hysterical farrago that by now it was assumed and being asserted in the news media that Combe was suspected of espionage. ASIO and the National and International Security Committee suspected him of no such thing: the very idea was absurd. But that was the public perception, and that was what now had to be legally tested in the Royal Commission. McHugh asked for a meeting with the Prime Minister, at which Gareth

Evans, Mick Young and Sir Geoffrey Yeend (the departmental head of Prime Minister and Cabinet) were also present. McHugh asked that the government and ASIO be separately represented,

> I've always remembered Hawke's decisiveness about this. Gareth Evans wanted a government counsel to control the case for the whole government. But I could see big problems, a conflict of interest between ASIO and the government. In the end, ASIO might have to wear the blame from the government's point of view. I didn't want to be in a position where [I was representing both parties]. I would have a conflict of interest. And Bob said to me, 'Is it your professional judgment that ASIO be separately represented?' and I said, 'Yes.' And he said, 'Well, it will be'—and Evans didn't like that. It was obvious from his face. But it turned out to be the right thing. There were a number of reasons. First, I realised that there were going to be two climaxes to the case: one would be the cross-examination of Bob, if he was called, which I thought was only a remote possibility, but obviously, the cross-examination of Combe was going to be a great climax. And although this is not a legal consideration—good lawyers take into account things outside the strictly legal application—I thought the government was going to have big trouble within the Labor Party itself if their counsel was the one who did the major cross-examination of Combe. So it would suit the government's purpose, I thought, to have ASIO's counsel do the major cross-examination of Combe.

Stephen Charles, QC, was appointed to represent ASIO. In McHugh's opinion ASIO, by not showing the transcripts to the government immediately, 'had really made a bad mistake and the government was going to have to wear it'.

The Royal Commission got down to business on 14 June in a frenzy of publicity. Headlines of the time read: 'I Have Been Destroyed: Combe Speaks Out'; 'Labor In Revolt Over Bugging'; 'I'm No Spy'; 'David Combe, Sacrificial Lamb'; 'Your Dad's A Spy'. The effect on Combe's family was appalling—at the time and for years to come.

Because much of the evidence being put to the Commission was confidential or secret, the hearings were frequently in camera, for hours or even days at a stretch. David Marr, whose book *The Ivanov Trail*, is authoritative, wrote, 'Like a great whale, the royal commission surfaced briefly from time to time only to descend once more beneath the waves where it remained almost all through July.'[7] Combe was still winning the sympathy war.

In the middle of July, the second bomb exploded. Jovial Mick Young, the man considered the heart and soul of the Labor Party, one of the funniest men who ever pulled a laugh in the Caucus or the House of Representatives, the one you could rely on to restore good humour in the most tense situation . . . *Mick*, Hawke's mate of twenty years, his drinking buddy who went blind man when women appeared in Hawke's hotel rooms, was unmasked as the leaker.

It was the other Mr Young, Neil, McHugh's junior, who was doing the legwork for the case, reading ASIO documents and conducting his own interviews, who found him out. Neil Young asked to see Hawke and laid out the facts. Hawke was devastated.

'I had asked Mick a question [on 10 May] and he'd looked me in the eye and lied,' he said.

Sir Geoffrey Yeend was called in, then hurried out of the office to get a copy of the *Crimes Act*. Yeend, Hawke and Graham Evans pored over the Act. It was obvious Young had breached section 79(3), for which the penalty is two years jail. There is always a personal price to pay for leadership: Hawke knew what had to happen next. 'It was the hardest thing I ever had to do in politics,' he said.

That afternoon he called Neil Young back to his office. Neil Young had with him a record of what Mick Young had said, to whom, when and where. Hawke asked Neil Young to stay in the room and called in Mick Young. Neil Young recalled,

> Bob asked Mick Young whether he'd had a conversation with Eric Walsh [lobbyist and former press secretary to Whitlam] and what he had told him. And Mick told Hawke exactly what he'd told me [earlier]. Didn't beat around the bush. He was quite frank and candid, and then Mick said he'd been considering his position and he thought he should resign from Cabinet. And my recollection is that Hawke did not ask for his resignation but Young said he'd been thinking about his position and he'd made that decision. It was a very professional and amicable discussion. I don't remember Bob being upset or angry at any point. The conversation was very professionally handled by Hawke and there was a very professional response, no nonsense, no bones about it, by Mick Young. The whole conversation would have taken probably fifteen minutes.

The sangfroid of the politicians in the presence of the young lawyer is remarkable, because both were dying inside. Mateship was the highest value in life for Young. He had just reached the pinnacle of his career, had been a minister for only six weeks—and his mate, Bob, had not just let him fall but would have pushed him had he not jumped. Like the rupture between Falstaff and Prince Hal, it was a tragedy unique to politics.

McHugh, more worldly than his junior assistant and more familiar with Hawke, recalled: 'Bob was very distressed about it all—whether it was because of his friendship with Mick, or whether it was the problems it was going to create for the government. He was certainly shaken by it.' In Caucus, Young's resignation caused uproar. Hawke was blamed for it.

Meena Blesing wrote,

> [Young's] resignation ... caused great shock waves in the Government, the press and the labor movement. Young was seen as a sacrificial lamb or goat—a John the Baptist—in this murky affair and it was feared that more heads would roll. There was talk of more Ministers being involved and it was all publicly a rather frightening and hush-hush affair.[8]

Young resigned on a Friday. Over the weekend Peacock, knowing how loved within the party Mick Young was, accused Hawke of 'hiding behind the facade of a Royal Commission' in the Young affair, asserting Hawke had 'sacked' Young.

Within a week the *Australian* published an editorial asking, 'Is this the way to run a country?' Hawke was under attack from every side. McHugh, who had thought to bring him into the witness box, if at all, as last of the ministers, decided, 'things were going too badly in the press and it was important that the Prime Minister come in first ... I thought if Bob Hawke made a very impressive performance then the whole atmosphere would change.'

The national media were in a frenzy of excitement when it became known Hawke would be going into the box. This was the moment when the sultan would get his flogging.

Hawke recalled, 'When I walked into the room to give evidence you could have cut the air with a knife.'

McHugh said,

> It was one of the best tactical decisions I ever made in any formal case, because Hawke was a superb witness. There's no doubt about it. And that was really the end of Combe. At the end of the day [Hawke spent almost three days in the witness box] it was all over. After his performance there was no way that Combe was going to succeed.

David Marr, the most pukka of the press sahibs, a trained lawyer and no fan of the Prime Minister, wrote,

> No one present had seen a prime minister in the witness box before … Hawke here was facing professionals, hired guns of the Bar. But he was at home. Hawke had spent more of his career in the roughhouse of arbitration tribunals than he had in parliament. The forum of the royal commission suited him perfectly … [he] had drilled himself superbly for the occasion and had the facts, down to tiny details, at his fingertips … Hawke was an exceptional witness … he could always see the question coming, and chose at times to answer a slightly different question.[9]

Cross-examination is one of civilisation's darker arts, but Hawke understood it. Poor David Combe did not.

McHugh recalled,

> I felt very sorry for Combe and the position he was in, and I didn't like the job of cross-examining him, however I was going to have to do it. But when he was giving his evidence he actually volunteered this

statement about Bob getting $1500 for some speaking engagement, and I thought to myself, 'You bastard!' There was no need to say that. It was an irrelevance, it had nothing to do with the Royal Commission; it was just saying that Bob was greedy and charging money and it wouldn't go down well with the hoi polloi in the Labor Party. My mood changed from sympathy to neutral. It steeled me, and put me in a better mood to cross-examine him.

Combe's volunteered information, inaccurate as to the sum (which Hawke had declared and on which he had paid tax), did indeed have the effect Combe had anticipated: there was more anger in the party and the press, and questions in parliament against which Hawke had to defend himself. But Combe, having moved from a position of being unable to win, had, by raising the combative spirit of a skilled cross-examiner, assured himself of a horrible defeat. He spent eleven days in the witness box and left it a shattered man. His wife noted in her diary,

> he had been forced into agreeing ... that he was indiscreet, self-aggrandising, greedy; he wanted to get rich. He had practically concurred with the whole ASIO argument in his efforts to go along with [ASIO's counsel] in the vain hope he could still clear himself.

Their marriage broke up; Combe fell into a slough of despond.

'I was deeply depressed during the case,' he recalled years later.

> I felt betrayed by the party and by people I'd known for years. The media was camped on the front lawn and

you know, you'd put on a happy face, but feeling like shit. But that's how I was raised: stiff upper lip.

In the first week of December 1983, the Royal Commission's report exonerated the government of all its presumed malfeasances and found that David Combe's relationship with Ivanov had 'serious implication for national security'. It found that there was no further reason to blackball Combe's lobbying, but it also found that Mick Young had breached the *Crimes Act*. The Attorney-General, Gareth Evans, recommended Young not be charged. There was a storm of abuse in parliament—'a stench about this government, a stench of dishonesty, a stench of duplicity, a stench of downright deceit, subterfuge and cover up', said Andrew Peacock. He was attacking the Prime Minister especially over Mick Young, whom, having taken his punishment, Hawke proposed should now return to the ministry. The wound to their relationship had not healed and never would completely, but Hawke, who so shrank from hurting vulnerable people that he could be emotionally timid himself, was doing all he could for Young. He defended him in parliament, but he was at a psychological disadvantage because he was traumatised about sacrificing Young in the first place. His speech was hot but off-key. Hawke was not and never would rise to become a great parliamentary speaker. It was the young Treasurer, Paul Keating, who had spent all year immersed in economics and had played no part in the spy drama, who strode into the fray and skewered the Opposition. Keating turned the attack back onto Peacock with the vehement contempt for which he was to become notorious. Peacock, he said,

> could not rise above his own opportunism or his incapacity to lead. He made a public issue of the matter ... The Opposition [took] a decision to drag David

Combe's name into the public arena. That is why there is a Royal Commission report. There would have been no Royal Commission, no report and no briefing of Mr Combe ... had the leader of the Opposition not breached the commitment he gave ... [at the security briefing] to the Prime Minister ... the Government did everything to protect Mr Combe's name. It was only after exposure by ... Jumping Jack Flash from the National Party ...

The Treasurer went on to refer to Peacock as 'slinking' and 'crawling'; he raised the Opposition leader's past embarrassments over his wife's behaviour and his resignation as Minister for the Army in the Fraser government.

Mr Justice Hope had exonerated the government; Keating beat the Opposition to a pulp.

John Dawkins, both hard-nosed and soft-hearted, had been troubled by Combe's plight but had no way to help him—until the end of 1985, when as Minister for Trade, he offered Combe a job abroad. In December 1985 David Combe accepted the post of trade commissioner to Canada. Combe's broken marriage had repaired, and his wife and four sons accompanied him. He had, at last, his 'job for the boys'.

2

WHILE THE ROYAL COMMISSION into the Combe–Ivanov Affair was making its inquiries, Australia became, on 26 September 1983, the first country to beat the United States for the most prestigious yachting prize in the world, the America's Cup. For most of its 132-year history, the race series had been a refined addiction of American, British and European multi-millionaires, virtually unheard-of by the Australian public. But in the early 1960s, Sir Frank Packer, the Sydney press baron, became an addict himself. He publicised the sport in his newspapers and magazines and by 1983 the race had captured the public's imagination. Australians were proudly supportive of the national boat, *Australia II*, which needed to beat yachts from the UK, Canada, Italy and France to become the official challenger. There was a renewed sense of pride in Australian abilities and potential.

The final series of races was held off the east coast of the United States and when it seemed that Australia had a chance of winning, hundreds of thousands of people from Sydney to Perth, from Darwin to Hobart, stayed up most of the night to watch a live telecast. Serendipitously, Cabinet was scheduled months earlier to meet in Perth on what turned out to be the day after the last race. Hawke spent all night watching the decider in his hotel room and later that morning went to the Royal Perth Yacht Club where, at the request of members from the club, he donned a jacket of red, white and blue, with *Australia II* and the Union Jack printed all over it. Photographs and television footage of the Prime Minister in the flamboyant jacket, cheering wildly, flashed across the country. 'I'll wear it to the next Cabinet meeting!' Hawke said. When a journalist asked if he feared people might be sacked for taking a day off work because they were tired and hung-over, Hawke responded: 'Any employer who sacks an employee for not turning up to work today is a *bum*!' There was sanctimonious tut-tutting from the usual suspects, but the electorate at large was delighted. More than two decades later, people who had been children at the time would recall being thrilled by the Prime Minister's naughtiness. Hawke's star continued its rise. 'He bestrides us like a Colossus,' a public servant noted at the time.

When parliament closed on 6 December, with the Hope Royal Commission successfully concluded, Hawke gathered a couple of his economic advisers together to focus their full attention on something much more daring than a sickie.

When the Labor Party won office, a newspaper headline had asked, 'Will Hawke Cast the First Stone?' It was a reference to John Stone, the permanent secretary of the Department of Treasury, whom Hawke had known and disliked since their school days at Perth Modern. The feeling was mutual. Stone was a highly intelligent, fierce right-winger with a dominating manner. Senior bureaucrats are selected after rigorous academic exams—Stone was a Rhodes scholar—and are experienced in bureaucratic infighting. But no bureaucrat can stand up to the aggression, developed over decades of training in the struggle for power, that attends a political leader. Both sides know this; politicians often see bureaucrats as employing the weapon of the weak—manipulation—and can be apprehensive of their nimble manoeuvres. They can also be driven half-mad by bureaucratic passive defiance. Chairman Mao, it is said, launched the Cultural Revolution in 1966 in a frenzy of frustration with his own mandarins' refusal to implement reforms. (The Chinese mandarins, it should be noted, understood economics, while the chairman did not.) John Stone's overt aggression made him an unusually scary mandarin. A senior government economist recalled,

> Graham Evans and I were having a leak in the urinal at Parliament House, right at the end of the Summit, saying to each other how good it had been and what a good base it had laid for policy things we wanted to do, and a gruff voice yelled out from behind us, 'You blokes should be ashamed of yourselves!' It was John Stone.

For Labor, Stone was a Number One Class Enemy.

Hawke, having long reflected on how important the public service was to effective government, decided to trust Stone—if not his political judgment, at least his honour and integrity. Being incorruptible and a guardian against corruption, being truthful and objective no matter the circumstances—in short, having honour—is to good public servants what a fighting spirit is to good politicians. Hawke believed that Stone, whom he described as 'a very good technical economist' was honourable, that he would serve a Labor government as diligently as a conservative one. The Caucus, with an indrawn breath, accepted his decision on Stone. The public service greeted news that Stone would remain as head of Treasury with delight: to them it demonstrated that the new government had learned from past mistakes. For his part, Hawke was completely confident he had the means of keeping Stone's headstrong and domineering nature in check. Not only was he himself more economically educated than any former Australian prime minister, he had on his staff an economist whose intellect he found exhilarating. The Prime

Minister enjoyed his conversation above all others—loved his mind and liked him physically: his tall, virile physique—he was a talented Australian Rules footballer—his candid blue gaze, his frequent laughter that a wide gap between his two front teeth made as engaging as a happy child's. He was Dr (later Professor) Ross Garnaut. Garnaut, too, had attended Perth Modern; he had been the school captain. As a seventeen year old, in 1964, he had remarked to Kim Beazley Senior that Hawke would make a good future prime minister. Beazley Snr corrected the boy: after the usual parliamentary apprenticeship (five to seven years), Hawke would make a good Minister for Labour.

Hawke had met Garnaut in New Guinea in 1966 when Hawke had been invited to lend his talents to an industrial dispute that became known as the local officers' wage case. Garnaut, an ANU postgraduate student, was in Port Moresby doing a research job in the vacation. Garnaut said,

> The next and more substantial contact was when Bob was working on the Crawford Study Group for Structural Adjustment, in the late 1970s, and John Crawford used to bring me along at lunchtime to meet people, and I had a few yarns to Bob then. He was very much engaged in the ideas that both Crawford and I were bringing before the committee ... [ideas] on the positive opportunity in Asia for Australia.

There had been a tendency in public policy discussion to see the beginnings of rapid growth in East Asia as being an economic threat to Australia, but Garnaut presented an alternative perspective that Hawke found both attractive and persuasive. Garnaut's generation of students at the ANU viewed the deeper engagement of Australia in Asia as a change that had to come. The key issues for students interested in policy in the late 1960s involved undoing the historical mistakes Australia had made in relation to race: the treatment of Aboriginal people, the White Australia policy, apartheid in South Africa, and a fearful approach to Asia. These were all in accord with Hawke's personal views, pursued through the trade union movement. The same issues led Garnaut to study trade. His PhD thesis had been on Australian trade with South-East Asia; trade issues had been the whole of his professional life.

Of the economy—as it was when Hawke took over—Garnaut said, 'We'd made a historic mess.' Protectionism, once such a nice idea, had become counter-productive. Like a lot of young Australians, Garnaut had been excited by the election of the Whitlam government and gratified with what Whitlam did for Australian foreign policy. But he was deeply disappointed by Whitlam's mismanagement of the economy. 'I spent a fair bit of time thinking, and some time writing, about what needed to be done about our macroeconomic situation,' he said.

> It always included a need to open up more in the financial sector and in trade, and it always included a need for more budget discipline, a lot more care in what we spent money on, and always included the need to have a more flexible wage and industrial relations structure, supported by a social democratic budget. But I felt fairly pessimistic that Australia would ever do anything about it.

Fraser was always enlightened on racial issues and far ahead of his party in this area, but he had set back the economic debate and he and his Treasurer, John Howard, had run an undisciplined budget process. Early in the 1983 election campaign Garnaut wrote to both Hawke and Keating about the likely problems that would emerge in the regulated exchange rate system, quoting the enormous flight of capital that had occurred in the early days of the Mitterand government (elected a few months earlier in France), and the destabilising capital flows in Sweden after its new government's announcements of social democratic programs. In Australia, at that time, each month a note would be hand delivered to the prime minister, telling him what the secretary of the Treasury, the governor of the Reserve Bank and the main economist in the Department of Prime Minister and Cabinet had decided the exchange rate of the Australian dollar was to be. 'The focus required on this area of policy was quite ridiculous,' Garnaut said. The antiquated practice had also created a competition in the business community for outguessing the government officials, thus causing speculative capital flows.

In his letters to putative Prime Minister and Treasurer, Garnaut also said that an anticipatory devaluation at the very start of the government would probably be necessary. It would need to be supported by a high degree of wage restraint to ensure that the inflationary effects of the devaluation did not pass through into the cost structure of the economy. 'I thought there was a risk of a lot of destabilising capital flows at the time of the formation of the new government. Now, as it happened, that capital outflow began during the campaign.'

When Hawke and Keating met on the Monday after the election, a feeling of crisis had already developed among bankers and the business community. The new Prime Minister and Treasurer decided to devalue the currency by the amount that Garnaut had suggested: 10 per cent.

A day or so later Graham Evans rang Garnaut to ask him to come over for a chat with the Prime Minister. They had a long conversation on the issues facing the new government, at the end of which Hawke asked,

> Is there anything I've been saying, or in our program, that would make you uneasy about taking on the role as

my economic adviser? You don't have to worry about protection: I know your views on that, and we'll get there, but not until we've got employment moving in the right direction. We have to do that first.

Garnaut recalled,

I said, 'Well, I'm pretty uneasy about the whole macro-economic framework that you've been elected on—this big fiscal expansion. Malcolm [Fraser] has already fired up the Budget so much that before long public expenditure will be putting a lot of pressure on things, and if you put in place the whole of your existing expenditure program on top of that, you'll blow the head off the place.' Hawke replied cryptically, 'You don't need to worry about us doing that.'

It was only days since Stone had given Hawke the note warning that Labor was heir to a deficit, kept secret by the Liberals during the campaign, of $9.6 billion. Privately, Hawke had already decided to jettison most of the spending promises in Labor's platform. But ditching election promises was a matter of great delicacy, with ministers, in the party and in the electorate, which he intended to reveal only as necessary.

Garnaut said, 'So we agreed there were no inhibitions to my taking on the role as his adviser.' Hawke would describe him later as 'the co-architect' of the government's landmark economic reforms. (The Prime Minister's other economic adviser was the very able and influential Ed Visbord from the Department of Prime Minister and Cabinet.)

Garnaut and Visbord were set to work immediately on ways of reducing the huge projected deficit and Garnaut spent Easter 1983 at the Hawkes' house in Sandringham, where he and the Prime Minister worked together from early morning to midnight over several days on what turned out to be the government's first budget statement, delivered in May. Their only interruptions were for meetings with a succession of state premiers.

In his initial letters to Hawke and Keating, Garnaut had raised the issue of the exchange rate system. It sounds Dickensian these days, and it already was in 1983. From early in the year discussions began on how to reform the antiquated, dysfunctional system for determining the exchange rate. 'In the end the only change that would clean it up was a floating of the dollar and a lessening of exchange controls,' Garnaut said.

But this could not be achieved without first psychologically preparing the business community. In May 1983 when discussion began in earnest, floating the dollar was not seen as urgent. In the second half of the year, there were larger speculative capital inflows, and they continued to grow. Speculative investment is destabilising, and these ever-greater inflows, attracted by the artificial exchange rate, caused things to come to a head in October. There was a meeting in Hawke's office with Keating and Stone. Stone was against a float on principle, for the cogent reason that once the currency floated, Treasury would lose control over monetary policy. Garnaut recalled,

> Paul wasn't against it per se, but he was still pretty dependent on Treasury through that first year, so he let Stone carry most of the argument. At the meeting I suggested floating the forward rate, which would give a clear signal [to business] that soon we would float the whole thing.

The next day, at a meeting of business economists in Melbourne, Hawke announced the government would float the forward rate, 'and from that time we were just waiting for the best moment', Garnaut said. But money kept flowing in, in waves.

The next crisis came at the end of the first week of December 1983. It was obvious to Hawke and Garnaut that the float could not wait any longer: the question was whether Keating and the Treasury could be persuaded to act. There was a long discussion in Hawke's office, ending about midnight, which was inconclusive. Garnaut said, 'We in the PM's office were disappointed that it hadn't been decisive, and after Paul had left we said, "You know, we can't keep buggerising around like this."' Hawke's chief of staff, Graham Evans, wrote of:

> Peter Barron [one of Hawke's political advisers] meeting with the then Treasurer on the night before the decision to float the exchange rate ... to establish whether or not 'he was in the cart' (an event which has since given rise to enough works of fiction to start a library!)

Garnaut recalled,

> So Peter Barron was sent down to bring Paul back. And Bob said something like, 'We're buggerising around!' and Paul said, 'Well, I've just had the Reserve Bank in my ear saying a similar thing—so yes, we'll do it.' By then it was well after midnight. Paul phoned the bank people and said, 'Come up to Canberra tomorrow.' There was a series of meetings, the bank announced the markets would be closed all day Friday. It was announced, and by Monday the dollar was floating.

There were surprisingly few objections because few people understood what had happened. Garnaut said,

There was some muted anxiety from the industrialists; the farmers hadn't worked out what it meant. It was sort of breathtaking, and so the main commentary was from positions of awe, rather than criticism. The people who understood it best were those in the merchant banks, the investment banks, who liked it and took the benefit from it. And they immediately came in with plenty of positive commentary. My memory is that once it was done and was positively received it gave Paul a lot of confidence. He had taken a position contrary to John Stone, it had turned out to be a political success, and I think that was crucial in building his confidence.

The decision had such a strong psychological effect on Keating that forever afterwards he would claim that floating the dollar was his idea and he had to persuade the Prime Minister to go along with him (Graham Evans' 'works of fiction'). Bill Hayden, who had been Treasurer in the Whitlam government, recalled, 'I wrote in my autobiography that it was Keating's idea, because Keating said it was. And Peter Walsh [Finance Minister] got in touch with me and said, "You're wrong, you know. It was Hawke who did those things."' Hayden added,

> Keating was terribly worried about it, because Stone was against it. He came and saw me and said, 'I want to talk to you about floating the exchange rate. How do you feel about it?' I said, 'I've always supported it. I've made speeches about the way Fraser used to rig the exchange rate to keep the dollar up and he did that through high interest rates. So count on me. I'm on side.' But I had misunderstood Keating's reason for coming to talk to me. He wanted me to be on side with him to *oppose* it.

Until this time Hawke had hankered after having Ralph Willis as Treasurer, for Willis' skill and knowledge, and had raised the issue with his political advisers from time to time. They told him it was non-negotiable: the New South Wales Right, which had overturned Hayden in Hawke's favour, still insisted on Keating. Paul Kelly, the political commentator and author, recalled, 'This is a hyper-sensitive issue which I don't think ever came out at the time, but the discussion [in Hawke's office] was, "What do we do if Paul's not up to the job?" Paul was struggling.' Keating had confessed to the Prime Minister that he was terrified during Question Time in case the Opposition asked him for economic details he would be unable to give. Fortunately, the Opposition was in too much disarray to realise it could severely embarrass the Treasurer and the government, and the dreaded questions were never asked. So Hawke set out, according to an insider, to 'strengthen Keating, give him confidence and win his friendship'. John Bowan, the Prime Minister's adviser on Foreign Affairs, recalled,

> In the old Parliament House we'd be in those little cubby holes of offices and at Question Time Paul would put on one of his virtuoso performances and then he'd come walking down the corridor to go and have a session with Bob. And Bob would tell him how wonderful he'd been. They would bask in this mutual admiration.

The relationship between Prime Minister and Treasurer was on Hawke's part warm and avuncular. His elder daughter, Sue, recalled, 'Paul was the only man Dad encouraged to take the limelight from him. He had an indulgent feeling to Paul.' He called the Treasurer 'Paulie'; Keating called him 'Uncle Bob'. Hawke was proud of Keating, fourteen years his junior, and regularly introduced him to foreign leaders as the future of the Labor government. Keating had plenty of rough edges, for in his bones he had the Irish Catholic anger of how it hurt to be pushed to the margins of society for generations, to be humiliated into second-class lives—deprived, even in egalitarian Australia, of a place at the table in matters of social importance. Hawke was keen to expand Keating's geopolitical grasp and invited him to come to Asia, the initial leg of Hawke's first overseas visit as prime minister. It was Asia that had first opened Hawke's eyes to another world, one so foreign it had made him question the core of his identity. But Keating was still very green. Graham Evans, running Hawke's office, noted: 'The Treasurer informed us he would not be joining the prime ministerial party in Asia, "because Asia was somewhere you flew over on your way to Europe".' Keating would change his mind later, and became an Asiaphile. He sparkled with intelligence and had a natural elegance of movement that made him visually pleasing as a foil for Hawke's shorter, stronger body and hard jaw. 'Paul's a mixture of a hired killer and someone you could imagine as a parish priest,' Bowan said. 'A terrific guy. Very warm and decent. And charming.'

The relationship of Prime Minister and Treasurer, while warm and strong with the cement of comrades in arms, had from the outset a hidden undertone of rivalry. Hawke had ruined not only Hayden's plans for his future, but Keating's also: Keating had backed himself to succeed Hayden after a term and a half, or two—as he had told Hayden to his face—and had been a late, unwilling convert to Hawke's ascendancy. Keating recognised in Hawke a leader much tougher to unseat than Hayden, one who would not be farewelled nearly so soon.

Garnaut recalled,

> I knew Paul better than Bob at the beginning, because when Paul had been shadow Minister for Resources and Energy he took a lot of interest in my work. One of the

big policy issues Paul pushed then, in fact the biggest one, was the resource rent tax, which I had designed. Paul used my material, and whenever he needed a battering ram in Caucus he would drag me over to play that role. So we had a fair bit of contact. When he was putting his staff together Bob set up a process requiring a couple of references from others for each new staffer, and Hayden and Keating felt they knew me well enough to provide references. And on my very first hour in the office Paul Keating came into my room, a small cubicle in the old Parliament House, and closed the door and said, 'Ross—if you and I play our cards right, we'll run this show.' So he was inviting a close relationship. And it was a close and productive relationship through that first year. But I must say I was taken aback by his remark. A little bit surprised. I didn't know how to interpret it, so I just tucked it away as one of those things you think about.

Not long after the election, the columnist Peter Robinson had noted that Hawke was an anomaly in Labor politics:

> By history and by definition, the Labor Party is a party of conflict—a political movement aimed always at 'fighting'—fighting what used to be called 'the class war' ... Its passionate oratory almost invariably centres around the righting of wrongs, the correction of injustice, the battle against overwhelming capitalist power. The entire thrust of the Hawke philosophy is, in fact, foreign to these basic Labor assumptions ... His rhetoric ... concentrates on national unity, the pride of all Australians in their nationhood and the need to work together for

future generations ... It is a theme he has been hammering away at ever since he came into public life ... which he has pursued with such evangelical zeal that many political cynics concluded he was just too good for the real world and would never get anywhere in politics. So much for cynicism.

By the end of that first year in power, the government and the Prime Minister were more popular than ever. Hawke was named Australian of the Year. In January 1984, the *Australian* ran a headline 'Hawke Is the Man Who Is Bringing Us Together' and inside, 'People believe there is change, there is hope.' There was an excellent team of ministers, probably the most talented in Australian history, becoming even stronger later when Hawke moved young Kim Beazley into Defence. In those days a Labor Prime Minister had to accept as ministers men and women chosen by Caucus; his only discretion was in how he allotted portfolios. But his personal office was at his own discretion: there Hawke assembled a cast of erudition, sophistication, cunning and power. Most importantly, all of them saw it as their job to call the shots as they saw them and not as the Prime Minister wanted to hear.

There was Hawke's chief of staff, Graham Evans, and his chief economic adviser, Dr Ross Garnaut; his Foreign Affairs adviser, John Bowan, a passionate, witty, well-read former diplomat, a self-described 'music lunatic', whose ear had won him the apocryphal reputation for knowing every note of every symphony ever written. He was also a sports fanatic, which created a strong bond between him and the Prime Minister. Hawke decided to revive a tradition that had died with Menzies, a Prime Minister's XI cricket team. Evans, assisted by Bowan, helped him select it. 'I think if cable TV had existed then,' Bowan said, 'the government would have fallen to pieces because Bob would have been up all night watching the golf and the tennis.' Hawke had two political advisers: Peter Barron, of the New South Wales Right, and Bob Hogg, of the Victorian Left. Barron was and is one of the most fascinating characters in Labor politics, for he has an octopus' knack of invisibility, rarely giving interviews or allowing an opinion to be attributed to him and never writing anything down. He later went to work for Kerry Packer. Communications ministers and shadow ministers spoke of seeing Barron 'flit out of the room' on their approach—having already advised Packer, they realised, on how to handle them. Barron was stocky and fair-haired, with a pudgy face and blue eyes in which, from time to time, an imp could be seen turning cartwheels and laughing. As a youth he had worked in Paddy's Markets in Sydney before becoming a tabloid journalist, then a press secretary to the New South Wales Premier, Neville Wran. The fruit and vegetable markets, a ragged, poetic, semi-criminal world of hungry expectation and quick wits, had helped form Barron's intellect and sympathies. He was shrewd, straight talking, funny, very likeable—and would never step back from a fight. One of his jobs early in Hawke's time in office was to close the door to people who, because of past association, presumed they had as much access to the Prime Minister as in the old days. The millionaire industrialist, Sir Peter Abeles, a friend with whom Hawke did want frequent contact, quickly ran foul of Barron, whom he urged Hawke to sack. Abeles was a large, dignified man of deeply serious demeanour, who bore himself with the quiet majesty of a Rolls Royce. He had a heavy Hungarian accent. He would pause in conversation and in the silences one could almost hear the wheels of some mighty machine turning; when he next spoke, a deeper, unanticipated layer of thought would be revealed. But while Abeles knew a lot about business and the world, he was unversed in Labor politics. He complained 'That Barron is not—' searching for the expression in English, but ending with a literal translation from Hungarian '—not *room clean.*' He meant 'house-trained'. Being not house-trained was exactly how Barron was most useful. A very senior public servant observed of Barron,

> If he's got a point to make, he can make it in three words where most people would need three sentences. He's very direct and you can't miss the message he's giving you. He's a combination of being really, really smart and astute politically and in other ways, but also of knowing if there was a bad decision coming down the line. He would kill it in three words. Bob used Peter to deal with issues that arose with some of the really strong ministers. It was a very strong Cabinet, and some of them had very strong views. When there were issues bubbling, especially from the New South Wales Right, or Keating, they would talk to Peter first, and if he thought what they were telling him was crazy he'd just say so and they'd go off with a flea in their ear and would think again. He protected Bob from having to deal with a lot of stuff that was going on.

Ross Garnaut recalled,

> It was a relatively small office by modern standards but it was a pretty interesting group. The work environment was made much more productive by Bob's very open approach. He had from the beginning what I think is a very important characteristic for a prime minister, but a rare one, he did actually want to hear what people were thinking, whatever that was, whether it was positive or negative. We presented truth exactly as it was, unspun, and often loaded with awful political management challenges . . . It was a very open office in terms of exchange of views. Sometimes shockingly so. Although I was used

to being open and candid, I was open and candid in a gentle way. Peter Barron would use the language that I later learned was characteristic of the New South Wales Right. I remember after one Caucus meeting Bob came back shaking his head, saying, 'Those bloody troglodytes from New South Wales!' and Barron said, 'Bob: they might be troglodytes. They might all be as thick as planks, but I don't want ever to hear you call them troglodytes again. You're Prime Minister because they put up their hands when we want them to.'

(In retelling, Garnaut almost certainly deleted Barron's favourite adjective, 'fucking'.)

Barron understood the way bureaucrats would return with an issue that a political adviser believed was settled with the Prime Minister, and change his mind. 'Peter was very good at knowing when to have the last word. He'd make sure somebody didn't get let in to the prime ministerial presence after a decision had been made,' a colleague recalled.

All agreed that Barron was sometimes crude in his language.

At a time when it was such a bad word even red-blooded men in anger rarely used it, Barron regularly called people 'cunts' to their faces; he was allowed outrageous behaviour rather in the fashion of a Shakespearean king's fool. Like the fool, Barron was always the politically smartest guy in the room, the one to speak unwelcome truths. Once, travelling interstate, he was so frank and fearless in his advice to the Prime Minister within the hearing of the Commonwealth driver that Hawke summoned him to his hotel suite and verbally decapitated him. Hawke's temper when unleashed, which it rarely was, was ferocious. But always, as soon as the storm was over, sunshine returned, with no hard feelings. Michael Duffy, known as 'Black Mick', a Minister for Communications, recalled, 'I had rows with Bob and I'd think,

"Jesus, he'll never speak to me again." But the next time we met he had completely forgotten about it.' Hawke was, all his staff agreed, a very amiable and fair-minded boss. They were loyal to him, and to each other.

Bob Hogg, from Victoria, had been given the job of weeding out undesirables from among Hawke's associates before he became party leader. Power brokers in the Victorian branch of the party wanted Hawke rid of, Hogg said,

> sycophants and back-slappers, some of them just grubs, others of dubious value, people who made him feel comfortable, put him in too much of a comfort zone, rather than in a critical zone. Politics is about ideas, and these people had no ideas.

Hawke, ever optimistic about himself and human nature, was and would remain vulnerable to toadies and the company of people who praised and apparently adored him. 'If somebody was nice to Bob, he thought that person liked him,' an observer remarked. 'If somebody was nice to Keating, Paul thought, "What's he after?"'

The risks from adulation and lies are a constant danger to people with power. The vanity of political leaders is tempted day and night, for everywhere they go they are flattered. It was all the more important that Hawke surrounded himself with men (and one woman, Jean Sinclair) who spoke frankly. Hogg had been an enemy. He had despised Hawke over the question of uranium mining, which Hawke supported, and which at the time was still the most bitterly divisive issue in the ALP. Kim Beazley recalled being spat on as he walked down the steps of his Canberra hotel in 1984 by anti-uranium activists attending a party conference. ('How we got ourselves into such a knot over uranium is a mystery—when you consider that Jim Cairns, Whitlam's Minister for Trade in the early '70s, was trying to sell Australian uranium to the Shah of Iran,' Beazley said.) The ALP, so long out of power, was filled with people whose political idealism had become reckless and unreserved, untouched by any pragmatic need to maintain economic order. Hogg said,

> I was a product of the Cold War period, of the left persuasion on social issues especially. After I went to work with Bob when he became PM, very sane, rational leftish people said, 'How can you work for that shit?' I said, 'He's the fucking *Prime Minister*.'

Hogg's political fire was concealed by a diffident manner and a soft, kind face under a Beatle haircut. He resembled a stocky brown-eyed pixie. He recalled, 'After about three years the same people said to me, "You were right, you bastard." When you look back on those years [the 1970s and early 1980s] you wonder, "What on earth were they going on about?"'

Geoff Walsh was Hawke's press secretary, but also functioned as a de facto third political adviser, and was another quietly spoken good-looking young man, with a wry sense of humour and sharp political nose. Walsh later made a tribute to Hawke, describing his time with him as 'the richest work experience in my life ... Your optimism and ambition for this nation and its people ... your compassion and genuine delight in the company of your fellow Australians was a source of wonder and inspiration.'

In addition, the Prime Minister had two lieutenants, each in control of a large faction in the Caucus. One was Senator Robert Ray of Victoria; the other Graham Richardson. Ray was a former teacher, a calm, pipe-smoking, brown-skinned man who projected an aura of quiet menace. He had a very dry wit and, and as a lover of junk food, an ample girth. Keating referred to Ray as the 'Fat Indian'. The Victorian Right was smaller and less important than the New South Wales Right, so Richardson had a larger role to play with Hawke, although the Prime Minister respected Ray in a way in which he could never respect Richardson.

If Garnaut was Apollonian in intellect and temperament, measured and restrained and of unimpeachable character, Richardson was his dark opposite: Dionysian. To the Left wing of the ALP and Left-leaning journalists, there was little to distinguish between Richardson and Mephistopheles except, perhaps, the devil cut a more dashing figure. Richardson's face had been lacerated in a car smash when he was sixteen and stitched back together, but it was a pink potato all the same. It was Richardson's personality that was intensely attractive. Full of vitality and brisk intelligence, shrewd, earthy and humorous—although given to gloating on how clever he was—he kept bad company, was guilty of numerous moral delinquencies, was loyal to friends, a fighter, frank, a man determined to claim his right to avoid the disappointed life he had seen the men of his father's generation live. He was also a gifted liar. Most importantly, he could 'count': that is, he could discern, by tone of voice, by light of eye, who was lying and who was speaking honestly when he asked for support. He was, in a way, an archetypal trickster, a man who knew that, despite fervent belief to the contrary, the world was essentially irrational. He seemed to understand the bottomlessness of human desire. In his youth in ALP headquarters in Sussex Street, Sydney, he was nicknamed 'Consumption Man' because of his appetite for junk food. He and Barron were best friends, very alike in their shrewdness, wit and irreverence, but Barron was more playful and blithe of spirit.

There were two other key members of the Prime Minister's inner sanctum: Sir Geoffrey Yeend, the secretary of the Department of Prime Minister and Cabinet, a dignified mandarin who had served Whitlam and Fraser and whom Whitlam praised as 'the *second-best* politician in Canberra'. (No prize for guessing the best, in Whitlam's mind.)

Last, and importantly, there was Graham Freudenberg, Hawke's speechwriter. Freudenberg had been Arthur Calwell's speechwriter, Whitlam's and Neville Wran's. He had a love of history and the party, a lovely, prosodic writing style, a rather fey manner, and an addiction to cigarettes and drinking cans of beer while he worked. He and Jean Sinclair were very close. Jean, who had been Hawke's secretary and personal assistant since 1973, was the most low-profile member of Hawke's staff, but she held in her memory more than a decade of his life, habits, family problems, friends and indiscretions, and in this respect was senior to all the others. It was to Jean they turned when unusual problems arose. Her discretion was legendary.

According to all the staff, it was a very happy office. On a typist's birthday, there would be a cake and a song and a kiss from the Prime Minister. When there was tension between Sir Geoffrey Yeend and the politicals—especially Barron—it was diffused with humour. Yeend had, Hawke said, a love–hate relationship with Barron, whose political brilliance Yeend recognised. For his part, Yeend's gravitas caused Barron agonies of temptation. On an official visit to the Cook Islands, Barron, having arrived before Yeend at the hotel in which the Australian party was to stay, took the manager aside to warn him an international conman would soon be arriving, claiming to be 'Sir Geoffrey Yeend': under no circumstances should he be checked in or the manager would never see his money again.

Barron installed himself in a large armchair in the lobby to observe what ensued at the reception desk. Yeend turned up and announced himself. Unfortunately, he was not booked in, he learned. Puzzled, he persisted. Finally, asserting his natural authority he had the manager summoned. The manager confirmed the hotel was full, and there was no booking in his name. At this point Yeend broke the habit of a lifetime and insisted that the Australian Prime Minister be informed. With a po-face, the manager gave way to the sheer force of conviction of the knight. Barron, hiding in the armchair, was in stitches, but vanished just as Hawke, dragged away from reading in the sun, arrived in the lobby.

Walsh recalled,

> It was a fabulous place to work. There was such a sense of purpose. It was a team that didn't need any artificial, contemporary team-building exercises to create it. There was mutual respect for the qualities that each person brought to the task. Where there were difficulties, they didn't linger ... There were tensions because you had Left and Right, New South Wales and Victoria, idealistic and pragmatic, and lots of neat divisions, but there was more that Peter [Barron] and Bob [Hogg] agreed on than they differed on. Because in the end they were always thinking, 'How do we turn this into votes? How does this get us re-elected? How is this going to be perceived by all the small interest groups?'

This team of invisibles was the dramatis personae who played their roles in the wings and behind the set, working the stage machinery, dressing, coaching and prompting.

Garnaut said,

> It was a respectful office. Bob used to drag us into all of the discussions, especially on the economic things. It was sometimes uncomfortable, because he'd bring together people he thought needed to be part of a discussion and would, with everyone present, ask them to put out their views. And he'd sit back, sometimes with his feet up on the desk, smoking a cigar, listening. On economic policy matters that often required me to say things that were the

opposite of what the Treasurer was saying, which wasn't great for my relationship with him, but Bob wanted to hear both sides. 'What do you think about that, Ross?' 'What's your view, Paul?' And this brought us into direct conflict. I always said exactly what I thought; I had no doubt what the Treasurer was thinking. Bob would get the discussion going, listen to everyone, and after thinking about it for a while would sum things up. Sometimes he'd say, 'Well—I agree with Paul.' Or, 'I agree with Ross.' It was all right for my relations with Paul if Bob had agreed with him, but if he had summed up against him, that was very bad for my relations with the Treasurer ... Bob handled discussions with [other ministers, such as] Button [Industry], with Susan Ryan [Education], Walsh and Dawkins in the same way. Paul was the only one who resented it. And he did resent it.

Keating had an intuitive, artistic mind that arrived at conclusions through leaps of insight, often of dazzling originality. But having had scant formal education, he was untrained in and unfamiliar with the practice of freely testing ideas that is foundational to academic intellectual enquiry. He often complained to others about the presence and influence of Garnaut. Even a quarter of a century later, he would refer to it with irritation, as a black mark against Hawke. The fact was that Hawke and Garnaut were soul brothers; Hawke and Keating never were.

But these tensions between the Prime Minister's office and the Treasury were ephemeral in the context of the major work of reforming the nation upon which all of them were bent. Paul Kelly said,

Keating had been infused with a great sense of confidence after the float. It really made him as Treasurer. It was a good period for [the government]: Hawke was a confident Prime Minister, Keating was now confident about the Treasury job. You had a constructive and cooperative phase in their professional alliance.

By the end of 1983 Hawke had launched a national conversation on the importance of change, including science, technological innovation, education and trade as part of the economic structural reform story he elaborated. Hogg, Barron and Walsh had urged him from the outset to be frank with the electorate, which chimed with his own inclination. Hogg said,

> The thing that, by far, made him the best prime minister I've ever seen is that he took to heart the early advice that you had to explain to the people what you were doing. Why were you doing it? Is there going to be pain? He did that across the board. He was an educator. And that educative role was essential.

In his speeches Hawke connected all areas of the economy, pointing out its weaknesses and potential weaknesses, strengths and potential strengths, so that, over a period of years, and with the help of financial journalists, the Australian electorate became one of the most, if not the most, economically literate in the world. Keating backed him to the hilt with his own salesmanship. Bill Hayden recalled, 'Paul was a super salesman. If he wanted to persuade you of something with which you disagreed, you'd have to hang onto the arms of your chair. He was the most persuasive bloody salesman I've ever come across.'

At the time of Federation, Australia was one of the two richest countries on earth but had gone steadily downhill until the 1980s, when the Hawke government halted the decline and the nation began climbing back towards the rich list. Hawke's first years of government were spent stripping the economy of hang-overs from the past. Kim Beazley recalled,

> Basically, we were still in lock-step with the paradigm established in the 1950s under Bob Menzies. It had been tinkered with at the edges, there had been lots of studies done on what was the problem in Australia, there was endless chatter about how the structure on which we had survived and prospered had basically run out of steam, but there was no will or policy direction in the Australian political process. Bob changed all that.

Hawke was assisted by talented ministers but, as many noted, he encouraged their talents. Other prime ministers before and since have had cabinets that were never allowed to reveal their talents. As soon as the ministry was selected Hawke called them together to say: 'There are only two circumstances in which I will become involved in your portfolios. First, if you ask me, and second, if an issue arises that has a whole-of-government implication. His method was to talk individually to each minister about priorities and the direction of the portfolio. The road map being clear, he then left the minister to get on with the job.

Peter Walsh, Minister for Resources, dismissed at a stroke a system for setting the price of domestic crude oil that had been in place since the days of John Gorton's prime ministership (1968–71). Walsh was a dour, tough character, an economic rationalist, robust and down to earth. His blunt management style is revealed in a Parliament House account of how he dealt with a very tired staffer. Megan Stoyles, a gorgeous blonde who had worked for the Whitlam government and was almost as famous for her mischievous sense of humour as for her large breasts, was Walsh's press officer in the early 1980s. On learning one night that Ms Stoyles had passed out in the Non-Members Bar, Walsh stomped in and without a word heaved her over his shoulder like a bag of potatoes and stomped out again. He was not the sort of minister to be defied or mystified by bureaucrats.

But in Trade and Industry, the bureaucracy was able for months to stonewall their new minister, Lionel Bowen, on changing a practice that had been introduced by the Whitlam government and left in place by Fraser. The Department of Trade had to approve the price of any export contract in the resources sector. It provided plenty of work for the bureaucracy—which engages endlessly in turf battles for more staff and more authority—while many businesses also found it congenial. A staffer recalled,

> It was a comfortable sort of arrangement where companies didn't have to be very clever at negotiating. They were told what the price was. In that area Bob really had to say to Lionel Bowen how things were going to be in future. It wasn't quite a meeting of minds, but Lionel never made a big issue about it, he just accepted it.

The forum in which ministers learned they would have to curtail their budgets was the Expenditure Review Committee (ERC). The ERC was established soon after the government took office and was in full swing by May 1983. Its purpose was to cut all the fat it could from the government's program. Hawke chaired it. The other members were Keating, Walsh, Willis and Dawkins, at the time Minister for Finance. Dawkins, from a wealthy West Australian family, was an intelligent, complex man whose nature combined courage, strong sympathies for the underdog and in his convictions a certain brutal rage. Like Walsh, he was a head kicker. These two were the hard cops of the ERC. Ralph Willis was the soft cop. Keating, in the early stages, was too inexperienced to contribute much, so it was up to Hawke, Walsh and Dawkins to make the tough decisions. ERC meetings were held in the Cabinet room. Dawkins, as Finance minister, was in charge of the one department that shadowed every other department and knew more about what was happening financially in the government than any other minister, on occasions even more than the Prime Minister. He frequently knew more about a department's expenditure than its own minister did. He recalled,

> It was a matter of bringing these new ministers in and pinching their money. It just had to be a fairly brutal process but it really was done with a great deal of co-operation, and was a very important part of making the new government. It established the discipline we needed.

On occasions Garnaut would be called in to explain to a minister the economic necessities the government was facing. In May 1983, in the midst of the Combe–Ivanov distraction, the ERC produced its first expenditure review statement, announcing a big reduction in spending, but also reintroducing a universal health care system, Medicare. Hawke had to leave the ERC from time to time to attend to other business but it sat almost daily for six weeks, from the end of the Summit, until the statement was ready. 'We were hardly ever out of the bloody Cabinet room,' Dawkins recalled. 'We'd start in the morning and quite often go through late into the night.' In June, July and through to the first week of August, the ERC sat again, almost daily, preparing for the Budget which, in those days, was delivered in early August. Hawke began calling ERC sessions 'Erk!' meetings.

Sector by sector, Hawke worked through the economy. It was clear at the time of the election that Australia had serious problems at both the micro and macro levels. Macroeconomic policy balances the economy's total demand with its capacity to supply; if the macro balance is out of kilter it is impossible for the nation to improve overall. Hawke's view from the outset was that the macroeconomic situation had to be going in the right direction, and employment growing, because that was the necessary base of everything else. Microeconomic policy reform is concerned with efficiency at the level of an industry or a firm, or a union or the labour market, and is the engine of economic growth.

While the Summit and the Accord had as their first focus the macro economy, behind that and simultaneously there was recognition that barriers to efficiency had to be removed across the board. In steel production, in research and development—miserable by international standards—and in education. Australia's proportion of children completing high school, 37 per cent, was the lowest in the OECD. Changes in attitude in the labour market, with an end or at least a diminution of confrontations and strikes, were essential to raising productivity. Hawke knew this only too well from his decades in the trade union movement. He was determined that attitudes and relationships within individual industries had to change, that government policies had to be adjusted to achieve higher productivity. With higher productivity, the nation could become prosperous again.

But there were many instances in which good economic policy could not be reconciled with good politics. Hawke had *an* answer to this problem, but there is no complete answer. Geoff Walsh recalled,

> Bob insisted that if people were impacted for something that was in the medium- or the long-term good of the country and the economy there was a responsibility to ensure that they were adequately protected. But there is often a crunch, when you can't get that neat resolution. For example, Bob's speech in Japan in early 1984, announcing tariff cutting: in the Labor Party there were a lot of people who had a deep interest and commitment

to the continuation of the manufacturing sector and the membership of their unions, and all the consequences that had for the internal dynamics of the Labor Party.

He added, 'Garnaut won that one.'

Hawke knew that reforms made in 1983–84 would take up to a decade to have their main effects, but as Garnaut noted, he 'underwrote long time-perspectives in policy ... he expected his government to be around to absorb the benefits [of reform]'. The benefit of the tariff cuts and the general economic reforms were paid to the nation in the late 1990s. 'People just couldn't see the benefits earlier,' Walsh lamented. By the time the reforms did start to make the economy soar, Hawke was out of office.

Garnaut recalled,

> Bob had ideas on what needed to be done in each of these areas [of science, technology, education, resources, etc.]. Typically, a couple of members of staff, with Bob, would have a chat about the sort of agenda he would try to lead, we'd get the department to get together some basic material, then have a lengthy discussion with the minister. After a fair bit of focus there would be an understanding with the minister on the way things would go. And that worked very well, with one minister after another. Bob's role as the leader of Cabinet is often described as being chairman of the board and giving ministers a lot of rein, which is certainly a fair characterisation—but it was in a framework that had been worked out fairly elaborately earlier on, before the issue ever came to the Cabinet room.

By the winter of 1984 Hawke had reason to be delighted with the progress his government had made. The recession was over. Unemployment was falling; job vacancies were growing; strikes were fewer; the Opposition was having problems adjusting to its diminished status. With exceptions, the news media were somewhat awed and certainly respectful. The party's national conference had seen another bitter anti-uranium fight, which Hawke had won, and most importantly the conference had agreed to opening the banking sector by allowing in fifteen foreign banks—a huge win for the pro-Hawke, modernising, anti-protection forces.

Government was still strenuously hard work: sixteen hours a day was normal for the Prime Minister, but there was a mounting number of small and larger goals successfully achieved. And always, he could tune himself into the glorious, exhilarating sensation of holding in his hands the nerve fibres of historical action. His popularity rating was 75 per cent, the highest in Australian history.

Then, in a moment, it collapsed in ashes. The staff had to struggle to keep the Prime Minister politically alive.

Fame is the enemy of family life. The Hawkes' family life had been unusual from the time they moved to Melbourne when Hawke took the job of ACTU advocate. 'From that first wage case, in 1958, I had pretty much rock star status,' he said. He worked hard, drank hard and played hard while Hazel stayed in the background, running the house and rearing the children. She was a down-to-earth woman who kept her emotions under firm control and had no illusions about her husband's philandering. But she was proud to be the wife of a man of outstanding ability who, materially, was a good provider. In an era before mothers worked outside the home, this carried much weight. They owned (with a mortgage) a large house with a tennis court and an in-ground swimming pool and Hazel drove a second-hand but handsome Mercedes. She shared his dream of one day living in The Lodge and years later explained why she had not divorced him for his many affairs: 'When you're on a good thing, stick to it,' she said. It was a practical, intelligent attitude to a difficult situation. Neither was happy in the marriage, however, and the household tended to dysfunction. After the firstborn, Susan, the Hawkes had a son, Stephen, then a daughter, Rosslyn. Rosslyn was an adorable toddler whom Hawke liked to keep on his lap or close by when he was studying for wage cases. She grew to be pretty, quick-witted and empathetic, looking exactly like Hazel in her youth. She was full of gaiety and humour: 'Don't touch me! I'm a work of art!' she exclaimed after having her hair and make-up done professionally for a party. Friends doted on her. She adored her father, but threats to his life, public attacks and sneering at him in the media were the constant background to her primary and early secondary school years, causing her acute anxiety. Police guards were posted outside her school when a man threatened to murder Hawke's children.

By the early 1970s huge numbers of schoolchildren were experimenting with cannabis; parents were apprehensive, but more or less powerless against the force of peer pressure. Hazel knew both her daughters were smoking dope and, encouraging them to be open rather than secretive, made a joke about it by having a marijuana leaf pinned to the kitchen notice board. Hawke disapproved of marijuana, which he never tried himself, but he had no scientific ground to argue against it, and as his own drinking was reprehensible it was left as one of those family issues best avoided. At the age of fifteen, Rosslyn left school and home for a gypsy life in the drug houses of Sydney. Hawke and Hazel lived in a state of denial that she was taking hard drugs, but there was no denying the spectral waif Hawke went searching for and eventually found, with the help of Sir Peter Abeles, in a squat house in a Sydney lane. Back at home, her teenaged indiscretion became a family secret. She regained her lovely appearance, fine skin and glossy hair, married a young man from a respectable family and presented her parents with their first grandchild, a son. On 1 August 1984 she gave birth to a second son.

Meanwhile her elder sister, Sue, living in Japan at the time of the 1983 election, had returned to Australia and to Left-wing political activism, and had recently been convicted for possession of marijuana. She was waiting on an appeal.

It was obvious to everyone who knew Rosslyn and her husband, who partied with the Brett and Wendy Whiteley crowd, that they were using heroin—everyone, that is, except her parents, who clung steadfastly to the belief that their daughter did not use hard drugs. The news from the hospital in the first week of August that the new mother was so wasted by heroin she could soon be dead fell on Hawke like an axe. Although he saw less of his children than most fathers, and from the late 1970s there had been a civil war between him and his two elder offspring over uranium mining, his children were, nevertheless, sacred to him.

The news about Rosslyn was like tumbling into a nightmarish fable: at the height of his power, the king's daughter is cast under a spell; a demon is taking revenge on him, on her, on her children, because he failed as a guardian of the sacred.

Hawke told only Jean Sinclair, Paul Keating, a few of his most intimate friends—Abeles being one, plus a couple of others in the Jewish community on whose devotion to family and discretion he knew he could rely. He told no one else on his staff. But most noticed that something was wrong: the Prime Minister was unusually quiet and seemed distracted and nervous. He shrank in on himself.

At this moment there arrived a weird confluence between Hawke's private life and national public events. By the beginning of September 1984 a public storm about drugs was brewing. In 1980 Malcolm Fraser had set up a Royal Commission into the

Ship Painters and Dockers Union (SPDU), in the hope of uncovering the nest of vipers that union certainly was, and of embarrassing both the union movement and the Labor Party. He appointed Frank Costigan, QC, to head it. With zeal appropriate to a Jesuit, Costigan pursued his inquiries, unearthed the vipers but then, to the horror of many supporters of the Liberal Party, discovered their billion-dollar eggs: a vast tax avoidance system known as 'the bottom of the harbour scheme'. It was the tax evasion of choice of thousands of prosperous Australian citizens. During the Fraser years avoiding tax had become a middle-class sport: the tax system was so ramshackle and so full of holes that the temptation to cheat was irresistible. In the chatter of tens of thousands of dinner parties, tax cheating was rebranded as financial savvy. One's doctor and lawyer were doing it. But respectable citizens did not know, or care to know, that a direct line led from their tax accountants to the thieves, thugs and murderers of the Ships Painters and Dockers Union. It was SPDU men who enabled the whole rotten system to operate.

There was huge embarrassment and anger in the Liberal Party when John Howard, the Treasurer, passed retrospective legislation to outlaw the bottom-of-the-harbour and other tax rorts.

But then the situation got messier. Costigan himself had suffered the anguish of a drug-addict child and like every parent in the same predicament nursed a burning hatred for drug dealers. When he stumbled over the fact that the multimillionaire press baron Kerry Packer was having huge amounts of cash delivered to him, Costigan demanded Packer appear before the Royal Commission, which Packer did in February 1984. Costigan's time was running out: the Attorney-General had told Costigan he must wind up by June 1984. (This may account for the shoddiness of the 'case summaries' that were handed to the National Crime Authority, the permanent body established to replace Costigan.)

Enter Brain Toohey of the *National Times* (the journalist who had first floated the Combe–Ivanov story). Someone from within Costigan's team gave Toohey cases of material, including copies of case summaries that asserted Kerry Packer, whom the *National Times* called 'The Goanna', was a drug lord, the importer of pornography and involved in the death by shotgun of a former Queensland bank manager. There was a frenzy of gossip and speculation; Packer was publicly abused by strangers; once, immobilised under a cape in a barber's chair in the window of a Double Bay hair salon, he had to endure the finger pointing and screamed abuse of a group of young people on the street outside.

Andrew Peacock, meanwhile, had found, he believed, a site from which to launch an attack on the Prime Minister: the winding up of the Costigan inquiry, with investigations to be passed over to a national crime authority, was happening against a background of accusations of corruption against police and politicians in New South Wales. Peacock, who had been rather limp as Opposition leader, used letters asking for a time extension from Costigan to Hawke to launch a censure motion in parliament. He accused the Prime Minister of undermining the fight against the drug trade, of protecting 'some of the most powerful criminals in Australia', of being 'a perverter of the law' who 'associates with criminals and takes his orders from criminals'. Hawke stalked from the chamber in fury: if anybody hated drug dealers, he did. As he left, Peacock called after him 'little crook', a slander for which Hazel would never forgive Peacock.

The *Costigan v National Crime Authority* debate ranted on, with Hawke threatening legal action if accused outside parliament of criminality. Already the *National Times* had run a story that the Prime Minister's daughter, Sue, had a drugs conviction that by now had been overturned on appeal; it insinuated corruption of the legal process. At a press conference a week after

Peacock's censure motion a journalist asked Hawke 'if it made a mockery of the political system if politicians [i.e. Peacock] felt inhibited in making statements because of threats of legal action [i.e. by Hawke]'. With television cameras trained on him, Hawke replied, 'In public life you cannot, it seems to me, entirely abandon the rights that you have, because it is not only a matter affecting yourself,' he said. His eyes filled with tears. 'You don't cease to be a husband. You don't cease to be a father. My children and my wife have a right to be protected in this matter.' Tears began flowing down his cheeks. He was then asked if he was upset by the *National Times* article about Susan. Openly weeping he replied,

> Of course I was, because like any father I love my daughter. I trust her and she was completely exonerated by the processes of the law. I had no contact with the judge or anyone involved in it and yet you have this insinuation that affects her. Of course, I'm upset.

The question had referred to Susan, but Hawke had answered thinking of Rosslyn. He was thinking of her day and night, of how to save her and his infant grandsons, who could soon be motherless.

Geoff Walsh shut down the conference as soon as he could and, mystified, shepherded Hawke away. Laurie Oakes, writing for the *Age* commented,

> politicians on both sides were unsure about the electoral impact of yesterday's prime ministerial weeping. There is no doubt, though, that it changes the nature of the organised crime debate ... The tears were real and it made extraordinarily moving television. The millions who saw it will be less likely to give credence to

Opposition claims that the Prime Minister deliberately curtailed the Costigan Royal Commission to protect people financing drug importations and distribution.

The press conference was the start of a full-scale crisis in the office because Hawke, after a month of silent self-flagellation, could no longer conceal the family secret. Nor could he function as national leader. He had gone straight from the interview to a meeting with the Malaysian Prime Minister, Dr Mahathir Mohamad, who hanged people for possession of heroin, and burst into tears, weeping in Mahathir's arms as he told him the story. The staff were appalled. When Hawke called them together to explain the situation they were more annoyed than sympathetic. The Prime Minister had collapsed.

It was as if the guiding hand of destiny in which he had so long and so fervently believed had suddenly bunched into a fist and punched him in the face. Both his elder children, Left-wing in their sympathies, especially Stephen, had argued bitterly with him over uranium at the ALP conference two months earlier. Stephen, eponymous with the first Christian martyr, had suffered a kind of martyrdom all his life as 'the son of . . .', repeatedly flattered or abused on account of his father, to whom he bore a striking physical resemblance. He had taken his mother's side in the dysfunctional family and when he left home changed his name to her maiden name, Masterson, until people recognised him anyway and began calling him 'Steve Wink-Wink Masterson'. Then, having reverted to 'Hawke', he gave his own children their mother's maiden surname so there would be no grandchildren named 'Hawke'. Their grandfather could not comprehend how difficult it was to be labelled the son, or even grandson, of a rock star, and was deeply hurt.

After Hawke's public tears, Peacock was criticised within the Liberal Party for having 'gone too far'. His deputy, John

Howard, tried to defend him, saying, 'Mr Hawke should remember that he is not the only parliamentarian who has a wife and children.' The ever-vicious Wilson Tuckey from Western Australia weighed into the fight with:

> Australians are entitled to the guarantee that their national leader has the moral fibre to carry the pressures of national calamity. After the Prime Minister's 'I want my mummy' performance today, it is clear Australia has no such leader at present.

Keating, a savage team fighter at any time and in an emergency especially dangerous, deflected the attack from the Prime Minister and turned it back on the Opposition with scalding invective. From his upbringing in the Catholic church, he was as familiar with the mighty language monuments of Christendom as with contemporary gutter slang, and he pressed both into the service of his oratory, describing the Opposition's attitude to tax avoidance as 'a dog returning to its vomit', a reference of fascinating horror to those unfamiliar with the second Book of Peter 2:22. To Howard, Keating said, 'I will squash you like a rat.'

Meanwhile in Hawke's office the staff were slow to realise that the Prime Minister was in the grip of depression. They were so used to him riding like a horseman whom some talisman protects from every fall that they were almost blind to what was in front of them. Hawke was contemplating resignation and at one stage even suicide.

How long his depression lasted is contested. Hawke says he was 'down' for about six weeks; some staff members thought six months; Richardson, after he had turned against Hawke, said more than a year. Garnaut said, 'I think a year, or even six months, is bullshit: you just have to look at the record of what was happening: Bob's work in Asia, against protectionism, in education—where he needed endless discussions with [Education minister] Susan Ryan, who was nervous about the teachers' unions.' With disdain Garnaut added, 'They were solid reforms which Richardson wouldn't have noticed.'

As yet no explanation had been made to the electorate about the Prime Minister's emotional state. During a radio interview in Sydney with John Laws, Hawke choked up and did so again with another well-known television and radio man, Clive Robertson. Rosslyn, who unlike her brother enjoyed the excitement of publicity, volunteered to go on national television and explain she had been the cause of her father's distress. The hardheads in the office vetoed the idea immediately. One of them remarked,

> She was too naive to realise they would have crucified her. She wouldn't have had a day's peace for the rest of her life: the media would be watching her every time she stepped out the front door.

Her husband, Matt, then volunteered for the job—but it was discovered he did not own a suit, and for such a serious occasion a suit was deemed essential. Geoff Walsh was a similar size: he was to lend Matt one of his suits. Finally, Graham Evans realised that the best spokesperson would be Hazel and it was she who, with dignity and self-control, explained that their daughter had a drug problem. The nation took her to its heart from that moment on.

Political reporters, who had sat staring at their laps when Hawke wept, seemed relieved to be let off the hook of needing to ask more questions; the public treated the episode 'as one of those things that can happen in any family', Walsh said. Hawke won a large measure of public sympathy.

But behind the political scenery, things were going from awful to frantic. The Caucus was panicky because their jobs depended on the Prime Minister's charisma and it seemed to be evaporating. A leader's authority lies in his *personal* responsibility, which, as Weber noted, 'he cannot reject or transfer ... Ultimately there are only two kinds of deadly sins in the field of politics: lack of objectivity and—often but not always identical to it—irresponsibility.'[1] Hawke, unable to control the dam-burst of emotion, had fallen into deadly political sin. The staff were increasingly annoyed in private, while in public defending him. After Walsh's explanation to journalists that the Prime Minister had not choked up again during a speech, he just had a bit of a frog in his throat, a grim joke went around the office about 'the optic frog'—as in: 'we had another optic frog moment today'. Barron was appalled at what he saw as self-pity.

If any of the staff, beyond the security men, were present when Rosslyn, distraught and hysterical at being separated from her infant children, was loaded on to a private jet and flown to the United States for treatment, all were too loyal to their boss to admit it, even twenty-five years later. For Hawke the moment was lacerating. Normally he could switch off from subjects as easily as flicking a television channel, but from this episode he could not. Wanting to get it out of his mind seems to have contributed to his decision to go to the people again.

By September 1984, the government had a technical excuse for calling an early election. Hawke decided to have an eight-week campaign. Richardson said, 'We thought the length of the campaign was crazy, but he just wouldn't listen.' The staff and the election committee tried to convince themselves that a long campaign was worth the risk because the Prime Minister, being so extroverted, would benefit from getting out among people. *They* would cheer him up.

There is a reason that politicians of all persuasions refer to their work in military terms: battles, campaigns, strategy, tactics, troops, rank and file. It is equally obvious that, if launching a war, one should design it to be as short as possible. Richardson said, 'Hawkey thought, "The longer it goes my mastery over Peacock will show, and I'll increase my majority." And everyone said, "That's bullshit, Bobby. We're a government, we don't give the Opposition room to shoot at us."'

What's more, by now Peacock had some targets. Middle-class abuse of welfare payments had built up over decades in Australia and become egregious during Fraser's years. There were instances of millionaires claiming aged pensions. The government was determined to undo middle-class welfare in favour of giving more to the needy. The 1983/84 Budget introduced an assets test for pensions that inaugurated needs-based welfare as a central theme of the decade—but caused outrage from the Coalition, the Democrats and even some sections of Caucus who had large numbers of retirees in their electorates.

Grey Power was born out of the 1984 election.

Peacock pressed relentlessly on the issue, loudly assisted by a campaign in the Melbourne *Herald*. People were deadly serious about the right of the affluent to government hand-outs, for Fraser had taken the view that once something had been given to the electorate, it could never be taken away. It was the perfect situation for a Liberal tax scare campaign, at which Peacock excelled. John Button accidentally helped him along on 17 October when, in the Senate, Opposition Senator Fred Chaney asked a series of scaremongering questions: 'Will the Government give an assurance that a capital gains tax, a wealth tax or death duties will not be imposed following any review of the taxation system ... ?' John Button replied, 'It is very difficult for me to give an undertaking in respect of capital gains taxes, wealth taxes and death duties.' The fat was in the fire and the Opposition fanned it vigorously. Hawke, campaigning in Perth, needed to quench it as quickly as possible. He announced on radio that there would be a 'Tax Summit' after the election, at which everyone would be entitled to put forward views about reforming the tax system, just as they had at the Economic Summit.

Geoff Walsh, travelling with Hawke, rang Graham Evans in Canberra, explained what had happened, and passed on the message that Hawke wanted Garnaut to begin work on an outline for the Tax Summit. 'It was,' said Evans, 'policy on the run.'

Geoff Walsh recalled, 'From a dream run in 1983, the '84 campaign was a nightmare.' The early election, little more than halfway through the government's term, irritated the electorate, and the enormous length of the campaign irritated it even more. But from the very beginning there was another irritation, and that was in the Prime Minister's right eye. Hawke had played cricket at Kingston Oval in Canberra on the weekend the election was announced and, batting, had mistimed a hook shot, with the ball smashing his own spectacles and driving glass into his eye. In agony and half blind, he was taken to hospital. The surgeon who removed the glass said had it gone a fraction deeper he would have lost the sight of his eye altogether. It was an event that seemed to echo Kafka's story, 'The Penal Colony', in which condemned men have a description of their crimes cut into their flesh with glass. Hawke had been blind to what was happening with his daughter. Now glass had inscribed 'unable to see' in his eyeball.

Hawke said, 'I was an emotional mess and my eye was driving me mad throughout the campaign. I found it almost impossible to concentrate.' But by now he was practising a stiff upper lip and few realised he was in pain. Geoff Walsh, who travelled with him, noted, 'He was clearly uncomfortable and at times a little short.' Hawke spent a minimum of time with the news media travelling with him, whereas Peacock and his new wife, Margaret, fraternised and had fun with their travelling circus.

Before the election was announced Hawke and the party had assumed Peacock would be easily beaten. In the *Bulletin* of 16 October Richard Farmer summed up ALP thinking in a cover piece headlined 'Hawke's Biggest Headache: A Record Poll Majority'. The summary beneath it read: 'With the prospects of a general election loss virtually disregarded, Labor's federal leaders are contemplating a quite different challenge—how to cope with a record majority.' Labor polling confirmed a Morgan poll that the government could win 100 out of the 148 seats in the House of Representatives. The years of existential outsiderness would soon be a distant nightmare and the party looked forward to a decade of Labor government, a political luxury that, until this moment, had been beyond their dreams. For Hawke, victory would be the vindication he yearned for: restoring Labor's honour as the natural party of government, one that could unite the nation in the cause of enlightened self-interest.

Farmer noted that an important part of Hawke's thinking was 'a belief the more the electorate sees of Peacock the less voters like him, and consequently, the greater Labor's likely victory'. Most of these opinions were in error. It is always an error for a government to assume it will win and, worse, to allow the electorate to know it holds that assumption. It is always an error to underrate an opponent. It is always an error to count chickens before they hatch. As Kim Beazley said, 'Had there been something of an expectation that we could lose, we would have changed strategy. Since then, many a Labor government has saved itself by crying poor, but we weren't so sophisticated in those days.'

Richardson recalled,

> At that stage Hawkey's ego was as big as all outdoors, and I think he had an extraordinary view of himself, that the longer the campaign went, the better he'd go.

He saw himself as the emperor and his subjects would all dutifully bow down at the right time—except a lot of them didn't.

Peacock fought well and beat Hawke in their debate, largely it was said, by looking manfully into the camera, something that Hawke, with his sore eye, could not do. Walsh said,

> It was a campaign that lacked the energy and point and punch we'd had in '83. You couldn't repeat that, because the circumstances were different, but Bob didn't do as well as he expected. We all had a share in the blame for that.

Besides Peacock, Keating campaigned well. Stone had taken early retirement in August and this may have contributed to the Treasurer's sense of freedom and strength. What he brought to a campaign in which pensions were a major issue was, in Kim Beazley's words,

> his love of old people. I've never seen anyone, even Bob, better with old people. Paul genuinely respected and loved them. He looked on old men as repositories of wisdom. And they responded to that. The election transformed him.

Keating had been the darling of his grandmother. As a youth he had gone, week after week, to sit at the feet of the aged giant, Jack Lang, a hero to Keating's father, a man old enough to be his grandfather; Keating was born, in a sense, thanks to the tutelage of Lang and to the respect Lang showed him, always addressing the young man as 'Mr Keating'. It was Lang who taught Keating to look intelligently upon himself, who opened the world to him. Theirs was that strangely intimate but elusive relationship between a student and a teacher when Sirens sing an enchantment in the background. It was Lang's strong old voice that unveiled to Keating the possibilities of what the world could hold for him. Lang had lived through, and was in power, in one of those incendiary periods of history, the Great Depression, and had been shockingly burnt by it, sacked as Premier of New South Wales, expelled from the Labor Party (by Curtin), humiliated and reviled. He was a man with a grievous sense of deprivation. It was Lang who warned Keating when he got into parliament, 'you haven't a moment to lose'.

The election of 1984 was a psychological turning point for Keating. The tempo of his dream, which had slowed to a saunter when Hawke became leader, picked up again.

On the Monday after the election, the *Age* editorial's headline summed up the situation: 'Hawke shaken, Peacock stirred'. In a cartoon Hawke was shown crowned, draped in kingly robes, but with sticking plaster on his cheek, a tooth missing, his robes torn and wearing a penitent's sandals. Michael Gawenda wrote, 'Nothing could disguise the disappointment. The smile looked like it had been sculpted on to his face ... He had won even if it had not felt like a victory at all.' Hawke's enemies would paint the 1984 election result as poor. More accurately, it was a realistic result, less than hoped-for, because rather than deliver a swing to Labor there was a 1.4 per cent swing against—but because of recently introduced electoral changes there was an informal vote of 12 per cent, mostly in Labor electorates. In addition, a redistribution meant a loss of two seats in any event. The government was still comfortably in power at the end of the night of 1 December, with a 16-seat majority. But the magic aura that had surrounded the Prime Minister had lost its brightness and he would never be 'Mr 75 per cent' again.

While his public life had taken a battering, his private life was improving. His little grandsons were living at The Lodge. They were to be a source of joy for Hawke and Hazel, bringing a springtime of family life and happiness. After months of hard work in a Californian clinic, Rosslyn overcame her addiction. She returned to live with her parents and care for her children. The fugue of death and despair was over, but its damage to Hawke would never be completely undone. In time, his right eye lost 95 per cent of its vision. Politically he was no longer a god.

But he determined he would win the 1987 election.

3

IN MID-APRIL 1984, on Palm Sunday, an estimated 600 000 Australians marched in cities around the nation 'Against Nuclear War'. The Nuclear Disarmament Party, whose only policy was expressed in its name, came within 6000 votes of winning a Senate seat in the election in December of that year. Hugh White, a defence analyst and journalist at the time, later an adviser to the Defence minister, then the Prime Minister, made the droll observation, 'Nuclear war wasn't actually *the policy* of the Hawke government, but somehow people thought it was a good idea to have at go at us about it anyway.'

The real issue was the American alliance, especially since Reagan had entered the White House four years earlier in 1980 (he would stay there until 1988). Hawke personally was determined that the Labor Party must establish its credentials to govern in the Cold War that, with the Reagan administration, had been growing noticeably warmer. Hawke's government had been elected on a platform that promised to 're-examine the ANZUS alliance to see if it still meets Australia's purposes'. Once the Labor Party had assumed office, the defence chiefs gave Hawke a briefing about what the American bases in Australia—Pine Gap,

Narrunga and North West Cape—actually did. Hawke became, in Beazley's words,

> immensely conscious about how vital the bases were to the United States and to the Western alliance generally and as a result, recognised two things: one was that the bases were basically useful for a whole range of stabilising policy directions in the global political system—that they assisted in making things like arms control stability possible. The second was, he realised that with the United States, if you got too far offside there would be no half measures with them: you would end up in the doghouse. He utterly despised New Zealand's playing games with the nuclear warship visits. He thought that was pissant politics.

The bases, because they were American, and top secret, were a magnet for leftist activists. In the party, Beazley explained,

> The Right took the view that the US alliance was critical, that we needed to pay a price for that relationship and that we were prepared to pay a price. The Centre Left position [Hayden supporters] was: that's probably true, but we ought to be optimising the extent to which we leverage it. The Left position was: it's all just unacceptable.

In December 1984, immediately after the election, Hawke promoted Beazley to Defence minister. Beazley recalled,

> The next day a couple of my senior officials came to me and said, 'Minister, there is something we think you should know.' And they told me about this MX missile test which had to be supported by Australia.

It was the beginning of one of the worst crises of all the years of the Hawke government. John Bowan, Hawke's Foreign Affairs adviser, was to say later, 'When I die and they open me up, they will find "MX" engraved on my heart.' He felt personally at fault for advice he gave the Prime Minister, and for the way he handled the press.

Defence is the largest department of government and, because of its size, complexity and technical detail, presents the greatest difficulties for a new minister. The warrior's eternal mystique is part of the problem, but so too is the continuity of experience for war fighting: the Australian Defence department boasts a proud tradition of baffling and browbeating its ministers, especially about weapons it wants the taxpayer to buy. To add to the problem there is constant friction between the armed and civilian wings of the department, the civilians having perfected a subtle weapon known as 'the snow job': enormous numbers of papers, reports and analyses that need to be read. Beazley, who came to be internationally respected as the best Defence minister Australia ever produced—the best in the world, according to the United States Defence Secretary Caspar 'Cap' Weinberger—had come to the job after decades of personal interest in military matters. He was so intellectually and psychologically well equipped it seemed some field marshal of the past had been resurrected in the guise of a huge, genial West Australian politician. 'Kim was overwhelmingly good. It was like Snap! you could almost hear it happen when he took over,' White said.

> He always thought strategically. For Kim the armed force is never an end in itself. There's always the question: what are the political objectives we're trying to achieve with the armed force? One of the distinctions between people who do this well and those who don't is that the latter become obsessed with the armed

force itself. They forget it's meant to serve a political purpose. Or they get obsessed with the operations themselves, and forget they're meant to be serving a political purpose. For example: what exactly are we trying to do in Afghanistan? Are we sending Special Forces there for fun? ... With Kim, he never lost sight of the reason for action. His view was you had to act not just for domestic political, but for a national political strategic purpose.

On 14 December 1984, when Beazley was told of the proposed MX missile test, he recalled,

> I said to these guys, *'WHAT DO YOU MEAN BY AGREEING TO THIS! YOU KNOW IT'S AN AMERICAN TRY-ON!* All they need to do is change the azimuth of the rockets and they can perfectly well test the MX. The Yanks are trying to assemble all flags.' And they said, 'Yes, we know that, but it was Bill Pritchett's [the secretary of the Defence department] idea and it was picked up by Malcolm Fraser and it went through your security committee ...' So I went up to see Bob and said, 'Mate: this is bad news.' And he said, 'Awww ...'

The background to Hawke's own support for the MX test was that, while Hawke was in Washington in 1984, George Shultz, the American Secretary of State and an old friend, had taken him aside and, out of the earshot of Hawke's aides, had asked him to agree that Sydney could be a staging base for reconnaissance flights to monitor the missile splashdown. Hawke had agreed. Weinberger and Shultz were delighted and thanked Hawke.

Beazley continued,

I said, 'Mate, this is a weapon that will be interpreted as a counter-force; it will be seen as an effort by the United States to achieve superiority in all their rockets. *We* are for MAD [the policy of 'mutually assured destruction' preventing any side from starting a nuclear war], a stable balance. We're going to have hell to pay on this. It'll leak, and there will be a scandal.' ... The Caucus in those days was a much more emotional beast than it is now. And Bob said, 'Oh well, that doesn't matter. We'll just get down and fight for it.'

Bill Hayden remembered,

Bob said he didn't see anything wrong with the Americans using Australian support to launch the missile. And I said, 'Jesus: I wouldn't do that! It's going to send the party into fits.' You see, a lot of moralising had developed in our long period in Opposition, and nobody had tried to straighten them out.

According to White, Hayden underestimates his contribution as Foreign minister to educating the party and the electorate about the American alliance. He said,

Bill established a whole line of argument which had not been present in the Australian debate before and that was: our support for the joint facilities serves Australian interests directly, by supporting agendas we have in arms control and disarmament. There was an element of political convenience in that argument but it was true. Bill made the announcements. Bill's department produced the paperwork and so on. But as soon as Kim took over as Defence minister, Bill backed off and Kim reached out and grabbed it. It became Kim's issue.

But the situation continued to develop. Hayden recalled,

Anyway, Bob wouldn't agree about the tests. No! No! He banged the table and said, 'Listen! I want you to get in there [the Caucus] and fight. *FIGHT!* Hold the fort. Don't back down.' And I thought, 'Jesus—that's all right for him.' And the whole issue opened up and all hell broke out.

Keating was strongly backing the Prime Minister. Richardson recalled, 'Paul was literally telling them all to get fucked. "We'll stand the Caucus up" and all that stuff. I remember having a huge argument with Keating over the MX. He was totally gung-ho.'

The journalist who broke the story was, again, Brian Toohey. In the *National Times* on Sunday, 1 February 1985, Toohey, reporting from Washington under the headline 'Sydney Role in U.S. Missile Tests', noted that the MX could deliver twenty times the explosive force that had obliterated Hiroshima. By the next day, every newspaper, radio and television station in the country was running the story, harping on the theme that Hawke would have to say no, since the test would fly in the face of the government's disarmament policies, and create ructions in the party. The media campaign continued all week.

Hayden continued,

Beazley came forward defending the decision in his way, which was quite intellectual, and then the weekend came up and I thought, 'Most things don't survive the weekend.' I was still going strong. I went on TV with Richard

Carleton on the ABC on Monday and defended the decision very vigorously. Huh! Next morning my principal private secretary told me the declared CIA officer from the American embassy had rung to congratulate me. *Bloody hell!* Anyway, the thing just blew. Blew its head off. There was no way we could hold the line.

Frequently for Hawke, as for any prime minister, the fiercest battles in getting government policy accepted were against his own side. As the political apophthegm has it: 'Those opposite are our Opposition; our enemy sits behind us'. Hawke had been able to enforce Cabinet solidarity, a luxury Whitlam had not had, but the Caucus was another matter. It was the job of the faction bosses, Richardson and Ray for the Right, to keep the Caucus in line. It would be political death for Hawke to be rolled in Caucus, which was growing increasingly fearful; some of it was pumped up, Beazley said, 'by the KGB and Muscovite agents of disinformation who were floating around the place'.

At a news conference in Sydney, Dr Helen Caldicott, a leading anti-nuclear activist, described the agreement to co-operate with the MX test as 'a suicide pact'. The Victorian premier, John Cain, said federal ministers had no 'moral authority' to make the decision without consulting the rest of the party; the New South Wales branch called a rank-and-file meeting on the issue. Richardson said,

> We couldn't hold the Right. If you can't hold the Right, you've got no chance of getting the Centre, and of course you'd never get the Left. At least a third of the Right would have broken. Alan Griffiths [a law and economics graduate from Melbourne, still a backbencher] led the charge—it was twenty-five years ago, but I've never forgotten. Alan Griffiths: one of our rock-solid

blokes. He wasn't someone accustomed to revolution, but he was absolutely adamant. We were dead.

To cap it all, Sir Joh Bjelke-Petersen announced that if Hawke backed down he would allow the P3 aeroplanes needed to monitor the splashdown to fly from Queensland.

Beazley said,

> Bill and I put endless pressure on it. We did press and radio interviews defending the position. The view the pair of us took was, 'The US won't let us off the hook.' In an environment in which the New Zealanders were kicking over the traces on the nuclear ships issue, when the Americans were bracing the Europeans to take Pershing missiles on the Continent and cruise missiles in Britain—this was *not* an environment in which the United States was going to back off. I remember meeting the Americans and saying, *'Just fire the bloody missiles!'* and they said, 'Oh, no. They won't be ready for eighteen months.' So we were going to have to put up with this crap for another eighteen months. Anyway, Bob was about to go overseas, to Japan and then Washington, and he got Richardson to do the numbers. I spoke to Richardson and he said he thought he had a majority of three votes in the Caucus. So I said to Bob, 'It's going to be pretty bloody tough in Caucus,' and he said, 'Aw, no: I've made up my mind we'll have to get out of it.' I said, *'Mate! You can't do that!* The Americans won't let us off the hook.'

Neither Beazley nor Hayden realised that Hawke was holding out as strongly as he was because of his long-standing friendship with the American Secretary of State, George Shultz, whom he had known since his ACTU days. 'He didn't want to fail Shultz,' Richardson said.

Shultz was one of the great men of the twentieth century, and continued to be so in the twenty-first when, well into his ninth decade, he worked on international nuclear disarmament. As a marine in World War II, he had led the American forces ashore at Pulau in the North Pacific and was fond of remarking, 'There's no such thing as an ex-marine.' He was a warrior by nature, a Republican, a sophisticate who—way beyond the conventions of his status and class—had a tattoo somewhere on his body; he was politician, diplomat and a man of profound sagacity. He spoke slowly and thoughtfully, usually in a soft voice and often after a long pause during which his remarkable blue eyes, the colour of aquamarines, gazed like a sea captain's towards some distant horizon. Henry Kissinger, always sparing in his compliments about others, said if the United States were in danger, Shultz was the man he would like to see in charge. At Stanford University, Shultz taught a course in diplomacy that was famous for its insights. 'His knowledge of geopolitics was encyclopedic,' Beazley said. Shultz and Hayden more or less loathed each other and had many shouting matches. Hayden referred to Shultz as 'the German pork butcher'. What Shultz called the Australian Foreign minister to his face was *'STOOPID'*. White recalled, 'In press conferences, when they had to sit side by side, the hostility was just radiating off both of them. It was right up there with John Howard and Bill Clinton in terms of negative chemistry. But it was quite effective diplomatically for Australia.'

Hawke, as so often in a tight corner, was about to turn his weakness—not wanting to disappoint Shultz—into a strength.

Beazley recalled,

> Bob arrives in Washington. For some reason he decided to confide in me—reasonable, I guess, as I was Defence

minister. So I had one of those weird nights. I had my two little girls over from Perth staying with me in a hotel in Sydney and Bob was on the phone to me *all night* to discuss what had been said by whom and to whom. Each time the phone rang my little girls, aged about four and six, would wake up and crawl into bed with me and then start flicking through the television channels and get onto the X-rated movies. I'm desperately trying to talk to the Prime Minister and to seize control of the remote from them, while on the screen people are shagging the arse off each other. Terrific! It was a *dreadful* night. But only Bob could have pulled it off. He convinced Shultz that if the test went ahead, then serious issues would come on the table about the joint facilities, and that there would be a groundswell of opinion in Australia against them.

Hayden recalled, 'Bob rang me at 4 a.m. and said, "Look, we're not going to allow the tests." And that was it.'

When Hawke announced that Australia would not be supporting the MX missile tests the news media frothed: 'Hawke caves in: No to MX tests' was on the front page of the *Australian*, which ran a side story 'Breathtaking victory for the anti-nuclear camp'. One cartoonist, making fun of the fact that American presidents of the past had called Australian prime ministers by the wrong names, had a flunkey announcing to the United States leader, 'Mr Bob Chicken to see you, Sir'. Others drew Hawke tied in a knot with his own arms and legs. Peacock announced that 'Australians would never again trust Mr Hawke in international affairs after his handling of the MX missile'. A poll showed that only 9 per cent of people thought Hawke's performance as prime minister was 'excellent', while 64 per cent rated it as 'poor' or 'average'. Reflecting anger in the party against Hawke, a cartoonist drew the ALP as a frog, its tongue flashing out at a fly: the Prime Minister.

Richardson said,

> If a leader backs off something, the media present it as a disaster for him. But it isn't really. It's just a few days of bad publicity. The far bigger disaster is getting rolled and having your leadership totally undermined. Leaders have to cop a few days of bad publicity now and again. That's what being a leader is about.

The hysteria whipped up about the MX crisis was blamed for a dive in the Australian currency—'Missile Confusion Undermines Dollar' according to the *Australian*, on 8 February—although the more likely cause was that markets were beginning to react to Australia's external payments situation; nevertheless, the dollar was down, and this had serious implications for inflation, and the Accord.

Hawke was blamed.

The day before the Prime Minister returned to Australia, Keating, who had played no public part in the MX Affair to date, stepped forward and told the party, through the news media, to '*Shut up!*'

Beazley saw the crisis at its conclusion as one of the most positive turning points in Australia's relationship with the United States.

> These days everyone wanders around examining their navels, trying to work out the relationship between Rudd and Obama: is it going to be better than the one between Howard and Bush? or was that better than the one between Keating and Clinton? Nobody used to talk like that in the 1980s. Nobody was looking around

for a close relationship between Bob and Reagan, Bob and Bush Senior. In fact, the view in Australia was, 'Yes, keep the alliance, and a degree of independence. Agree on fundamentals, but keep our national policies and the way in which *we* see the world.' So the first of those close personal relationships that I've come across historically between an American and an Australian politician was the Shultz–Hawke connection. It was the first. And it was deeper than any of the others because it did something that none of the others have ever done: it caused the United States to surrender a very important strategic policy to allow an Australian politician to get off the hook. What Bob managed was a miracle.

The MX crisis brought to the fore public debate in Australia about the American bases. Founded on the work Hayden had begun, Beazley steered discussion within Australia and with the Reagan administration; his imaginative power united with his depth of military knowledge transformed the bases issue from one of Big Brother–Little Nobody into one of equality between the United States and Australia. By the end of Beazley's term as Defence minister, the American bases had become the 'joint facilities'—in name and in fact. This is a relationship of equality that, even in 2010, has not yet been negotiated by the British for the American bases in the UK. In the late 1980s, Dick Cheney, the American Secretary of Defence, visited Australia and Beazley, instead of meeting him in Sydney, asked him to fly straight to Pine Gap for a briefing. The Australian Defence minister knew what was about to happen; the American did not. A beautiful woman stepped forward. 'She was gorgeous: a mane of blonde hair,' Hugh White recalled. She was the briefing officer. When she began to speak Cheney's head spun round to stare at Beazley. 'She's an Aussie!' he exclaimed in a stage whisper.

White recalled, 'I was standing right behind Cheney. It was a *very telling* moment.'

After the MX crisis, the next major challenge for the government, and for Hawke in particular, was the 'Tax Summit', promised during the election campaign. There was now a mandate to reform the taxation system. Treasury was more excited than it could remember: with Keating, it had as its champion a politician who, once convinced on an issue, would fight relentlessly. Treasury was only too aware of how jerry-built the tax system was; for a decade its economists had been itching to dismantle most of it and rebuild on the firm foundation of a value-added tax, bringing Australia up to date with most of the rest of the OECD countries. The moment, it seemed, had arrived.

Garnaut had been working since October on a framework for the Summit (as had economists from the Department of Prime Minister and Cabinet, and Treasury). His original note on the framework included both a broad-based consumption tax and death duties—'not that we would *include* those things, but that we should consider everything', he said. But the Treasurer and the New South Wales Right regarded death duties as a political suicide tax, and they were struck from the list as taboo, never again to be mentioned. Hawke had announced nine principles during the election: no overall tax increase; more cuts in personal income tax; a crack-down against tax avoidance and evasion; a simpler tax system; a more progressive system in which tax was paid according to capacity to pay; no disadvantage to welfare beneficiaries; no indirect taxation expansion that might prejudice wage restraint; a package that facilitated investment and employment; and, finally, proposals that had wide community support. It read like a list for Santa Claus. Out of delicacy, the really big present had been omitted. The *big* gift Treasury wanted was a broad-based consumption tax (its purer form, a value-added tax, being deemed too difficult even to consider). 'The Keating–treasury tactic,' Paul Kelly wrote, 'was to hijack the tax agenda. The treasury was not interested in an analysis of options; its mind was set.'[1]

Keating and his advisers believed Labor could win the next election, due in 1987, by outflanking the Opposition on tax reform: increasing the tax base and making deep cuts in personal income tax; appealing to the less affluent by an attack on the tax shelters of the wealthy and rounding this off with a well-aimed kick to the shins of the prosperous: a capital gains tax.

But within a few months Hawke and Garnaut began to suspect Keating and Treasury had helicoptered away into cloud cuckoo land. So, in the end, did most of the rest of the Cabinet. The scene was set for an internal battle.

Keating's tactic, Kelly wrote,

> was to destroy Labor's options ... Keating's aim was to generate such a momentum for reform that ... retreat would be seen as political cowardice and that biting the tax bullet would become the lesser electoral risk ... It was a classic hijack.[2]

Keating had frightening strengths and equally frightening weaknesses as a politician: his weapons of scorn and bias were unparalleled, seeming at times as refined as a civilised vice. His rhetorical skills for attack and salesmanship were of the highest order; he was a man of passion and imagination—and had he not been a politician would have been 'a mad inventor', according to Beazley. But Keating lacked a sense of proportion. With little formal education, his intellect had led him to hobbies, one after another, all his life: car engines; budgerigars; the life of Winston Churchill; rock music and, as his taste matured, classical music and its visible sister, architecture. He loved clocks and the decorative arts of the Second Empire in France. Especially these: over the years he was to collect enough for a small museum. He had begun life as a beautiful dark-haired child from a working-class suburb that struggled enviously to become middle class and he had grown into a beautiful dark-haired political tough—'that boy is a political killer', Kim Beazley Senior had remarked when first he had seen Keating, aged twenty-five, in Parliament House. And all the time the young man was assiduously transforming himself from his modest beginnings into the Bankstown version of a gentleman—with a good dose of Johnny Rotten up his well-tailored sleeve. Keating wore beautiful clothes; he had a natural eye for elegance both elaborate and simple; his wife, Annita, was a stately, multilingual European, with whom he enjoyed mutual devotion; he was courted by the rich and powerful, and revelled in the company of artists. His life was a dream come true. But it was even more than that, for it seemed as if Keating's very soul bore traces of the brilliant Second Empire: Paris—the capital city he most loved and studied so well he could draw maps of it from memory—had been rebuilt during that brief and shining age of Napoleon III when good music was promoted for its uplifting effect on the labouring classes. The emperor had wanted to transform his society, but unfortunately he had also declared war on the Prussians. France was left 'in pieces'. There was, in Keating's nature, something of the same lust for transformation as displayed in the Second Empire: he had transformed himself; now he would transform the country. He wanted a *different* Australia. Hawke, on the other hand, aimed for reform: he wanted a *better* Australia. If Hawke had a motto for the nation it would have been that of the Roman Emperor Hadrian: 'Humanity, Liberty, Happiness'. It's difficult to know what Keating's Australia may have been, because the country he envisaged has not yet come into being.

Hawke was, in Paul Kelly's description,

> A balanced and diligent Prime Minister, assessing issues on merit. People today underestimate the extraordinary chemistry and atmosphere of the time: the crusading element in Keating was amazing. Hawke, I think, was concerned at how far out Keating had gone on this issue; Keating would talk in terms of 'putting his job on the line' over it. [The Tax Summit] was the first evidence we saw of a remarkable phenomenon of the Keating political character, which we saw later in his Prime Ministership—a really crusading element, wanting to move beyond the limits of the system to transcending new policies. Which he can then impose on the system ... In a sense, it's a variation of the Whitlam crash-through-or-crash.[3]

Keating and his supporters were ever after to present the Tax Summit as a time when Hawke showed that, underneath, he was weak. It was a view important to their self-esteem, because the other explanation was that Keating was reckless.

Immediately after the 1984 election, the Prime Minister had held a meeting at The Lodge with Keating, Garnaut and other advisers. From this meeting a task force had been set up to draft a White Paper for the Summit. Kelly wrote, 'It was an immediate battle.'[4] Treasury was on one side, Garnaut and Ed Visbord from Prime Minister and Cabinet on the other. '[They] grew more hostile with each task force meeting.'[5] Peter Barron and Bob Hogg, Right and Left wings of the party, were dubious about the Treasury idea of introducing a series of new taxes, each one potentially alienating a part of the electorate.

At the outset, Hawke laid down a condition: whatever was finally adopted as the reform, it would have to be in place completely before the 1987 election, with no loose ends onto which the Opposition could attach a wrecking ball. Garnaut said,

> He wanted to be able to implement changes crisply, to have them all up and running a year or more before the next election. That was tremendously important. Bob made very clear that we needed crisp answers to the questions of income distribution. We still had high unemployment and high inflation and the big game was still macroeconomic reform: winding down inflation; economic expansion to mop up unemployment; wage restraint through the Accord and the support of the ACTU. If all that was to come out of the Tax Summit was a consumption tax added onto wages you'd bugger the rest of the program. But Treasury didn't hear that. They didn't want to hear the conditions.

Partly because of the hyped drama of the MX missile crisis, the dollar had fallen, which increased inflation, which in turn meant it would be more difficult for the ACTU to support wage restraint.

Garnaut, having himself put a broad-based consumption tax on the agenda, was convinced by April that it was more trouble than it was worth, a danger to everything that had been achieved so far.

> I started saying that the whole package was not going to meet Bob's conditions, pointing out that we had a big inflationary impulse but we really did have to deliver on wage restraint or we'd simply lose the big game.

Keating meanwhile was assuring the Prime Minister and others that the ACTU was on side. But Garnaut, who had his own sources, was hearing a different story, as was Willis, and they were reporting to Hawke that Keating was either being misinformed or was deluded by wishful thinking. All factions expected that, at the Tax Summit, business would be supportive of the reforms. Keating, busy lobbying the ACTU and welfare groups, was confident he could take for granted the endorsement of the Business Council of Australia.

The White Paper, still including the option of a broad-based consumption tax, was put to the Cabinet in mid-May, causing disbelief. There were three meetings and, according to Kelly, twenty-three hours of discussion,

> before Keating emerged victorious with Cabinet endorsement of his option [C] as the preferred government position ... only Hawke, Gareth Evans, Kim Beazley and Susan Ryan supported Keating's position; it was carried against the numbers. Keating talked, seduced and intimidated the Cabinet into submission, leaving a legacy of bad blood. It was a decision devoid of conviction. Most ministers were unenthusiastic and some were horrified.[6]

Ralph Willis said,

Bob's approach to Cabinet was consensus, to let people have their say and not to have his own say until he had the feel of the meeting—or if he didn't like the way it was going, he would steer the discussion and argue the points. Paul's was: 'Well, this is what I think—and you all should think the same.'

Hawke knew he had to back up his Treasurer to save Keating's face in Cabinet, while reasoning that the Summit, through a free play of ideas, would be the final arbitrator. But his less-than-ecstatic support for Keating's 'tax cart', as it had become known, annoyed the Treasurer who, in frustration, began to refer to the Prime Minister as 'Old Jellyback'—this, despite the fact that without Hawke's backing Keating's cart would be a write-off. Peacock picked up the 'Jellyback' tag and used it in parliament, as did Wilson Tuckey. Behind Hawke's back, Keating was speaking so vituperatively of him that Bill Hayden, not a man to carry stories, sought out Ross Garnaut, to warn the Prime Minister's office, 'Look, it doesn't matter to me what Keating says about Hawke, but I think it's bad for the government.' It seemed the parasite of grievance that ate Jack Lang had passed from teacher to student, and was now consuming the Treasurer from within.

Hawke opened the Tax Summit on 1 July, with an appeal to its 160 delegates to restore 'equity, efficiency and integrity' to the tax system, adding, 'All Australians require an assurance that the least privileged among us will not suffer as a result of the changes. I give that assurance unreservedly.'

Next up was Bob White, president of the Business Council of Australia (BCA) who, for a week before the Tax Summit had tried to contact Keating, but the Treasurer had been too busy to take his calls. That was a mistake, because what White had to say lobbed a hand grenade into the tax cart. The BCA rejected the proposed reforms holus-bolus, because they didn't go far enough—and once the BCA had bridled, every other sectional interest felt at liberty to do so too, each from its own narrow point of view.

John Hyde, the Opposition's intellectual leader, wrote,

> Like the cast of a Greek tragedy, Tax Summit participants remained true to their flawed characters destroying something that most of them wanted then or came to want within a few years. Keating should have anticipated

the selfishness and political incompetence of the business community... while he worked in detail with the ACTU, he did little to ensure that the business sector did not destroy his summit in a manner that was foreseeable.[7]

The cart was running downhill fast; to Hawke, who had been giving Keating his head for months, it was obvious that the Treasurer was no longer in control of his vehicle. That evening 'events moved with speed and drama as Hawke began a series of private talks to locate a compromise', Kelly wrote.[8] The talks continued on the second day, inconclusively, then, on the morning of the third day, the *Bulletin* magazine came out with a Morgan poll that showed the Opposition leading Labor by 8 per cent—and, for the first time, Keating being more popular than Hawke. This was the inevitable result of Hawke's lower profile and Keating's higher one during the months leading up to the Tax Summit. Kelly described the shocked mood within the party and the government over the Morgan poll: 'If debate about Keating's package had done such harm what fate for Labor after its implementation?'[9] The Prime Minister had given the Treasurer every chance to drive his tax cart home, had supported him during the drafting of the White Paper, in Cabinet and at the Summit—and the result was this: a looming electoral defeat. Hawke realised that he must take the power he had given Keating away from him.

Bill Hayden, who had been vociferous in his opposition to the consumption tax, said,

> Paul is a typical Irish political conniver ... [but] I thought he was taking on too many fights at once. In politics, if you take on too many fights you can get done on the lot of them, instead of just the ones you should get done on.

Lined up against Keating and Treasury were business, the ACTU, the Centre Left and the Left of the party, the welfare lobby, John Stone—now, on the loose from his public service bridle, kicking down doors as a media commentator—and the canny populist, Sir Joh Bjelke-Petersen, who wanted a flat tax. Of these, from Hawke's point of view, the ACTU was of paramount importance because of the big game in which it was decisive: wage restraint.

That night the Prime Minister, without telling Keating—whom he thought had temporarily lost all sense of objectivity—visited Simon Crean, president of the ACTU, and Bill Kelty, its secretary, in their hotel rooms to work out a compromise. Keating and his advisers still believed they had the unions on side, although all week Crean and Kelty had been telling them the situation was very difficult. Hawke said,

> When I arrived at the hotel that night I asked Bill Kelty to restate the ACTU's position for me. Bill did not mince words. The ACTU would not accept Option C ... With that, the consumption tax was dead.

Eyes and ears are everywhere in Canberra and the story of Hawke's visit by night to his old colleagues leaked: Keating was to learn from the morning newspaper that his planned transformation of Australia's tax system had vanished, like a dream.

Hawke, whose heart had been broken open by the shock of his daughter's plight, was still and would remain for years, easily prone to tears. His depression had lifted but there remained with him a deepened sense of the pains of life: he was a more sensitive man than he had been, which is not always an advantage for a political leader. He knew how badly he had hurt Keating and how deeply Keating bore hurts. His voice trembled with emotion at the Tax Summit that afternoon as he announced that Option C was dead because it did not meet the condition set out at the very beginning for 'wide community support'. But Keating was gracious and reached out to pat Hawke comfortingly. Keating was the trusted colleague to whom, in his deepest misery, Hawke had reached out, father to father, to confide about Rosslyn. Until the end there would stay with them a subtle bond of affection—and hatred.

During the press conference that followed they did an impressive double act as brothers in arms. Hawke, feeling tense, was strident and Keating, feeling devastated, was funny. Referring to his 'tax cart' he said, 'It's a bit like *Ben Hur*. We've crossed the line with one wheel off, but we have crossed the line.' Nietzsche remarked: 'A joke is an epitaph for the death of a feeling.'

In private, Keating's slaughtered dream cried out for revenge. Kelly wrote that Keating

> abused Barron and complained about Garnaut. His loathing for Hawke's office … intensified. His senior advisor [Tony] Cole had a screaming match with Barron … From this night onwards Keating, typically, manufactured his own history. He insisted that he could have won—but for Hawke's betrayal.[10]

Ironically, eight years later Keating implicitly acknowledged that Hawke had been correct when he fought furiously against a consumption tax proposed by the Opposition.

But a line had indeed been crossed. Prime Minister and Treasurer would still fight side by side as a formidable duo, but their tender feelings for each other had died. In earlier days they could often be seen hugging, holding tête-à-têtes, touching each other's hands and arms with an easy intimacy. Keating's pat on the arm at the Tax Summit seems to have been his last moment of affectionate display for Hawke: in future he would see almost all the Prime Minister's actions with the jaundiced eye of malice.

In the roiling waters of politics, this was neither unusual nor unexpected.

Meanwhile, from the wreckage of his cart Keating constructed over the next two months a new tax package that was, in fact, an impressive reform—so much so it convinced members of the Opposition that it would be electoral poison, especially after they mauled it in the Senate. Keating's tax reforms, the Opposition believed, would deliver to them the next election. Peacock had eagerly adopted the idea that Hawke was a weak leader and that but for minor reasons *he* would have won the 1984 election. Peacock was a vain man whose care of his appearance and dress gave the impression he spent more time on fittings with his tailor than on fitting himself for the prime ministership. He had a reputation for laziness. On 5 September 1985 a plain, hard-working but more formidable politician inside the Liberal Party overthrew him. John Howard became leader. Now Hawke and the government had a serious adversary.

4

Both Gough Whitlam and Malcolm Fraser were well regarded in China: Whitlam for opening diplomatic relations with the People's Republic in 1972, and Fraser for striking the first bilateral aid agreement. Fraser had invited the Chinese Premier, Zhao Ziyang, to visit Australia in April 1983, supposing he would be the prime minister to greet the Chinese leader. But it was Hawke—and from the moment of Zhao's arrival the Chinese and the Australian leaders took to each other *yi jian ru gu* (first sight, like old days) as the Chinese proverb says. The times were opportune. Just over four years earlier China's supreme leader and the last of its imperial rulers, Deng Xiaoping, had decreed that China would open to the West and move to a market economy. He had done so against huge opposition within his own government. Psychologically, the country was still entangled in a puzzle of ideological knots. Few of its leaders had ever been outside its borders. Its people were forbidden to travel abroad. The bulk of its gigantic population was backward, poor, superstitious and paranoid after centuries of mismanagement, Western attack, warlordism, two revolutions—the first republican, the second Communist—occupation, the worst famine in human history, and three decades spent in Chairman Mao's laboratory for social engineering and intellectual adventure. An entire generation had been robbed of an education thanks to the decade of terror known as the Cultural Revolution. Like the religious of medieval Europe obeying dictates of the Church, millions still embraced suffering and poverty as virtues: the party had instructed them to do so. But in December 1978, Deng had declared, 'To get rich is no sin' and dismissed ingrained concepts of good and bad Communists with a proverb: 'It doesn't matter if the cat is black or white, so long as it catches mice.' China's third revolution in one century had been proclaimed.

By the early 1980s, the obstacles it faced were vast: in its own neighbourhood China had no diplomatic relations with Indonesia, South Korea or Singapore, while the Chinese people's feelings for Japan, the world's second-largest economy, were embittered with memories of the Japanese occupation that stretched from the late 1930s to 1945. China had very few interpreters of foreign languages, no system of commercial law—and thanks to its centuries of turmoil (although having once been a peaceful, law-abiding empire)—the country now barely understood the concept of the rule of law. It had state guest houses for foreign heads of state, but the hotels it needed for foreign businesspeople were still of a standard to give Swiss hoteliers toothache. Lacking foreign language staff and with cultural differences so vast they seemed planetary, phone calls and housekeeping were often pantomimes ending with Western visitors puce with rage while a smiling Chinese writhed in silent fury at them. (The Westerners, by losing their temper, had lost just as much face as the Chinese, but being unaware of this, kept going.) The 'Western food' in dining rooms was punitive. China existed outside the stream of history as far as the Western world was concerned, still regarded as Napoleon's 'sleeping giant'; in the twentieth century, it seemed a giant kicking around in a comic nightmare of little red books and running dogs.

During the 1970s Left-wing trade union leaders urged Hawke to go to Beijing but he refused until the Gang of Four were in jail or dead. (The Gang of Four was a group inside the Communist Party, led by Mao's wife, known in the latter stages of the Cultural Revolution for their cruelty and ambition to seize control of China after Mao's death. They were overthrown in a coup d'état in late 1976, tried and imprisoned. 'Four' in Chinese sounds the same as 'death', so they were, to Chinese ears, 'the death squad'.) When Hawke did visit the country, in 1978, he was captivated by the people and the potential he saw in them.

'My first visit was the beginning of a deep friendship towards the Chinese people,' he said. 'China was a poor and insignificant economy with hundreds of millions living below the poverty line, but I had the feeling that they would harness their mighty resources of human capital and become a great world power.'

From their first encounter the Chinese liked Hawke. Intuitively, it seemed, they recognised he was non-racist and had benevolent feelings towards their country. Physically, Hawke was not so big as to be intimidating; his body was trim rather than shambling like many Westerners; his high forehead was a sign of intelligence; his nose was curved at the tip rather than pointy, which is considered ugly; he had a warrior's hard, piercing gaze; prolific eyebrows of the correct, strong shape for a leader; ears with large fleshy earlobes, a sign of high status and good luck; his face was without unlucky moles, and he was very friendly. He allowed himself grey hair, a look that was both exotically Western and rather bohemian to the Chinese eye. Over the decades, thanks to many television and newspaper interviews, Hawke became one of the most recognised foreign faces in China and could not walk down a Beijing lane without people shouting 'Hou Ke! Hou Ke!' and calling friends to come out of their houses to look at him.

From Zhao's initial visit a rhythm developed: each alternate year a Chinese leader would come to Australia and in the intervening year Hawke would go to China. Australia was, from the Chinese point of view, a perfect gateway for its opening to the West. A developed English-speaking nation that had never been a colonial power was in alliance with the United States and had good relations with its Asian neighbours. China in 1983 was a land power. Although Communist, in Cold War terms China was an asset to the alliance because its adversary was the Soviet Union, which threatened China from the north and west, and also from the south, via the Soviet client state, Vietnam. President Nixon had 'played the China card' during his phase of the Cold War, bringing China under American protection vis-à-vis the USSR. It was a brilliant move, but the Americans remained nervous about their Communist ally, on tenterhooks that Nixon had been too clever, and that the Chinese may have a secret understanding with the USSR. For Republicans, the concept of alliance with *Communists* created mental nausea. They jumped at Chinese shadows. Hawke's good relations with the Reagan administration were known in Beijing and on several occasions the leaders, once their relationship with him had blossomed, asked him to take messages of reassurance to Washington. From Hawke's point of view, China was a highly desirable trading partner: it was in the same time zone as Western Australia and offered the biggest market in the world for Australian products. One of its ambassadors never tired of telling Australian politicians, 'If you sell a single pair of socks made from Australian wool to every Chinese, you won't need to sell wool to anyone else in the world.' But it was on iron and steel, not wool, that the commercial friendship was founded.

In his earliest days in office, Hawke had spoken about 'enmeshment with Asia', which at the time was greeted with cynical chortling from press sahibs and other gurus. With the exception of Japan, 'Asia' was poor, backward, overpopulated and had been asleep for a couple of hundred years.

Zhao's first visit to Australia had been a getting-to-know-you exercise at which nothing was decided. Chinese culture is intensely hierarchical, and Chinese leaders of those days and even now can be, by Australian standards, rivetingly formal. For centuries the motto of Chinese rulers has been 'First awe, then soothe'. Leaders observe a strict dress code of dark suit, subdued tie and black shoes. There is no mention of family, of recreations, of private interests. No personal issue is permitted to appear even fleetingly from behind the official mask of office—at least until feelings of trust are established. An agenda for discussion is worked out by aides in advance of a meeting; each side says their piece, there are pleasantries, an exchange of gifts, photographs and a banquet. If a leader is visiting a building, the aides will check it in advance so that the size and layout of the rooms, whether there are stairs, and how many, are known. Surprises can cause confusion, even loss of dignity, and the horror of loss of face.

In February 1984 Hawke visited South Korea, Japan and China and just before calling on Zhao told the Australian ambassador in Beijing that he wanted to raise with the Premier an idea for co-operation in the iron and steel sector. The ambassador was aghast: 'You can't do that, Prime Minister! There have been no preparatory discussions. The Premier will think we have ambushed him.' Hawke listened impatiently to a treatise on the protocols of the Middle Kingdom. At the end of it he took Ross Garnaut, who was travelling with him, aside. 'I'm going to say it anyway,' he said. Hawke had judged that Zhao liked him enough to accept a surprise.

When Hawke raised with the Premier the idea of closer links in the iron and steel industry, Zhao was fascinated. At the time, almost all Chinese iron ore and all its coal were domestic, but it was of low quality and consequently Chinese steel mills' productivity was poor. Australia was keen to find markets for its iron ore and steel, so Hawke proposed to Zhao that China could improve its steel industry, especially in the coastal provinces, by importing Australia's high-quality iron ore and coking coal. As Garnaut remarked, 'This was *radical* stuff.'

Mother China had a deep ideological belief that she must be self-sufficient in rice and iron, lest she once more found herself at the mercy of enemies who could starve her children or beat her to death. Hawke proposed the two countries ease into the new relationship through a joint venture in iron ore production as a way for China to gain confidence in using imported raw materials. Garnaut was taking notes of the discussion and recalled,

> A few times Bob stopped for Zhao's response and Zhao said, 'No, no—keep going.' He wasn't taking notes himself at all. So Bob talked through all his points, which took about half an hour, and at the end Zhao just started answering them in the order in which Bob had raised them. And on the iron and steel stuff he was very expansive, saying, 'It's a good idea, let's work together on that.'

Zhao proposed a joint study group as a way of China getting to understand Australia's capabilities as a supplier of high-quality material, and Australia getting to know China's needs for industrial development. From this conversation began the enormous trade in raw materials that was to fuel Australian prosperity and give jobs to tens of millions of Australians and Chinese as yet unborn.

Zhao was a reserved, serious man, a protégé of Deng Xiaoping, but as he and Hawke saw more of each other he increasingly relaxed. He was the leader of the reformists in government and deeply interested in the nuts and bolts of reform. As he felt more confident in the Australian leader, he allowed their conversations to move to discussion of the ideas that really excited him, inviting Hawke to share his own ideas and experience on reforming the Australian economy. They began moving further and further outside the confines of their strict, premeditated roles. It was a relationship that was as poignant as it was thrilling: two men from enemy ideologies striving to found modern economies and uplift their people through mutual co-operation. On Hawke's trip of 1984, Zhao engineered a meeting for him with his superior, the General Secretary of the Communist Party, Hu Yaobang. Hu was a tiny, excitable extrovert, 'like a bright-eyed sparrow', Hawke said, very popular with the Chinese people and one of the last of the great eccentrics of Chinese politics. As second in command of the largest country on earth, he was somewhat more important in world affairs than the Prime Minister of Australia. But he paid Hawke an unusual compliment. They were scheduled to have their first meeting in Nanjing when a storm made landing there impossible. Hawke had to fly on to Shanghai. Hu flew down to Shanghai himself so the meeting could still take place. It was obvious that Zhao had spoken highly of Hawke to his boss. Again, there was an instant rapport: *lao pengyou xiang yu* (old friends on first meeting).

Hawke invited Hu to visit Australia, which he did in April 1985, in the midst of the discussions about the White Paper for the Tax Summit.

Meanwhile, agreement had been reached on a Sino-Australian mining joint venture at Mount Channar in Western Australia, the first investment China had ever made in a foreign mine. Hawke repaid Hu's compliment by flying to Perth to meet him and his right-hand man, Hu Qili, after dinner in a restaurant overlooking the Swan River. The next day they flew to Mount Channar. Hu found it all highly exciting and exotic. China is grey and dusty. Australia is in technicolour. Hu Yaobang marvelled at skies as blue as a Ming vase, at the endless red landscape and the huge, well-fed workers with their sunburnt faces and brawny forearms pelted in yellow hair. To everyone's delight he put a rock in his pocket to take home as a souvenir. The party then flew on to Whyalla to visit the BHP steel mill from which, in due course, China would buy 40 per cent of production, thus keeping the city going until the Australian domestic market improved. At Whyalla the word was around that Hawke would be visiting and most of the town turned out to greet him. Hu was thrilled. He assumed the people had come out to see *him*, and that the waving and smiling and cheering and photograph-taking were all being staged in his honour. He waved and smiled right back, his exuberance, Hawke said, 'was wonderful to see'. Australian informality was intoxicating for mainland Chinese of those days, burdened as they were by etiquette, protocol and fear of loss of face. The Chinese saw a young and innocent people living an insouciant, rapturous life amidst glorious natural beauty. In one sense, they saw us more clearly than we saw ourselves: by 1985 Australia was already living way beyond its means.

On Hu's return to China the bureaucratic machinery suddenly shifted up several gears, in Australia's favour.

In late 1985, after the tax reform package was finalised, Hawke appointed Garnaut as ambassador to Beijing. Garnaut said, 'Hu was politically really important. While Zhao was the one who managed government and made the reforms happen, Hu was cleaning out the old Cultural Revolutionaries from the Party, embedding the new approach.' (More than thirty years after 'The Terrible Decade', as the Chinese call the Cultural Revolution, what one did or failed to do during that time still determines how high one can rise in government in China, and often if one's business will prosper. Nobody says, but everyone remembers: you saved my grandmother from starvation; you beat my uncle to death.) After Hu's visit Australians in China who had been battling the bureaucracy suddenly found that doors opened and insoluble problems evaporated. Cultural and educational exchanges became easier; a group of Chinese was allowed to attend Writers' Week at the Adelaide Festival. Australians were allowed to tour China in supervised groups.

Garnaut said, 'People down the chain of command were saying, the Boss likes the Prime Minister of Australia, and likes Australia, so we'll make it happen.' In two years, from 1984, there were more than twenty-eight delegations at ministerial level and economic co-operation expanded from iron and steel to wool, non-ferrous metals, transport and communications, and to coal. Six technical co-operation programs had been concluded and fourteen more were underway.[1]

Garnaut was in charge of arranging Hawke's reciprocal visit in May 1986 by which time Australia was, in his description, 'flavour of the month'. In April 1986 John Bannon, Premier of South Australia, had visited Beijing and made a courtesy call on the general secretary, who had shocked everybody except Bannon, who did not fully grasp the significance of what was happening, by saying, 'Let's have a meeting in my house in Zhongnanhai.' Garnaut said, 'It was unheard of. Like setting out for an official visit to the Queen, and having her say, "Oh why don't you stay for a sandwich at lunchtime?"' Bannon duly went to the political holy site, Zhongnanhai. At the end of their meeting, Hu had said, 'It's spring, and the first blossoms have appeared. Why don't we walk around the lake?' During their stroll Hu had made it clear, by referring to issues he had discussed with Hawke, that this had been the reason for his pleasure in Bannon's company. He mentioned he would like to see Australia–China trade doubled by 1990. The Beijing diplomatic corps, Garnaut reported, 'were green with envy: a mere state premier had been treated better than any of their heads of government ever had'.

When Hawke arrived a few weeks later, Hu and Zhao made room in their schedules for unusually long discussions, and Hu set out to reciprocate Hawke's courtesy. Hawke had arrived in the west, in Chengdu. Hu flew across China to meet him there and arranged a banquet with *knives and forks*. He knew Hawke was at ease with chopsticks, but he was being hyper-polite in providing cutlery. He was also making a political point: Hu wanted the Chinese to give up the unsanitary tradition of plunging chopsticks into a communal food bowl, a known way to spread hepatitis, and thought the Western cutlery was a necessary reform. But in 1986 the knife and the fork were such rarities in China that only the social elite could manipulate them, so the Chengdu banquet, photographed and televised, turned into a lesson for the nation: knife, right, fork, left. Plunge fork into food, steady it with knife. Et cetera.

It was during the formal discussions on 19 May between Hawke and Premier Zhao Ziyang that Hawke raised the possibility of Chinese students studying in Australia. At the time only a handful of postgraduate students from China and Australia had studied in each other's countries. Hawke wanted Chinese schoolchildren to come to Australia to qualify to enrol in Australian universities as undergraduates. It would be good for bilateral relations, he believed, and a great financial boost to the tertiary sector, which had been desperately in need of funds since Whitlam made university education 'free': free, that is, for students, expensive for taxpayers. Hawke had talked long and hard to his Education minister, Susan Ryan, about the need for her to stand up to the teachers' unions opposed to the idea of fee-paying foreign students 'on principle'. Premier Zhao welcomed the suggestion and agreed that, when Ryan visited later that year, it could be further explored. None of them imagined then the bonanza Chinese (and other foreign students) would be for Australia. By the early twenty-first century education had burgeoned into a $15 billion export industry.

In China—then and now—leaders, both domestic and foreign, are accompanied by hordes of advisers, aides, bodyguards and general fusspots who watch over them with such solicitude for their welfare they could be little children who might suddenly, through inattention, trip and hurt themselves. Leaders will have their heads protected by a white-gloved hand each time they enter a vehicle; every step on a staircase will be pointed out to them lest they slip, and they may not go to the bathroom unaccompanied. A female leader will have her handbag held by one of several female assistants who wait outside the cubicle and prepare running water or a little wet towel for her hands. Honour guards of beautiful, long-limbed young women in cheongsams split to their thighs welcome and farewell leaders, one presenting a bouquet while thirty others applaud. No other nation displays respect with the dramatic panache of China.

When that Chengdu banquet with its knives and forks was over, Hu dismissed his army of aides and invited Hawke back to his apartment in the state guest house. There were three Australians: Hawke, Garnaut and another diplomat, Richard Rigby, fluent in Mandarin, who was to act as translator. The Chinese were Hu Yaobang and the Vice Minister, Zhu Qizhen. Their translator was Gao Qikai.

Garnaut recalled, 'They just talked and talked. It was completely unknown for the Chinese leadership to do this. It didn't happen with Khrushchev or Tito. Hu talked until midnight, and the conversation covered everything.' At first they discussed the United States, Hu saying that the Chinese leadership 'would like to have separate, in-depth discussions with members of the US leadership, but they are always in a hurry'. The theme of China's frustrated attempts to form a genuine friendship with America wove throughout the night, with Hawke listening sympathetically, while constantly making clear his unshakeable friendship with the American leadership; he offered to convey Hu's message to Reagan, and to tell his friend, Shultz, that Hu and Zhao craved serious get-to-know-you discussions with the United States. Hu told Hawke he had tried to point out to the Vice President, George Bush, that in the Third World (a term China had invented), American prestige was slipping because of United States heavy-handedness. He told Hawke he had said to Bush, 'You've got more money than friends.' It was meant as a playful opening to a serious discussion over United States foreign policy. But Bush stood on the dignity of American imperialism, replying, 'No we don't—we have more friends', and that was the end of that, Hu said. He went on to ideas about solving the issue of Taiwan, the most intractable problem between the United States and China. He described Chinese alarm at recent American arms sales to the Republic, asking rhetorically, 'were all these arms designed to allow Taiwan to launch war against the US, Japan or the Soviet Union? No! They [are] only for confrontation against the mainland.' The discussion turned to the problems of the Korean peninsula, of American support for the Contras (the anti-socialist counter-revolutionaries) in Nicaragua and the recent bombing of Libya by the United States. Hawke argued back to Hu that Libya was planning terrorist attacks against American targets wherever it could find them—including in Australia, thus revealing to the Chinese leader secret Western intelligence. Hu responded with intelligence on the situation in Cambodia and Vietnam. As Hu continued to fret over American foreign policy, Hawke gently pointed out that the United States had existential problems to deal with: 'The US has a sense of isolation,' he said.

> Power, and great power, causes many people who come into contact with it to feel uncomfortable, and this can lead to the United States feeling isolated. If the US feels

that China understands what it has to face, this will help it to respond favourably.

Hawke had recently had an audience with Pope John-Paul II and told Hu that the Pope had mentioned he would like the Holy See to have relations with China. Hu said, 'Bob, that's not a problem. All the Pope had to do is recognise Beijing is the capital of China.' (The Vatican continues to assert that Taipei is the capital of China.)

Hu Yaobang then remarked, 'The Soviet Union thinks it's the Pope of Communism.' It was his opening to a long conversation about the USSR, and China's analysis of its future—which proved to be extraordinarily prescient, for the Chinese had studied their worst enemy closely and calculated it would collapse internally from economic mismanagement. Hu also spoke movingly of Chinese social history, saying,

> For more than 100 years the Chinese were oppressed by the three big mountains: Imperialism, Feudalism and Bureaucratic Capitalism. Chinese people will never allow oppression by another mountain. If the Chinese leadership does not respect the wishes of the people we will be toppled.

He added, 'It is often more difficult to deal with the Soviets than the Americans,' and concluded by saying, 'Well, Prime Minister, I have shown you all our cards.'

The next day they flew to Nanjing and walked around the city together, drawing crowds of people excited to see the General Secretary. Hawke pretended they had turned up to see him, waving and smiling like Hu at Whyalla; that evening he and his host again talked long into the night. During these discussions, at which the same group of people gathered, Hu spoke about Sino-Japanese relationships, on which Richard Rigby was an expert. At one stage Hu said, 'We have to get over our feelings against Japan. We need to develop peace and prosperity together with Japan.' His sentiments of forgiveness for Japanese atrocities during its long occupation of China were so generous that Rigby, a professional diplomat, had tears streaming down his cheeks as he translated. The Chinese leader asserted to Hawke that China, 'for a minimum of thirty years would be buying Australian iron ore, steel and wool' and asked Hawke to do what he could to increase Chinese imports to Australia, 'because we lack foreign currency'.

Although the fact of these talks remained secret, within the diplomatic corps the word went round that the Australian Prime Minister had received 'unprecedented courtesies'. Garnaut said, 'It was a wonderful time to be ambassador.'

But China had neither policies nor regulations to deal with the agreements its leaders had made for the iron ore and steel venture and an investment in the Portland aluminium smelter in Victoria—in fact, Chinese foreign exchange laws made such investments illegal. Zhao and Hu instructed the bureaucracy to grease the machinery and problem after problem eased away. Several times Garnaut went to see Zhao with obstacles that seemed insurmountable and Zhao would either telephone officials or, on occasions, take the matter to the State Council for new legislation to be passed.

Zhao Ziyang had told Hawke the Chinese proverb: 'Ruling a big country is like frying a small fish'—that is, it's easy to ruin. Shanghai, China's most cosmopolitan city, was and is the centre of avant-garde thought and action. It was there that the Communist Party had been born after student unrest in 1919. Deng's reforms announced in December of 1978 had created a surge of wealth in China, but with it came a surge of corruption—the latter endemic in any society lacking the rule of law. At the time, per capita income was $US400, while the Chinese Premier was paid only five times this amount (although provided with many perquisites). The country was used to a degree of economic equality that by the 1980s was rare in the rest of the world. The surge of prosperity after opening to a market economy threw this accepted and cherished situation out of kilter, and in late 1986 students in Shanghai began demonstrating over rising prices and corruption. Deng became alarmed that Hu was not dealing with the students firmly enough, and that the city could run out of control. Deng, like Hu, was a physically tiny man, a veteran of the Long March and a pragmatist with a deeply grounded horror of mob rule. He had been jailed and bashed during the Cultural Revolution; as additional punishment Red Guards had thrown his son out a window, crippling the boy for life. As well as Deng's horrific personal experience, there was an ideological gulf between him on one hand and Hu and Zhao on the other. The younger men believed that with economic reform would inevitably come demands for greater social freedom and political accountability that the government would have to deal with. Hawke and Zhao had spoken of this on several occasions. But Deng believed it was essential to do one thing at a time: economic liberalisation came first, politics at some later date. He described in a proverb how China was to manage its progress: like a man gingerly crossing a river, feeling out with his toes the river stones on which to step. Deng feared the conservatives in the party, who loathed his opening of the economy to the West, would use Shanghai's social unrest as excuse to throttle economic reform.

Hu Yaobang had always been something of a loose cannon, another reason the Chinese people loved him: he was a leader they could relate to as a human. Others were distant, awesome demi-urges. Around the time of the Shanghai unrest, Hu was on a trip to New Zealand where he announced the very big news that the

People's Liberation Army would be cut by 1 million troops. The decision to slash the size of the army had already been taken, but was still officially secret. Mentioning it provided enough ammunition for Hu's enemies in Beijing to criticise him publicly.

Deng took the hugely unpopular decision of sacking Hu. He replaced Hu with Zhao Ziyang.

Shanghai got the message and the students, dismayed and sullen, left the streets.

But there was a much sadder aspect to the disgrace of Hu Yaobang: the party held private denunciations of him in which he was accused of the crime of revealing state secrets to foreigners. 'That was, I think,' Garnaut said, 'a reference to some of his intimate conversations with Bob. It wasn't the reason, but it was the excuse they used inside the party, after the event, once they'd decided to kick Hu out.'

Hu's disgrace jerked the wheel of history. It began turning in a stormy gyre. Its thunder would burst three years later, in 1989, in the very centre of Beijing, in the huge plaza in front of the Forbidden City known as Heaven's Gate: Tiananmen.

At the beginning of his 1986 trip to China, while he was still in Tokyo, Hawke had his own troubles. An economic crunch, decades in the making, had arrived. On 13 May the Bureau of Statistics revealed the trade figures for April: the national current account deficit had leapt to $1.48 billion, 6 per cent of GDP. The economy had been expanding, but to finance the expansion the nation was borrowing more than it was earning in exports. Australia was in debt up to its ears.

Hawke had been given the figures before he left for East Asia and had discussed the situation with both the Treasurer and the rest of the Cabinet. 'The figures were certainly no cause for celebration, but we were determined to deal with them without panic,' he said. Cabinet had agreed that funds to the states would have to be cut, but they would leave that argument until the forthcoming Premiers' Conference, when Hawke and Keating would make it in public. The decision was to do nothing to spook the markets and to buy time for grappling with the underlying problems that had caused the huge debt. Since February 1985, the Australian dollar had lost 40 per cent of its value. The loss felt all the more queasy because the nation was unused to its currency riding the waves of the international markets—rather than standing more or less still on the Treasury wharf. (Paul Kelly discusses these problems in fine detail in his magnum opus, *The End of Certainty*.)

In Australia, the day after the figures were publicly released, the Treasurer travelled to the semi-rural electorate of Burke and it was there, in a reception centre, that John Laws, reigning king of Sydney radio, tracked him down for an interview over the telephone. It was an era before mobile telephony was ubiquitous; Keating took the call in a kitchen, where the sound of plates and saucepans could be heard crashing in the background. But what currency traders heard was the sound of a crashing Aussie dollar. The Treasurer, making a spur of the moment decision to impress the electorate with how serious the situation was, let his supple tongue run loose, uttering a phrase which for evermore would be associated with his name. Australia, he said, could face the prospect of becoming 'a banana republic'. He may as well have used a twenty-dollar bill to light the stove.

It is the job of political leaders of every stripe to arouse disapproval and mockery by disrupting social stagnation, since they are, or should be, agents of social evolution. Their actions are to shock the community into reaction against prevailing beliefs. But the shocks must be administered gingerly.

Within hours of Keating's interview, the dollar had fallen three cents, and would keep on falling in the days and months ahead. It was not quite what the Treasurer had intended, but at this stage of his career it was difficult to know—some thought, even for the man himself—just what he did intend. Keating, after his successful reassembly of the wrecked tax cart into a reform package, seemed in the same combative state of mind as he had been before the Tax Summit. He was perhaps still angry with Hawke about the ACTU rejection of his favoured option, a consumption tax, which he believed Hawke had engineered, and which he and his staff interpreted as the Prime Minister being scared of an argument with the Treasurer. In combat, every action suddenly looks different: prudent hesitation appears to be specious cowardice, while reckless audacity is reframed as courage. In private, Keating was calling Hawke names and metaphorically beating his own chest: in his eyes, *he* was the man who was really running the country, and had been doing so ever since Hawke's depression of late 1984. That Garnaut was now out of the country and not available, with his steady gaze and long, smiling silences, to unsettle the Treasurer in economic arguments inside the Prime Minister's office may have lent extra weight to Keating's feeling that *he* was the silverback.

Keating shared his sentiments about Hawke's weakness with people from his office and some in the press gallery. Inevitably the stories found their way back to the Prime Minister's own staff, notably to Peter Barron, who had many sources of information inside and outside Parliament House.

Perhaps the real trigger for Keating's reckless mood had been a succession of low blows from the Liberal thug, Wilson Tuckey. Tuckey had discovered the skeleton of a dead romance in the Treasurer's closet—in the early 1970s Keating had proposed to a girl then changed his mind. Since the very opening of parliament in February 1986 Tuckey had attacked the Treasurer inside the House with offensive insinuations, including that he had fathered an illegitimate child. Such suggestions were bound to disturb the feelings of Keating's wife and children. 'Paul was more devoted to his family than any other man I knew in politics,' Hawke said. Once Tuckey had discovered the Treasurer's Achilles heel, he bit it at every opportunity.

The Opposition, which had sunk back in the polls once the government's tax reforms were recognised as a success, seemed to have decided on the tactic of disrupting parliament, a common enough response to the frustrations of Opposition. In 1983 Labor had promised to create 500 000 jobs in three years, and had more than succeeded, creating 608 000 jobs by February 1986. Keating was trying to advertise in parliament the government's achievement when Tuckey hit his sore spot. The Treasurer struck back furiously, calling the Opposition 'animals', 'this rabble', and threatening them with 'a few New South Wales ALP rules'. And that was on the first day. The next day, during some cut and thrust between Keating and the leader of the National Party, Tuckey again leapt into the fray with an irrelevant reference to the Treasurer's former girlfriend. Keating responded with 'The loopy crim ... is at it again', 'you stupid foul-mouthed grub' and 'you piece of criminal garbage'. He was visibly shaken and outside the chamber ranted about Tuckey and what he would like to do to him. Tuckey continued using his weapon against Keating for years, the tongues of both men vigorously exercised for the injury they could do each other. 'The tongue is a little member and boasteth great things ... It is full of deadly poison,' the Bible warns. Tuckey's tongue, in due course, would bring ruin on his own party. Meanwhile, he tried to poison Keating's personal life with it.

Hawke was in Tokyo when he got the news on 14 May about the 'banana republic'. He was angry with Keating's clumsiness because of the panic he knew it would set off, and for the difficulties it would cause him in trade talks in Japan. 'Paul had turned a weak currency, as the Aussie was at that stage, into a collapsing currency,' he said. In addition the Budget process had begun, a period during which the government tries to keep economic decision-making to a minimum while prime minister and Treasurer concentrate on Budget strategy.

But while Hawke was angry with Keating, he was more sympathetic to him than was his staff. He knew from personal observation how protective of his wife and children Keating was and understood the impotent rage Keating felt towards Tuckey. Hawke still harboured avuncular feelings for Keating, who was his undisputed heir-apparent, and he was much more willing to indulge a man fourteen years his junior than one his own age. He was concerned about the Treasurer's health, both out of friendship and because he knew how much good health one needed as prime minister. Until the moment in December 1990 when Keating spoke disrespectfully of Curtin, Hawke would in private ask medical friends and others who used alternative medicine if they could help with Keating's numerous small but debilitating physical problems. Hawke had been robust since his teenage years. Even during his heaviest drinking, in the 1970s, when he sometimes collapsed from overwork and lack of rest, Hawke would bounce back from exhaustion and respiratory infections after a good night's sleep. As everyone who knew him recognised, Hawke had the proverbial constitution of an ox.

Hawke enjoyed working. His work habits as prime minister delighted the public service. He always read his briefs, he could absorb quantities of detail seemingly without effort; he could concentrate on whatever he was reading in the noisiest environments, he travelled with ease, unaffected by time zones, heat or cold, he could fall asleep within minutes in cars, boats, trains and aeroplanes. The Lodge had a tennis court on which he and Hazel and visitors played on weekends, and he played cricket when he had time. Keating was not robust, played no sport and was plagued by minor complaints, sore eyes, tinnitus and chest infections. He did not have the stamina to work as hard as Hawke, nor did he have the temperament for hours of reading briefs. But both Treasurer and Prime Minister shared a tenacity to complexity and nothing could interrupt their concentration once it had located its chosen difficulty. Keating loved to read figures, but how he gained the rest of the information he needed was, for many who worked for him, a mystery. 'I never knew how he got his information,' a public servant said. 'He read almost nothing.' Keating was a classic intuitive, able in a few minutes of observation or conversation to absorb as much as a non-intuitive collects in an hour. It was a strength but it had a considerable drawback: it was imprecise and it deprived Keating of a wider range of views.

Keating's other weakness was that he could not work for long periods without physical depletion and needed to escape from the tension of high office by immersing himself in hobbies and music. Hawke would zone out from politics into the cryptic crossword puzzles that he carried with him and could do anywhere for a few minutes at a time. Keating needed to get away from people altogether, to refresh himself in the meditative solitude of a symphony. The Tax Summit and its aftermath had exhausted him; now Tuckey's attacks on a sensitive issue, the early Budget process and worry over the current account deficit were the cause, Hawke believed, for his mishandling of the Laws interview. What the Treasurer had actually said was,

> If in the final analysis, Australia is so undisciplined, so disinterested in its salvation and its economic wellbeing, that it doesn't deal with these fundamental problems, then the fallback solution is inevitable because you can't fund $12 billion a year in perpetuity every year, and then the interest on the year before that, and the interest on the year before that, the only thing to do is

to slow to a canter. Once you slow growth under 3 per cent, unemployment starts to rise again. And then you have really induced depression. Then you have gone. You know, you are a banana republic.

If only he had held back the flourish of these few final words, but Keating could rarely resist the bravura of his own rhetoric.

Hawke was travelling with his politicals. Unlike their boss they were certain that Keating, although misjudging his shot, had nevertheless aimed to hit Hawke. They believed, because they were being fed information by press gallery journalists, that back in Australia Keating was presenting himself as the real man in charge, asserting there were two leaders now: one a figurehead, the other doing the hard yards.

Keating compounded the uproar over the banana republic and falling dollar when two days later he announced an unscheduled meeting of the Advisory Council on Prices and Incomes to discuss all aspects of the economy. 'Everything is up for discussion as it relates to economic policy, the economic outlook,' he told the media. Already in a febrile state, the media described the proposed meeting as a 'mini-summit'. The Treasurer issued no correction. There were three interlocked problems now: first, Keating had not mentioned to the Prime Minister his plan for a mini-summit; second, he had not discussed it with his Cabinet colleagues; third, his proposed mini-summit looked like a panic measure to divert attention from his banana republic remark.

This was all an enormous distraction for Hawke and his staff dealing with difficult trade issues with Japan.

From Tokyo, Hawke phoned the deputy Prime Minister, Lionel Bowen, and told him to take charge of the situation. Bowen, also of the New South Wales Right, was a former lawyer, a devout Catholic, a man of great calm, modesty, common sense, wit and good humour. Within an amiable exterior, there was a steel core. Hawke asked him to call a meeting in the Prime Minister's office for a conference call with him in Beijing. When the Treasurer and other ministers had assembled, Hawke announced there would be no mini-summit, no special meeting of the Advisory Council on Prices and Incomes, that there were not two sources of policy-making in the government—the Treasurer on one side and everyone else on the other—and that economic problems would be handled in the normal way, in Cabinet, upon his return.

Hawke's staff were unhappy that he had not been tougher on Keating, but he said, 'My main concern was *not* to be tough on Paul. I needed to settle things down and stop him taking the government off on a dangerous sidetrack.' The other thing Hawke knew about Keating was that the Treasurer *did* get sidetracked: he could have his attention attracted by, then riveted, to something—a hobby, a piece of music, a new set of headphones—to the exclusion of the day's work.

Sandy Hollway, who would later take over as Hawke's chief of staff, was on the trip in his then role as a Foreign Affairs officer. He recalled,

> From the time we hopped on the plane at Fairbairn until we got off again, I was beavering away on speeches and notes for all the places we were visiting, but I became aware that there was some other issue running that was much more important than the China visit. I didn't realise at the time, but it was when Keating made his 'banana republic' statement. And I remember this distinctly: that whole issue was a subtext to the entire trip. Bob was getting on with the foreign policy and trade stuff very professionally, but this other issue was running. Barron was on that trip. And Hogg. I remember we got to the last night and I walked down the hotel

corridor back to my room, all my work finished, and passing Peter Barron's room there were clouds of cigarette smoke seeping under the door. I poked my head in and there was Peter with an ashtray full of stubs, working the telephone back to Canberra. And I said, 'Peter, what are you up to!' He replied, 'Just putting the guns on the hills, Comrade. Putting the guns on the hills.'

The news media, gazing into the mirror of cheap reflections that human malice so enjoys, had made much of the second falling out between Hawke and Keating. 'I was annoyed by Paul's looseness of language, and his presumption in calling a meeting. But I didn't regard either as an ongoing obstacle to our own relationship. I think Paul understood and accepted my reaction,' Hawke said.

The next day, when Hawke arrived back in Canberra, Keating came straight to his office, shook his hand, and they sat down together to talk. Keating told Hawke that on top of his other worries his wife needed an operation, but was holding off until the Budget was finalised. The Treasurer had four young children for whom he would be mother and father while Annita was out of action. Hawke assured him of his continued regard for him, and they got on with the business of framing the Budget. Whatever the intent of Keating's adventure, and there has been disagreement over his motives ever since, both men knew that disunity was death. They in fact enjoyed working in harness, knowing they were a brilliant team. Keating was one member of government for whom Hawke's door was always open, and who sought frequently to call in on him, not as often as in the first term, but still very often. They continued to discuss ideas and their personal lives right up and into 1991. Rosslyn, living in Canberra, saw Keating often in the course of her job in the business-class lounge at the airport and retained a strong affection for him throughout his dispute with her father. 'I loved Paul,' she said. 'He was always such fun.'

After Hawke left office a documentary series called *Labor in Power* negatively distorted the relationship of Prime Minister and Treasurer (and almost completely discounted Hawke's achievements) but the series was so well produced it gained a specious authority as factual, being shown and reshown on ABC television and the History Channel. A friend of Hawke's, a senior lawyer who had persuaded him to trust the ABC producer and co-operate with him, wrote to apologise when he realised how misleading the series had been. In 2010 a TV docu-drama, *Hawke*, portrays the Hawke–Keating relationship as moving from twilight to dark, without showing the affection and years of sunlight that had shone between them.

Keating had embarrassed himself by using the banana republic analogy, but ironically its effect in the longer term was a net gain, since—by overstating his case at a critical moment—he made the nation focus on its very real, chronic problems, thus creating an easier political atmosphere in which to introduce reforms. His point was rammed home a few months later in August 1986, when the international credit-rating agency, Moody's, downgraded the Australian government's AAA rating, effectively making it more expensive for the nation to borrow money. But by then an economic tempest was raging and Hawke and the government were in the fight of their lives to save the nation from a financial capsize.

The situation was so dire that finance journalists were forecasting the IMF was poised to intervene in running the Australian economy.

While Australia had created many of its own problems over decades by taking easy options—chiefly high tariffs that led to uncompetitive industries, and a protected industrial relations system that led to low productivity—the crisis of 1986 was brought to a head by external events. The United States had a huge trade deficit, due in part to its economy staying open during the Cold War years, for both economic and political reasons, and because it was already squandering money on oil. The post-colonial world of the 1950s and 1960s had descended into confusion and poverty for a decade or so, but by the 1980s many 'developing countries' were developing fast and their agricultural and mining products were both feeding their own people and flowing into world markets. The nations of Western Europe found themselves with 'beef mountains' and 'butter mountains' and other agricultural goods they could not sell, while parts of Africa starved. The Europeans' solution was to subsidise their farmers, which was politically sweet for governments in Paris and Bonn. Meanwhile, in the United States, Republican Congressmen were pitching to the mid-west, to seats to the west of Illinois, where grain and beef grew. Naturally, their farmers wanted subsidies too. For the first time since the 1930s, powerful elements in the American Congress began flirting with protectionism. There was a frightening groundswell of opinion for the United States to place import barriers across the board. This would have the effect of halting the American trade deficit, and of causing havoc in the economies of virtually every non-Communist country in the world. Reagan passed the Farm Bill, justifying it on the grounds that to overcome European protectionism America needed to take the fight up to them. It was electorally convenient for the Republican Party, and quite disastrous for Australia, caught in the crossfire between the United States and Europe, a war that Japan joined as a third force. By the early 1980s the world agricultural market was rigged. Just one incident exemplifies how rorted the system was: the European Community dumped sugar at US$0.05 a kilogram, wrecking the economy of the Philippines and traumatising sugar towns right up the Queensland coast.

Government was suddenly much, much harder. Hawke said, 'We had to face up to some really tough decisions: every minister was told he or she must cut costs and we spent *hours* upon *hours* in sittings of the Expenditure Review Committee.' Ministers reacted differently to the problems now confronting them, some unable to come to terms with what was happening. They had to go to the ERC, one by one, and argue their case for every dollar. Barry Jones, the Minister for Science and Technology, brilliant and original in many areas, was one who was unable to cope with the iron laws of economising. Ralph Willis, the gentlest member of the ERC, recalled,

> Barry would come in and say, 'It's perfectly obvious why this money is needed for Science and Technology', and we'd say, 'You explain to us exactly why.' And he'd get in a huff and reply, 'Well—if you can't see this for yourselves, what's the point of talking to you!' *Sleepers Wake!* and all that stuff. And we'd say, 'Right. Piss off. That's one less issue on the table.' It was a pity, but Barry was just too emotional about his portfolio to be able to argue for it, and as a result it lost out. There were a number of ministers like that.

Hawke had the unpalatable task of persuading the unions to accept not merely restraint in their wage demands, but in fact a cut in real wages. He made a major speech on 11 June in which he explained that with Australian inflation now running at 9 per cent, when the rest of the world's was only 3 per cent, there was no way that wage earners could be compensated fully for increases in the CPI.

But just when things seemed as if they could not get worse, they did: on 28 July 1986 the dollar fell 10 per cent in twenty-four hours. Hawke recalled,

Four

> We had just finished three months of grinding Budget deliberations in the ERC, and were about to put the Budget to bed. The ERC members were together in the Cabinet room when the dollar began to fall. There was Paul, Peter Walsh, John Dawkins, Ralph Willis, John Button, and me. Paul had a portable Reuters screen and he began calling the drop in the dollar like a referee calling the count on a boxer who's hit the canvas. It had been at 63 cents, then it went through 60, 59, 58 … It finally stopped at 57.15. We felt like stunned mullets. It was very depressing.

Because of the floating of the Australian dollar, this was the first time an Australian government had had precisely this experience. There was no precedent to guide them. Senator Walsh, by this time the Finance minister, said later,

> I was closer to despair than I'd ever been in politics, because I thought we'd been a good government … and yet we had been hit with this, and we didn't really deserve it—and how the hell were we ever going to get out of it?

The solution was to reconvene the ERC and 'slash and burn' (in Hawke's words) their way out. It is difficult for a government of any hue to cut costs, but for a Labor government it is especially challenging: the ALP balances exquisitely between ethos and pathos, between its noble, dignified, universal moral aspirations and its inherent feelings of pity and sympathetic sadness for the downtrodden of the world. Small gestures, let alone large ones, can pitch Labor people from one extreme to the other. Hawke said,

Philosophically, the party had been brought up on the notion of government playing an expansionary role. The party expected a Labor government to spend on health, education and welfare. I had to tell them, as did other ministers, there was no money to spend. It caused much discomfort among the faithful.

During a horrible fortnight the ERC cut another $1.5 billion from the Budget. One decision was to save $70 million by lifting a ban on uranium sales to France. The French had made a contract with Queensland Mines to buy uranium at a fixed price, but when Labor policy banned uranium sales, France bought its uranium elsewhere, and more cheaply, leaving the Australian taxpayer obliged to compensate Queensland Mines for the cost of the ban. Hawke despised what he had always seen as an unintelligent, emotional fad about uranium mining, a field of disinformation—much of it ploughed over decades by agents of the USSR—into which were sown the deadly weeds of paranoia. He was personally delighted to have an opportunity to dismiss the ban—an idea that had originated with John Dawkins, who was now Trade minister—especially because, Hawke said, 'Labor's policy was penalising the Australian people: our taxpayers were subsidising a prejudice that served absolutely no purpose. The French were simply buying cheaper uranium elsewhere.' But in the party there was anger. By small degrees more and more of the ALP faithful were feeling uncomfortable with Hawke. In the two previous years budget deficits had been 2.5 per cent and 3.2 per cent; now the ERC cut spending to zero, but only Hawke and Keating knew how drastic the surgery was. They kept it secret, even from the Finance minister, Senator Walsh.

The ERC also decided to levy fees on tertiary students on a capacity-to-pay basis. This too had been Dawkins' idea but Hawke backed it wholeheartedly, as he had always regarded the phrase 'free university education' introduced by Whitlam, as pernicious nonsense. 'It's never free,' he had argued.

> It's a question of who is paying—and most of the time it's working-class people, through their taxes, paying for middle-class kids to get the education their own children will not. I had the inequity of all this brought home to me one day when Frank Lowy [third-richest man in the nation] said to me how absurd it was that his employees, through their taxes, were paying for his wife to do a university degree.

For many in the party, however, university fees in any form ranked as treachery both to the Labor ethos and to Whitlam's legacy.

The news media hammered the government—and the Treasurer in particular became fresh prey for the ever-questing vole, Brian Toohey. The *National Times* launched an investigation of Keating's friendships, creating an impression that the government from the top down enjoyed consorting with the wrong sort of person—namely the very rich. It published photographs of Hawke and Keating in dinner suits at a function where millionaires were also guests, with the insinuation that they were behaving improperly: by being present, by wearing dinner suits, by having 'rich mates'.

It was the same old sahibs-versus-the-natives (admittedly, the native rulers) mentality, but it was damaging to the government all the same. As Keating was to object, 'One photograph of me and the Prime Minister at one function in a dinner suit is republished and rebroadcast 1000 times.' The media made it appear that the Prime Minister and Treasurer almost lived in black ties after dark, whereas Hawke was at his desk until midnight most of the week and Keating was at home playing with his children or listening to music. However, dinner-suited leaders caused predictable outrage on talkback radio. By 1986 a new money class was already springing up, seemingly out of the cracks in city pavements: men who had been paper shufflers or 'on the tools' were now driving Porsches and taking skiing holidays in Aspen. Suddenly all kinds of people did not know who they were, or where they fitted in to the new social hierarchy—and this released the social poison of envy. Hawke was less vulnerable to it, because of his down-to-earth working-man's image, but Keating, with his elegant suits and beautiful ties, was so unpopular both in the electorate and in the Caucus that Hawke was warned that Keating could not win a contest for deputy prime minister if Lionel Bowen stepped down.

Politics on its surface is an ever-restless ocean. Its deep currents are mostly invisible. And, invisibly, while the Hawke government was doing much to reconstruct the economy and re-establish Australia's role in the world, the Opposition began tearing itself to pieces.

5

ONE OF THE NEW money men of the 1980s was a Gold Coast developer called Brian Ray, friendly, charming, determined and generous, a mate of Kerry Packer, an enthusiastic risk taker, both in business and in life. Mostly he was a millionaire, but sometimes he was broke. He was a leader of Queensland's white-shoe brigade, a group of entrepreneurs whose patron saint seemed to be Jay Gatsby. They had made lots of money very quickly and enjoyed its conspicuous consumption: designer casual clothes worn with the classic 1930s accessory, white shoes. They were masters of a small, tropical universe—from just across the Tweed River then on and on up north for a thousand kilometres, anywhere there was land to develop for housing or tourism. Brian Ray had come to the attention of the Costigan Royal Commission in 1984 when, as a bankrupt, he lent Kerry Packer $250 000 in cash; this had led to the notion that Packer was a drug dealer and all sorts of other innuendo being enthusiastically bantered about. But just how a bankrupt happened to have on hand a cool quarter to lend to a multimillionaire was to remain a mystery both men would take to their graves.

Another friend of Ray's was Queensland's National Party premier, Sir Joh Bjelke-Petersen, whom he had met in the early 1970s, and with whom he formed a strong friendship. Ray could rightly be called 'visionary' as a property developer; like many people who experience outstanding success in one field, he had confidence he could succeed in another. (Hawke in his younger, more egotistical days, at a time when Australian fiction writers were enjoying a resurgence in national esteem, liked to assert, 'I could write a novel.') In the second quarter of 1986 when Keating was making his 'banana republic' statement, Ray, fired by hatred of Keating's taxation policies, his admiration for Bjelke-Petersen, and the premier's own ambition, envisioned an Australia with Joh as prime minister. Ray had a meeting with Joh to discuss what their next step might be. It was to bring into the loop Mike Gore, another white shoe, a former car dealer who had made it big time, and been bankrupt, who loathed the Hawke government and revered the capitalists' friend, Bjelke-Petersen. Gore, Ray and Bjelke-Petersen were of that cohort of successful men, shrewd in business but deeply ignorant of history and of how a national economy actually works, arrogant and parochial, who believed with almost touching innocence that they could run a country. Now it seemed that their day, the Day of the New Capitalists, had arrived. They would revenge themselves on the Canberra Socialists who had imposed the fringe benefits and other tough-on-business taxes, and who were hurting the battlers (the social strata from which these men had sprung) through the increasing cost of living.

Bjelke-Petersen was already seventy-five years old and, as an old political soldier, now gloried in memories of his salad days when, with a flash of brazen political cunning, he had helped destroy the Whitlam government by appointing a Trojan horse to the Senate in 1975. He dreamed of destroying Hawke— but more dramatically: *mano a mano*. He, Joh, would run for the prime ministership at the next election. There was a small hurdle to overcome first: John Howard was the leader of the

Liberal Party and Ian Sinclair the leader of the National Party. It would be necessary to dispense with their services, but Mike Gore saw this as a marketing exercise. He paid for some high-quality market research that showed that Andrew Peacock and Joh Bjelke-Petersen were a winning team, compared with stolid, bespectacled Howard (not yet forgiven in conservative circles for outlawing bottom-of-the-harbour tax evasion) and the virile but shop-worn Sinclair. Hawke was leading Howard 70 per cent to 16 per cent as preferred prime minister in May 1986.

In July Mike Gore, now the organiser of the secret 'Joh for Canberra' campaign, as it became known, revealed the plan to astonished senior members of the National Party. Joh was facing a state election that polls showed he would win only with difficulty. To imagine that, at his age, coming from the National Party, rather than the Liberal Party, he could go on to defeat Hawke and the Labor Party was, to say the least, imaginative.

It would be some months before the campaign would go public, but whispers of it came much sooner to the ears of Hawke, who was incredulous. 'I thought there must be a God,' he said.

He was back on top of his game, but he was facing a sea change in his private staff during 1986. Three years is usual for political staffers if they are to avoid burn out or loss of objectivity. During the banana republic spat, Keating, in tones of contempt, had named those who ran the Prime Minister's office, a 'Manchu court'. The description was reported in the press, leaving people somewhat puzzled, since the Prime Minister's staff were on good terms with the Treasurer. Graham Evans, Hawke's senior officer, recalled,

> When I first went to work for him in 1983 Bob said, 'I haven't been in Parliament long, so I will have to rely on you a lot' ... I never thought about Keating's calling

the PM's office a Manchu court at the time it happened, but later I did. I wondered, 'Why is Paul [attacking Bob's staff]?' It wasn't that he had problems of access, or disagreement about policy issues: so why? What's the motive? And I think Paul was aware that Bob had a very good and loyal staff, and if he, Paul, were to push himself forward, a significant obstacle to that would be the people around the Prime Minister. Paul realised that while Bob had a competent and loyal staff he was not likely to make the sort of errors that would open him up to criticism of his performance.

Keating's staff, which also consisted of outstanding people, had nevertheless let him down badly by allowing the Treasurer to overlook submitting his tax returns at a time when he was thumping others over tax, and in miscalculating a claim for parliamentary allowances. Later, two staff members wrote books about Keating[1] that, while not intentionally derogatory, were not helpful to his reputation. Hawke's staff considered the authors traitors to their boss who, like Hawke, was considerate and affectionate with his office. Keating's jibe had most particularly been directed at Peter Barron, who had taken charge of managing the banana republic crisis in a way that would prevent the Opposition from driving a wedge into the government. In the process Barron had upbraided the Treasurer with a savagery that Keating was accustomed to hear coming only from his own lips.

By the end of 1986, Evans, Barron, Garnaut, Walsh and Hogg had all gone on to other jobs, their time spent on Hawke's staff setting up their careers for life. Somewhat quixotically, when the last of the courtiers, Hogg and Walsh, were about to leave, Keating arrived unexpectedly to thank them and the rest of the Manchus for their great contribution to the government. One of the newcomers, press secretary Stephen Mills, was to write,

Their departures deprived Hawke of considerable accumulated experience and made him more susceptible to the increasingly dry economic advice flowing from the bureaucracy. But in a certain way it also liberated him. The first generation ... having been in their jobs as long as Hawke had been in his, they were quasi-equals; they had seen him when he was still a novice and they had seen him in his bereft phase in 1984. As they peeled off, Hawke seemed to gain in self-assurance; the longer he remained prime minister, the more comfortably he managed the responsibilities and workload of the job.[2]

Yeend had retired and in the new head of Prime Minister and Cabinet, Mike Codd, a fellow West Australian, Hawke had a magnificent strong right arm. Codd not only filled the gap left by Yeend, but in intellectual prowess added the delight that Garnaut once provided to Hawke's quiet hours of discussion.

Codd is a tall, reserved man with a quiet voice who had worked for prime ministers John Gorton, Billy McMahon, Gough Whitlam and, under Malcolm Fraser, had been appointed head of the Industrial Relations department. Someone very powerful in the trade union movement had taken such an intense dislike to him that, when Hawke won office, Codd was virtually the only senior public servant to be put out to grass. He was made head of the Industries Assistance Commission. By rumour, he was a blue-nosed Tory. But in late 1985 Hawke dispatched Peter Barron to look Codd over as a possible replacement for Sir Geoffrey Yeend, who was due to retire. When Barron returned after half-an-hour's chat with a favourable report there was shock in Hawke's office. John Bowan exclaimed, 'I thought he was the devil incarnate!' By 1987 the Prime Minister's staff recognised Codd for what he was: a highly intelligent, honourable, hardworking public servant with a good political nose.

Times were tough for the government. It was losing its electoral base in droves—those who had been subject to the enormous pressures of restructuring the economy and who, despite Hawke's best intentions, did not feel, and had not been, fully compensated for what they had lost. Graham Richardson noted,

> our fortunes were starting to decline; after three years of dominating the Opposition, our ascendancy was beginning to sink. The fallout from the [1985] tax package was considerable: workers felt short-changed by the taxing of staff canteens and employer-provided motor cars, employers were angered by the extra taxes they were having to pay to keep their workers happy. Virtually everybody ignored the benefits that flowed from the tax package, such as lower tax rates for all and the raising of the lowest tax threshold which meant that 100 000 people no longer had to pay any tax at all.[3]

An internal report by Bob Hogg noted,

> The electoral coalition of support we took years to build is almost completely alienated ... we have lost youth, the low income blue and white collar workers, to a lesser extent the aged, and we have lost the middle ground in a big way.[4]

Young people saw the government as cynical and lacking Labor idealism.

Hawke's response was to fight to win back the minds—the hearts had never really left him—of the people. From mid-1986 he launched himself into an intense schedule of visits outside Canberra—to schools, factories and shopping centres. His message was that the nation faced a hard slog. His speechwriter, Graham Freudenberg, recalled,

> The economic crisis of '86 was the other side of Hawke at the Summit: that is, Hawke at the Summit, the optimistic, outgoing leader. Hawke at the mid-'86 crisis was quite stern. No prime minister had spoken to the Australian people in those terms since Curtin.

Hawke was still so popular that at one Sydney shopping centre a crowd gathered in such a surge a Hawke staffer feared there had been an accident. Asking what had happened, he was told 'We're here to see the Prime Minister!' But while Hawke, in personal popularity, was a mile in front of Howard, the government was a mile behind the Opposition. In late November, Hawke convened a Sunday meeting of the full ministry at which he read out to his team of twenty-seven men and women just how big a battle they faced to win the following year.

> The mood we have to create for the next year in the conduct of government business is one of stability, certainty, decisiveness, cautious and realistic optimism ... It is essential that the government control the middle ground—and that the Opposition be excluded. There need to be twenty-seven voices selling the government rather than twenty-seven voices selling twenty-seven pieces of government.

He told his ministers they needed to 'get out of Canberra more' and have as much contact with their electorates and with traditional supporters as possible.

By the end of the year the Coalition's 7.5 per cent lead over Labor had, on one poll, narrowed to 1 per cent. Hawke was still three times more popular than Howard. An important turning point for young people in late 1986 had been the government's renewed emphasis on the environment. In the 1983 campaign, Labor had fought hard against the building of the Franklin Dam in Tasmania, winning many votes on the mainland and losing every single seat in the island state, which, like Queensland at the time, danced a few steps behind the salsa.

But during 1986 a most unlikely character had turned green. In April Senator Bob Brown, a Tasmanian independent at the time, through the Tasmanian Wilderness Society, which he had founded, invited Labor backbencher Senator Graham Richardson to fly by helicopter over some of the Tasmanian forests that both the Liberal and Labor parties in Tasmania were keen to log. Richardson already knew from party research that there was a huge, untapped number of idealistic young people across Australia who wanted the environment protected. Neither of the large parties had tapped into their yearning and Richardson realised the Opposition, because of its ties to business and its contemptuous attitudes to 'tree hugging', would have difficulty in doing so.

He wrote of his first experience of the majesty of Tasmania's trees,

> we flew over some of the world's most beautiful forests and stopped for a lunch of soggy sandwiches near a small mountain lake ... Bob Brown wanted chunks of forest, or preferably the whole area, put into World Heritage classification and protected forever ... by the time we arrived back in Hobart I was a convert ... I wanted to become a warrior for his cause. That was a bad day for the logging industry in Australia but a very good one for me, the environmental movement and the Labor Party. It didn't take too long to work out that we had a perfect convergence: what was right was also popular.[5]

Richardson always promoted himself as a tough operator, which the Left took at face value, and loathed. But there was a softer, genuinely empathetic side to him, best seen some years later when he was Minister for Health and, in the words of Mike Codd, 'became passionate about Aboriginal health. Genuinely passionate. He could have achieved an awful lot in that portfolio, but he had to resign.' His resignation was due to scandal, and the shadow of scandal seemed to be Richardson's kismet, pursuing him into his seventh decade.

But it would be insulting to Richardson to attribute his greening in 1986 to purely idealistic motives—unless they were the ideals of winning votes, keeping Labor in government and advancing his own career. The 'perfect convergence' of which he wrote was even more exquisite than he suggested. As the New South Wales Right's faction boss, Richardson had counted the numbers and knew that the current minister, Barry Cohen, was weak in Caucus support and not highly regarded in the environmental movement. The greens wanted a fighter, and Cohen simply did not have the fight in him that Richardson had. Urban to his toenails, more at home in a Chinatown restaurant than by a woodland stream, Senator Richardson flying above the virgin forests of Tasmania saw not just beauty, but his chance to be promoted out of the ruck: *to the ministry.*

But there were pitfalls for an Environment minister: forestry workers, who were traditional Labor voters, would lose their jobs.

On returning to Canberra, Richardson took Senator Brown to talk to the Prime Minister.

Just two days earlier Hawke had appointed a young economist, Dr Craig Emerson, to his staff, who, on hearing that Brown would be talking to Hawke about environmental issues, asked if he could sit in. Hawke agreed, and from that moment Emerson became something new in a prime minister's office: the environmental adviser. There was a touchy issue to resolve: the Hawke government had signed a memorandum of understanding with the Liberal government of Tasmania to allow logging. Emerson recalled, 'Brown told the PM, "This logging means the destruction of the national estate."'

Hawke and Emerson studied the memorandum and to their delight discovered that the text said one thing, and the attachments said another—which allowed the federal government room to attack the agreement and begin intervening in the Tasmanian government's permits for logging. It was not quite cricket, but it was good politics. The government took a decision that it would protect the national estate. The Wilderness Society was thrilled.

Emerson recalled,

> We were flying by the seat of our pants at the outset. Whether what we were doing was Constitutional was moot. Anyway, we said to the Tasmanian government, 'You've got to stop logging these places.' And it was on for young and old. A real shit fight. But the Wilderness Society backed us all the way.

By December 1986 a glimmer of optimism for a Labor victory in 1987 had appeared.

Then at the end of the month, at Christmas, the change in Labor's fortunes became surreal. On Christmas Day the white-shoe brigade set out in one of their privately owned helicopters to fly to Sir Joh Bjelke-Petersen's farm at Bethany to deliver the premier their special Yuletide gift: the blueprint for how he would take over the Australian government in 1987.

New Capitalism's Saviour mulled things over until New Year's Eve.

On 1 January, in the *Australian*, came the astonishing news that Sir Joh Bjelke-Petersen would be running for federal parliament, that a hundred groups were supporting him, that he would introduce a flat-rate tax—and that any time the Canberra Socialists wanted to call an election, he would be ready to take 'em on.

Sir Joh had launched a populist crusade to appeal directly to the people; he intended to sidestep party structure as a trifle beneath his contempt. For good measure he attacked former and current leaders of both the Liberal and National parties: Malcolm Fraser, John Howard and Ian Sinclair.

The sahibs and memsahibs of the press gallery were ecstatic: here was a story better than any since Combe–Ivanov: a home-grown People's Revolution! The downtrodden of the earth, uneducated white men and women in horrible jobs or without jobs, and millionaires who were having taxes extracted from them by the Canberra socialists as unwillingly as if their money were their fingernails, would join in a mighty tide rising across the nation to sweep away socialists and milquetoast leaders of the Liberal and National parties as so much flotsam after a storm. Des Keegan of the *Australian* described Sir Joh as: 'this remarkable man [who] is clearly going to shift the debate substantially towards personal freedom after 20 years of weak, grasping and undemocratic leadership'.

On 1 February 1987, Sir Joh told a rally, 'I'm starting the bushfire here today and the media is going to fan it.' He was certainly right about that. The Joh campaign was page one for weeks on end and talkback radio ran wild. Most journalists restrained themselves to simply reporting what was happening, which was astonishing enough, but some of those who had appointed themselves opinion-makers went for Joh's throat. On 3 February, Richard Carleton announced on ABC radio,

> The Premier of Queensland, a man who can't string together three words in the English language, a man who

believes in water-powered cars and quack cancer cures, this man is stomping the country preaching voodoo economics and flat earth finance and he's being listened to.

And so he was, but his audience was not confined to rednecks. Members of the left-wing intelligentsia were so alarmed there were some public and many private expressions of anxiety about the possibility of concentration camps for homosexuals and the need to flee abroad.

The 1980s were, for many, already a decade of anxiety and uncertainty not simply because of the vast economic reforms the Hawke government was instituting but because people did not know what to believe in any more. The churches had become lifeless relics, the morality and social cohesiveness they once embodied wasting as the power of their rituals faded. By the 1980s the women's movement of the 1970s had disrupted the emotional basis of personal life at a deep psychological level by altering the power relationship between men and women. This accompanied a disruption of power relations between parents and children and a drug culture, begun in the optimistic innocence of the 1960s, which had by the 1980s grown mad, demonic and criminal. Money seemed the only security, the only way for people to measure their value to each other, to belong. The new money class, the cutthroat merchant gentlemen driving Italian and German sports cars, squiring flashy women and ordering Bollinger at lunch, seemed to show the way forward. A lifetime of certainties about Australian society had been overturned in a few years.

On 7 February, Sir Joh announced, 'I am determined to turn politics upside down in Australia ... [I have] a lot of experience and I know what I am doing.'

Labor research showed that most of Joh's support was coming at the expense of the Coalition, but a disturbing percentage of it was from the ALP, from unskilled male workers with low education and low incomes. If it's a truism that a man with a fortune is in need of a wife, it's equally true that a poor man will be lucky to find one. Unskilled men had suffered most from the feminist revolution, and from economic restructuring. They felt abandoned to the scrap heap of society, without a hand to help them up. Until Sir Joh! A Channel Nine television poll showed 72 per cent of 204 000 callers supported Sir Joh. The figures were dubious, but could not be entirely ignored as Channel Nine was the most popular national station. On 18 March a credible poll, by Morgan, showed that an Andrew Peacock–Sir Joh team could win 52 per cent of the vote, while the existing Coalition leadership of Howard and Sinclair would win only 42 per cent. It was not clear if Peacock or Sir Joh would be prime minister, but the electorate did not seem to mind. They wanted a saviour.

Sir Joh was on a roll.

While Labor's research was pessimistic, the Prime Minister became increasingly annoyed with Labor's pollster, Rod Cameron, because Hawke believed Cameron was mistaken in his advice to the government. There was a large personal element at play: Cameron, whom David Combe believed had betrayed him in evidence he had given in the Ivanov Affair, had by now turned against his Prime Minister. According to Richardson, Cameron 'considered himself the equal of or better than pretty well all the politicians and party officials with whom he worked' and was openly backing Keating against Hawke. Relations between the pollster and the Prime Minister were by 1987 'poisonous' in Richardson's view.[6] In Hawke's office, the new political advisor, the very able Bob Sorby, had argued vehemently since January that the Prime Minister should call an election as soon as possible, which would be March 1987. But Hawke wanted to wait, and he had hit upon one of his unexpected manoeuvres: instead of the advertising company the party had used for the past thirteen years, he would arrange to appoint a brilliant maverick, an anti-Labor radio and advertising wild man, John Singleton, best friend of the white-shod Brian Ray, to run Labor's ad campaign. When the Prime Minister first proposed Singleton ('Singo' as he became known throughout the nation) to the 1987 campaign committee its members were flabbergasted. Bob Hogg, working as a consultant at the national office, was horrified, and expressed himself vehemently opposed. Others concurred. Singleton was famous for his love of drink, beautiful women, racehorses, having fun and making and spending lots of money. On radio he had frequently attacked 'the socialists' and had actually founded a half-baked populist political party in the 1970s to attack the Whitlam government. The objections to him as Labor's champion for the election were loud, but Hawke hammered through his reasoning: Singleton was uniquely gifted in advertising, sharp as a scalpel, always original—and now he was on Labor's side ('to the death, mate', he had told Hawke). If Sir Joh was weird, Singo was weirder. And much smarter.

Sullenly, the Labor election committee agreed.

Hawke was focused on winning, and on restoring the good repute of the Labor Party in the process. He had decided that the longer he let the Joh for Canberra campaign run, the stronger Labor could become. But it took nerve. Bob Hogg said, 'Bob hung on and on, until July, which was the right thing to do, because the Joh campaign ran Howard ragged. If Bob had listened to his advisers and gone in March the outcome could have been different.'

As Hawke had calculated, the Coalition began hitting and biting each other in public. The Liberal president, John Valder, called Sir Joh 'a political terrorist in the Colonel Gaddafi mould'; Ian Sinclair called him 'the Norman Gallagher of the National Party'; Andrew Peacock, smooth and cynical after too many years believing in nothing in particular, announced, 'Sir Joh is a great Australian, a great patriot who always—and I mean always—puts his country first.' Sir Joh said Peacock would challenge Howard for the Liberal leadership and referred to Howard as 'a silly little boy'. Peacock denied he was about to challenge. Howard sacked Peacock from the shadow ministry. Joh then announced that his son, John, would accompany him in the storming of Canberra, which prompted Bill Hayden to request that Sir Joh on arrival in Canberra should also, in emulation of the Emperor Caligula, appoint to the Senate his horse.

By now the weather had turned cold and Canberra's lovely summer roses were blown. Hawke announced the election for 11 July—mid-winter, a time never before chosen for an election. This of itself was news, and a show of prime ministerial daring.

A few days earlier, Sir Joh had attended the Premiers' Conference in Canberra, which, the white shoes had planned, would be his real launching pad into federal politics. But Hawke, backed by Keating, savaged Bjelke-Petersen's economic proposal for a flat 25 per cent tax to a point of grave public humiliation for the Queensland premier. It was a tax welcome only to the rich. 'I remember saying to Paul: "This is too good to be true,"' Hawke said.

At that conference Sir Joh suddenly knew beyond doubt that he was fighting out of his class; he was on a hiding to nothing.

Then, on the day after Hawke's election announcement, Howard made a fatal political mistake. On 3 June, from fogbound Canberra, he set out to fly to Queensland to speak personally to Sir Joh. His plane had to wait hours on the tarmac before it could take off. Howard should have seen the bad weather as an omen, and disembarked. But instead of publicly dismissing Sir Joh as a populist ratbag, Howard believed he needed to appease the premier, to persuade him to make no more waves during the election campaign. When he finally arrived in Brisbane, Sir Joh treated Howard with contempt. The premier knew his own campaign was sunk; he believed Howard's was also—and that Howard and Sinclair deserved to lose.

For the government it was more fun than a circus. Hawke laid it on with a trowel, telling parliament,

> The desperate early morning dash ... by the Leader of the Opposition to Brisbane is the action of the weakest leader in the history of Australian politics ... This man, this silly little boy, goes up to see the thug, to see the Norm Gallagher of conservative politics ... and he says, please, Sir Joh, will you anoint my campaign? Will you say no longer I am a silly little boy? ... He knocks on the door of the thug, the Norm Gallagher, and says: Norm, Norm, here I am, the silly little boy ... He says, 'I'll take it all back. Joh, I won't any longer call you a thug. I won't say you are ... the worst conservative Premier in Australia. Do you remember, Joh, that I said you were suspending the laws of arithmetic? I will now take all that back.'[7]

Mick Young joined the fray:

> The Leader of the Opposition should not have gone to Queensland this morning; he should have gone to St Vincent's Hospital to see whether the staff could find his spine ... the Leader of the Opposition, helped by the fog at the Canberra Airport, rubbed ointment on his knees and went to the altar of the white shoes. He has carpet rash from kneeling in front of Joh this morning saying, 'Please, don't upset our campaign too much.'[8]

Singleton, as Hawke had predicted, fashioned a dashingly original advertising campaign, with a battle hymn that encapsulated the feeling of hard times for ordinary people,

'Together, Let's stick together, let's see it through'. The song and the ads, plus disciplined campaigning from the government, helped to deliver Labor a majority that increased from 16 to 24 seats.

Years later Howard remarked in a tone of gallows humour, 'Bob Hawke should contribute to the Joh Bjelke-Petersen Memorial Fund.' Although he felt cheated of victory in 1987, Howard was too realistic a politician not to recognise later that history had, in fact, been kind to him: had he succeeded in 1987, he would have been a one-term leader, in charge of a mutinous crew, trying to steer his ship through an economic storm that was building into a cyclone.

Hawke's election victory in 1987 was a high tide for him and the government. Graham Freudenberg, whose knowledge of federal government history was peerless, remarked,

> One of the outstanding things about Bob was there's never been a prime minister who enjoyed the job, had sheer joy in it, as much as Bob. He exuded the spirit of fun and sheer zest for it. I don't mean having power and the appurtenances, which of course he enjoyed, he loved. But just the sheer joy of being prime minister for THIS PEOPLE. *The Australians*.

Hawke surged with the renewed energy of a man who has stuck to his vow, and succeeded. His vision of the Australian Labor Party as the natural party of government, and his dream of ordinary Australian people leading lives of greater happiness, justice, freedom and prosperity was coming true. In photographs he appeared younger, more vital and buoyant than he had since 1984. In winning three elections, he had outdone his hero, Curtin. He was now, officially, the most successful Labor prime minister.

Hawke said,

> I was thrilled that the Australian people had endorsed the ideas I'd developed and, in many cases had had to persuade my party to embrace, in what was a historic event. I felt excited and ready for the challenge of a third term.

Hawke saw his task now as pushing through further economic and social reforms; like Curtin and his successor, Ben Chifley, he and Keating were laying the foundations of a New Australia. But there was a vital difference: Hawke was not about to drop dead from the strain of office, as Curtin had, and Keating was no Chifley when it came to loyalty to his leader.

The triumphant 1987 election was, in Paul Kelly's words, 'the big turning point' in the relationship of the Prime Minister and the Treasurer, for it was after that Hawke victory 'that Keating's mind really starts to turn to leadership . . . and it starts to prey on his mind'.

In February 1983, Hawke had ruined Keating's long-laid plan for taking over the leadership from Bill Hayden 'after a couple of terms', as Keating told Hayden to his face. At the time Hayden thought to himself, 'Well, *how kind* of you.' From 1983 onwards, Keating had been waiting for his moment to arrive. Everybody, including Hawke, believed it would come. But from many accounts, both from those who admired and those who disliked him, Keating became obsessed with the idea that after the 1987 election and before the 1990 election, it had to be his turn to take the helm. All power tends to corrupt; power denied also tends to corrupt.

Richardson, who was close to the Treasurer in those days, wrote,

> Keating ... has never understood the concept of being in a position of weakness: he just keeps going and expects his position to improve by virtue of its inherent correctness; if it's his position, it must be right.[9]

Keating had the intransigence of a born leader but as an autodidact he was untrained in the hard intellectual struggle against one's emotions and assumptions to see another point of view. Together with his personal charm, his ferociously held convictions gave him powers of salesmanship of extraordinary force, and slowly this force would be brought to bear upon the Caucus.

At first, only those closest to Keating knew of his mounting frustration, but as Richardson noted, 'Keating cannot hide disappointment, so his private rhetoric on Hawke got worse and worse.'[10] Keating began sharing his sentiments with colleagues and a critical few of the gallery sahibs. Unlike Hawke, who enjoyed discussion but not talk, Keating was a relentless talker whose telephone calls to journalists and editors would sometimes stretch to an hour. The more he talked, the more he saw himself as the victim of Hawke's unreasonable determination to remain prime minister, when in his own mind, he, Keating, was the true leader. Evidence to the contrary—Hawke was the most popular prime minister in polling history, even after five years of hard reforms, and Keating was highly unpopular—had no impact on the Treasurer. A kind of pathology was taking hold of him and his staff, but in 1987 it was all but invisible; Hawke, as was his custom with bad news, chose to ignore it. He dismissed Keating's increasingly vicious remarks about him as gossip he did not want to hear. Publicly, he and Keating were still a brilliant team; privately they continued to talk to each other as intimates, Hawke fretting about Keating's health, particularly his tinnitus, a cruel affliction for a man who so loved classical music.

Unlike the Opposition, the government had not promised tax cuts during the election campaign; its message had been sombre and wintery to match the hard times the country had been experiencing due to the collapse in the terms of trade. There was only one area in which the ERC and Cabinet agreed more money must be spent, and that was on the children of poor families. It was to be, and was in fact, the greatest social reform of the whole Hawke–Keating era, a multimillion annual allocation to be added to existing social security child payments, integrating them into a single system that would significantly benefit 500 000 families and more than one million children. Hawke had announced it, the Family Allowance Supplement, as the centrepiece of his policy speech at the Sydney Opera House on 23 June. There was spontaneous, roaring applause in the auditorium as he described *con brio* what would be done. But unnoticed by everyone that day, and for many months afterwards, the Prime Minister had committed a grievous political sin. Later several staff members would claim the guilt was theirs—but it was Hawke who would have to take the punishment. In the behind-the-scenes madhouse of preparing for an election launch and condensing the policy speech to thirty minutes for television broadcast, those proof-reading the final draft that Hawke would read from an autocue had missed the fact of a small but important change in wording. Hawke was meant to say, as was written in the printed speech circulated to the media, 'We pledge that by 1990 there will be no financial need for any child to live in poverty.' (This was achievable, and the government delivered on it.) Instead, the speech Hawke read from said, 'We set ourselves this first goal: by 1990 no child shall live in poverty'—a pie in the sky for the tens of thousands of children of dysfunctional families sunk in addiction and mental illness where the family allowance was spent on alcohol or drugs. It would be two years before a thousand times over, and over again, the phrase 'no child will live in poverty' would be flung back in Hawke's face. The softening words, 'we set ourselves this first goal' were always omitted, making him seem an even worse political shyster. If 'MX' is engraved on John Bowan's heart, 'no child will live in poverty' will be engraved on Hawke's. 'I was deeply hurt,' he said,

> because the welfare community acknowledged publicly and told me privately that this was the most significant improvement in child assistance ever. Many mothers confirmed the official judgment. They wrote me letters of thanks. I remember one mother approaching me in a shopping centre to say the new entitlement had changed her life. She had tears in her eyes as she thanked me.

In October 1987, three months after the election, there came the greatest stock market crash since 1929. It threw every government in the Western world into turmoil, with fears that it was the start of another Great Depression.

But in spite of the difficult times, being in government was glorious. Sandy Hollway, who had replaced Graham Evans as Hawke's principal private secretary, recalled it as 'the sweet spot'. Despite the Treasurer's personal frustration, the government was confident and cohesive, the faction system worked smoothly, the ministry carried no dead wood, the public service machine purred along, the Opposition was in a shambles and the Prime Minister could now afford to concentrate on his second great ambition: lifting Australia's profile in world affairs.

6

Soon after first winning office, Hawke turned his attention to foreign policy issues. By 1985 Australia was an elected member, with a then-record majority in its support, of the Security Council of the United Nations. Much of the credit was due to the professionalism and debonair charm of Australia's ambassador to the UN, Richard Woolcott, a former Rhodes scholar, an elegant, witty career diplomat with the even, finely boned face that Americans call 'preppy'. He resembled the diplomat of popular romance: with his beautiful Scandinavian wife, Birgit, the Woolcotts cut a glamorous swathe through the cocktail and dinner parties of New York. But Woolcott could not have accomplished his feats of lobbying for Australia without the international respect the country was already commanding. Michael Costello, principal private secretary to the Foreign minister, Bill Hayden, recalled being present at Hawke's first visit overseas as Prime Minister: 'It was an incredibly exciting time: a new Labor government. I've never forgotten, we walked into the hotel in Jakarta and the foyer erupted into cheers.'

In 1983 Australia had voted in the UN to condemn the United States for its invasion of Grenada. Hawke was not happy with this vote—he would have preferred an abstention—but he accepted Hayden's argument that there could not be one law for the Americans and another for the Soviet Union, condemned a only a few years earlier in the UN for invading Afghanistan. The Soviet Union, which at the time seemed invulnerable in its worldwide power, had invaded the most strategic point in the Middle East, Afghanistan, at the end of 1979 while the United States was distracted by the sacking of its embassy in Tehran. The Soviets took the opportunity to install a puppet government in Kabul.

Woolcott recalled (of the Grenada invasion),

> We thought that even a close ally shouldn't invade another country and expect our support, particularly if we hadn't been consulted. In the short term, the Americans were very cross with us... Bob was extremely deft about the relationship with the United States. He sort of played the good guy and Hayden tended to play the bad guy. That worked pretty well.

Journalists and members of the Left liked to accuse Hawke of being a lickspittle of the United States but, as Costello—who was no Hawke fan at the time and who observed the relationship closely—remarked, 'I never saw him as such.'

The UN vote against President Reagan's decision to invade Grenada allowed Andrew Peacock to create a drama in parliament, accusing the Hawke government of being an untrustworthy ally of the United States. 'The Americans knew they had sort of broken the rules,' Woolcott said, 'but thought they had the right to act to prevent what they believed was a looming Communist threat, because the Communists, in addition to Cuba, had got hold of Grenada.'

At the time of Australia's election to the UN Security Council, the Iran–Iraq war was devouring hundreds of thousands of young soldiers, many as young as fifteen. As a member of the Security Council, Australia was among the countries that drafted a resolution, then in Woolcott's phrase, 'sold it' to the Big Five, the permanent members. This resolution paved the way for ending the war. Australia took on Malaysia, and won, in a major fight over the Antarctic Treaty, and the French over obstruction to independence for New Caledonia, another win but only after a 'highly abrasive' fight.

Two huge chess games were in play in the 1980s: one in the Middle East, still ongoing this century, the other in South-East Asia.

It was in the South-East Asian game that Hawke decided Australia could play a constructive role.

Costello recalled, 'Bill came back from a meeting with Bob in 1983 and said, "Well, Bob tells me he wants me to take a big initiative to solve the Cambodian problem." I said, "Should be a piece of cake, Bill."' Costello, then in his thirties, had the tall, imposing body of a front-row rugby player, a shock of russet hair and an open, friendly face to which laughter came easily. He towered over every Asian he met, which in many Asian countries is considered offensive, but he would end up a trusted negotiator.

To describe the politics of Indo-China in 1983 as venomous is an understatement. Labor sentiment added to the government's difficulty in making any constructive moves in Indo-China, the party feeling being 'red raw', in Costello's description, on the issue of Vietnam and Cambodia. Indeed Cambodia stirred passions across the political spectrum.

In 1975 the Khmer Rouge had taken over Cambodia and launched an orgy of murder that included emptying the capital, Phnom Penh, of inhabitants and declaring the history of the country to have been abolished. They announced a new calendar with

1975 as Year Zero. Millions of citizens were tortured or slaughtered; everything Western was destroyed—even traffic lights, which had their 'eyes' ripped out. In the grip of blood lust, and with the acquiescence of China, the Khmer Rouge began raiding into Vietnam. The Vietnamese, toughened by years of warfare and almost giddy with victory over the United States, repaid their ancient enemy by invading. In late 1978 Vietnam installed a government in Phnom Penh, led by Heng Samrin. But waiting in the wings was a former brigade leader of the Khmer Rouge, Hun Sen, who would outmanoeuvre Heng Samrin and become prime minister in his place. Hun Sen had already swapped sides and also moved sideways, from being a Khmer Rouge fighter to fighting against the Khmer Rouge (a battle in which he lost an eye), then joining the invading Vietnamese forces. China denounced the Cambodian government as a Vietnamese puppet.

In 1983 Cambodia had a government that was the vassal of Hanoi; it had large Vietnamese forces occupying its territory and three factions of guerrilla fighters on its borders: the Lon Nolists, who, under General Lon Nol, had deposed the ruler of Cambodia, Prince Sihanouk; the Royalists who supported the prince (at the time in exile in Beijing); and the Khmer Rouge, who called themselves the Party of Democratic Kampuchea. These three made up a somewhat fractious coalition called the Coalition Government of Democratic Kampuchea, or CGDK. (The Khmer Rouge had renamed their country 'Kampuchea'.)

The United States had been furious over its humiliation in Vietnam. Militarily the South, backed by America, had been holding off North Vietnamese forces with ease. But after the disgrace of the Republican President Nixon over the Watergate scandal in 1972, the Democratic Congress voted to withdraw from Vietnam and within six months, drained of fighting spirit by the psychological collapse of its ally, the South surrendered.

Costello recalled that, even more than a decade later, in the mid-1980s,

> Reagan and the Republicans felt absolutely beside themselves with rage about this. Their sense of betrayal was almost like that of the German high command at the end of World War I. It was incredibly important in American domestic politics.

The Reagan administration took the stance: 'my enemy's enemy is my friend'. Despite the appalling atrocities of the Khmer Rouge, America supported the CGDK as the legitimate government of Cambodia. This suited the Chinese, for several reasons. All the neighbours of Vietnam were frightened of its fighting forces—even huge China, which had attacked it twice in the late 1970s and on both occasions received a horrible shock. As a Thai general explained to Bill Hayden, 'You always knew where the Vietnamese had been because there was blood everywhere.' Other Indo-Chinese were so terrified of the Vietnamese that in refugee camps Vietnamese refugees were accommodated in separate areas from the Cambodians and Laotians, who feared even the glance of their eyes.

The Thais were desperate for the Vietnamese to leave Cambodia, because just over the hills they were too close for comfort. Thailand had an army that looked very smart on parade, but its general staff had no illusions about how it would cope with a Vietnamese assault.

Added to all this was the tension between China and its dangerous next-door neighbour, the Soviet Union. All through the 1960s and 1970s, both the Soviets and the Chinese had worked hard to make Vietnam their ally, but centuries of Vietnamese resentment against China, whose vassal it had been, ended with an alliance between the Soviet Union and Vietnam, revealing to the West the bitterness of the Sino-Soviet split. The Soviet–Vietnam alliance became a nightmare scenario for China when the Soviet Union invaded Afghanistan, for China was now surrounded on its northern, north-western and southern borders by its enemy. The Soviet Union was obliged by treaty with Vietnam to support it militarily: China turned to its ancient text and the bible for contemporary Chinese businessmen, *The Art of War*. It set out to bleed its small enemy, Vietnam, in order to cut a vein in its big enemy, the Soviet Union. China voted in the UN in unison with the United States to uphold the CGDK as the legitimate government of Cambodia. More importantly, China gave material support to the Khmer Rouge: money and arms. The Chinese intended to destabilise the government of Cambodia and 'they did it very effectively', in Costello's view. Meanwhile the Thais were also doing all they could to work with the Chinese against the Hun Sen government in Phnom Penh. 'The Thais really didn't give a big rat's about the Khmer Rouge or the Cambodians, whom they'd dominated and exploited for centuries,' Costello said. 'They were just terrified the Vietnamese would come across the border.' To top it off, Singapore, buoyed by the sheer force of will and intellect of its prime minister, Lee Kuan Yew, was riding herd on the other ASEAN countries over Vietnam–Cambodia. Although Lee was not a military man, there was no other South-East Asian leader or Foreign minister who could stand up to his rapier intelligence and Western legal training. Singapore demanded that Vietnam–Cambodia be treated as a pariah, while 'Singapore-registered cargo boats dumped kilotons of consumer goods in Cambodia's harbours', Hayden noted in his memoirs.[1] He considered the Singaporeans 'sheer humbugs'.

For years Australia had been voting in the UN the same way on Cambodia as the United States and China: that the Khmer Rouge in its CGDK coalition was the legitimate government of Cambodia, that Vietnam had illegally invaded and it must withdraw. The Soviet Union and its allies voted the reverse. All this was occurring some years before the film *The Killing Fields* had exposed the horror of Khmer Rouge atrocities to the Western public. But among policy buffs it was such a passionate issue that in 1981 Andrew Peacock, then Foreign minister, had resigned over Australia's UN vote for the Khmer Rouge and had challenged Malcolm Fraser's leadership of the Liberal Party. In the ALP there were screaming matches about Australia formally supporting the Khmer Rouge. Personally, Hawke thought it disgusting, but like Fraser before him, he was conscious of the dogmatic and prejudiced position of the United States.

He wanted Hayden to find a way through.

When Hayden returned from that 1983 meeting with the Prime Minister, he explained to his secretary,

> It's to do with Vietnam and the United States. We have in the party platform an absolute commitment to resume aid to Vietnam. If I do that the Americans will go absolutely nuts, and I don't want to start this whole government off by getting the Americans furious with us. If we undertake an initiative on Cambodia we can say to the Left and we can say to Vietnam it would be a very bad idea for us to resume aid to Vietnam because we need the Americans on board to support a solution to the problem in Cambodia. And we need the countries of South-East Asia on board to support the solution: they'll all be very upset if we resume aid to Vietnam as our first act. So can we put it on hold?'

Hayden said Hawke had explained this as the background to what the Prime Minister described as 'just like a big industrial dispute. Mate, you get all the parties round the table and you just talk and pretty soon you'll have a solution.'

Hayden, always downbeat, was highly amused. But as Costello noted, 'It showed one of the best sides of Hawke: his optimism, his belief that if you try hard enough you can do it.' Despite misgivings, Hayden set out to try, noting 'the risk of total failure, and the dismissive hoots which would inevitably follow ... were no justification for fudging the challenge'.[2]

Foreign Affairs officers were aghast when their new minister explained what he and the Prime Minister wanted to do.

Hayden, accompanied by Costello, attended his first ASEAN Plus meeting, in Bangkok, in 1983. Shultz was representing the United States. Before the meeting a quiet word had gone out that Australia intended to raise the Cambodian issue. The Americans already had doubts about Hayden, who recalled, '[Paul] Wolfowitz [the assistant Secretary of State for East Asian and Pacific Affairs] was going around South-East Asia telling people in government that I was a secret Communist'.

Costello recalled,

> I was sitting in the chair behind Bill, who was seated at the table. He puts his proposition on the table. He is highly apprehensive. The ASEANs, who knew what was coming, turned their faces to wood and said nothing. Obviously, they had set up George Shultz to do the talking—not that he needed much encouragement. So George launched into this bitter criticism of the initiative. 'Is Australia really part of this show? Whose side is Australia really on?' All the usual things they do. 'The whole of ASEAN was as one with the United States and Japan, and here was Australia ...' blah, blah, blah. And at the end of it he came up with this line, '*And you know, I've got to say, this proposal is just STOOPID.*' People think Bill is a little bloke—and he did look that way on television—but he's a big guy, an ex-Queensland copper,

and at that moment he looked every inch his size. The back of his neck was going redder and redder. He said, *'Well, Mr Secretary, not as STOOPID as your efforts in Vietnam*. You created this situation! The United States of America, by its action in Vietnam and the bombing of Cambodia, created this nightmare!' He just gave it to Shultz: Boom! Boom! . . . So it was a very bad start to the Hayden–Shultz relationship. But he had clear instructions from Bob that he wasn't to give up, because otherwise we'd have to resume aid to Vietnam, which would have created a bigger problem. Anyway, Bill being Bill, he just kept going from then on.

Hayden said,

After Shultz had had a go, the Korean Foreign minister ripped into me. Then Sit, the Thai Foreign minister, chose to disagree in a very elegant, Thai way. So there I was, the flak-catcher for Bob Hawke . . . Shultz gave me a hard time for a few years, but then he settled down. The Americans didn't like me . . .

Costello recalled,

We went round and round and we were getting nowhere. Then Bill went to Vietnam, which we'd been to a number of times and met with the Foreign minister, Nguyen Co Thach, a brilliant, smooth, sophisticated man. He persuaded Bill to go down to Ho Chi Minh City and meet the 'Foreign minister' of Cambodia, whom we officially regarded as an illegal Foreign minister. The Foreign minister was Hun Sen.

Hayden took up the story,

> From Hun Sen's response I thought we might get somewhere. So I went to Bangkok, went straight to their Foreign Affairs department to tell them. I was waiting outside the meeting room and they began playing a tune I thought I recognised.

Hayden had quickly got the hang of how oblique Asian manners were.

> I asked, 'Anyone know that tune?' 'Yes,' said one of the assistants, 'It's called "Bring in the Clowns".' I thought, 'Oh Hell!' I went in, and the Thai Foreign minister was white with rage. 'How could you do this to me! How could you! I just want to ask you a question, Bill: whose friend is Dallas? Is she Madam Hun Sen's friend? Or is she my wife's friend? And whose friend are you, Bill? Are you Thailand's friend? Or are you Cambodia's friend? Are you my friend?' ... I got back to Australia and the Opposition put up a censure motion against me. And I was very tired, jet-lagged, and Bob said something like, 'Oh well—you're for it today. They're going for you. I'll lead our side.' And he was good. Defended me.

The press had persisted in trying to present the Hawke–Hayden relationship as tense, but Hayden added, 'Our relationship was always good, in my view.'

Hayden, after his interview with the Thai Foreign minister, with whom he and Dallas had until that moment enjoyed a warm friendship, decided he had done all he could about Cambodia; he was at a dead end. Costello said,

Regional balance of power considerations, global balance of power considerations and American passion and emotion meant that it wasn't possible to shift anybody. It just wasn't. The geopolitics wouldn't allow it. The regional politics wouldn't allow. American politics wouldn't allow it. Bill had got a huge kick in the arse for meeting Hun Sen—the Thais made sure of that.

Hawke turned to the Chinese to seek a lever. In his long late-night talks with Hu Yaobang in 1986, the Soviet Union was front and centre in Chinese concern, but Cambodia was interwoven with Sino-Soviet tension. Chinese intelligence on the Cambodian situation was of the highest quality. Hu, knowing Hawke's feelings about Pol Pot, head of the Khmer Rouge, tried to reassure him by saying, 'I can tell you, Prime Minister, that it is a real fact that Pol Pot has already retired from the leadership.' He went on to say that the CGDK forces had agreed that, were they able to defeat Vietnam and take over government, a free economy, not socialism, was the essential future for Cambodia. He was optimistic that the CGDK's 70 000 guerrilla army could better the Vietnamese. Hawke disagreed. There was in existence already an eight-point plan for peace talks, but as Hawke pointed out to Hu, in parts the plan lacked clarity. 'What,' Hawke asked,

> would be the status of the Khmer Rouge forces [if they agreed to] discussions? Would they still be armed? If so, people would fear a return to the excesses of the past ... While we acknowledge the sincerity of the Chinese view, we have doubts about how much optimism we can justifiably have about the CGDK to force Vietnam and Heng Samrin to the bargaining table ... We feel it requires too much optimism to believe that

the CGDK can force negotiations. Perhaps, therefore, we should be applying our minds to an honourable and reasonable way of resolving this stalemate.

They went on to discuss the problems within ASEAN for any Cambodian solution. In April 1985 Malaysia had suggested there could be separate rooms for the CGDK and Heng Samrin, with someone acting as runner between them, but Thailand, Singapore and the Philippines opposed the suggestion and Vietnam flatly rejected it. So did Hu Yaobang. Hawke responded,

> I can only express the hope that your optimism about the CGDK's capacities are justified. I must repeat, we have some doubt … Does the General Secretary see any reason to believe that the Soviet Union will change its position [of expanding its presence in Vietnam, and propping up Heng Samrin]?

Hu replied, 'No.' Hawke asked, 'Do you see any prospect for change in Vietnam? They are having their party Congress later this year. Are there any grounds for optimism here?' Hu replied,

> There is much dissatisfaction amongst the cadres and masses with the present Vietnamese leadership. It is also a fact that Le Duan [the leader of Vietnam who had approved his country's invasion of Cambodia], who is seventy-eight years old, is not in good health. It is now a race to see who can last longest.

They concluded the meeting with an agreement to keep in touch on Cambodia.[3]

The stalemate continued for several years. Then, as Costello remembered:

> We come to 1989, and guess what? The Soviet Union is collapsing. And it's 'Bye bye, Vietnam. You're on your own.' The Vietnamese say to themselves, 'We can't afford to keep our army in Cambodia,' and they decide to fall back. And suddenly, everyone's confronted with this terrible situation: the people who are going to take over will not be Prince Sihanouk and the Royalists, will not be the Lon Nolists—it's going to be the Khmer Rouge. They have the weapons and the grunt. Hey, we don't like this! But nobody could work out what to do.

At a conference in Paris the French proposed a quadripartite interim government to run Cambodia until there could be free and fair elections. Costello said,

> Hun Sen, who was the prime minister by now, said, 'Three of you, and one of me? I don't think so.' So that didn't fly. By this stage, in Australia, the Caucus was going nuts, absolutely nuts. Caucus was saying, 'Australia has *got* to change its vote.' The Americans were saying, 'Don't you dare!' ASEAN was saying, 'Don't you dare!' So what are we to do?

Hawke appointed Gareth Evans Minister for Foreign Affairs on 2 September 1988, as Hayden had left parliament to take the office of Governor-General. On 1 September the Prime Minister had appointed Richard Woolcott head of the department. During their meeting Hawke had asked Woolcott to assist Evans until the new minister—in whose abilities Hawke

Six

had total confidence—had a grip on his portfolio. Costello was no longer working on Cambodia, but he remained interested, and he was close friends with Hawke's foreign policy adviser, John Bowan. Bowan was concerned by the pressure on the Prime Minister coming from Caucus. One night he invited Costello to dinner at his house in Canberra where they worried at the Cambodian issue. Costello was due to attend political–military talks with the Americans in Hawaii, before going on to Japan. He recalled,

> About halfway through the second bottle of port we dreamed up this mad idea that instead of spending four days on the beach in Hawaii, I should go to Hanoi and talk to the Vietnamese Foreign minister, whom I'd met several times when I was working for Bill. Meet him to see if he and I could come up with something. At that point in the evening it seemed we had a great idea: to create a supreme national council, and make that the representative Cambodian authority. Get it to delegate all its power under certain terms and conditions, to be negotiated, to Hun Sen's government as the interim authority, and then have an election. For every ministry there would be a UN shadow minister and a UN shadow administration to oversee the Hun Sen regime and prevent it impairing the free and fair election. Plus there would have to be a substantial UN peacekeeping and peace maintenance forces, and UN control of all the factional armies. It was one of those ideas that only come when you're drunk. Anyway, we went to Gareth and he said, 'Why not? Try anything.' I presume he talked to Hawkey about it. So, we got the mandate, and off I went. I didn't have a single briefing note. Absolutely nothing.

In Hanoi, Nguyen Co Thach found the plan interesting. He told Costello,

> We trust Australia on this because we know you're allied with the US and we know you're friends with the ASEAN and we know how you vote in the UN, but we also know you are trying hard. You showed you did with Minister Hayden, you did everything you could. So we trust you.

He suggested Costello go down to Ho Chi Minh City where he could talk to the Vice Foreign Minister of Cambodia, Sok An. Sok An, who was a close ally of Hun Sen's, whose children were to marry each other, told Costello, 'You may not believe me, but I'm telling you: Hun Sen is his own man. You will have to convince him.' Shortly afterwards Costello received the message, 'Hun Sen would like to see you. Come and see him.' Nobody from Australia, the United States or any of Australia's ASEAN allies had gone to Phnom Penh since the 1970s, when it had fallen to the Khmer Rouge. Cambodia was a pariah state. Hiding in its jungles was an army of guerrilla fighters armed by the United States and China. Costello requested permission from Australia; the delicacy of the issue demanded it be cleared not just with Evans, but with Hawke. A return cable said, simply, 'Go'. He was off into tiger country.

Costello plus a note-taker from the department and an Australian solider were driven from Hanoi to the Cambodian border, where a man on 'a very large white motorcycle in a funny uniform, with his gaiters sort of falling off, escorted us through the Khmer Rouge areas'. Costello had insisted on taking the soldier with him, and that the soldier come to the talks wearing uniform, 'because I knew they weren't going to believe some crappy civilian, particularly on the military stuff. Our soldier looked very fierce. He wasn't wearing formal military dress. He was wearing the stuff you'd wear in the field.' The roads were bad and it took two days to reach Phnom Penh but they did so without any sign of the jungle armies.

Finally Costello was face to face with Hun Sen, a slightly unnerving experience as it is difficult to know which of Hun Sen's large brown eyes is real, and where his gaze is directed. He was in military uniform, as Costello had anticipated, and looked every centimetre the war-toughened fighter he was. After the first day of talks, when Costello had explained the plan, the Cambodian leader responded, 'I am prepared to take this seriously. The only reason I'm seeing you is because Bill Hayden saw me all those years ago, and took such punishment for it.'

The peace process in Cambodia, which in due course would see Gareth Evans nominated for a Nobel Prize, was underway.

There were many more hurdles to clear—with the Chinese, who by this time were angry with Australia and with Hawke personally over his reaction to the Tiananmen Square killings—with the members of ASEAN, with Prince Sihanouk and with the Khmer Rouge. Their representative agreed to meet Costello but when the Australian asked his first question the guerrilla took out a notebook and read a forty-seven minute diatribe. Costello asked a second question. The Cambodian opened his notebook again and read the same diatribe for another forty-seven minutes. Costello tried a third time and received the identical response.

At least Thailand was no longer maintaining its rage. As soon as the Vietnamese army left Cambodia, Thailand was, Costello said,

> Keen to re-establish relations. They didn't give a damn who was running Cambodia, didn't care if it was Hun Sen or Sihanouk or the Khmer Rouge. They just wanted to get back in there and resume stealing their timber.

Throughout these tortuous negotiations, which dragged on for months, Hawke gave Evans his full support, which in turn empowered Costello to bravely go where no man had been before. One cable from the Australian Foreign minister to his negotiator read, 'Your instructions remain as they have always been. Follow your nose and see where it leads you.' Costello said,

> I wanted to talk to the Chinese, who were isolated at the time because of Tiananmen. Nobody was speaking to them, not the Americans, not us. And once again Hawkey came though. Straight away. 'Yep: we'll take the flak for talking to China.' It wasn't Gareth's decision, it was Hawke's.

Finally, after years of conferences and shouting, the goal was accomplished thanks to Gareth Evans' brilliance as a draftsman and a last throw of the dice by Costello. The Khmer Rouge were insisting on the framework for peace that had, largely, been drafted by Evans. But Hun Sen refused, saying he wanted to negotiate further. By now the Americans had moved away from the Khmer Rouge, but were still refusing to speak to Hun Sen. All the parties had arrived in Jakarta for a final conference. Costello recalled,

> I went round to see Hun Sen. The only reason I felt confident doing it was because I had this instruction to follow my nose. I said to him, 'What's your price to sign the treaty in its entirety?' He said, 'Get the American ambassador to pay a formal call on me.' So I went to the Americans and said, 'If you'll do this we can get a signature tomorrow.' They cabled the President of the United States [George Bush] for permission and the next day the American ambassador called on Hun Sen.

The leader of Cambodia emerged from the meeting to announce, 'I will sign.'

Costello added,

> Remember this: officials do their thing. They can do it well or ill, they can bugger things up. But they suffer few consequences. It's the politicians who get the heat. They are the ones who have to answer for what's been done. There is no particular credit to me, but enormous credit to Hawke and Evans.

In early 1988 Hawke had been prime minister for five years and had almost completed the task of restructuring the public service, reducing the number of departments from twenty-eight to eighteen. This included amalgamating Foreign Affairs with Trade. In acronym-loving Canberra FA had become DFAT, presumably because FAT was too tempting for wits. Hayden was still Foreign minister. Woolcott recalled,

> I was brought back [from the UN] by Bob Hawke and Bill Hayden [who would still be the Foreign minister for a few more months] with the specific instruction of trying to make this melding of two rather different bureaucratic cultures work. I think we did. I think the amalgamation was a great success. The philosophy behind it was very sound. It was that Australia was a major trading nation. It needed much closer co-ordination of foreign policy and trade policy, and it would work better if they were under the same roof. As time passes, people almost forget there used to be two separate departments. Creating DFAT was a very

sound move because it really strengthened our position in the World Trade Organization, in what was then the Uruguay Round [of global trade negotiations], and enabled us to move ahead with the formation of APEC, the Asia–Pacific Economic Co-operation forum ... Australia's currency had collapsed in 1986, and that really motivated the Prime Minister to call for the establishment of an Asian-Pacific economic co-operation forum, because he was afraid that the way the global economy was moving there was a risk that the world would break up into three blocs: the yen bloc, the dollar bloc and the deutschmark bloc, and Australia—and New Zealand for that matter—would find themselves excluded. This was part of the driving force, the need to have better institutional arrangements, which led him in January 1989 on a visit to Korea to launch the idea of APEC.

Sandy Hollway, Hawke's principal private secretary in 1988, recalled,

The idea of some sort of Asia–Pacific community had been kicking around the academic community for about nine months. It wasn't right on the radar screen, but the idea was there. And I remember we were preparing for a visit Bob was to make to South Korea, Thailand, Pakistan and India, and as was customary, many months before the trip we were sitting around in the office talking about how the trip would work: what appointments Bob wanted with ministers, what speech opportunities there were. And it became obvious there were opportunities for major speeches in Seoul and Bangkok. It's very important to remember that at the time a huge thrust of

Bob personally and of the Hawke government generally was Australia's economic relationship with Asia. Bob had invented this phrase that he continually used, 'enmeshment with Asia'. Multilateral trade negotiations were also a constant preoccupation: how to liberalise international trade? So the thing that naturally always sprang to our mind was economics. I was talking to Bob late one night in Canberra and one of us said, 'You know, this trip might be the time for Australia to stand up and say we should have some kind of community for the Asia–Pacific. It was a very embryonic conversation.

Hollway envisaged a kind of Asia–Pacific OECD; the OECD studied and issued reports on matters such as intra-regional transport, economic management and financial flows.

I remember thinking to myself, There is a model which is utterly defensible, and it's a no-lose proposition—even if we don't get anywhere—because *forever* the Australian government will be on record as having stood up and declared that it wanted Australia to be part of Asia.

Gareth Evans was not scheduled to accompany the Prime Minister on the Asian trip because he was due in Washington for talks with, among others, Jim Baker, President Reagan's Secretary of State. His right arm, Woolcott, was to stay in Canberra minding home base.

Hawke travelled with a team that included his head of Prime Minister and Cabinet, Mike Codd, who recalled,

The thing senior public servants *pray* for from prime ministers is opportunity: opportunity to offer a view and be part of any discussion around policy suggestions that are going forward—because if you're engaged in that process it not only inspires you, the message goes back to the department and to other people in it, who have the job of fleshing out what's being proposed, and they all feel they are part of the government machine. Bob was very good throughout his time at doing just that, and one example is the formulation for APEC. We flew into Seoul one afternoon for a meeting next day with President Roh Tae-woo. And as was Bob's usual way, that night he drew in people from the team to chew the fat and discuss what major issues he should raise with the President next morning, and what we should try to get out of the meeting. John Bowan was there, Sandy Hollway was there and I was there. It was about 10 p.m. We talked about regional co-operation, the fact that the Asia–Pacific would be the growth region of the world in the next few decades, and how to get more cooperation. We talked about needing something a bit more than the OECD, but not a body that required a huge machine to run it. And the proposition about what might be put forward, initially to President Roh, emerged from that discussion. Everyone in the room felt they were engaged in the process of developing the idea. It was remarkable: you often have PMs or leaders who have a great idea, but rarely do you have people who do that, who then think, 'How can we successfully implement it? What are the hurdles? What are the issues that can come up?'

There were plenty, the first being China's towering hostility at the time to Taiwan, its 'renegade province', and the Chinese refusal to recognise Hong Kong as an independent state empowered to represent itself. There was also the problem of

Hawke and Hayden at a press conference after the unsuccessful leadership challenge in Canberra, July 1982. (Newspix)

Hawke and Hazel in the tally room on election night, Canberra, March 1983. (Courtesy of Bob Hawke)

Victorian State Secretary, Bob Hogg in the ALP office during the successful 1983 election, March 1983. (The Herald and Weekly Times Photographic Collection)

The first Hawke ministry, Canberra, March 1983. Front row (left to right): Peter Morris, Mick Young, Paul Keating, Don Grimes, Sir Ninian Stephen (Governor General), Hawke, John Button, Lionel Bowen, Ralph Willis. Second row (left to right): John Brown, Michael Duffy, Arthur Gietzelt, Stewart West, Neal Blewett, John Kerin, John Dawkins, Tom Uren, Gareth Evans, Brian Howe. Back row (left to right): Susan Ryan, Peter Walsh, Clyde Holding, Gordon Scholes, Barry Jones, Chris Hurford, Kim Beazley, Barry Cohen, Bill Hayden. (Courtesy of Bob Hawke)

Mick Young and Paul Keating in the tally room on election night, March 1983. (Courtesy of Bob Hawke)

The first caucus meeting, March 1983. (Courtesy of Bob Hawke)

Director General of International Labour Organisation Francis Blanchard, Geoff Walsh, Hawke and John Bowan, Geneva, June 1983. (Courtesy of Geoff Walsh)

Celebrating the America's Cup victory, Perth, September 1983. (Newspix)

Sir Geoffrey Yeend, Hawke and General Secretary of the Communist Party, Hu Yaobang, Beijing, February 1984. (Courtesy of Bob Hawke)

*Keating and Graham Richardson, Canberra, July 1984.
(NAA, A6180, 23/7/84/42)*

*Hawke and Keating enjoy a lighter moment during the Tax Summit debate,
July 1985. (Newspix)*

From left to right: Peter Barron, Graham Evans, Sir Robert Cotton, Hawke, Neil McInnes, Ross Garnaut and Tim McDonald at the White House with Vice President George Bush, President Ronald Reagan and Secretary of State George Shultz, Washington D.C., February 1985. (Courtesy of Bob Hawke)

Commonwealth Heads of Government review meeting regarding South Africa, London, August 1986. Front row (left to right): Margaret Thatcher, Lynden Pindling, Kenneth Kaunda. Back row (left to right): Rajiv Gandhi, Brian Mulroney, S.S. Ramphal, Hawke, Robert Mugabe. (Sahm Doherty/Getty Images)

Hawke celebrates election victory, July 1987. From left to right: Craig Emerson, Jackie (Rosslyn's boys' nanny), Sue, Hawke, Rosslyn, Hazel and Roger Martindale (Head of security). (Rick Stevens/Fairfax)

Hawke playing golf with George Shultz, San Francisco, October 1987. (Courtesy of Bob Hawke)

Hawke with President Gorbachev, Moscow, December 1987. (Courtesy of Bob Hawke)

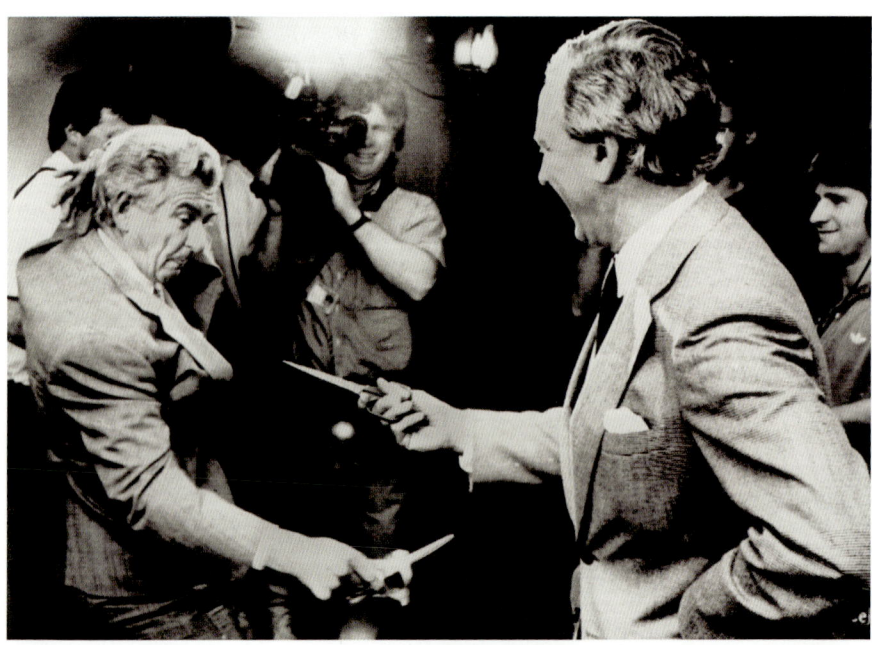

Hawke and Peacock at the opening of the radio alley in the new press gallery at Parliament House, Canberra, November 1988. (Newspix)

Hawke celebrates his birthday, Old Parliament House, Canberra. Among those in attendance were: Michael Lavarch, Allan Griffiths, Peter Walsh, Kim Beazley, Paul Keating, Ted Lindsay and Barry Jones. (Courtesy of Bob Hawke)

Hawke on Christmas Day with his four-year-old grandson, Paul Dillon, at Kirribilli House, Sydney, December 1988. (Fairfax)

Richard Woolcott (bottom left) and Craig Emerson (top right) were among those present with Hawke at a lunch hosted by President Mitterrand, Palais de l'Élysée, Paris, June 1989. (Courtesy of Bob Hawke)

Hawke welcoming Nelson Mandela to Canberra, October 1990. (NAA, A8746, KN31/10/90/15)

Hawke's close friend, Sir Peter Abeles, the chairman of Ansett, February 1990. (Newspix)

Mike Codd, Head of Prime Minister and Cabinet. (NAA, A6180, 3/7/86/1)

Michael Costello, principal private secretary to the Foreign Minister. (NAA, A6180, 10/6/93/1)

Hawke arrives at Richmond RAAF base to thank airforce pilots for their help during the pilots' industrial dispute, August 1989. (David Bartho/Fairfax)

Hawke with speechwriter, Graham Freudenberg, Parliament House, Canberra, November 1991. (Bob Finlayson/Newspix)

Hawke with President George Bush, Barbara Bush and Hazel at the Canberra Embassy, January 1992. (Barry McKinnon/Newspix)

Hawke with President Jiang Zemin, Beijing, October 1993. (Courtesy of Bob Hawke)

Hawke at the BOAO Forum for Asia press conference, Hainan, February 2001. (Courtesy of Bob Hawke)

Rudd, Hawke and Gillard at the 45th ALP national conference when Hawke was presented with life membership, Sydney, August 2009. (Kelly Rohan/Newspix)

the United States. If Australia were to propose that the United States should be part of the group, thereby presenting itself as an American 'deputy sheriff', then the members of ASEAN would baulk. Malaysia, in particular, harboured strong anti-American feelings, partly based on its pro-Palestinian stance. Its Prime Minister, Dr Mahathir, often seemed possessed of a general aversion to white people. In former colonial countries a reef of fear and hatred of Europeans lay just beneath the surface and it was easy to raise anti-Western passion. Codd said, 'We decided to leave Taiwan out of it, because it was just impossible at that stage to talk to China about Taiwan; we decided we wouldn't say if we thought America should be in or out.'

Hawke already enjoyed a warm relationship with Roh, he and Hazel having been guests at the President's house where they played tennis with Roh and his wife. 'When I outlined the APEC concept to Roh it was to a man who was prepared out of friendship and trust to discuss seriously any proposal I raised with him,' Hawke said. At their meeting the next morning Roh 'gave immediate and effusive support ... going out of his way to make it clear ... he wanted to be seen to be identified with it'. Hawke and his staff thought an envoy from Australia should travel from country to country, explaining the concept to each leader. Roh agreed.

Based on the President's positive attitude, the speech Hawke was to give the next day at a luncheon of Korean business associations was rewritten to present a clear, strong case for regional co-operation on trade, economic and social issues, to be driven by an intergovernmental vehicle. The United States and Taiwan were not mentioned.

In Washington there was outrage.

Unfortunately for Gareth Evans, because of his flight and the time difference in the era before wireless technology, he arrived unaware of what had been said in Seoul. The smooth, hard-nosed, gentlemanly Secretary of State, Jim Baker, later to become famous as *consigliere* to the Bush family, treated Evans to a tongue-lashing. Woolcott recalled,

> Baker bawled Gareth out about how could Australia, a friend and ally, take a major regional initiative in the Asia–Pacific, not *only* without the required consultation with the United States, but not even *including* the United States in the list of countries involved?

Evans' red-beard temper was famous throughout the Australian government and public service. He was known for primal shouting and throwing things at walls. What he had to say to his staff and the department in Canberra after this interview has not been revealed but, as Woolcott remarked, 'He was rather unhappy.'

Meanwhile, Hawke flew down to Bangkok. Codd recalled, 'The Americans were going *bananas*. They were *so angry*. We were very keen that Thailand, as one of the ASEAN countries, should bless the general idea, which the Thai Prime Minister did.'

As the trip progressed everyone realised that if Hong Kong and Taiwan were excluded because of Chinese objections the plan would be empty, and would fail. Within governments and in the press, discussion and comment began to call openly for these two tiger economies to be members of the group.

Hollway continued,

> I remember arguing very strongly, not that it took much argument with Bob, that if we're serious and if we want to project the Prime Minister as a serious player rather than somebody who's just shooting the breeze, we need to be ready immediately to follow the speech up with some serious diplomacy. Richard Woolcott was the obvious man for the job.

Six

For years Woolcott had enjoyed the reputation of being able to walk on eggshells. Hollway continued,

> Some of the ASEANs were nervous about the Americans because the Malaysians were so cranky about them. The Japanese were saying, 'Sounds interesting but we're pretty wary of this unless the United States is happy.' It took about a micro-second to realise that Dick Woolcott would have to go to Washington.

Woolcott said,

> The upshot was I was nominated as the Prime Minister's special envoy to go to all the countries concerned and deal with them. That worked out very well with two exceptions, China and Malaysia. In unfortunate timing I arrived in Beijing just before the Tiananmen Square issue and called on the new Premier, Li Peng, as the students were occupying the square.

Li Peng was the adopted son of China's first premier, Zhou En-lai, who had intervened to save the life of Deng Xiaoping when Red Guards wanted to execute him during the Cultural Revolution. Li had met Hawke on a visit to Australia in 1988 and for once the magic of Hawke's personality had made no impression. Li, widely described as very reserved, was alarmed by the speed of the vast reforms in China being made by Zhao Ziyang, Hawke's close friend and a man Li despised. He had advised Garnaut, 'I wouldn't waste my time with him.' Indeed, Li intended to depose Zhao and a palace coup was brewing in Beijing in 1989, well before the students occupied the square. Because the granite foundation of China's civilisation is inter-generational responsibility, Chairman Deng, owing his life to Li's father, owed a debt to Li. Li had far greater access to Deng than his superior Zhao Ziyang and it was Li Peng's advice that would persuade Deng to authorise the killing of the students in Tiananmen Square, and the permanent house arrest of Zhao Ziyang.

Woolcott said,

> I made my pitch about what the Hawke initiative was and he said, 'Well, you should inform Mr Hawke that this is not acceptable to China since it includes Hong Kong, which is a British colony soon to revert to China, and Taiwan, which is an inalienable part of China.' If it wasn't acceptable to China that would be the end of it. We had to think very quickly.

Woolcott was as quick as a cat on his feet. He said,

> I had a couple of guys from Foreign Affairs with me and we conferred for a moment, then came up with something slightly different. We said what Mr Hawke wanted was to have a ministerial meeting of major *economies*. Not countries as such, but *economies*. Premier Li sort of softened and said, 'We can think about that.' He asked me then to talk to the Foreign minister, Qian Qichen, along those lines, which I did.

Meanwhile, as Hawke and his staff had hoped, the ASEAN nations began to say publicly that the United States should join. 'It *had to* come from them,' Codd said. The leaders of the push were Lee Kuan Yew of Singapore and President Suharto of Indonesia. Having decided that a regional economic forum was a good idea, Suharto, the strongest, most suave, most respected and intimidating of the ASEAN leaders, exerted his authority over Dr Mahathir, who abandoned his fight against America. In Washington Woolcott explained Australia's apparent unfriendly behaviour. As there was a warm regard that had been established over more than five years between Reagan and Hawke, who loved telling each other jokes, and Hawke and Baker, who had a few fine stories of his own, the row blew over.

The first APEC meeting, attended by the United States, the members of ASEAN, Japan, South Korea, Hong Kong and Taiwan—but without China—was held in Canberra in November 1989. China by now was a pariah in the United States and other Western nations over the Tiananmen massacre, and it was not until 1991, at the third APEC meeting, held in Seoul, that China acceded. Woolcott said,

> China had made one more proposal, which was accepted. China asserted it was inappropriate that Taiwan be represented by its Foreign minister, because Taiwan was not a country, and therefore could not have a Foreign minister. But a Trade minister would be acceptable.

(There is no word for 'logic' in Mandarin, which perhaps explains the delicacy of Chinese reasoning.) The knot was undone: Taiwan and Hong Kong attended as major economies, not as countries. Woolcott said,

> If Bob had been at that meeting he would have been proud. It was the first time China and Taiwan had met at an international conference. It was an interesting moment, because once they got through the preliminaries, out in the corridors they began chatting away to each other, and it went very nicely. APEC was basically Bob's idea. Twenty years on it has its critics,

but it's been enormously useful in the business communities, in Australia and the other member countries, and in things like harmonising customs regulations, producing a major trade database and generally in being a useful pressure group for trade facilitation and liberalisation.

APEC over its two decades has assisted in the creation of wealth and welfare for millions of people in the Asia–Pacific region. Paul Keating built on APEC, taking the initiative in 1992 to raise it from an annual ministerial meeting to a leadership meeting. In 2009, APEC had twenty-one members representing 2.7 billion people, 40 per cent of the world's population, while its GDP was 55 per cent of the world's total. Throughout Asia, Hawke is known as 'The Father of APEC'. Garnaut commented, 'Bob's establishment of trust with Chinese and many other leaders created the launching pad for APEC.'

Hawke took another major foreign policy initiative in 1987, as daring as his ambition to try to fix the Cambodian mess, but an issue in which he was involved day by day and hands-on. This was the fight against apartheid in South Africa.

He had publicly fought against apartheid from the moment he was in a position to do so, on acceding to the leadership of the ACTU in January 1970, when he called for a union boycott of the rugby tour of Australia by the South African Springboks team scheduled for the following year. The pro-apartheid slogan of the time was 'Don't mix politics with sport'. As Hawke pointed out, the Springboks team was a perfect example of politics mixed with sport: no blacks were allowed in it. In the 1970s and in years following, there were violent protests for and against apartheid and Hawke was subjected to a barrage of racist hatred, including a bomb threat to an aeroplane on which he was a passenger. His predecessor as prime minister, Malcolm Fraser, had been as anti-apartheid as was Hawke, and like Hawke had been unable to make any progress against the adamantine will, backed by an immense treasure of gold, diamonds and oil, of the white South African regime. The biggest, richest, most heavily armed and strategically located country in Africa was immovable. Hawke realised he was in need of a lever, and preparing for the 1987 Commonwealth Heads of Government Meeting (CHOGM) the thought suddenly struck him of what such a lever might be.

At the CHOGM of 1985 a ginger group, made up of Prime Minister Rajiv Gandhi from India, Brian Mulroney from Canada, and Hawke, had formulated a communiqué that, with great difficulty, they persuaded the formidable British leader, Margaret Thatcher, to sign. The communiqué announced an Eminent Persons' Group to negotiate with the South African government over apartheid and, if this did not work, a stage-by-stage application of sanctions against the regime. Hawke nominated Malcolm Fraser as Australia's representative on the Eminent Persons, but the group got nowhere in its attempts at negotiation with the South African government. In 1986, to the disgust of Mrs Thatcher, sanctions began. She believed apartheid was the only viable system for the time being for South Africa, that sanctions would not work and to the extent they did, the only people to suffer would be the black population. Small as she was, and titanic as he was, Thatcher the Ice Queen seemed to tower above Malcolm Fraser in their meetings about South Africa. Brian Mulroney, built along the lines of an Aberdeen Angus bull, also received the Thatcher freeze. In a very uncomfortable meeting, held in Malborough House, London, in 1986, Hawke made life bearable for himself by a surreptitious exchange of notes with Geoffrey, later Lord, Howe, the British Foreign minister. They competed in lampoons of the Iron Lady. Hawke and Thatcher, both of whom enjoyed a fight, actually liked each other personally, while disagreeing about almost everything politically.

On his return from London Hawke had to report to parliament on 21 August: 'Specific and meaningful action has not been taken to dismantle apartheid. A new State of Emergency has been introduced. Nelson Mandela and other detainees are still in jail...'

Although the Eminent Persons had failed, international feelings against South Africa were now following the Commonwealth lead. In August 1986 the United States Senate voted in favour of strong measures against South Africa, the European Community was considering sanctions, and Japan was quietly adding its voice. Another year of sanctions went by and the South African government was, if anything, more intransigent. For a price, rogue traders and countries around the world were willing to break the sanctions. Thatcher, to date, was proved correct.

The tenth CHOGM was to be held in October 1987 in Vancouver. Hawke would be accompanied by various advisers, the most senior being his head of department, Mike Codd. Like Hawke, Codd was the son of a clergyman, an Anglican, whose ministry had been in Subiaco in Perth, the same district in which Clem Hawke was a minister for the Congregational church. He said,

> Long before I worked for Bob my father told me about his conversations with Clem, initiated by Clem, who was very interested in consensus on major social issues. He wanted to get the other denominations in the Subiaco area to be singing from the same hymn book, and approached my father about putting a joint letter forward to the local papers about not drinking on Sunday, which was one of Clem's passions. But my father actually liked a beer, including on Sundays, so he wasn't terribly encouraging on that issue. The other one was to do with sport on Sundays. Clem had this

drive for achieving change in attitudes by having consensus views put in front of the community.

Codd recalled,

> A couple of days before the CHOGM started we were having a meeting, at night, and Bob started talking about the financial support for the regime, the bank loans they had, and if that could provide a lever. I got some work done and a brief came back to Bob that said there are major loans from American and European banks that are due to be rolled over in about eighteen months. The view was, if the banks refused to roll over those loans it would cripple the South African economy. And the business sector, if it got some hint this was about to happen, would put *huge* pressure on the South African government to do something to stop it. So that was the embryo.

But these were views from within the Australian government, not those of professionals in the field.

Codd continued,

> Bob said, 'We need a meeting with some of the other members to talk about this, but we can't have Brian Mulroney, because he's the CHOGM host and the tradition is you can't involve the host in a controversial issue. And obviously we can't have Thatcher, because she's out on an island about apartheid.' So it was to get together Robert Mugabe, who back then had not yet gone mad, Kenneth Kaunda, Rajiv Gandhi plus Sonny Ramphal and Chief Anyaoku from the Commonwealth Secretariat. So one night before the conference had started we gathered

this small group and Bob, who had had further briefing on the loans situation, outlined the plan. They were all very enthusiastic about it. And Bob said, 'Well—now we've got this far, we must find someone who knows the financial system to come and tell us what is doable, and if so how? I know Jim Wolfensohn, an Australian [who had become an American citizen in 1980] who's running a small investment bank in New York. Will we try him?'

And they all agreed, so Bob rang Wolfensohn and without telling him much on the phone, asked him to come to Vancouver. Jim got on his private jet and was there by the following evening. They all sat down together and Jim was so helpful. He did think this would have a major, major impact on the South African economy and he felt it was doable if the right people spoke to the right banks. He offered personally to approach some of the American banks, who were big lenders to South Africa, but asked us to get somebody else to deal with Europe. Then he got on his jet and flew home.

As Wolfensohn needed to return to New York as soon as possible, there was no opportunity for Codd to raise security issues with Hawke. As soon as they were alone together Codd told Hawke they had failed to alert Wolfensohn to something rather important: if the South Africans, who had a wide-ranging intelligence service, were to discover what was afoot, not only could Wolfensohn's own business be attacked, his life could be at risk. The apartheid regime was not squeamish about assassinations, either at home or abroad.

Codd said,

We needed some follow-up with Jim immediately—first to alert him and to make sure he understood how serious the situation was. We knew the South Africans were very active and that they would be trying to listen in to what was happening in Vancouver, or to pick it up in one way or another, so we had to act very fast. Second, we needed a secure channel to keep communications with him open, and decided the Australian consul general in New York, John Taylor, would be the man to use. We were to drive this on behalf of the others. So it was late on Thursday and the leaders were all due to go off together on the Friday afternoon for their weekend retreat.

The retreat is a leaders-only conference, without staff. Hawke decided that Codd should fly immediately, on Thursday night, to New York to see Wolfensohn. He had to travel commercially so as not to draw attention to himself. As it happened there were only economy seats available, and Codd, who is more than 1.85 metres tall, was forced to hop from Vancouver to Seattle, to Chicago, and finally New York. He met the Australian consul general at 10 a.m. on Friday morning, then met Wolfensohn. Codd said,

> I wanted Jim to be absolutely clear what sort of stuff goes on in the real world when these big issues are at stake: he needed to get his head around just what he had let himself in for, because he had generously volunteered and put his own reputation at stake with the American banks he needed to deal with.

Wolfensohn accepted the risk to his business and possibly his life, and on Friday night Codd went to Kennedy airport to fly back to Vancouver. 'But as usual,' he said,

> out of Kennedy on Friday night it was chaos and we sat on the tarmac for an hour, then we circled Chicago for

an hour, so I missed the last connection out of Seattle to Vancouver. There were security perimeters around the hotel in Vancouver because Rajiv Gandhi and Margaret Thatcher, in particular, were targets [Gandhi was later assassinated]. I had to get on a bus then fight my way through security somehow.

Codd had spent his scant free time in New York in buying what he modestly described as 'some flimsy gear' for his wife. He recalled his excruciating embarrassment when, 'At every checkpoint they pulled this stuff out and inspected it. Eventually I got into the hotel at about 3 a.m.... At no stage did Margaret Thatcher discover what was going on.' The execution of the plan to have international banks boycott South Africa was, Codd said,

an example of the idea that you need expert advice about how to get something done. Within days we had appointed Tony Cole, who was my deputy on the economic side, a highly competent, respected fellow who went on to become head of Treasury, to deal with the European banks. He worked especially with the German banks, the biggest lenders to South Africa, and so between Tony and Jim we actually got the banks on board. We had very secure communications networks set up with the other leaders to keep them informed of progress. And the impact was just as we expected on the South African business community. None of us was there in South Africa, so we can't say for sure that this was *why* apartheid came down, or exactly what percentage of the reason it was, but there's no doubt in my mind that it was very, very significant because the business community was saying to the government, 'You've GOT TO move.'

In 1990 the South African Minister for Finance, Barend du Plessis, admitted that the banks' disinvestment was 'the dagger that finally immobilised apartheid'.[4]

Codd added,

> I think it was a very, very clever idea in the first place. It was the most powerful individual weapon that had been used against South Africa, and the execution of it was done very effectively. If ideas are in the least bit controversial, and most good ideas are, just announcing them will never work. Bob had a good idea and he won other people over to it, he got the right group committed. Some leaders can't do that: they have an idea and just throw it into the Cabinet ring, without talking to anyone beforehand, and opposition sinks it. This was an object lesson in leadership by Bob.

In February 1990, President de Klerk announced that Nelson Mandela had just been freed from prison after twenty-seven years, that the African National Congress was a legitimate political party and that the government would negotiate with it. In October that year a tall, graceful African stepped into Hawke's office in Canberra, a smile on his face, his arms open to embrace the Prime Minister. Taking a seat he said, 'I want you to know, Bob, that I am here today, at this time, because of you.'

7

MANDELA HAD CHOSEN AUSTRALIA as the first country outside Africa to visit after his release from jail. The friendship between him and Hawke flourished and years later Mandela would become International Patron of the Bob Hawke Prime Ministerial Centre in Adelaide. But well before their first meeting in 1990 Hawke had known that apartheid was on its deathbed—it was formally buried in February 1991—and began to think ahead to the problems South African could face. Sandy Hollway said,

> He was thinking ahead about it in a way that no other country did. It's a very important story. It wasn't an initiative that changed the world, but in terms of demonstrating an attitude about getting out ahead of a problem—if we're bringing this system down we've got a responsibility to help its successor up—of thinking creatively, it's a very good example.

Africa, which at the beginning of the 1960s seemed as economically promising as Asia, was by the 1980s a continent in precipitous decline, a mess of mismanagement, corruption, violence and—defeating all attempts at modernisation and decency—the knot of tribalism.

Hollway said,

> Africa economically, in too many places, was a basket case—and Bob said this couldn't be allowed to happen in South Africa. So he wanted to figure out what we could do to help a future black government in South Africa to manage its economy decently. And he sent me and Ross Garnaut and Doug Sterkey from DFAT to talk to the ANC, to the business community, to the government, about what we could do by way of advice and assistance.

At about 3 a.m., when the flight from Perth was midway across the Indian Ocean, Garnaut, who had been reading the economic brief on South Africa, nudged Hollway awake. 'We may as well turn around now,' he said. 'This place is stuffed.' But they ploughed on and the assistance given at Hawke's instigation to South Africa during a time of critical transition was just one of many unpublicised initiatives, mostly in Asian and Pacific countries, that helped them and established Australia's prestige in the region as an intelligent, creative nation committed to benevolence. This was the Australia that Hawke wanted the world to see and to recognise as the *real Australia*.

Hollway added of the work Australian economists, bureaucrats and other advisers did in South Africa, 'Of course the difficulties were formidable because half of the people now running the country had been out in the bush fighting, or had been trained in Moscow.'

Hawke held strong views on Moscow's economic efficiency and especially on its trustworthiness in negotiations. In 1979 he had suffered his single-most mortifying humiliation as a negotiator at the hands of Muscovites. They had promised him that a group of Jews, desperate to leave the Soviet Union, would be allowed to emigrate and Hawke announced this joyous news to the Jewish world. There was an ecstasy of relief and happiness. But Moscow had played him for a sucker. The so-called 'refuseniks' were not allowed to emigrate after all and were still in Moscow more than eight years later when Hawke met the new tsar, Mikhail Gorbachev.

The international news media was in the early stages of turning Gorbachev into a superstar but, as Hawke knew, the media, like the wind, blows where it lists, one hears its sound but cannot tell whence it comes nor where it goes. He had good reports from both Margaret Thatcher and Ronald Reagan, both of whom were edging forward on arms reduction talks with Gorbachev. Hawke, as leader of a Cold War alliance nation that would be due for almost immediate attack in a hot war, was keen to judge for himself. But protocol decreed he should not meet Gorbachev, who was the Secretary General of the Communist Party, but instead the Soviet Prime Minister, Nikolai Ryzhkov. Hawke was determined to talk to the man who mattered, and before leaving Australia sent Michael Costello and Sandy Hollway to Moscow as an advance team whose job it was to arrange a meeting with the Secretary General and to ensure that no barrier would be put in the way of a meeting between the Australian Prime Minister and the refuseniks. They succeeded. Before leaving for the USSR Hawke also spent hours in conversation with Bill Lane, the United States ambassador to Australia, a Republican and fierce anti-Communist, reassuring him that his visit to the 'Evil Empire' would in no way be detrimental to the alliance.

John Bowan, Hawke's Foreign Affairs adviser, said,

> Bob had this fantastic ability to adjust himself to the situation: if he had to spend four and a half hours reassuring

Bill Lane, he'd do it. If he was with Lee Kuan Yew, who considered himself an intellectual master of the universe, Bob would turn into an intellectual master of the universe. And he could go to the pub with a bunch of wharfies. He wasn't drinking alcohol at all, but he would somehow give the impression that he'd had one or two himself and was really comfortable with these blokes who were boozing up.

Hawke's years of building Australia's international role got off to a good start in Jordan in January 1987, and on the same swing through the Middle East meetings went well in Egypt, Hawke being the first Australian prime minister to visit Cairo since Menzies' disastrous intervention in 1956. But he ran aground in Israel, where his brief, disagreeable meeting with the Prime Minister, Itzak Shamir of the right-wing Likud Party, instantly established that both men disliked each other.

On the very day in 1983 when Hawke was sworn in as Prime Minister, he had said in a radio interview he believed he might 'have a part to play' in negotiations between Israel and Arab nations by making an official visit to the Middle East. The holy grail was a Grand Bargain: a trade of land seized by Israel in 1967 in exchange for peace with the Palestinians, specifically their acceptance of Resolution 242 of the United Nations that stated Israel's right to exist within secure and recognised borders. The politicals on Hawke's staff and the Department of Foreign Affairs were appalled that the Prime Minister wanted to revive his passion for Israel. John Bowan, who took up his job as Foreign Affairs adviser just a couple of days after Hawke's 1983 remarks, said,

> Bob saw himself as a fixer and thought he could perhaps fix the Arab–Israel dispute. My job was to keep him out of the Middle East for as long as possible. There was a

general fear among the powerful people in the office that if he got into the Middle East, God knows what he might do. I remember sending him a note letting him know that everybody—the entire staff—felt that he should not go to the Middle East.

Since the late 1970s Israeli intellectuals had been arguing that their country could have any two of three attributes, but not all three: it could encompass Greater Israel, the land it had seized from Palestinians in 1967; it could be a Jewish state; it could be a democracy. It could not be a Greater Israel Jewish democracy.

By the mid-1980s Hawke had come to this view himself. He believed Israel was trapped in a race against time and Palestinian population increase, in danger of losing its greatest virtue: democracy. As usual there was a 'peace process' underway; as usual, it was going nowhere. Israel's future, as Hawke perceived it, was so alarming he decided to tackle the issue in a speech to the Hebrew University in Jerusalem, where he was to receive an honorary doctorate. But when he showed the Australian ambassador a draft the envoy was horrified. He ruled thin red lines through page after page.[1]

From long experience Hawke knew that, beneath their macho swagger, Israelis were terrified of their Arab neighbours, especially the Palestinians who lived under Israeli occupation, and that they turned skittish and thin-skinned at any criticism from outsiders. He agreed to boil down his full message to one question: 'How will Israel solve the great issues of political principle and human rights, not to mention the demographic pressures, entailed in its role as administrator of occupied territories?' Abstract and academic, the speech caused no offence, and the Australian news media travelling with him missed its underlying significance: that Hawke's views on Israel had changed. The media was after an emotional story. They were hoping that the

Australian Prime Minister would fall into a tearful state when confronted with imagery of the Jews' appalling history. Photographs of Hawke weeping were guaranteed for page one and the lead item on the television news. Stephen Mills, Hawke's speechwriter noted, 'After he inspected the Holocaust memorial in Jerusalem there was intense media speculation about whether there was a tear in his eye—and if so, whether it could be put down to emotion or to the cold morning.'[2] But Hawke had the present and the future rather than the past on his mind, and was determined to raise the issue of where he believed Israel was heading.

After Hawke received his honorary doctorate, he was accorded a state dinner in the Israeli parliament, the Knesset, and intended to raise in that forum the issue of Palestinian self-determination and the future establishment of a Palestinian state. In an unprecedented breech of protocol the President of Israel, Chaim Herzog, insisted that Hawke censor his remarks. Hawke refused, pointing out that the speech had already been circulated to the media, but he agreed to soften the text by inserting the suggestion that a Palestinian confederation, rather than an independent Palestinian state, would be the most likely outcome of the peace process. The next morning, in East Jerusalem, he met a group of Palestinian leaders and was impressed by their realism: they were, he believed, people with whom Israel could, and should, negotiate, and that to refuse to do so was both immoral and would lead to violence. That night he dined privately with Shimon Peres, a Labor Party leader, and a man with whom he could talk unreservedly. Hawke proposed a simultaneous act of recognition by the Palestinians and the Israelis as a basis for negotiations. Peres wholeheartedly agreed. Bowan said, 'While Bob had started out [his prime ministership] with a partial view, skewed towards Israel, he ended up with a very well-balanced view.'

Hawke left Israel with an ominous sense that the nation he had admired and supported so long and at such expense to himself was now, under its right-wing government, moving in a direction away from not only peace, but from its own principles and ideals, the very qualities to which he and so much of the West had been so attracted in the first place. Israel was transforming into a country he found difficult to recognise, gripped in a solipsism that could become self-deception.

The year ended in Moscow in December where, thanks to the efforts of Michael Costello and Sandy Hollway, he was to meet Gorbachev.

The interview was scheduled to last twenty minutes, but such was the leaders' rapport it stretched to three and a quarter hours. There was much at stake for Hawke. He had established Australia as a country for 'reality testing' between China and the United States. If the meeting with Gorbachev went well, Hawke would be in a position to play the same role between Moscow and Washington, passing on messages that neither side wanted to give directly to the other for fear of rebuff, but would do so through a trusted intermediary. 'You could make suggestions in good faith and could explore them without prejudice. And you could kill off bad ideas without fear of international embarrassment,' he said. Off his own bat he urged Gorbachev to push both the Arab states that were committed to the destruction of Israel and Yasser Arafat, leader of the Palestinian Liberation Organization, another Soviet client, to accept Resolution 242 of the United Nations. At the time every nation in the Middle East, plus others including Malaysia, rejected Resolution 242. Hawke said,

> I argued to him he should use his influence with the Arab states and the PLO to recognise Israel *in return for which* Israel would recognise the right of the PLO to speak for the Palestinians. He accepted the logic of what I put, but made the wry observation, 'Prime

Minister, you must understand, they don't always accept my recommendations.'

In his meeting with the Soviet leader, Hawke also brought up the issue of the refuseniks. He intended to persuade Gorbachev to consider the wretched group of Jews whose plight he had first raised in 1979. The excuse for refusing them exit permits was that, as scientists, they knew state secrets. One of them had been asking to be allowed out since 1971, had long since retired, and any state secret he might have known was by 1987 completely out of date.

Hawke emerged from his meeting with the Soviet leader so enlivened that for the first time since he had given up alcohol he felt like a glass of champagne. He was excited not because he believed Gorbachev was approaching his reform of the USSR in the right way—Hawke believed Gorbachev had put the political cart before the economic horse, and told him so—but because he had recognised the hand of history resting on the Russian's shoulder. 'I had been with a man of destiny,' he said. 'I knew he was *the indispensable man* for closing down the Cold War.' He found Gorbachev, he told the Australian media, 'engaging', 'stimulating', with 'a quickness of understanding', 'an attractive preparedness to recognise past weaknesses', and that he was 'sincere' about reforms. He said there had been 'vibrance' in their conversation. Gorbachev had told Hawke something he did not pass on to the media: that the Soviet Union was 'in a pre-crisis situation'.

Back home Hawke's comments caused John Howard, leader of the Opposition, to accuse him of looking 'through rose-tinted glasses'. Howard declared that the Prime Minister had made 'a monumental error of judgment' for declaring he would welcome 'constructive involvement' with the USSR. History put egg on Howard's face rather swiftly when a few days later there was a Gorbachev–Reagan summit from which the

American President emerged smitten with admiration for the Secretary General.

Hawke did not reveal to the travelling media in Moscow that during their meeting Gorbachev had promised to give serious consideration to the list of refuseniks with which Hawke had presented him. On the last morning of his visit, amidst the splendour of the Australian ambassador's residence, an art-nouveau mansion once owned by a sugar merchant, Hawke had an emotional reunion with the group of old and shabbily dressed refuseniks he had last seen in 1979. Many were now ill and feeble. He told them his thoughts on Gorbachev and that the Secretary General had agreed to give consideration to their plight. Late that afternoon as the Australian entourage was preparing to leave the state guest house, Gorbachev's interpreter unexpectedly turned up. He was middle-aged, which is old for an interpreter, and a man whose thought processes it had seemed to Hawke were virtually a continuum of the Secretary General's, such was the lightning fluency, the flow and counter-flow of his translation. He brought wonderful news: five of those on the list Hawke had given Gorbachev would be allowed to leave immediately.

By the following May almost all, more than twenty refuseniks, were free. It was a triumph for human rights and for persistence. The Jewish communities in Australia and around the world were ecstatic about their release and the World Jewish Congress voted to award Hawke an honour. He stood at the pinnacle of respect in the Jewish community. His old friend, Isi Leibler, the founder of Jetset and a man whose passion for the release of Soviet Jews seemed to drive the very breath of his body, arranged a great celebration in Melbourne for Hawke. Leibler was of aggressively sharp intelligence and for years Hawke had enjoyed mentally sparring with him. Leibler flew the liberated refuseniks to Australia for the grand occasion, which was envisaged as a homage to the Prime Minister, champion of justice and human rights. 'It was to be a lap of honour for him,' Bowan said.

Hawke, however, had what he considered a better idea. He intended to tell his audience what he had wanted to tell the Knesset seventeen months earlier: among other things, that Israel was violating the human rights of the Palestinians.

Years earlier, in the 1970s, his daughter, Sue, who was active in a number of left-wing causes, had asserted that if her father ever heard firsthand the Palestinians' side of the argument, he would be as sympathetic to them as he was to the Israelis. Hawke was such an Israelophile, especially after the Yom Kippur War of 1973, the idea sounded outlandish. But now he had heard the Palestinian side of the argument and he was determined not merely to rain, but to pour, on his own parade. 'They had to be told,' he said. 'I'd proved my friendship and I thought it the duty of a friend to speak the truth as he saw it—and that truth was the universality of human rights apply to the Palestinians as to the Israelis.'

John Bowan recalled,

> Bob wrote the speech he wanted to give at the dinner, and you had this ironical situation that his staff, most of whom had a much more pro-Arab view of the Middle East than Bob did, trying to talk him out of saying what he wanted to. In one sentence he was comparing the Palestinians in the occupied territories with the blacks in South Africa and the Jews in the Soviet Union. His principal private secretary, Sandy Hollway, Bob Sorby, his political adviser, and I were all horrified.

By May 1988 the Palestinians had launched an uprising (the first intifada) in the West Bank and Gaza, exactly the violent reaction Hawke had feared would eventually but inevitably be the response to Israeli oppression in the occupied territories.

At his lap of honour ceremony in Melbourne, Hawke said, 'Our sense of celebration is necessarily muted ...' and referred to the intifada as providing proof that the principles on which Israel was built 'do not sit easily with the role of master of occupied territories and subject peoples'. Around the room there were sharply indrawn breaths. He continued,

> The Palestinian in the occupied territories, as the Jew in the Soviet Union and the black in South Africa, has his aspirations to be fully free. The friends of Israel around the world are fearful that in a real sense we may be witnessing again, after thousands of years, a giant eyeless in Gaza.

The temperature in the room dropped, Hawke's staff noted, 'about twenty degrees'. The audience began muttering to each other but their guest of honour went on, 'Is there not emerging the danger of Israel being blinded to the threat to its very soul and the vision of its founders?' The audience by now was so angry they were on the point of booing. The staff muttered, *'There goes the Jewish vote.'* Bowan said, 'Bob knew exactly what he was doing. Sometimes he just did these things.'

Leibler was dismayed and furious. When the ceremony was over, Hawke returned to Leibler's house in Caulfield, where they argued for about three hours. The friendship, begun in the early 1970s, never recovered.

In the same month, May 1988, the Queen opened Canberra's new Parliament House, which had cost $1 billion and was the most expensive building in the country. Shaped as two huge boomerangs when seen from above, it had 4500 rooms and was, for both the upper and lower ranking inhabitants of the old Parliament

House, a glorious new workplace. Hollway was the last chief of staff for a prime minister in the old House, and the first in the new. He said, 'We'd had people crowded together in ship-galley-width rooms, trying to handle phone calls, write speeches and hold meetings. And that was the Prime Minister's office.'

For junior backbenchers, independents and members of a splinter party, like the Democrats, the old House had been a ghetto: Senator Don Chipp, the leader of the Democrats, had been accommodated, with another senator and a shared staffer, in a tiny room in which the air conditioning did not work, where private conversation was unthinkable. In Canberra's 36-degree summers, Chipp would remove his jacket and tie and open his shirt four buttons down and still be perspiring. Hollway said,

> It was weird. My office was next to the PM's office and the way for me to know whether he was meeting with someone, or whether he was in the bathroom, was to look though this spyhole in the wall: it amplified the room and I could see a distorted figure in there. It was absolutely bizarre. It had been there since Curtin was PM, when someone had come up with this bright idea about how to know if the boss was busy. So when a staffer or a minister came and asked, 'Can I see the PM?' I'd go and have a look, and say 'Yes' or 'No'. In the new Parliament House, I had a monitor under my desk and I could glance down without anybody realising what I was doing. The physical environment of the new office was far superior for the good running of the government.

Hawke loved it. Unlike many parliamentarians who had spent most of their working lives in the old House, he had no nostalgia for it and he preferred contemporary domestic architecture and furniture.

After five years in government there were, Hollway said, 'a central core of ministers who were all extremely competent and by then pretty experienced, pretty confident, and not yet getting tired. They were firing.' The economic difficulties after the stock market crash of October 1987 meant that

> from early '88 economic advisers were just beating a path continuously back and forth across that corridor [from the PM's office] into the Cabinet room, and there were more and more ERC meetings. The economy was a *huge* preoccupation.

Nobody quite realised at first that a boom was gathering and that 'the most unpredictable year in an unpredictable decade' had begun. Like riding a bolting horse, it was a case of holding on, staying focused and hoping the beast would run itself out before hitting a wall.

In the calm of hindsight, it's easy to see that 1988, which caused economic chaos throughout the West, was the cloud of a storm that would burst in 1989, a year of shocks and wonders in which the world watched in astonishment as the proud towers of European Communism shuddered on their foundations, as the last emperor of China, Deng Xiaoping, decided that bloodshed was necessary, as the death of Allah's Voice on Earth, Ayatollah Khomeini, threw Iran into convulsions, as Nelson Mandela would be secretly freed from prison, as the tyrant Nicolae Ceauşescu and his fearsome wife were executed, as Germans clamoured for reunification—and the ancient empires of the East would begin inexorably to rise.

The government had intended to tighten monetary policy at the end of 1987 or in early 1988 but, because of the stock market crash in October, delayed doing so. Ralph Willis recalled, 'everybody was worried that if you tightened monetary policy on top of the crash you might hammer the economy through the floor'. This was the mistake made in 1929 that had created the Great Depression. Willis continued,

> So we held off for something like nine months after the crash before a tightening cycle got under way—and it was too late. It became a case of making up for lost time, which is diabolical with monetary policy.

He used a simile to describe the devil in monetary policy:

> It's like a brick tied with a piece of elastic. You want to move the brick, and you pull on the elastic. Nothing happens. You pull harder. Still no response. And harder. Suddenly the brick jumps and hits you in the face.

At some stage during 1988 Willis thought, 'This looks traumatic.' For the Cabinet and the ERC, and especially for the Treasurer, managing the economy was as difficult as it had been two years earlier, during the trade and currency collapse. But by now Keating was fed up with playing second fiddle to Hawke. He was forty-four years old and it was time, he believed, for him to become prime minister.

All Keating's hopes were invested in Hawke's retiring during the third term so that he, Keating, could lead the government into a 1990 election. He believed Labor could not win a fifth election, but if he took over in 1988 he would have the satisfaction of being prime minister for five years, before almost certain defeat at the polls in 1993. Always either borne aloft or whipped raw by his imagination, Keating already believed he was the *real* prime minister, and that Hawke was a mere figurehead. He began to gather supporters for his cause, among them John

Dawkins, the very able, aggressive and unpredictable Minister for Education and Training. Dawkins said,

> Bob had this great ability to engage with people in the broad, in this sort of matey way, and everybody thought he was their best friend. Keating, in contrast, had an incredible capacity to actually engage with small groups: he'd sit down at the table and he'd have them eating out of his hand in no time. There was an intensity about him, and an intensity about his discourse which was very engaging.

Dawkins held long discussions with the Treasurer on what the job of prime minister required. Dawkins said,

> You really only have to do one thing a day, if that. You have to do a couple of things a week, but they've got to be things that matter. And you can do some of them from Canberra—you don't have to go around shopping centres, and all that stuff.

For Hawke, such an idea was risible. *He knew* the hours he worked and was concerned that Keating did not have sufficient stamina. Keating frequently skipped meetings or turned up late. Compared to the prime minister's job a Treasurer's is relatively easy, most of the work being done by officials; a number of very successful Australian Treasurers have been famously lazy: after a learned or amusing performance in Question Time, they could mentally sign off for the rest of the day. Only around budget time or in crises did they have to work consistently. The Prime Minister's heir apparent presented him with a dilemma: brilliant in Parliament, the government's greatest weapon for verbally demolishing the Opposition, a good campaigner, Keating lacked the boundless vitality he would need, Hawke believed, to keep him going day after day. There were few people with whom Hawke could or did share this view, which he had developed over five years of observing his partner. He said,

> Paul had many outstanding and some unique positive qualities as a politician, but he lacked what I considered the sine qua non for doing the prime minister's job successfully. He did not have the constitution or commitment for the continuous hard work the job requires.

The mutterings and verbal backstabbing of Hawke, which had been growing bolder since his 1987 victory, grew bolder still. Geoff Walsh, former press secretary who had rejoined Hawke's staff as political adviser, was astonished when he walked into Keating's office one day and saw written on a large whiteboard, 'The Lodge in 88'.

It is hard to overstate the influence a senior politician's staff and advisers have in these affairs. In the years before he challenged Hayden, Hawke himself once remarked of his beloved and trusted confidante, Jean Sinclair, 'Aah—she just wants to be the prime minister's secretary.'

The staff stand to gain status in the same ratio as their boss, and their plotting, scheming and leaking to the news media, plus the encouragement they give their champion, are critical in political fights. Their vicarious lives tend to deepen staffers' pains and triumphs. So 'The Lodge in 88' it was in the Treasurer's office. Keating believed he could either persuade or bluff Hawke into giving him the leadership during the year. He held an ace: if he did not get the job he wanted, he would resign and go to Paris, he said. A Treasurer's resignation, unless on grounds of health or family crisis, is a blow to public confidence that governments must try to avoid. But, as Paul Kelly wrote, the Hawke camp ... had the challenger beaten before he began. Hawke and his advisers had operated on the assumption that Keating might mount some form of challenge ... [Hawke's] tactic was to keep the loyalty of the dominant NSW faction, Keating's own base. Hawke's political aide Bob Sorby, appointed on the advice of Graham Richardson, worked closely with Richardson during 1988 to ensure that there was no defection to Keating ... While Richardson stayed with Hawke, Keating was stymied.[3]

But Keating, who believed in his own point of view with unshakeable intensity, carried on as if the prize was already his. It sometimes seemed that within his heart there blundered about the huge old man, Jack Lang, Keating's political father, with iron will and iron muscles, his actions motivated by a kind of unrestrainable blindness. Keating devised the Budget he delivered in August 1988 as a vehicle for him to win the 1990 election. He characterised it as 'bringing home the bacon', announcing on the first page, 'the nation is successfully emerging from its most severe economic crisis in a generation ... we are now well on the way back to prosperity'. His career as Treasurer was about to end in triumphant flourish, he thought. But reading the budget papers, economists and economically literate journalists recognised it as better politics than economics. And worse was to come, for within three weeks Keating's own officials were to warn him his numbers did not add up. Kelly noted, 'Keating ... was looking for a virtual [landslide for himself in 1990], an election win which would increase Labor's majority and set up the Keating government for many years.' But the Budget, in fact, was a horrible mistake.

Hawke never attempted to micromanage the government nor interfere with his ministers but was now fed up with

Keating's public rhetoric, his claims to glory, and his private threats to 'take the Paris option'. He decided to bring the subterranean rumblings from Keating's supporters up into the light. 'My patience, which had been considerable, was not, however, limitless,' he said.

The morning after the Budget a Morgan poll showed Labor ahead of the Coalition 47 to 42 per cent, and Hawke leading John Howard as preferred prime minister 69 to 18 per cent. The Treasurer was still very unpopular with the electorate, despite his attempts, since 1987, to soften his image. The Prime Minister took three opportunities that day in answering questions to remark that there were many competent economists in the government and that if Mr Keating wanted to live in Paris he would not be irreplaceable. Keating was furious and, in a brief conversation with Hawke in the Prime Minister's office, announced their relationship was 'dead and buried'.

Richardson quickly organised a peace treaty of sorts, persuading Hawke to go back on television and recant about Keating's indispensability, which Hawke did, but as a very poor liar Hawke was so effusive as to be quite unconvincing—certainly to Keating, who saw Hawke's praise as insincere. That night Richardson rang Keating from his car phone to persuade the Treasurer to bury the issue, pointing out that the Prime Minister had done the right thing. Keating objected that Hawke had not meant what he said. The cat's cradle of Richardson's loyalties—to the Prime Minister, to the government, to his political tribe in New South Wales—were demonstrated in this phone call, in which he and Keating fell into the male-bonding speech that members of the New South Wales Right use with each other. Richardson referred to the Prime Minister as 'the cunt'; Keating called Hawke 'an envious turd'. As it was Keating who lusted after Hawke's job and perquisites, envy seems more attributable to the speaker than the turd. The phone call was intercepted, recorded and offered for sale to the press gallery. Hawke had a transcript of it within a day.

He read it on a flight to Sydney, where he was to address a dinner, but grew so angry he spent forty-five minutes beforehand on the telephone shouting at Keating, while the two hundred guests waited. Later that night he spoke to Keating again and suggested they meet on Sunday afternoon, 28 August, when Hawke was back in Canberra. Before their meeting Kim Beazley, whom Hawke loved like a son, and who loved and admired both the Prime Minister and the Treasurer, talked to each in turn. Both assured Beazley they would be civil with each other.

Keating arrived determined that Hawke should promise him a transition in late 1988 or early 1989. Hawke said he would stay on and win the 1990 election. He did not accept Keating's assessment that the 1990 election was virtually unwinnable; he said that if Keating made good his threat and went to Paris, Dawkins could replace him as Treasurer. What's more, Hawke believed that the Opposition was still in a parlous state. The Melbourne businessman, John Elliott, a Church shoe rather than a white shoe, had taken over as Liberal Party president, and had told Hawke at a dinner at Government House what a mess it was. (Elliott, as it happened, was plotting to overthrow the current leader, John Howard, and become prime minister himself at the 1990 election. He did not mention this to Hawke.)

Keating did not accept Hawke's analysis of how weak the Opposition was; Hawke told Keating he had, with time and effort, established himself as an Australian leader who could play a constructive role internationally and he intended to do so right through until 1990. Keating said Hawke was neglecting leadership at home, and that if he had to keep being Treasurer until then, 'I'll be going ga-ga.' Keating's fear, according to Kelly, was that he would, indeed, be physically and mentally burnt out by the time he became leader, and that his whole team would be exhausted. The meeting ended in a frosty stalemate, with a promise by both men to keep up public appearances.

But Hawke's counter-threat to Keating to make Dawkins Treasurer in his place was evidently alarming to Keating and required swift action. It seems he talked to Dawkins that night, for next morning on the *AM* radio program, Dawkins called on Hawke to set a timetable for transition. Dawkins then went a step further: he decided to front the Prime Minister and ask him to step aside to give Keating a clear run at the 1990 election. He had arranged to be accompanied by Peter Walsh and John Button, both ministers anxious about an orderly transition and to avoid a rerun of the internal ructions over Hayden's leadership. But at the last moment they changed their minds and Dawkins went alone. The Minister for Employment, Education and Training was a man with the psychological freedom that wealth may confer: he could walk out of parliament any time he wanted to (and would later, when he became disillusioned with Keating). His encounter with Hawke was, according to both men, friendly: for many years Dawkins had worked closely with, and had enjoyed support from, the Prime Minister when other ministers were attacking him. He was an attractive target because he belonged to no faction. In every portfolio he held—Finance; Trade; Education, Employment and Training—Dawkins was outstandingly effective, prepared to take hard decisions without fear of being disliked. 'I was the only minister Graham Richardson was frightened of,' Dawkins said, 'because he knew he couldn't manipulate me.'

Hawke listened then told Dawkins he believed that, as Prime Minister, he still had a significant contribution to make, especially in international affairs. To Dawkins' mind, international affairs were largely the problem: Hawke was focusing too much attention abroad. 'It's the curse of leadership,' he said.

> It happened to me when I was Trade minister. It's incredibly infectious to get involved in international stuff, to be rubbing shoulders with all these famous people and to believe you're making a difference. In some cases, you actually are making a difference—but it takes an enormous amount of time and effort and personal commitment and personal relationships.

Oddly, Dawkins thought, Hawke used the current turmoil in Poland as an example of an arena in which he could help, which seemed 'to be a little bit off track from our point of view'. The Prime Minister was passionately interested in it because the Polish turmoil was due to the trade union, Solidarity's, struggle against Poland's Soviet-controlled government. At meetings of the International Labour Organization in the late 1970s Hawke had helped nurture the formation of Solidarity, then only an embryo, which came into the light in 1980. Now it was a mighty warrior in the Cold War, a conflict that Hawke, as leader of a nation at risk, fervently wanted to come to an end. Events in Poland were, however, as Dawkins said, an irrelevance to most Australians. He thought Hawke almost fey in talking about a country so far away that few in the electorate could have found it on a map. He and Hawke were speaking and thinking on politically different levels.

Hawke changed tack. He argued that Keating was not physically strong enough for the pressures of the job. The ministry was familiar with the plague of minor illnesses and potential illnesses the Treasurer endured, for some of which he sought unusual treatments. According to his biographer, John Edwards, Keating took up jumping on a trampoline as a prophylactic against cancer cells in the body. One of Keating's most notable, and often most attractive, characteristics was his refusal to accept received wisdom, including that of science. Dawkins did not seriously consider Hawke's assertion that Keating lacked the physical strength needed to be a successful prime minister. 'I came round more to Bob's view later,' he said in 2009.

They parted amicably. 'He at no stage demonstrated any kind of anger or irritation to me,' Dawkins said, adding,

> I don't know what it was that led me to tell [Paul] Kelly about it. I suppose it was a kind of an instinct that, I don't know, I just sort of talked to him about it and then of course it ended up in the paper. It wasn't supposed to. It was supposed to be off the record.

There is a touch of madness to all successful politicians, especially on the Labor side, since their purpose is to shift society and they can't achieve this aim if they agree with the status quo. Hawke prided himself on being 'a little bit mad'. Dawkins too scored well on the 'slightly mad' scale. His belief that Paul Kelly, whose reputation for trustworthiness is immaculate, may have quoted him when he was speaking off the record is eccentric. Parliament was sitting and Kelly's report in the next morning's *Australian* brought delight to the hearts and whimsy to the tongues of the Opposition. One of Hawke's many nicknames was Old Silver. The wittiest gibe during Question Time came from Ian Sinclair, who said this was 'not a case of "Hi-ho, Silver," but "Heave-ho, Silver."' Dawkins recalled,

> Bob and I made it clear that we were friends, we were sitting next to each other, sort of hugging each other, to deflect the Opposition ... basically, after I'd spoken to him I accepted that he wasn't going to move. I didn't set about to wreck the government.

But in the view of the Hawke camp, he did.

Hawke was embarrassed he had so misread his Education minister, while his staff and supporters were enraged: they too had not realised Dawkins was already a Keating general in the war of succession now taking shape. They dismissed the idea of Dawkins as a possible future Treasurer. Dawkins said afterwards, 'I did wonder what I would have said, but it would have been a close-run thing. If [Hawke] had asked me to be Treasurer and I'd declined, I would have felt bound to leave the government.' Keating had promised Dawkins the Treasury in a government led by him.

The noise from Keating's camp was that Hawke was not giving leadership at home. Certainly, there had been a change in atmospherics at the peak of government. After the 1987 election Caucus had promoted all the faction bosses—Richardson and Ray of the Right, Gerry Hand of the Left, and Peter Cook of the Centre Left—into the ministry. Hawke promoted them into Cabinet, where their presence altered the whole government power balance. Dawkins said that ministers were frightened to speak against a faction boss seated at the Cabinet table because preselection depended on him. Meanwhile, according to Beazley, the backbenchers were under the thumb of less formidable factional overlords, and were more prone to indiscipline. It was a flaw in the Labor system, not present in the Coalition, that the Caucus elected the ministry and the prime minister could only allot portfolios to the ministers he was given. In a Coalition government, the prime minister holds the whip over his entire government. John Howard later said that the most important part of his job as Liberal leader was choosing and discarding members of his team. This was a power that neither Hawke nor any previous Labor prime minister had ever held. (In 2007 Kevin Rudd simply announced he would be picking his own ministry, and so eager was the party to win no one raised a voice against him.)

Meanwhile, Keating's 'bacon budget' was transforming into a live and greasy pig. It was not his fault alone: both the Treasury and the Reserve Bank had badly miscalculated. They had all predicted lower inflation and a lower current account deficit. But both were rising. Catching the budget pig was going to be tricky and potentially dangerous.

Keating spent much of September abroad, during which he contemplated his future. He had failed to bully or bluff his way into The Lodge and the Caucus was not supporting him, but as he believed in his bones he was destined to be prime minister he decided to take the option Hawke had offered: a handover after the 1990 election. Both men now despised each other. Keating decided he must nail Hawke down to a promise, witnessed by another, for the deal to stick or else Hawke would string him along until he was totally worn out. It was impossible, even for Keating, not to recognise that Hawke's well of stamina was almost inexhaustible and that his skills of evasion were similar. It took more than a month before Hawke could find time in his diary for a meeting with Keating.

Finally, on the evening of 25 November 1988, three grave-faced men arrived at Kirribilli House, the Prime Minister's Sydney residence. They were Keating and his witness, Bill Kelty, secretary of the ACTU, and Hawke's witness, Sir Peter Abeles. The deal was that Hawke and Keating would work as a team until the 1990 election, which Hawke expected to win; then, after a suitable time, but before the end of 1991, he would step down. Keating would then, after the formality of election by Caucus, become prime minister. Hawke's one proviso was that if the deal were leaked it was null and void. Keating agreed. Nothing was put on paper.

For the Treasurer, the Kirribilli pact was a disappointment: his 'Paris option' card had not worked and the thing he had wanted so fervently to avoid, spending another two years grinding figures, while his wife and four children lived in a cramped Canberra house, would have to be endured. For Hawke it was a triumph: as Prime Minister, he had, after an initial error, successfully steered the government through treacherous waters; he had called Keating's bluff and won. He had a leg-rope on his Treasurer and his Treasurer's supporters for the next two to three years. Personally, Hawke now had clear psychological air and could, without worry about disloyalty to distract him or his staff, pursue success at the next election. Privately he was elated by the Kirribilli pact. When every waking hour is spent in the grip of difficult and practical issues, both trivial and great, life becomes disenchanted. With his new-found freedom of action he recovered a sense of spaciousness. His philandering had been cramped since he moved into The Lodge, restricted to just a couple of women. He decided he was feeling so good he could feel better still, and began to expand it. Keating, for his part, manfully accepted the setback, but his language showed how psychologically rattled he had been: he made a weird, vehement attack on John Howard, likening himself and Hawke to a pair of black widow spiders weaving a web to trap the leader of the Opposition.

But winning the 1990 election was looking more and more dubious inside the government: the nation ate, drank, partied, sported fast cars, big yachts and big shoulder pads, all with a feverish excitement that made economists' blood run cold. The boom the government had meant to avoid was gathering force. Hawke remained optimistic for he had set himself the goal of winning a historic fourth term—and this would cement Labor's reputation as the party of government, and his own place in history. Only Sir Robert Menzies, who fought a Labor Party crippled by its splitists, the DLP, would have won more elections than he. While Australia remained a democracy Menzies was unlikely ever to be outdone. So, although winning a fourth term would only win second place, it was of the utmost prestige for the party and the leader.

8

The New Year began calmly enough with the former vice-president of the United States, George Bush, assuming the presidency in January. Bush was a tall East Coast multimillionaire of aristocratic appearance who had been a much-decorated navy pilot in World War II. He was personable, well educated and thoughtful, with a broad knowledge of geopolitics. But as a leader he could never match the luminous power of Reagan's personality—the sunshine smile, the jokes, the actor's perfect timing with a line, the deft, ineffable charm—all tailored, as if by Providence, to soothe the troubled breast of the American people. With Reagan gone, so was George Shultz, whom Bush replaced with Jim Baker. Hawke had met and respected Baker, but did not enjoy with him the long, warm friendship he had had with Shultz. His friendship with Bush, however, was more intimate than it had been with Reagan; an extra benefit was that Hazel and Barbara Bush clicked when they met.

The year 1989 was the bicentenary of the French Revolution, of which it is alleged Zhou En-lai, when asked in the 1960s had it been a good idea, replied, 'It's too soon to judge.' It would turn out that 1989 was another revolutionary year that would reveal the long view of history of Chinese leaders—but in a manner the rest of the world found horrifying.

On 19 April, the General Secretary of the Communist Party, the sparrow-like Hu Yaobang, died, his death arousing grief the length and breadth of China. Ordinary citizens everywhere openly wept in the streets for Hu. The grieving populace idealised their lost leader and began to yearn for change. They were angry with corrupt officials and their corrupt children. There had been a bout of inflation in 1988 that had raised the issue of corruption. In China's two-tiered price system of those days, the well connected could buy steel, for example, at the state price, sell it at the market price and pocket the difference. 'It was,' a foreign observer said, 'a very easy way to steal money.' In the big cities students, artists and musicians began discussing alternative ways for China to be governed and whom they would like to see running the country. Unknown to Hawke until two decades later, a popular choice for at least one group of Beijing activists was the Prime Minister of Australia, Houke Lober.

A young American, Josh Klenbort, who spoke Mandarin and was staying in the capital, recalled,

> There was a lot of idealism in the air in the months between April and June of 1989 ... It was a moment when people believed that almost anything could happen. It was a very positive feeling for a vast majority of people. My friends in the artistic community were all very pleased and excited and there were lots of ideas in the air that nobody had dared to think for many, many years. Everyone was very optimistic about what the outcome could be. They would have regular get-togethers at a restaurant or at somebody's apartment and during one of these informal forums the idea popped up that China should have a foreign prime minister, a foreigner

as head of government. Of course, this sounds completely preposterous today, and it would be. It would've been even then—but it was a measure of the times that people had such an open mind. The idea was not that Chinese people are incompetent or that they are not capable of running their own country. Far from it. But they did feel that the cultural and historical pressures on China were too great for the period of change they were going through. That was the root of the thought. It makes a lot more sense than the idea itself ... They drew up a short list of foreign leaders, and Bob Hawke was on it. He had visited China a couple of times in the '80s as Prime Minister and he had invited Chinese leaders down to Australia at least three times. It's hard to remember now, but this was not normal back then. The world had yet to start tramping to Beijing to meet the leadership of the Chinese Communist Party. China was still something of a footnote. In trade relations China's percentage of exports and imports in world trade was in very low single digits. Its foreign reserves would have been $10 to $20 billion. It was an important Cold War country, but it wasn't important politically in the world. It just wasn't. They were still very poor. So when a foreign leader did go to China it got a lot of press. It was a good opportunity for people who were more liberal to get on the front pages and talk about how China is opening up to the world: here we have these foreigners visiting us—that sort of thing.

Hawke's physical appearance seems to have been in his favour. In the late 1990s, a Chinese press photographer gushed to someone in Hawke's entourage, 'Mr Hawke is very handsome. He is the most handsome man I have ever seen. I think he is the most handsome man in the world!' The photographer wanted a picture of himself with the Prime Minister, but his flattery would have been utterly ridiculous had it not contained an element of truth. Hawke's mane of silver hair and thick eyebrows made him easy to recognise for the Chinese, to whom into the 1980s and even the 1990s all Caucasian males looked more or less identical, the slang for 'foreigner' being 'big nose'.

In 1984 Zhao Ziyang had done Hawke the honour of inviting him to review troops of the People's Liberation Army drawn up in Tiananmen Square, which is bounded on one edge by the Great Hall of the People and on another by the Forbidden City. On 21 April students from Beijing, Shanghai, Xian and Nanjing began protesting in the square.

In Canberra, Hawke, already sad about the death of his friend Hu, began to feel anxious about the situation in Beijing. After his meeting with Gorbachev eighteen months earlier, he had predicted to his chief of staff, Sandy Hollway, that the Soviet Union was going to be a train wreck—such an unfashionable view at the time that Hollway kept quiet about it, as did Hawke. A collapse of one pillar of the Communist world would inevitably shake the other. Cables from the Australian ambassador to China, Ross Garnaut, advised Hawke that his friend Zhao was being blamed for the inflation in 1988, while Zhao was objecting that it was the policies of Deng Xiaoping that were the real issue. This was risky on Zhao's part, for in China there is a tradition that The Boss is never wrong: problems are the fault of underlings.

Referring to the students gathering in Tiananmen, Garnaut said,

> Normally there would have been a big police and army presence to control what was happening in the square. The Chinese sit on these things. But there were two very important visits in May of that year: China was

hosting a board of governors meeting of the Asian Development Bank, and there were all these VIPs in town—the secretary of the US Treasury, and so on. They were meeting in the Great Hall of the People.

The Chinese leadership knew it could not be seen to be intimidating peaceful demonstrators under the very noses of the world's bankers. Immediately after the Asian Development Bank meeting, Gorbachev was due to arrive, the first Soviet leader to do so since Khrushchev's disastrous visit in 1959. For Deng Xiaoping a visit by the 'Pope of Communism', as Chinese leaders sardonically referred to the leader of the USSR, would be the crowning moment of his career. Gorbachev was no ordinary pope either, but the most charismatic political leader in the world (outside his own country, where he was cordially disliked).

Gorbachev's visit was a cause of excitement across China. The world media had arrived in Beijing for the bank meeting and stayed on for the Soviet leader's visit. So, once more, police and troops could not be sent to clear the square, lest China be seen in a negative light in the world in which it now sought acceptance. With so many foreigners in town and the weather getting hotter, more students were filling the square, many of them just curious. On 12 May, the first day of Gorbachev's visit, Zhao pleaded with the student leaders not to damage the Sino-Soviet summit. They ignored him and called their followers to go on hunger strike. In China fear of famine is bone-deep: the mere suggestion of skipping lunch to get a job finished is alarmingly impolite, while a hunger strike arouses such age-old fears it is of almost magical potency. The hunger strike brought tens of thousands of sympathisers to the square, and not just students, but people from government departments and urban residents. Weeping grandparents appeared on Chinese television, pleading with the young people to stop their madness. On 19 May, with

Gorbachev's visit over, Zhao went to the square to try to calm the growing hysteria and persuade the hunger strikers to desist. He was too late. Li Peng believed the country was already riding a tiger and on his advice Deng Xiaoping decided to impose martial law. The announcement was made on 20 May. Zhao refused to endorse it. On 24 May, Hawke was horrified when he was informed that Zhao had been stripped of office. The students became more febrile and headstrong and erected a ten-metre tall Goddess of Democracy statue in the square, their version of New York's Statue of Liberty. Meanwhile, under the martial law order, soldiers from other provinces were being transported to the capital.

On the night of 3 June the guillotine was raised. On 4 June it fell.

Deng is reported to have said, 'We spill some blood now and we'll have twenty years to complete the reforms.' Zhao Ziyang, fifty-nine years old, was placed under house arrest. He would spend fifteen years, the rest of his life, a prisoner.

In Canberra, Hawke was distraught: the People's Liberation Army had shot dead an unknown number of their fellow citizens, China's international reputation was mud, his friend was branded a criminal—and, according to a raw intelligence report he had just read, the PLA had run down civilians with tanks, squashing them into the roadway as if they were worms. (The report, like much raw intelligence, turned out to be false.) Hawke had spent seven years patiently building the Australia–China relationship, doing all he could to assist China emerge into the modern world, winning no domestic political kudos for his efforts but keeping at the task because he believed in it. In three days of violence he watched it all collapse.

Hawke cancelled his planned October visit and, with Beazley's approval, put defence co-operation on ice. Without asking for Cabinet approval, he decided to extend the visas of all

Chinese students already in Australia, to the delight of approximately 30 000 who would ultimately benefit—and to the disbelief of Immigration department officials who had to sort it out. On 9 June, just after reading the gruesome raw intelligence about tanks squashing unarmed citizens, Hawke was to speak at a service in Parliament House to memorialise those slain in the massacre. As he spoke of the killings, reading from the report he had just received, he began to weep profusely. It was a television moment authentic in a way rarely seen. Gleaming in the blue-black room, tears and translucent filaments of mucus flowed from his eyes and nose, creating an image people would not forget, especially the Chinese. In their 4600-year history, the Chinese had never imagined one day to see a white man, the leader of a foreign country, weeping for them.

In Australia the feeling was a guilty embarrassment about Hawke's tears, and fury with China.

At the official level in China, Hawke's tears caused anger. Li Peng, who had now been promoted to Zhao's job, told Garnaut he found Hawke 'a difficult man'. He did not need to mention that the seven years of exquisite friendship were over.

'The old intimacy was never restored,' Garnaut said.

Many Australian businesspeople (including Sir Peter Abeles, who had been extremely active in China) left. The Chinese economy went into recession. But Deng kept sending out the message: 'Come back. We want to open up to the world.'

Garnaut said,

> Despite what had happened, such a strong base had been laid that nothing was actually lost: it was built on. I think how Bob handled it was terrific: he did some symbolic things, but did nothing to damage the future. A really important thing historically is that Bush found it very helpful to follow Bob.

The United States Congress had worked itself into a paroxysm of righteousness over the Tiananmen massacre and was demanding that China's punishment must hurt. Hotheads thundered for trade and investment to be terminated. In a press conference journalists badgered the new President with questions about cutting off trade, and where he stood on human rights. *'Did he stand for human rights?'*

Bush, who had been ambassador to Beijing and knew the need for China to modernise, replied that the United States had to be careful to do nothing to set back Chinese market reforms. He cited as an example of a measured response the action of Australian Prime Minister Hawke. Garnaut said, 'The Europeans did more negative things, but the Japanese reaction was very similar to ours. So we and Japan set the tone for the USA, and that really was critical in allowing the reforms to keep going ahead.'

Within six months, a Chinese Trade minister was on an official visit to Australia. But Hawke would never return to China as Prime Minister.

The Australian economy had taken off when monetary policy was eased after the stock market crash of October 1987: jobs were increasing, investment spending was enormous, an asset bubble was expanding, executives were awarding themselves monster salaries, and home loan interest rates had risen to 17 per cent.

In the *Age* of 10 June 1989, Michelle Grattan asked, 'But when will the economy slow? When will rates fall? How certain is it that the landing will be "soft" rather than "hard"? Don't ask the Prime Minister. He doesn't know.' Hawke had been out testing the electoral waters in regional Victoria, where the crowds, as ever, loved him. The story's headline was 'PM still has that magic, but voters need answers'. Glenn Milne of the *Australian* made a sharper point when he wrote, 'a paradox that will dog

[Hawke] until the next election [will be] how to explain to voters that an economy that is performing too well is somehow threatening the living standards of ordinary Australians'. In his 1988 Budget, Keating had promised tax cuts in 1989. These would further accelerate the economy but, ignoring advice to scrap his promise, Keating went ahead with the cuts in July 1989. The Treasurer's economic policy at this moment became oxymoronic, but it made political sense for Keating, for by now he and the ACTU were, in Paul Kelly's words, 'hostages to each other'.[1] The Treasurer's career had become dependent on the ability of Bill Kelty of the ACTU to deliver wage restraint. To achieve wage restraint, Kelty had to depend on Keating to deliver tax cuts and more money in the way of welfare. If 1988 was Keating's most difficult year in terms of thwarted ambition, 1989 was his most difficult for managing the economy.

A couple of months earlier Hawke's Labor Unity faction (the Right) strongly opposed the privatisation of Qantas and its domestic offshoot, Trans-Australian Airlines, which, after decades of being government cash cows, were running dry; the herd needed culling and revitalisation, which would be expensive. Privatisation of government-owned assets was an ongoing, constant struggle within the Labor Party, especially between Hawke and the Left. The objection was sentimental and often based on ignorance, as in the case of Qantas and TAA. Bob Hogg, by now the national secretary of the party, and a member of the Left, had studied the issue. 'I had to remind them,' he said,

> that Chifley set up the domestic airlines to force competition on the railways, to make them lower their prices. That was the reason. There was no great socialist ideal. Governments in that period had to set up new industries, but once they had matured there was no role for government.

But Qantas was a cherished symbol; the party would not listen. A cartoon showed two trade unionists walking past a newspaper poster that read 'Hawke: on Qantas sale'. One asks the other, 'What's happened to his soul?' to which the reply is, 'Privatised'. The rejection of privatisation was a disappointing setback for Hawke. Within weeks it would fade to invisible as a new, much more vexatious airline drama began to unfold.

Australia had a lazy domestic airline policy going back to 1957: it was a duopoly of Ansett-ANA, privately owned, and TAA, owned by the government. The pair operated as carbon copies of each other, flying the same routes, charging the same inflated fares, leaving and arriving within five minutes of each other. But although they were happy to gang up against their passengers, neither would risk grounding their aircraft by ganging up against their pilots' pay demands. The result was that Australian domestic pilots were on astonishingly high salaries by international standards for the number of hours they flew: an average of 36.8 per *month*. At the beginning of 1989 they demanded a 30 per cent pay increase; in February they went on strike for a day to show they were serious. Hawke had disliked the Australian Federation of Air Pilots ever since his ACTU days when the pilots' union had refused to join the umbrella body, considering themselves a cut above. They were quite willing, however, to pocket the gains that other trade unions had fought to win. Community values are destroyed by free riders. Hawke decided he had to fight and defeat the pilots' union or risk a nation-wide wages breakout that would wreck the Accord and fuel inflation. In mid-August, Keating's 1989/90 Budget, with a $9.1 billion surplus, few spending promises and enforced superannuation savings of 6 per cent, was greeted as a sign of the government's responsible economic management. It was a clear sign that Keating now realised how badly he, his department and the Reserve Bank had blundered in 1988. Hawke and Keating sold the Budget around the country, performing side by side with such displays of bonhomie that the new shadow Treasurer, John Hewson, referred acerbically to a 'dog and pony show'. The Opposition had been up to its internecine tricks again. Plotters, including the tempestuous troublemaker Wilson Tuckey, had secretly organised a coup against John Howard, replaced him with Andrew Peacock in May, then boasted on national television of what they had done and how they had done it. In a few minutes, Peacock's moral authority was shattered. The effect on the electorate, and on the press gallery especially, was to increase cynicism about politics and politicians.

On 23 August, just after the government had successfully sold the 1989/90 Budget, all 1645 domestic pilots resigned from their jobs. This crippled air transport, undermined the burgeoning tourism industry, drove hundreds of travel-dependent small businesses towards the wall, and the flying public and the Prime Minister to fury.

But Hawke held a card the pilots had not bargained for.

Hawke had always believed in the importance of friendship for its own sake; he was about to test it for the sake of the economy. His close friend, Sir Peter Abeles, was the chairman of Ansett, close to Bill Kelty and fully in support of the Accord. When the pilots first began threatening to go on strike if they did not get their pay rise, Hawke asked Abeles to stand firm. His friend agreed without demur and without consulting his board or any of his staff. The government ordered TAA to do the same. Hawke met the AFAP leader, Captain Brian McCarthy, and told him the world had changed: this time there would be no backing down by either airline.

Used to getting his own way industrially, McCarthy did not believe the Prime Minister. His union had already advised members to put their financial affairs in order, pay off mortgages and other debts, be ready to take jobs overseas if they could, and be prepared for a long strike. Whatever it cost them, it would cost the companies $50 million a day and the pilots did not believe it possible that the airline managements could hold out longer than the union.

The day before the resignations, on 22 August, the *Age* ran a story, 'Pilots War: PM Backs Total Airline Shutdown'.

Then the pilots resigned en masse.

Their resignation, which followed Hawke's meeting with McCarthy, put the Prime Minister in a rage. During a press briefing he used inflammatory language, calling the pilots 'greedy' and 'glorified bus drivers', asserting they were waging 'war' against the wages system.

'Why the Wages Accord Is Tailspinning to a Crash' was the headline in the *Australian* in which Richard Blandy, professor at the National Institute of Labour Studies, Flinders University, argued, 'Bob Hawke's confrontationist approach has served only to weld the pilots firmly together.' Des Keegan wrote in the *Financial Australian*,

> Mr Hawke's contempt for the pilots' skills is a dangerous punt that could lose him and his party their collective shirts … Labor leaders are looking more and more like the generals who bled their armies to extinction through fog, mud, shot and shell in the trenches of Flanders …

On 27 August, the *Sunday Age* headline was 'MAYDAY! MAYDAY! The Full Story on the Biggest Industrial Battle Since World War 2'.

The public was used to Hawke the industrial peacemaker and shocked to see him as a union warrior again after all these years. He quickly moderated his language, but threatened to take the pilots to court, a traumatic step for a Labor leader.

He was supported in this by the Opposition. Under a cartoon of the Prime Minister as a kamikazi pilot, Paul Kelly wrote, 'Bob Hawke sees the pilots dispute as the single most critical threat to his economic policy and political position in nearly seven years as Prime Minister—an issue, quite literally, he cannot afford to lose.' On 29 August, the *Australian*, on its editorial page, had a cartoon of two Hawkes: the first was a gunslinger, saying, 'Okay, okay ... So I made the wrong choice from the arsenal when shooting from the hip at the pilots!' The second Hawke was a bare-chested Rambo declaring, 'It won't happen again!' Rambo–Hawke was armed with a bazooka.

Headlines were 'Tourism Loss May Hit $600m'; 'Houdini Hawke Bound by Pilots' Tightening Chains'. The few pilots who had refused to join the strike received death threats; the wife of one had a coffin delivered to her; another man broke down in tears in Sir Peter Abeles' office. Abeles, although his company had benefited from the two-airline policy inherited from Menzies, believed it was bad for Australia. He privately argued to Hawke, 'You can have one airline or you can have many: you cannot have two.' One of Abeles' closest friends told him, 'It's your own fault: you and your predecessor, Reg Ansett, have treated the pilots like princes—letting them fly first class and be driven around in limousines. Of course they can't believe what's happening.'

The strike would run for thirty weeks and cost hundreds of millions of dollars in the short term. (But in the long term, the aviation industry was reformed under the surveillance of businessman and aviator Dick Smith, whom Hawke appointed chair of the Civil Aviation Authority. By 1991, the reforms were saving more than $100 million annually in aviation costs.) The strike was finally broken by English-speaking pilots from the United States, England, Canada, India, Malaysia and Singapore, who took the offer of Australian jobs. It ruined the careers of hundreds of Australian pilots and the businesses of thousands of people who depended on tourism. As it dragged on and the pilots became more desperate and paranoid, they adopted political guerrilla tactics and issued death threats to Abeles, whom some claimed had engineered the strike for nefarious purposes of his own. They ranted on talkback radio, wrote letters to newspapers, and arrived en masse at venues where Hawke was appearing to shout abuse and jostle him, disrupting his 1990 election campaign.

To no avail. By the time the pilots' federation accepted defeat, the airlines had engaged other staff, and few of its members would be rehired. Hawke took no personal satisfaction in the pilots' defeat, although he maintained a certain satisfied disgust for Captain McCarthy for being an arrogant shepherd of his flock. The Accord remained intact.

For the country as a whole the seven-month strike was a time of inconvenience and irritation that tended to wash off on to the government. But even before the pilots had resigned, hardheads in the party were working on a strategy for overcoming the government's weaknesses. Its design owed most to the ingenious, blunt-fingered Machiavelli, Graham Richardson, the Minister for the Environment, whose soul had experienced a Damascene moment and whose sharp political nose had picked up a scent. By the 1980s, the Baby Boomers had exchanged their idealism of the 1960s for rank consumerism, but they had left flickering in a corner a candle of the old ideals: it burned for the environment.

Richardson knew that the Australian Democrats, who since the late 1970s had been the pivot of the Senate, would be of increasing importance until they died off (which he saw as inevitable) and were replaced by green independents. Almost alone, he had spotted the coming political shift. In conversations with Hawke, he told the Prime Minister what he had observed and believed; Hawke agreed with him, and had already off his own bat, based on advice from his office, set out to court the green vote. But herein lay danger for him in Cabinet, and in the party.

Virtually all the ERC ministers were opposed to environmental protection, so if the government were successfully to attract the greens it would be up to Hawke to persuade or to hammer environmental protection policy past the objections of his economic ministers. His style as leader was to allow Cabinet debate to flourish without showing his own hand. His fiercest detractors allowed he was an outstanding chairman of the Cabinet, guiding it with a light touch, summing up the arguments and only coming in to fight if he believed a wrong decision to be imminent. Once Hawke had declared, the debate was over: what the Prime Minister said, even if all others were opposed, became the government's decision and according to the rules of Cabinet solidarity, all had to adhere to it as their own. Hawke used his hammer sparingly to overcome his colleagues with his unpopular views, but it was always at a cost to his goodwill among them, so his normal method was to steer the arguments towards the view he already held, or if he had not preformed an opinion, to develop one from the debate itself. On environmental issues the large, mild-mannered Minister for Primary Industry, John Kerin, was so furious with Richardson's political influence in the year before Richardson was promoted to the ministry, that after one debate Kerin kicked the sideboard in the Prime Minister's office, declaring of Richardson, 'Fucking *backbencher!*' The dour, tough Finance minister, Senator Peter Walsh from Western Australia, was another who was rabidly anti-green. His view, a close observer remarked, was that the government, by supporting environmental issues, 'was screwing the most vulnerable workers, who go out in the forests. And this isn't really a Labor government.' Richardson and Hawke shared a view that Walsh, brilliant as a logician and analyst, had the worst political judgment they had encountered in a senior politician.

Walsh would later join a pressure group that resisted signing the Kyoto Protocol and rejected the whole notion of anthropogenic climate change.

Environmentalism would also meet obstacles in the heart of the party, since trade unions by tradition were opposed to environmental issues, which they saw as hostile to industry, thereby robbing them of jobs. But the urban middle class and young people of all classes were increasingly sympathetic to environmental protection, and likely to vote for it. Unrecognised by virtually everyone, a headline on 12 June in the *Australian* announced what a large part of the government's election strategy for the following year would be. It read, 'Power Hangs On Greens: Richardson'. He even explained its mechanics: 'What [the Greens] do with their preferences, particularly in the House of Representatives, may well determine our fate.' Neither commentators nor Opposition nor many in the ALP seemed to understand that Richardson was describing how the government could fight the 1990 election. To chase preferences rather than primary votes was a political idea of such originality it remained beyond comprehension—and from his own memoir, *Whatever It Takes*, it seems Richardson himself had not at that stage fully developed his thinking about it.

Hawke was a genuine green convert. He accepted the truth of the argument that Australia's environment was unique, fragile, damaged and of the highest value, and that the planet was an interconnected whole. After the economist Craig Emerson had joined his staff in 1986 and become his environmental adviser, Hawke had grown close to the young man and, enjoying his company, had tended to indulge him with listening to his ideas. Some staff were jealous of Emerson who, besides being something of a prime ministerial pet, was tall, dark and handsome, with beautiful brown eyes, a beautiful white smile and a boyish attraction for women that made other men want to thump him.

In the bitter, vehement and hysterical ALP uranium conference of 1984, Hawke and his supporters had won the adoption of a 'three mines' policy on uranium. This translated to the Left as 'pro-uranium'. In early 1986 Joh Bjelke-Petersen announced a new road would be built through one of the most beautiful wet tropical forests of North Queensland, the Daintree. The area was in the marginal Labor electorate of Leichhardt, where the local member, John Gaylor, pleaded with the government not to oppose Bjelke-Petersen, for the road was so popular with locals he could easily lose his seat. Emerson said,

> The public had in mind that Labor is pro-uranium mining. Labor will allow Bjelke-Petersen to drive a road through the Daintree. It was all going over like a shower of shit. The Left of the electorate had abandoned us.

By 1987 Hawke had begun to reverse perceptions of the government's commitment to the environment by halting logging in Tasmania. But as he had discovered by then, the environmental movement of the time, given a metre, demanded a kilometre. Richardson, after three years as minister, was driven to fury with green activists, losing his temper during a public meeting and shouting abuse at a woman. He shocked himself at how they had worn down his nerves. 'I was in a lift one day, and this woman said, "You dog! You shit!" And she spat on me,' he recalled. Hawke showed some environmentalists the door after a one-minute interview when, invited to put a case to him, they threw photographs of logging on his desk, saying, '*That's* our case!' Two exceptions were Philip Toyne and Peter Garrett of the Australian Conservation Foundation, who enjoyed the respect and trust of Hawke, Richardson and their staff. Both men were fighters who when they came to an agreement would not try to change it later or stab the government in the back with off-the-record press briefings.

Hawke told Emerson, 'I want a fixed agenda with them. I do not want this *elastic agenda* they are pushing. We need absolutely fixed, manageable targets that we can meet and that are good things to do.' The upshot was an environmental agenda of four major items: World Heritage listing and protection of the Tasmanian forests; of the wet tropical forests of North Queensland; of Kakadu National Park Stage II; and the rejection of silica sand mining by Japanese investors at Shelburne Bay in the Cape York Peninsula. The Shelburne Bay project would create long-term employment for only fifteen people and a section of the Great Barrier Reef would need blasting away to build a port. Oddly, of the four projects, the last was the most difficult for Hawke to negotiate through Cabinet. Emerson said,

> We were still going through the economic trauma [post-1986] and Paul was very worried about Japanese foreign investment. It had got to a stage where very senior people in Japan were saying, '*Shelburne Bay is a litmus test for Australia.*' Paul later tried to say he drove a lot of it. Well, he didn't. But he was not sitting there as a conventional Treasurer would, saying, 'My brief is to oppose all of this because it will damage the economy.' He was quite good. But it was really driven by Bob, me and Richo, and in the end, and again to his credit, Paul finally agreed to include it.

After the Shelburne decision, Keating came to Hawke's office and announced, Emerson said, '"That's it! No more! We're not going to be jamming any more green bits down people's throats. Just the four! That's all!" But four was all we wanted.'

By July 1989 Hawke's office had developed Richardson's idea about green preferences, and created an image known as 'the holding paddock'. Labor's primary vote had been stuck for months at 39 per cent, which in a normal election would mean defeat. The party's polling revealed the electorate was thinking, 'We will not vote Labor, but we're not convinced the Liberals are better.' Emerson said,

> So there were all these people in a holding paddock, not knowing whether to go to the Liberals or to us. We had to get them to walk out of the holding paddock into the Labor paddock with their second-preference votes.

Hawke's office, working closely with Simon Balderstone in Richardson's, wrote a comprehensive environmental statement that Hawke took to Cabinet, explaining to his colleagues that besides the four areas to be protected, the government had brokered an alliance between the Australian Conservation Foundation and the National Farmers' Federation for an initiative called Landcare Australia. Peter Walsh, the Finance minister, was suffering from shingles and so depressed by illness and about the wrong direction in which he believed the government was headed that he wanted to resign, but Dawkins dissuaded him. When Hawke announced the statement Walsh, in a fit of Celtic gloom, muttered, 'You know you've got a bad policy if the farmers and the greenies get together.' John Kerin's reaction was sarcastic pique. He immediately dubbed it 'The World's Greatest Environment Statement'.

Despite Kerin's cynicism, which news media parroters used to discredit it, the statement did, indeed, address the world: in it, for the first time, an Australian government spoke of the dangers of the greenhouse effect—but outside the Conservation Foundation and a few other green groups, it went unnoticed.

Eight

The Prime Minister delivered his statement in July 1989 in the town of Wentworth in New South Wales, at the confluence of the Murray and Darling rivers. It was a gorgeous landscape made ominous by the white death of salt creeping towards the river red gums. Red gums need regular spring floodwater but agricultural irrigation was already robbing them of this necessity for survival. The background made splendid television footage, but the commentary that accompanied the pictures that evening was jaundiced. Its tone was: 'In a blatant attempt to grab the environmental vote, Bob Hawke today announced ...' Emerson said,

> But the pictures were magnificent, and that's what people were taking in. Bob Hawke is going to save these areas: Kakadu, the forests. He's going to protect our fragile environment. And they loved it. Absolutely loved it. In a sense, the electorate didn't care whether he was doing it for political reasons, or cynical reasons, it was just something that needed to be done and this government was going to do it. He used a phrase I'd thought up while on holiday, which Stephen Mills [the press officer] decided to include in the speech. It was: *'We've taken too much from the earth and given back too little. It's time to say, "Enough is enough".'* So we pointed the TV cameras to that part of the speech and they just ran that grab. Bob delivered it with great weight and moment. And it was magical.

Richardson noted, 'By the banks of the Murray and Darling rivers, Hawke took a giant step towards re-election.'[2]

Quite unknown to the electorate, but of further irritation to his Cabinet colleagues, Hawke in 1989 had undertaken another environmental initiative that would be difficult to manage and would win the government not a single vote—but it would be of importance to the planet in decades to come.

One weekend Hawke and Emerson each took home a Cabinet submission for the Australian government to ratify the Antarctic Minerals Convention, an international agreement that would allow 'regulated' mining in the Antarctic. The regulations would protect the environment from damage, the Convention said. Enormous quantities of oil lay beneath the ice and, as no country clearly 'owned' the continent, it was booty to be snatched. Reading the regulations, both Hawke and Emerson individually realised the Convention was nonsense: how could the regulations be policed? And by whom? If there were an oil spill, how could it be cleaned up? Technologies for mining such an area without environmental damage did not exist. Instead of 'regulated mining' there would be a free for all for giant oil companies that would foul the last virgin area of earth.

On Monday morning, after discussing the paper with Emerson, Hawke decided to take it to Cabinet and oppose it, although Australia was already well down the road towards ratification. Emerson recalled,

> We were confronted with very strong advice from the departments of Foreign Affairs, PM&C [Prime Minister and Cabinet] and Treasury that we should hold our horses. Gareth [Evans, the Foreign minister] in particular objected. He pointed out Australia had been part of the process of drawing up the Convention for a very long time, and we could not just pull the plug. It would be disastrous for our relationships with the United Sates and Britain, in particular. They were passionate about it and were leading the charge. And lots of other countries had lined up. It was ready to roll.

There was no opposition in Australia to the Convention since the public was unaware of its existence. A lone voice had been raised on the other side of the world: that of the celebrated underwater explorer and inventor of scuba diving, Jacques Cousteau. Emerson said,

> We started out initial discussions with his son, and then we met Cousteau in Tasmania, then met him again, in Paris. Before that we met Rocard, the French Prime Minister. Bob sat in the garden with him at Matignon and talked it through and Rocard said, 'I'm on board.'

The French in 1989 were in bad odour in the Anglo-Saxon world and the South Pacific for bombing the Greenpeace ship *Rainbow Warrior* several years earlier. The explosion killed a man on board the ship. The French then lied about it, and tried to blame the British Secret Service. All of this added to a growing hatred of France for its nuclear testing on Mururoa Atoll. France paid Greenpeace compensation of some $8 million in 1987, but the stain of what the French secret service had code-named '*Operation Satanique*' still clung to the Republic. It was one thing to convince Rocard. It was another to convince the President, François Mitterand. Hawke said he 'loved' both Rocard and Cousteau from the moment he met them, but he found Mitterand 'a most disagreeable man, comprehensively up himself'. But Cousteau, a national treasure, was on good terms with the French President and laid the groundwork with him for Hawke's meeting.

Emerson said,

> Within a day of meeting Cousteau again in Paris we met Mitterand, who tried to wriggle out of supporting us. He was using weasel words. I remember giving Bob

a note saying, 'He's trying to wriggle away. You've got to nail him.' And Bob said, 'Well, François, we need to know whether you are with us in opposing this.' And when it was put straight to him he said, 'Yes, I am.' So that got the French on board.

As an international meeting and vote was needed for the Convention to be overturned, the next step was to gather as much support as possible to fend off the might of the British and Americans. Hawke said, 'My Cabinet, and especially Graham Richardson, thought it was mission impossible. They took the view that if the old boy wanted to have a go, good luck to him.' By now the media was aware of what was afoot, but was not sufficiently interested to report it. The *Australian* ran an editorial on 28 June under the headline 'Hawke's Icy Reception'. It read,

> the futility of the Federal Government's political posturing on Antarctic has been underscored by the short shrift Mr Hawke received for his ideas in London and Washington, Mrs Thatcher and President Bush rebuffed him ... True, the convention does allow for mining in the Antarctic. But it seeks to regulate it. In its absence, controls are non-existent. Antarctica sits there, ripe for the plucking. Mr Hawke insists otherwise, but the reality is that the outright rejection by Mrs Thatcher and Mr Bush sounds the death knell for Australia's Antarctic proposals. This is just as well, for Mr Hawke's plan would see negotiation started all over again with the objective of establishing an international wilderness park in Antarctic. In the meantime, the continent would be vulnerable. This is why the Minister for the Environment, Senator Richardson, recently said the convention would at least have 'kept the bastards honest' in the event of

any attempt to mine the Antarctic's rich mineral resources... After London and Washington, Mr Hawke should realise just how isolated he is on the issue, and just how hopeless is his tilting at windmills. He should, for a moment, think beyond the ALP's wooing of the 'green vote' and sign the convention before the deadline.

Undeterred by this advice Hawke's office, now with the support of Foreign Affairs, began a campaign with countries for whom Antarctica was a place so far away and so foreign they did not mind one way or another what happened there. They just needed to be asked nicely. Emerson said, 'We started with countries like Greece, Malta and Italy. We were either writing to them or ringing them, and one by one we built up the opposition, to the point where we met Al Gore.' Gore, later Democratic Vice-President and in 2007 a Nobel laureate for his environmental work, was already passionately interested in green issues. By 1989 he had founded a large, well-funded environmental research institute. He and Hawke took to each other immediately when they met at Blair House, where Hawke was staying in Washington. But when Hawke put the proposal to oppose the Convention, Gore objected, 'I'm being advised to sign, because it would regulate mining and that's much better than unregulated mining.' Emerson recalled,

> Bob said to him, 'Look—you *can't* regulate mining in the Antarctic. The technology has not been invented.' Gore said, 'Well, I can't give you a commitment now, but I will certainly take on board what you've said.' And about three months later he announced, on behalf of the Democrats, that they did not support the Mineral Convention. And in the end the Bush administration,

with whom we'd raised it, said, 'We'll just agree to disagree on this.' The Poms were the last ones hanging out, but it was all over by then. That was the result of just one Sunday and Monday morning, and setting out on a crusade: it can be done.

The parties to the Antarctic Treaty signed the Madrid Protocol on 4 October 1991 after two years of negotiation. The Antarctic was not to be mined for fifty years. Events since then have moved so far and so fast in environmental understanding it is likely that Antarctica will remain in its state of empty, measureless white beauty.

There was no political kudos in all this for Hawke: the Australian public remains largely unaware of his efforts. But there are two curious footnotes to the episode. Paul Keating told the author Paul Kelly that it was *he* who initiated opposition to the Minerals Convention. Kelly duly recorded this claim in *The End of Certainty*:

> In May 1989 the government, at Keating's instigation, decided to oppose the international treaty designed to permit but control mining ... In September 1988 when Keating met French prime minister Rocard in Paris they canvassed the idea of turning Antarctica into a protected international park—a proposal Keating pushed as his own, not necessarily that of the government ... and this became Hawke's own view.[3]

And in 2005, President Mitterand was posthumously revealed to have personally ordered the bombing of the *Rainbow Warrior*.

9

Both the Coalition and virtually all in the government were sure the Opposition would win the 1990 election. Warwick Smith, Liberal member for the sensitive Tasmanian seat of Bass, recalled that his party had been confident in 1984 that Peacock 'would be the giant slayer of this former union leader'. Tucked into their procrustean bed of dogma and ideology about the working class, many Liberals still thought of Hawke as a trade unionist. A union leader was a person so alien to their idea of the right man to run a country some were still finding it incredible that he actually was the Prime Minister. But Hawke was also alien to many in his own party: he had not followed the accepted method of becoming leader by spending years in the grind of parliament; he was committed to being a winner. Many of the rank and file of those days were so accustomed to what Whitlam had described as 'the eunuch's virtue' they found disturbing Hawke's conviction that only through power could ideals be implemented. At party conferences, he lectured delegates about their sacred cows. 'Bob was pretty much a meat-grinder of a politician,' Beazley said. 'He would hammer his argument into the turf.' Hawke applied to the ALP the same fierce, demagogic tone he had used as a young advocate before the Conciliation and Arbitration Commission. As Whitlam before him was unloved by much of the party until he was sacked by Kerr—whereupon he transformed into a Labor hero—Hawke too was quietly resented by many on his own side. Nor did the press gallery like him much. 'New members of Parliament assiduously court the press to establish their profiles,' Hawke said. 'When I arrived in Parliament I was already a national figure. The press gallery was never very happy with me because I never sought out their favours.' Some, like Alan Ramsay of the *Sydney Morning Herald*, hated Hawke. Ramsay had been on Hayden's staff and waged a relentless, decade-long campaign against Hawke, who considered it payback for his defeat of Hayden—which also entailed denial of the job of prime ministerial press officer to Ramsay.

Politicians and political journalists usually coexist in an atmosphere of tension—and of hypocrisy if the politician pretends to treat the journalist as an equal. This causes, as Max Weber noted, 'a relentless, albeit unacknowledged and denied inner turmoil for the political journalist: despised, he despises as a way of releasing his tension'. Unlike Keating, Hawke did not invite intimacy with the press gallery; unlike Keating his speech patterns were often contorted and made for bad copy; unlike Keating, he rarely provided the gallery with a witty quip; Keating, with his love of art, beauty, clothes and shopping was sexually unthreatening to female journalists, whom he wooed and wowed in long conversations, whereas Hawke had a sexual edge that made many women uncomfortable. With the exception of Alan Reid, Alan Barnes and Ian Fitchett, all of whom he had admired but who by his time in office were retired or had died, Hawke had only minor respect for members of the gallery. He admired Laurie Oakes for his scoops, Paul Kelly for his seriousness and Michelle Grattan for her industriousness. He made up for his somewhat aloof treatment of the gallery on overseas trips, when he took the news media with him. Trips on the prime ministerial plane were rollicking fun, thanks to the happiness of his office staff and his own high spirits. While he was teetotal, he vicariously enjoyed accounts of the adventures of his travelling companions and the all-night drinking and card games held on long-haul flights at the back of the plane. There were hilarious mishaps, especially in Asian cities, where members of the entourage, media and staff members got lost occasionally, returning with excuses along the lines of 'the dog ate my homework'. One serious senior man arrived late and exhausted for a morning press conference, his face covered in green glitter, a circumstance for which he had no innocent explanation. The staffers who sat in on lunches between presidents Reagan and Bush and Hawke often found themselves breathtaken at the raunchy banter amidst formal splendour, and the exquisite sense that history was standing, listening, at their elbow.

When Peacock lost in 1984, tensions in the Liberal Party had created seven years of internal chaos, but by 1990 Peacock had shoved aside John Howard and the leadership pretensions of Sir Joh Bjelke-Petersen and John Elliott and was back as Liberal leader. At his side he had a glossy young shadow Treasurer, John Hewson. Hewson was a professional economist, had been John Howard's economic adviser when he was Treasurer under Fraser, and was the only person in the parliament who could, with the authority of knowledge, attack Keating convincingly. He did so frequently, vigorously and aggressively, drawing sprays of rainbow venom from the Treasurer. When Hawke announced an election in February, the Liberal Party's internal polling was optimistic. Hawke had already agreed to debate Peacock, who looked forward to beating him once more, as he had in 1984.

For three men the 1990 election would spell political death or glory. For Hawke, victory would mean he had reached his highest goal: Labor would be the natural party of government domestically, a civilising force that aimed at the best and most intelligent version of the Labor tradition. Internationally, his government had gone far in establishing Australia in the eyes of the world as an independent, beneficent and innovative middle power, integrated into the newly dynamic Asian neighbourhood. Winning would crown a career built over more than forty years.

For Keating, whose political ambitions also went back to school days, Hawke's victory, ironically, would be his only chance of becoming prime minister. Keating knew that he could not call to himself the people's indulgent gaze, that he could not win from Opposition. He would need the power of office behind him.

For Peacock, 1990 would be the final curtain on his years of waiting in the wings, eternal man of promise, heir to Sir Robert Menzies, whose seat, Kooyong, the crown jewel of Liberalism, he had held since 1966. If Peacock lost, his political career would be dead. If Hawke lost, both his own and Keating's careers in politics would be dead. This was grimly amusing for those who were aware that by now Keating's envy of the Prime Minister verged on hatred, while he desperately wanted him to win.

Hawke called the election for 23 March, March being the month that marked for him eight years in office.

While virtually all professional politicians believed the election would have to be Hawke's last hurrah, just how he would pass from centre stage, how he would part from the Australian people with whom he had enjoyed 'a love affair' for so long, was an enigma. The Opposition believed he *could not* win a fourth time. The current account deficit was a weekly scandal for those who understood its significance, and an increasing percentage of the Australian population, educated in economics by Hawke, Keating and a handful of financial journalists, now did. With financial deregulation in 1984, the banks had launched themselves into a frantic competition for customers in both business and housing. Cash poured into the economy, fuelling the spending spree of the 1980s. Throughout the Western world an ocean of money was flowing. By 1990 interest rates were 17 per cent. The government, naturally enough, was blamed. Hawke's popularity was also adversely affected by the pilots' strike that was dragging on into the new decade. After the excesses of the 1980s, the 1990s began to show an irritable fatigue. The hangover was setting in. And meanwhile, the world had changed. The Cold War was over and, unrecognised for what it was—not just a bubble economy bursting, but a historic decline—Australia's biggest trading partner, Japan, was running out of puff by 1990. Within a few years it would be selling its golf courses, resorts, hotels and office towers in Australia at knock-down prices.

A salient but rarely mentioned fact was that the IT revolution was already underway. From the office, computers had invaded the home; personal mobile phones were becoming widespread and the noise and tempo of life were increasing. It was as if the dark, satanic mills of an earlier age had slyly transmogrified into fascinating toys, turning the houses people lived in, the parks where they walked and the cocooning interiors of their motor cars into places of work. Private time was beginning to vanish and a sense of peace and restfulness was going with it. For many, the new technology was thrilling, but there was an almost imperceptible sense of overload as householders moulded their lives to the challenges of their new gadgets. Married women and mothers now worked not to enrich their intellectual and social lives, as the women's movement had envisaged, but of necessity, to pay for the changes in lifestyle the 1980s had brought. The winners of the 1980s boom flaunted their wealth while the less well off discovered that luxuries in the 1970s—two cars, for example—were now necessities. AIDS scythed through the inner-city suburbs. After twenty years of liberty, sexual relations were once again fearful. Statistics on mental illness were rising. The Age of Anxiety had appeared.

Richardson commented, 'By 1990 the electorate had no faith in politicians or political parties. They would be choosing whomever they believed to be the lesser of two evils.'[1]

When the election campaign got underway in late February, the pilots developed a new tactic, holding banners for the television cameras that said: 'Vote 1 Abeles, Cut Out the Middleman'. Abeles—European, Jewish, highly remunerated, overweight, with a whale-sized head and heavy features—was an easy target for arousing hatred in anti-Semites, in Leftists who feared and distrusted power, and in ordinary people who, by and large, feared the very rich unless they were publicly known philanthropists. Abeles was philanthropic, but privately. There was a lugubrious streak to his personality, not unjustified in someone who at eighteen had been forced into a labour battalion in the Hungarian army, under Nazi control, and whose extended family had been murdered. His sweetheart in Budapest had vanished: also murdered, he assumed. As a very large man—he bought his clothes in what he called 'the elephants' shop' in Bond Street—he had a discomfiting intensity, holding one's gaze a few seconds too long. Among journalists there were wild stories going back to the 1970s that he was importing cannabis concealed in secret compartments in shipping containers, a rumour for which there was no evidence at all, according to Brian Toohey, who read boxes of material and case studies from the Costigan Royal Commission. 'There was nobody in the twenty-six case studies we reported [in the *National Times*] who could remotely be believed to be Abeles,' Toohey said in 2010. Hawke had always regarded the stories with contempt. He never attempted to downplay their friendship. But for those whose cosmologies swarmed with class enemies the Hawke–Abeles relationship was taken as a sign of evil afoot. In the ALP it damaged Hawke. As far back as 1982, Peter

Bowers of the *Sydney Morning Herald* had written, 'Hawke's relationship with Abeles is seen by his Labor opponents as unnatural, even sinister, and the Abeles connection is frequently used to discredit him.'

Hawke yearned for intellectual companionship all his life and, once he had abandoned academia, he often found it among European Jews. Garnaut wrote of Hawke in 2009, 'his is one of the few best informed, retentive and analytically clear minds with which I have interacted intensively'. While discussions in the Prime Minister's office and in Cabinet were often interesting, they were limited by pragmatism.

With Garnaut gone from his office, Hawke found in Abeles intellectual companionship. Abeles' urbanity, wry wit and deep affection for a man he treated as a beloved nephew—he had no sons of his own—made him a fine sparring partner for the Prime Minister. There was much over which they disagreed and Hawke was often intemperate in his arguments with him, which he never was with Garnaut. The industrialist stood his ground with the solemnity of a statue. One topic they rarely discussed was Israel. Abeles admired Hawke's support for Israel in the 1970s, and his rescue of Russian Jews while Prime Minister, but as a secular Jew, his own interest in the country was 'passive', according to Hawke. Abeles rarely visited Israel, and when he did found its inhabitants rude. By 1990 Abeles was showing irritation with Israel, remarking of its frequent fund-raising appeals, 'We [diaspora Jews] have paid for every tree in Israel twenty times already.' He spoke English slowly, sometimes puffing on a pipe or a cigar; he was an oasis of calm intelligence for Hawke, who teased out ideas with him and picked up international trends and gossip. As chief executive of TNT, a trucking company that employed 170 000 people worldwide, Abeles was in touch with business and national leaders from many countries. He was always in a jolly humour when he was with Hawke, and was himself given to bouts of cock-eyed optimism. But, from time to time, even he found Hawke's self-confidence unbearable. On one occasion he remarked, 'I tell you what, Bob: put on a false beard and moustache; I'll lend you a hat. Then sit in a coffee shop and listen to what they are saying about the government.' Abeles had learnt young a survival skill that he tried to impart to Hawke with little success: how to distinguish friend from foe. Hawke's political advisers were often appalled at how inept Hawke was in his discrimination about others' motives. Although agnostic, Hawke remained his parents' son, imbued with the Christian ethos of the brotherhood of man. He trusted people to a degree that would have been stupidity in others, and was for himself sometimes.

While the pilots were saying that a vote for Hawke was a vote for Abeles, the Opposition began chanting, 'A vote for Hawke is a vote for Keating'. Television advertisements showed a smiling Hawke who suddenly removed what was only a mask to reveal beneath it the face of Paul Keating. As the Treasurer was highly unpopular, Hawke needed quickly to silence this assertion. He did so by promising that were he to win, he would stay on and fight the 1993 election. In the circumstances he had little option, but it meant that if he kept his promise to the people, he would have to break his promise to Keating.

By 1990, Australian elections had become as staged as a Peking opera. Media commentators lamented constantly that the campaign was driven entirely by polling, by grabs for television's evening news programs, by defensive strategies. Labor, indeed, had much to be defensive about, for ALP state governments in Victoria, Western Australia and South Australia were in dire financial or political straits, or both. (The jewel, New South Wales, had been lost to the Liberals two years earlier, prompting, insiders believed, Keating's first attempt to unseat Hawke, as he feared his own time was running out.) In the same week that Hawke announced the federal election the State Bank of Victoria announced its merchant banking arm, Tricontinental, had lost $1.3 billion. It was taxpayers' money. The premier, John Cain, unable to come to terms with the disaster, insisted that no one was to blame, thus adding to the electorate's fury with him, his government and Labor. Richardson wrote 'the general public wore that stony look of insolence they get when they are about to hand out punishment'.[2] With state Labor beyond its reach for the time being, the Victorian electorate set out to punish Labor federally.

In Western Australia, the state government's association with the west's version of the white-shoe brigade, WA Inc., had turned from dream to nightmare as its cowboy capitalists went broke, dragging the government's reputation down with them. In South Australia, the State Bank was also due to collapse under its burden of debt. People there were edgy; the party worried it would lose more federal seats.

The Opposition only needed to make a case for Labor mismanagement. It did so, but not single-mindedly. It chose a slightly pompous slogan, *'The answer is Liberal'*. Keating punctured it instantly with the riposte, 'If the answer is Liberal, it must have been a helluva question.'

Because the government did not want the economy to be an issue, Keating was kept out of sight for most of the campaign, and the launch, in Brisbane, where Labor was popular, was low-key. It was to have no slip-ups like the 1987 'We set ourselves this goal: no child shall live in poverty'. The political world, as the Canadian writer and politician, Michael Ignatieff, noted, is a realm of 'sometimes lunatic literalism, where the slightest divergence between what you meant to say and what you actually said is a punishable offense'. One journalist, trying to be helpful, pointed out that Hawke's statement in 1987 could never have been misrepresented had it been possible to show a full colon on television. Nevertheless the Opposition, through parliament and the media, had managed to establish in the public's mind that Hawke had lied or made an outrageous promise to Australia's children, then cruelly broken it. Once the public is convinced of something, argument will not prevail and Hawke simply had to put up with the taunt throughout the election, and even into the following century. It was doubly bitter for him since his government had spent more on child support than any in Australian history. To the rage of the Finance minister, Peter Walsh, at the launch of the 1990 campaign Hawke made a further large commitment, $398 million, to child care. The drafting error of 1987, however, almost recurred. There had been an argument between the speechwriters, the young Stephen Mills and the venerable Graham Freudenberg, who at one point declared, 'It doesn't matter what the Prime Minister wants to say. This is what he *has* to say. Because this is what the audience wants to hear.' Their struggle delayed delivery of the final speech. Sandy Hollway, the chief of staff, recalled being in a Brisbane hotel on the night before the launch, co-ordinating the production of 200 copies of the speech, with attached supporting documents, for distribution the next day. There were, he said,

> only antiquated photocopying machines in those days and we worked until 3 a.m. I remember taking a nap on the floor at one stage. Everybody was working their heart out. All the photocopies were finally lined up when Craig Emerson came up to me and said, 'Can I have a word with you?' We went into the bedroom and he told me, 'We've got a problem.' I said, *'What!'* He said, 'I think there's an inconsistency between the speech and the supporting documents.' We didn't say anything to the other staff, but waited until about 5 a.m., when we

called the economist who would know the answer. Sure enough, there was an error in the speech. There was no time left to re-photocopy the whole thing. I had to say to the staff, 'Look, you have to go through every one of these and pull out page X and slot in a new one.' And I remember all those terrific admin people, who had slept only two hours, taking a deep breath and, as the sun came up, saying, 'Okay.'

Hawke's speech for the campaign launch acknowledged the pain of high interest rates, but presented them as an unpalatable fact of life in modernising the economy. He said 'anybody who tells the people of Australia that the future lies at the end of an easy road is not fit to be your prime minister'. He announced the government wanted to make Australia 'the clever country' (as distinct from 'the lucky country') and to that end would be establishing fifty world-class research centres. He declared, to wild applause, 'Medicare stays.'

Peacock had a disastrous start to his campaign when the deputy leader of the Liberals in the Senate, Austin Lewis, said on national television that the Liberals had been unable to convince Australians of their fitness to govern. Peacock sacked him immediately, but the damage was done. It gave Hawke an opening that stuck: 'If you can't govern your party, you can't govern Australia,' he said, turning it into a nostrum to be used at every opportunity. It was an observation that would return to haunt him.

Although many claimed after the event that they had believed Labor would win in 1990, aside from Hawke there was virtually nobody before the campaign got underway—Richardson and Keating included—who shared his optimism. The crunch moment would be the debate between Hawke and Peacock. Hawke's success in every endeavour is driven by three forces: optimism, will power and self-confidence, and the greatest of these is self-confidence. His team, aware of how highly strung he was, how a negative thought of his earlier failure in debate against Peacock could unnerve him and turn him shrill, were on tenterhooks. But Hawke was not now the nervous wreck with a glassed eye he had been in 1984. He was calm, focused and statesmanlike. He beat Peacock with ease. With their champion back on top, the campaign committee knew they had a fighting chance.

Journalists complained throughout the five weeks of electioneering that it was dull, lacking in sparkle and spontaneity. The most exciting event was when Hawke lost his temper while launching an environmental magazine. A staffer recalled, 'Some hairy ratbag wearing shorts and sandals started shouting at Bob, who made a gesture that knocked over a microphone, then got annoyed with all the microphones on the podium and swept them off with his arm.' The scene lasted only seconds, but was replayed so often on television that the rest of the week's campaign was a lost cause: the story for that week was Hawke's temper. His temper was, indeed, a constant source of anxiety to his minders during campaigns, when the pressure on a leader is most intense. He stopped smoking cigars leading up to the election, but nicotine withdrawal made him irritable and it was the staff who bore the brunt of his bad temper. He performed 139 election events, including ten visits to senior citizens clubs, hospitals, bowls days, child care centres; ten more to schools, TAFE colleges, Skillshare centres; and ten more to other community events, including the Derwent Hop Festival, the Family Fun Day at Morphett Vale and the Ballarat Begonia Festival. He also visited war veterans, farewelled RAN ships sailing for the 75th anniversary of Gallipoli, and toured various factories.[3] The staff kept him out of shopping malls and away from street crowds because polling showed that he would be in danger of verbal abuse. And whatever else had been announced that day, on the evening news the abuse and how Hawke handled it would be the lead story. He was kept in the dark about negative focus-group polling, lest it damage his self-confidence.

The campaign committee used every weapon it had, including a new and very popular one, Hazel. Initially uncertain in public, she was now forthright and had won respect over the years for causes, such as reforms in children's television, that she championed. She had also won the sympathy of women when, in 1989, Hawke had replied 'Yes' to a television question about whether he had ever had an affair. (He looked so contrite, even tearful, the interviewer did not ask the obvious follow-up, 'Just one?') Hazel made many appearances during the campaign and had a soft-focus personal column published under her name in some of the tabloid press.

Until the 1970s, campaigning had provided many moments of rambunctious fun, both for voters and for politicians. Menzies was famous, and celebrated, for his scintillating repartee with hecklers. Years after his death Liberals and even Labor politicians would repeat with admiration some of his wittiest put-downs. Everyone in Parliament House knew the possibly apocryphal story of the politician who introduced himself at an election rally by explaining, 'I'm the Country Member,' to which a voice from the back shouted, 'We remember!'

Television ruined all that.

Hawke's speechwriter, Stephen Mills, noted,

> The enduring image of the 1990 campaign was of Hawke, having delivered his policy speech ... standing on the stage with Hazel acknowledging the applause of the audience. As they stood there, holding the pose for photographs, their gestures and expression fixed, they seemed transformed into figures of wax.[4]

This is the pathos of politics: the theatre of keeping up appearances, of repeating the same speech over and over, forcing smiles, waving to strangers when one is tired, or bored or just wanting a cup of tea. 'Saying the same thing twenty times, as if you were saying it for the first time—that was the hardest part of campaigning for me,' Hawke said. Political leaders must inspire confidence. They repeatedly improvise by reacting to events as they unfold, trying to stop them spinning out of control. British Prime Minister Harold Macmillan, when asked what was so difficult about political leadership, is reported to have replied, 'Events, dear boy. Events.'

The ALP campaign committee was determined to limit the possibility of events during the election. This, of course, frustrated journalists, whose livelihood depends upon events. They griped about the influence of market research, none realising that the politicians interpreted research in a more creative and practical way than they did. Under a headline that said, 'Drowning in the sunless sea of market research' Phillip Adams, an influential commentator, wrote in the *Weekend Australian*, 'Hawke [used to have] a genius for articulating the collective dream of a nation. Well, you won't plug into that through market research ...' Actually, you will, if you're clever enough. Adams, like all his colleagues, had missed the genuinely interesting story that was under their noses: politics was being done differently in the 1990 election. As Richardson had first mentioned nine months earlier, the votes to win were the *green preferences*. This election would collect people's dreams and unconscious wishes, as elections always do, but quietly, in marginal electorates. Slowly and silently, the tens of thousands of people in 'the holding paddock' of the marginals were about to push the government back into office by voting Labor *second*. Warwick Smith recalled,

It was quite masterful. It was about enchanting the living rooms of Sydney, and to a lesser extent Melbourne, with the need to have a green agenda. While Peacock and others in the party had inclinations to be aware of the environment, they just had no marketing pizazz whatsoever, and they were left flat-footed by Labor's capacity to swing the votes on the green issue. In the late 1980s and early '90s the environmental movement was seen to be more extreme than it was later, and what Richardson and Hawke did was try and popularise green issues and say, 'Extreme Green is not good, but Extreme Development is not good either—and in Tasmania you've got Extreme Development.'

Smith had a desperate fight, often against Richardson, who campaigned vigorously in Bass—'picked my nose in public for me', Smith said—to retain his seat.

By 1990 Labor's marginal campaigning was so refined that in Western Australia, where there was an overall swing against the government of 4 per cent, it held marginal seats the Opposition could have won with merely a 2 per cent swing.

On a two-party preferred basis, the swing from Labor was only 0.9 per cent. In Victoria, furious with its state Labor government, nine seats fell. Had Victorians reacted like the rest of the country, Hawke would have won with the government's eighteen-seat majority unchanged. As it was, it came home eight seats ahead. But the number of people who had voted Labor was only 39.4 per cent, fewer than the 39.6 per cent who had voted Labor in the Whitlam disaster year of 1977. The message to the ALP was clear: its traditional supporters had deserted. It was a challenge for the party, but as Paddy McGuinness, having predicted a Peacock victory before election day, wrote immediately after it, 'If the Coalition has not managed to roll Bob Hawke this time, what makes it think that it will be able to do so next time?' He went on to write that Hawke, who was only sixty and very fit, could well stay on to fight the next election, then added the $64 000 comment, 'Of course, there is the problem of Paul Keating.'

But having achieved glory, Hawke blundered.

The exuberant maverick John Singleton, rabidly anti-Labor under Whitlam, had again run the party's advertising campaign and announced he was throwing the staff a celebration party. Singleton is a man who treats life as a cornucopia; he spends over his head. He seems to live by the injunction 'MORE!' More wine, women, song, wives, flowers for them, children, parties, fun, pranks, adventures, racehorses—and, in the twenty-first century, large South American parrots. For the dinner, Singleton hired Eliza's Restaurant in Double Bay, the shopping epicentre of Sydney's wealthiest individuals and just up the street from the electoral office of John Hewson, who would within days, everyone realised, become the new leader of the Liberal Party. Labor traditionally celebrated in hearty, sluttish, down-at-heel Chinatown. Eliza's could not have been a less appropriate venue for a Labor victory party. Hawke was uneasy about it. Singleton, archetypal larrikin, had become a close friend and the party owed much of its success to his agile brilliance in the last week of the campaign when the 'Vote Labor Second' strategy was finally unveiled. Seated with him in Eliza's, Hawke's uneasiness turned to ghastly embarrassment when a horseman wearing a spangled cowboy outfit rode up the steps of the restaurant onto its dance floor and began performing tricks. 'I hated it!' Hawke said later. Thrown off-key by the glitz, he made a speech of thanks to his staff in which he inadvertently insulted both his political officer, Geoff Walsh, and his environmental adviser, Craig Emerson. They had slaved throughout the campaign, getting hours less sleep each night than their boss, but while Hawke praised others he forgot to mention them. They were so annoyed they left the party, went out and got drunk and refused to return to Canberra with him.

This was trivial compared with Hawke's next blunder.

Graham Richardson wrote in his memoir that, after the election,

> Hawke's reception of me was very different from any I had received from him over the previous twenty years. My great friend whom I had served so loyally for so long, who had repeatedly acknowledged all I had done for him, was cool towards me for the first time, treating me like just another minister waiting in a very long queue [to receive a portfolio]. This took a while to sink in because, not unnaturally, I had thought I would be king of the kids for at least a week or two.[5]

He seemed to have forgotten referring to his great friend as 'the cunt' two years earlier in a car phone conversation with Keating. He supported his case for being hard done by with a quote from Peter Smark of the *Age* and the *Sydney Morning Herald*, who wrote it was no longer a Hawke–Keating government, but a Hawke–Keating–Richardson government 'because of my contribution to the victory'. Richardson went on to suggest that the article and others like it may have been the reason for the Prime Minister's unusual treatment of him. He told Marian Wilkinson, journalist and author, that years earlier when he had been a nobody, Hawke, already a Somebody, had 'treated me really well, and he was a hero. He was a major, major, major hero and treated me well.'[6] Not expecting kindness from strangers let alone major, major heroes, Richardson had responded with adulation, in thrall to Hawke's charisma.

In his memoir, Richardson wrote,

> Like all the other ministers though probably a little earlier than most I trooped into the Oval Office to stake my claim. I told Hawke that after the contribution I had made during the election campaign, I was entitled to a promotion, and the job I wanted was Transport and Communications.[7]

Hawke's old friend, Ralph Willis, had the portfolio but his management of it had been lacklustre; he needed a job more suited to his talent.

For months, Richardson had been telling colleagues and journalists that after the election he would be Minister for Transport and Communications. In Canberra this job had the sobriquet Minister for Mates—because its communications arm dealt with policy affecting the media moguls Kerry Packer and Rupert Murdoch, whose empires during the 1990s were about to undergo great changes. Pay television was to be introduced, while the third media empire, the once-great Fairfax, was on the brink of collapse. The two others were poised to loot it. The Minister for Communications would draft the policy to referee this competition between titans; a misstep could make deadly enemies for the government. Already Murdoch was shaking his fist at Labor by urging readers of his national paper, the *Australian*, to vote against the government in the 1990 election. Richardson's best friend was still Peter Barron, now on Kerry Packer's payroll as a political adviser. The government needed, somehow, to keep both Murdoch and Packer onside, especially Packer, because of the influence of his Channel Nine television network. (Although Packer had sold the network to Alan Bond, by March 1990 Bond had collapsed with the rest of the WA Inc. cowboys and Packer was ready to buy it back. The sale went through in July that year.) Richardson thought, not unreasonably, that he had the political skill to do the job, and had earned it. He had positioned himself to become the third most powerful man in government, so it was a shock when he sauntered into the Prime Minister's office, jaunty as a punter whose horse has come home at 30 to 1, to discover Hawke cold-eyed. More than a shock: it was a slap in the face.

Their former intimacy had cooled since Richardson had become a minister. Partly it was due to the pressure of work: Richardson, always industrious in whatever job he did, no longer had time to spend shooting the breeze with the Prime Minister at the end of the day. In the dynamic of their relationship there was also a deeper shift: as a minister, Richardson was officially a Somebody, no longer the star-struck fan. And there had been an incident over a bet on a putt during a golf game—they used to play together regularly at sunrise—that had left both men annoyed with each other. There was also Richardson's abuse of Hawke behind his back. Before the election Richardson had been saying openly that it would soon be time for Hawke to step down in favour of Keating.

Richardson continued,

> [My] claim was summarily dismissed ... The only job left, I was told, was Social Security ... It wasn't the refusal that upset me, it was the manner of it. I was being put in my place, and I couldn't—and still don't—understand why.

It is difficult to know how much of this statement is disingenuous. Richardson, from his earliest years as a New South Wales Right apparatchik, had revelled in the colourful, shady side of inner-city life. He seemed fascinated by gangsta chic. In her deeply researched biography, *The Fixer: The Untold Story of*

Graham Richardson, Marian Wilkinson provides a wealth of detail about his associations with a small number of thugs and criminals in the 1970s. Wilkinson records that, as a poorly remunerated young Sussex Street organiser, he supplemented his income with 'loans' from at least one of these men, and was paid thousands of dollars on fake invoices for work supposedly done by his wife. Richardson's parents had died when he was a young man; he matured, as Wilkinson portrays his life, in a sort of weed-filled prelapsarian Eden, innocent of the difference between good and evil in financial affairs. As he rose up the political ladder, he became a fund-raiser for the party in New South Wales, and herein lay a source of his power. Richardson always sought to project it as something inexplicable, mysterious and glamorous. Actually, it was mundane: he pulled the purse strings. He was the man who, controlling the slush funds, could provide money for a candidate fighting in a marginal seat, or for selection for a seat, or in a by-election. He had perfected an approach for soliciting donations to the party that exquisitely balanced the suggestion that, while the donor had better make a friendly gesture, no promises were being given in return.

But control of money was only part of Richardson's strength. The other part was his true virtue. There was a well of sympathy and kindness within Richardson that he concealed behind his tough-guy image but which was known to the hundreds of people whom over the years he had gone out of his way to help—insignificant people, battlers, who would never be able to repay him with more than their thanks. When he had the funds to do so, Richardson gave generously and anonymously to charities.

Richardson had the sweet, uncommon gift of gratitude. It was his gratitude to Hawke that had made him such a fan for so long. John Bowan, who had once done Richardson a good turn, recalled that years later he and Sandy Hollway were working on the Sydney Olympic Games Committee when they fell foul of the Olympics Minister, Michael Knight. According to Bowan, Knight wanted to sack them both. Richardson intervened, using his weight in the New South Wales Labor Party and his authority as mayor of the Olympic Village to dissuade the minister. It was only later that Bowan learned who had saved his and Hollway's jobs.

Hawke said, 'There were a lot of negatives to Graham, but I have never doubted he is a true Labor man. He genuinely wants to help the poor and weak.' And he truly, madly, deeply wanted never again to be poor and weak himself. He wanted to live glamorously.

By the early twenty-first century, after sixteen years in state government, the New South Wales Right had degenerated into a hybrid of Tammany Hall, ethnic gang and *opéra bouffe* and turned to a new premier to save it. Kim Beazley said,

> The New South Wales Right fought a lone battle for decency in the party for the best part of a century. They were basically always in the minority up until the 1980s. The Left always had the greater numbers. And the New South Wales Right was consistently trying to produce a Labor Party that had a halfway chance of winning an election decently. Basically they were totally connected to the thinking of the average middle-Australia Labor voter, and the Left wasn't. And then in the 1980s they solidified, and transformed, and emerged as the leaders.

Geoff Walsh recalled,

> When I worked in the national office, the New South Wales office was absolutely dismissive of us and talked about 'the way we do things in New South Wales', and that they had a higher level of political professionalism

in the presentation and execution of events, research and advertising. The Victorian Right was equally organisationally effective, but it tolerated more diversity. Victorian institutions tend to be more thoughtful, more diverse in a range of views.

In the course of a century of struggle, the New South Wales Right found its cohesion in a tribal spirit and an unforgiving attitude to outsiders. It was held together by passionate anti-Communism with a rancour that today can barely be imagined. When the ALP split in the mid-1950s, ushering in almost two decades of power to the Liberal Coalition, New South Wales did not split, thanks to the decision of the Right to heed the advice of Sydney's wily and astute Catholic archbishop, Cardinal Gilroy, acting through his bishop, James Carroll. (His 'right hand blesses the victims of his left' the Catholic-convert poet, James McAuley, wrote, in fury, about Gilroy's political role.) Branch-stacking for preselections, frequently presented as a recent evil in Australian political life, is in fact an ancient and noble tradition in both the Labor and Liberal parties. Beazley said, 'There were stories in the 1950s of busloads of nuns in New South Wales being brought in to vote in preselection ballots.'

For the New South Wales Right—cynical, self-righteous, narrow-minded and now powerful—it was but a short step to a sense of entitlement, from which abuse of power hatches like flies in summer. The title of Richardson's book, *Whatever It Takes*, sums up the Right's ideology by the 1990s: nothing was more important than winning. There were no principles to guard. There was only venal pragmatism. Richardson himself was a fine example of it.

Hawke, other than his suddenly cold demeanour, gave Richardson no reason then or later as to why he could not have the job he coveted. This was a blunder and arose from embarrassment: Hawke was trapped by a promise he had made to Sir Peter Abeles to keep confidential something Abeles had told him.

Hawke said, 'While I did not believe Peter would lie to me, and he had absolutely no reason to in this matter, I could not have the same confidence about Graham—an assessment with which I think Graham would agree.' He added, 'My duty as Prime Minister was clear. I could not risk the government's reputation by giving him the job he wanted.'

Instead he gave Transport and Communications to a man of peerless good character, Kim Beazley.

While state and local politics throughout Australia have frequently been known to be corrupt, there has rarely been the suggestion of corruption at the federal level. Hawke believed Richardson could be the man to break the mould. Despite years of speculation by journalists, who are always passionately interested in the media and obsessive about media bosses, it was not the communications side of the portfolio that influenced Hawke's attitude to Richardson, but the transport wing. Abeles had told Hawke that Richardson, already boasting he would be minister if the government were returned, had asked for a meeting in Abeles' Sydney office. Richardson arrived for the appointment dressed in a manner that TNT staff found astonishing for a Cabinet minister. He was wearing a suit and tie—and a shirt of royal blue satin. His reason for meeting Abeles turned out to be in the latter's view, as inappropriate as his shirt. Abeles rebuffed him. Wilkinson noted that relations between Richardson and Abeles became 'poisonous'.[8] Transport was a tough and highly competitive industry. Abeles told Hawke that other transport companies in Australia would be willing to oblige a minister in virtually any desire.

In refusing Richardson's request and warning Hawke about it, Abeles had his friend and his country at heart, since he did not need the enmity of a powerful Labor figure. Hawke, for his own sake, should have confronted Richardson with what Abeles had said, but he kept silent. It was an expensive silence since Richardson lived by the concept that he who turns the other cheek gets hit by the other fist. As he wrote of himself, 'nobody ever took a free kick at me without massive retaliation'.[9]

In Hawke's next move, he made an even greater blunder, according to Richardson.

Richardson had left Hawke's office in dudgeon. The Prime Minister, Richardson wrote, had been keeping open the post of High Commissioner to the Court of St James for Willis, whom the New South Wales and Victorian Right wanted dumped from the ministry. Hawke had refused, insisting that the Right in both states support Willis, whom he intended to promote to a portfolio suited to his considerable talent as an economist. If that did not work, Hawke had said that he would offer him London. Richardson had replied jocularly that if Willis didn't want to go to London, he would, 'in a flash'. The job's perquisites would be a mansion in the centre of a fascinating city, presentation to the Queen at Buckingham Palace, rubbing shoulders with the international big league, his lovely red-haired wife pampered with servants, gorgeous shops, lavish parties and easy travel to Europe. Richardson wrote that that night Hawke rang him to offer him the high commissioner's position. He was, he said, 'appalled, hurt, furious. Without taking any time to think about it, I just said, "No."'[10]

Hawke says he has no memory of offering London to Richardson and believes the story is a concoction. The Prime Minister's relationship with the Queen was warm—they shared a good sense of humour and love of racehorses and he was reputed to be Her Majesty's favourite Commonwealth prime minister. Hawke says he considered Richardson could have been an appropriate envoy since Her Majesty had clearly liked Doug

McClelland, the rough diamond whom Hawke had previously sent her. It was simply that he did not consider Richardson for the job at all. Richardson's written account sounds odd, since he had so recently acknowledged that the job was a plum indeed. His account begs the question: why would he reject it out of hand, as an insult?

That night, Richardson wrote, soon after the disputed phone call from the Prime Minister he made two calls himself. The first was to his very close friend, Peter Barron, to tell him of the day's events. 'I said to him: "I'll get this bastard, I'll do whatever it takes, but I'll get him."' Richardson's next phone call was to Paul Keating.[11]

Hawke meanwhile mulled over what to do about Richardson's sense of grievance over the ministry he had offered him and by the following morning had come up with another idea.

Richardson was having breakfast in a Canberra restaurant when he was summoned to the telephone by a call from the Prime Minister. Hawke wanted to discuss with him the Ministry for Defence. Defence is a mammoth portfolio, with the largest staff, the biggest budget, the most formidable subordinates and insubordinates. Beazley had been brilliant in it, sensitive to the mentality of both the brass and the infantry. He recalled that just before the 1987 election he had asked the Prime Minister to inspect a brigade in the marginal seat of Townsville. The visit would be politically useful to the coming election. But to Beazley's horror, Hawke began talking to a corporal, who opened his pack to show the Prime Minister what was inside. Hawke said, 'Oh—you've got a lot of equipment there. What do you think of it?' The corporal replied, 'It's a heap of *shit*. Sir.' As they moved out of earshot Hawke said, 'What sort of Defence minister are you! Four years in the job and you have one of your soldiers describing his kit as shit!' Beazley explained,

'Bob, for thousands of years the whole purpose of warfare has been to kill infantrymen. They're naturally a morose group. Next week there's a battalion of US marines visiting for exercises. This bloke's unit will go to the marines, who think the same about their own kit, they will swap kits, and they will both be happy.'

At another of Hawke's brigade inspections in Townsville, a regimental sergeant major with the voice of a Jurassic bullfrog roared, 'GENTLEMEN! I want to introduce to you now the PRIME Minister of Australia, Mr Bob MENZIES!' Hawke also inspected a military barracks. Each time the man running it referred to another service—the navy, or the air force—he spat on the ground. 'Bob left thinking we were all lunatics,' Beazley said. He desperately wanted to stay in the portfolio but Hawke was determined to broaden his experience, for already at the back of his mind he wondered if Beazley, rather than Keating, might replace him, since Keating could yet 'take the Paris option'. Inevitably, anyone who followed Beazley in the Defence job would, for months at least, be overwhelmed by it.

Richardson wrote that the Prime Minister told him he had offered Defence to Robert Ray the day before, but on reflection he believed Ray's 'legendary temper' could make him unsuited to the delicate negotiations with foreign governments that a Defence minister conducts.[12] Hawke says,

> I never thought Robert Ray had a bad or a hot temper. He was sharp and direct and many people felt intimidated by him, but his temper was not an issue. I don't believe I would have discussed Robert with Richardson in these terms.

Richardson wrote, 'We talked it through and I accepted.' As he left Hawke's suite a new press officer saluted Richardson and called out, 'Good morning, Admiral.' Richardson was chuffed: the man he used to love did, after all, still value him.

But Hawke's handling of Richardson was sliding from poor to disastrous. When he rang Ray to tell him he wanted to switch Richardson to Defence and Ray to Social Security, Ray flatly refused. Hawke knew he was right to do so, and knew that he was intellectually far better equipped for the job than Richardson. Hawke also knew that in a showdown with Keating he would inevitably lose the New South Wales Right, which would rally to the banner of its tribal brother. He depended on Ray to hold Victoria for him. Hawke said later, 'My handling of the Richardson and Ray portfolios was dreadful.'

He summoned Richardson once more. He could not be Defence minister after all, the Prime Minister said. He was stuck with Social Security. The pain Hawke had inflicted on Richardson two days earlier seemed, in comparison, a mere tap on the wrist. Now Hawke whacked Richardson's face, and did so with the same steel-eyed chill of the earlier meeting. Richardson was devastated, but as he refused to be the victim of any man, his rage was directed outwards. 'Nothing in politics, or indeed in any facet of my life, has ever made me as angry as I was that morning,' he wrote later. 'All I could think of was revenge ... I was now completely won over to Keating's side ... From that moment the Hawke prime ministership was doomed.'[13]

It was doomed, but as Richardson knew, Hawke was a hero. No hero can be destroyed by others: from the age of myths into and throughout history, the hero's reward for heroism is the freedom to choose his path to self-destruction.

Richardson, meanwhile, was too proud and clever to reveal how deeply Hawke had wounded him, and how much he now hated the Prime Minister. Indeed, he gave the impression of having copped his demotion on the chin and although disappointed for himself, was still on Hawke's side.

Publicly, the government was united but the inner circle knew otherwise. Keating's every second thought seems to have been how unjust it was that he was still denied 'his turn'. Privately, to his staff, to other ministers and to journalists, he blamed every difficulty in his life, even strains in his domestic affairs, on Hawke. He denigrated the Prime Minister constantly. Hawke in his own day had denigrated Hayden—but he had not Keating's fire-talented tongue. And he was never as talkative as Keating, who was famous for telephone monologues, always the super-salesman selling, selling, selling his point of view.

The show went on. By the second quarter of 1990, the government could boast it had created 1.6 million jobs and while the booming economy was beginning to slow, Keating promised a soft landing. He publicly attacked all those who doubted his handling of the Treasury, including the Industry minister, John Button, and the former Finance minister, Peter Walsh, with such an edge of furious scorn that more observant journalists realised his feelings were almost desperate. David O'Reilly in a *Bulletin* cover story of 29 May wrote,

> Quite simply there is a real prospect that, after seven years as the driving force of economic policy for Australia, Keating has got it all wrong ... Keating produced in parliament a display of intellectual and oratorial brutality that was almost overwhelming for those sitting in the galleries. At times he leaves his opponents seemingly mesmerised by his capacity to translate complex government policies into plausibly defendable positions. From there he turns a machine gun of invective on to any contradictions or political problems in Opposition arguments. In an hour-long Question

Time he made the pugnacious and ambitious Liberal Shadow Treasurer, Peter Reith, pale into retreat. In the next salvo he dismantled John Howard's latest foray into industrial relations policy. And he slapped contemptuously at Hewson.

Hewson's barrage of economic statistics inspired Keating to dub him 'feral abacus'.

Hawke had an ambitious fourth-term agenda for micro-economic reform, especially in Commonwealth–state relations, which was less publicised than it should have been for several reasons: one was that few journalists understood it; another was that Keating was unenthusiastic about supporting an initiative that had come from the Prime Minister and that could be seen as a further great reform. Another was that the government, and particularly the Prime Minister's office, no longer had the sharp edge in self-publicising that it had enjoyed after the end of the Combe–Ivanov affair. Senior Canberra journalists were bored and cynical about the government. For a politician, years in public life entail years of being satirised, lampooned and criticised. In time, only her or his flaws seem evident. The virtues are overlooked.

Meanwhile, the new leader of the Opposition, John Hewson, was a shiny, sharp cobra of a man. He drove fabulous cars and was known as 'Fast Lane'. He was a political greenhorn, which of itself made him interesting for the gallery. He was far more exciting than the greying team that ground out government business day after day. While Keating was fourteen years Hawke's junior, Hewson was almost twenty.

In April, Hawke enjoyed his greatest pleasure and his final moment of peaceful reflection as Prime Minister when, at break of day on the 25th of the month, he stood with a handful of Australian and Turkish veterans and thousands of young backpackers above Anzac Cove to honour the dead of seventy-five years earlier. Former enemies embraced; the young embraced the aged. It was a moment of human brotherhood, as if an age of peace yet to dawn had cast its soft light backwards onto the turbulent present.

A few weeks later Hawke suffered a private setback that temporarily did his standing as much harm as his world record in beer drinking had served him well over decades. He needed a prostate operation. The fact was widely reported. Suddenly, the leader who embodied the Aussie larrikin ideal of boozing, playing sport and womanising transformed into the face of the male terror of impotence. While the press gallery restrained themselves in what they wrote, what they said to each other—and what Keating had to say on the issue—was as vulgar as it was vicious. Three months earlier Hawke had been 'still young'. Now John Hewson referred to him as 'old' and 'losing his grip on the party'. Hawke and the government began falling in the polls soon after the election and by June Hewson outpolled Hawke as preferred prime minister 46 per cent to 38 per cent. Glenn Milne wrote in the *Australian* on 7 June,

> Consider some of the headlines generated in recent weeks... 'Time may be right for Hawke to go'. 'Keating shows the troops who's boss.' 'Hawke opens up leadership issue in quelling row.' 'Hawke is on trial' and the doozy of them all, 'Crusher Keating: How desperate is he?'

Milne went on to argue that, while Keating was restive and Richardson had deserted the Hawke camp, Keating did not have the numbers in Caucus for a challenge and Hawke was safe in his job. Laurie Oakes, in the *Bulletin* of 12 June, wrote, 'Hawke appeared older and frailer than before his surgery. Hardly a PR triumph.' Walking past a motor mechanic's shop in Sydney around the same time a Hawke supporter heard young tradesmen refer to 'our senile Prime Minister'.

Had Hawke taken Abeles' advice then, sipping coffee through a false beard, he could have decided it was the moment to bow out. But giving up was no more in his character than it was in Mrs Thatcher's. And, by mid-1990, economic upheaval loomed. The worst recession in sixty years was emerging. Ralph Willis recalled Grand Final Day in Melbourne the year before, chatting to a man who sold cars. 'How's business?' Willis had asked. 'Going gangbusters,' his companion had said. 'Can't hire enough staff. But I don't know where we'll be in six months. I haven't got a single forward order.' Willis had felt his blood run cold.

In the *Weekend Australian* of 23–24 June, the publisher, poet, intellectual and columnist, Max Harris, wrote:

> There is little but Band-Aiding that any Australian government can do to ameliorate the economic chaos and disorder that has become a world affliction. With hundreds of nations around the world in an economic mess, it is idiotic to blame the Government or to call for therapies for economic miseries over which it cannot have the slightest control.

Like summer lightning, the air flashed with signs of a boom busting. Perhaps economists and bankers resemble generals: they forever fight the last war. After the stock market crash of October 1987, there was a worldwide belief that monetary policy had to be loosened to prevent another Great Depression. The ocean of money that was let loose caused the boom. By January 1988 economists in Hawke's office were arguing that the October crash had not been the cataclysmic event it was supposed to be and the response had been overdone. They wanted interest rates tightened.

But the Labor jewel, New South Wales, was due for an election in March that year and the government, especially the Treasurer, did not want to raise interest rates before then. The decision to wait was both foolish—the New South Wales Labor government was beyond salvation—and a blunder. Craig Emerson recalled,

> Ross Garnaut came over from Western Australia and said, 'It's going to hit the wall.' I don't think anyone fully accepted Ross' view. But he was right. And by 1990 the economy was a bloody runaway beast. It didn't seem to matter what interest rate increases were made, it just kept going. By then it was too late: we were too close to the wall.

Immediately after the 1990 election, the economy gave a shiver of contraction. Some professionals understood; most did not for several months. Hawke would say repeatedly, in Cabinet, in the ERC, in his office, to the electorate, 'We tightened too much, too late.' It was his greatest regret as Prime Minister. His government's misjudgment of monetary policy was its greatest error. Keating meanwhile refused to apologise for his role.

The rumbling of decay in Eastern Europe that thundered in 1989 as the Berlin Wall collapsed kept rumbling through the early months of 1990. The world watched, fascinated, as country after country, collected over centuries by sabre, cannon, horses and tanks, broke away from the Soviet empire. Suddenly, like a sandcastle under a wave, the empire dissolved.

An eminent international policy analyst, Professor Francis Fukuyama of Johns Hopkins University, wrote an essay titled 'The End of History?' suggesting that the collapse of the Soviet Union marked the advent of Western liberal democracy as the end point of humanity's sociocultural evolution and the final form of human government. Fukuyama was too quick off the mark. Certainly the West had won the Cold War. But what exactly was the prize? It was not as obvious as he and jubilant US Republicans and a strange new intellectual breed called neo-conservatives, who had lived in the shadows for a decade or more, believed. But it was a time of great hope and great relief. The threat of 5000 nuclear weapons exploding in two and a half hours over the cities of Europe, America, Japan and possibly Australia vanished. But there began to emerge an uneasy feeling that the world was not shifting into a glory of liberal democracies. It seemed to be moving towards a hazy no man's land. The victory prize remained tantalisingly out of reach. History announced its puzzling reward nine months after the Wall came down. Early in the morning of 2 August 1990, President Saddam Hussein of Iraq invaded Kuwait, his army halting at the border of Saudi Arabia. If it crossed the border and prevailed against the Saudis' far smaller armed forces, Saddam would be a master of the universe. He would control the majority of the world's oil.

The prize for winning the Cold War, it seemed, would be more war. The booby prize: anarchy.

By this stage, the American economy was flagging and many spoke of 'imperial overreach'—that the United States had won the Cold War but had been weakened in the process and would now have to pull back from global leadership. Dr Hugh White, an international analyst and by now Hawke's Defence adviser, said, 'Nobody, including no Americans, assumed that with the end of the Cold War the United States would retain the global role it had played.'

Saddam Hussein and the Bush family would change all that.

A twisted seam of atavism ran through the vulgar tyrant who was President of Iraq. He believed himself to be, and represented himself to his people and to the wider Arab world, as a resurrected Saladin, the paragon of Arab chivalry. Even the Christian warriors of the Third Crusade—Richard the Lionheart among them—from whom Saladin won the Kingdom of Jerusalem admired his strategic genius, his justice and his compassion for prisoners. Saddam's evocation of glories past conjured from the vast empty spaces of the desert what sounded like the distant thunder of hooves. People wondered: in which direction was the horse of history galloping? Some said this way, others said that. Hawke was quite certain what he thought: the horse should be pulled up hard and guided into a stall. Saddam had to leave Kuwait, by a face-saving negotiated settlement if possible, by force if not.

Hugh White said,

> I remember sitting in my cubby hole in the Prime Minister's office when news of the invasion came in, and the first responses from America were very ambiguous. The first responses from [President] Bush Senior were very ambiguous. I said to someone, 'Well, this is what it's like after the Cold War: small countries get invaded by big neighbours and nobody gives a damn. This is a really bad model for the way the world works.'

That was Hawke's attitude too. On Keating's recommendation—he and Hawke were still spending time together, still discussing ideas—the Prime Minister had been reading William Manchester's biography of Winston Churchill. White believed the book influenced Hawke's thinking: that a strong international response mediated through the UN was essential to stop Saddam.

White had been a little too quickly pessimistic about the world's reaction, for on the day of invasion the Security Council, at last able to play the role envisaged for it in 1945, passed Resolution 660, demanding an immediate and unconditional withdrawal from Kuwait. A sigh of relief, even joy, ran through the international community. White said, 'You can't understand what happened in August through to December 1990 without understanding the *hope* that we could now build an international order in which the UN at last played the role envisaged for it.'

The Cold War had consigned the Security Council to the deep freeze. What the world's leaders and diplomats suddenly realised was that the Security Council had been, as it were, cryogenically preserved: it was still alive. It could be brought out, warmed up, and get back in business.

In speech after speech, Hawke stressed the importance of the reborn United Nations, telling parliament that now,

> with real hope in our hearts, [the UN can become] an effective international system against aggression; a system in which all countries, great and small, play a part. If we fail in this obligation, in this the first test of the new international order after the Cold War, the consequences for our medium- and long-term security and for that of many other countries are deeply disturbing.

Saddam ignored the UN and began looting Kuwait.

Bush rang Hawke to say he was having trouble persuading the Canadian Prime Minister, Brian Mulroney, to agree to support intervention because of Canada's huge wheat exports to Iraq. Hawke replied, 'We've got a bloody big wheat trade with Iraq too. Leave Brian to me. He's my mate.' He rang Mulroney and told him Australia was prepared to sacrifice its wheat trade and Mulroney agreed his country should also be willing to make the sacrifice. He told Hawke that Australia's action would be helpful in persuading his Cabinet to support the Bush initiative.

On 6 August the Security Council ordered a global trade embargo against Iraq. White said, 'Bob was very careful to make sure the Canadians were taking the same view we were, so if we lost the market, they would too.' A few days later, on 9 August, Hawke discussed Australia's other options with Gareth Evans and Robert Ray, privately giving thanks that Ray had refused to forgo the Defence job. He was already across the issue and told Hawke three ships could leave for the Persian Gulf within three days to help enforce the trade embargo. Early next morning Hawke rang President Bush to confirm Australia's support.

On 11 September 1990, the American President announced that he would use force if necessary to remove the Iraqi army from Kuwait. Saddam responded by seizing all the foreigners in Iraq and Kuwait as hostages: he would use them, he said, as human shields in front of targets that might be attacked by a UN force. Hawke said, 'There were about 150 Australians in Iraq and Kuwait and their safety became a constant anxiety for me and the government.'

Hawke, passionately interested in the Middle East since the 1960s, eager to help edge Israelis and Palestinians towards peace, often seemed like a temperance worker patiently explaining to a drunk the logic of teetotalism. Devoted to logical argument himself, he had not been able to accept that these lands that gave birth to civilisation, to writing, to all the prophets from Abraham to Mohammed, to the mystery of Golgotha, are indeed unique and intoxicated with something more powerful than the humdrum of enlightened self-interest. At first he could not believe that Saddam, who had a case to argue for his claim on Kuwaiti territory, could not be persuaded it was in his best interests to withdraw. Hawke was on good terms with the Crown Prince of Jordan, whom he thought might be able to act as a go-between. He talked it over with Bush, who agreed it was worth trying, and on 24 August Hawke rang Prince Hassan. The Prince was sympathetic but categoric. Saddam, he said, would not even consider the idea Hawke suggested: withdrawal, with the guarantee of an international tribunal to hear his claim against Kuwait.

Saddam was highly intelligent and cunning, but he was primitive. He could not imagine the world outside himself; he did not understand what a superpower is, or what it can and will do.

For three months, feverish international diplomacy ruled the news media while in the party and the Caucus there were heated, sometimes tearful, debates. It was only fifteen years since the Vietnam War had ended—objection to that war being the very reason many people had joined the Labor Party. The horror and shame of it still carried a weight in the community and even more in the party. 'It was a hard sell in the party,' White recalled.

> We were the Vietnam generation. We were very suspicious about the use of armed force. We were very suspicious about the idea of going off and fighting other people's wars. In the debates in the office, for example, Stephen Mills, a very dear friend of mine, represented the 'Hang on! Let's not get carried away' argument. A sociological thing happens when people start discussing the use of armed force. It's not like putting on a new tax, or changing the qualifications for the single mothers' allowance. Deep emotions get involved; the back of the brain starts to take over. It gets pretty blokeish very fast. The capacity to stand back, to make a rational, structured, logical, contestable argument as to whether this is a good idea or not quickly goes out the window.

The Left in Australia and throughout the world was beside itself with distress: over renewed militarism and the possibility of another war, over the sanctions (causing Iraqi people starvation, the death of Iraqi babies), over the hostages, over the idea that the world's response was 'just about oil'. Australian's most famous historian, Emeritus Professor Manning Clark, deemed a living national treasure, an icon of the middle class and the soft Left, wrote an article in the *Sydney Morning Herald* saying that Saddam Hussein and George Bush were just two people with a difference of opinion. Clark's own opinion carried great clout. There was intense fear, especially in Israel and among diaspora Jews, that, if under attack, Saddam would use chemical weapons against Israel. He had used them against his own people and against Iranians and he was already having Kuwaitis raped, tortured and murdered. A constant stream of well-meaning people travelled to Baghdad to beg for the hostages' release. Saddam would release a few but that, as Hawke said, 'only made the situation more unbearable for the ones left behind'. The Australian government refused to negotiate over hostages, which, within the party and Caucus was further cause for grief.

By mid-November Hawke realised war was probably inevitable. He believed that, for three reasons, Australia had to take part. First, it was unacceptable for a country, unprovoked, to invade another. Second, he, like many other leaders around the world, fervently wanted to support the UN in its renaissance as an international force for justice and stability. Third was his support for the Australia–United States alliance. But of the three, the UN was by far the most important, for it was the hope of the future for a civilised world.

On 29 November the Security Council passed Resolution 678, which gave Saddam until 15 January 1991 to withdraw from Kuwait. This was the War Resolution. After that, member states were authorised to use 'all necessary means' to reverse the invasion. The same day Hawke called together Robert Ray, Gareth Evans, Paul Keating—who since the election had been deputy Prime Minister as well as Treasurer—and John Button, leader of the government in the Senate. They were to agree on a position to be put to Cabinet. White said,

> It's hard now [in 2009] when we seem to send off troops at the drop of a hat, to remember what it was like for Australia to be a country that believed you didn't ever use armed force. But that was the country we were.

After Vietnam there had been a taboo on sending forces abroad. White added, 'A lot of people, including a lot of people in government, just didn't think it would happen: *we don't go to war any more.*'

Hawke was saying publicly that Saddam was a tyrant and as evil as Hitler—but it was difficult for Australians to believe in the evil of tyranny since, refugees aside, relatively few had experienced it. Two generations had grown to adulthood convinced evil was a construct designed to enforce obedience to Christian theology. The Left, the Centre Left and many others thought Hawke was blustering about Saddam. White recalled,

> People hung on to the thought that maybe Saddam is not that bad. Because if you believed he was, it was very hard not to believe that going to war was the right thing. And people didn't want to believe that, so they looked for ways to avoid it, and when people are looking for ways to avoid the obvious they'll believe the most remarkable things.

Hawke was confident a war against Iraq would be easy to win because the United States and its NATO allies had been planning to fight the Soviet Union on the north German plain for about forty years: they had forces specifically designed for such a war. The Iraqi forces were poor versions of Soviet divisions, and they were deployed on the flat, treeless landscape of a desert, the optimum terrain for tanks. White recalled,

> A lot of people said, 'Oh this will be a disaster: it will be like Vietnam again.' And I said, 'No it won't! There are some battles the United States are very good at'—and this was one of them.

The ultimate strategic objective could be defined in very precise military terms; there was a direct connection between the military operation and the strategic goal. 'The big proviso,' White said, 'was: "*Don't cross the border, guys*—because then you'll end up governing Iraq, and Iraq is inherently ungovernable unless you're prepared to operate in the same way as Saddam Hussein."'

Despite the prospect for military success the government could not be confident of avoiding casualties. Its ships could be blown up by mines in the Persian Gulf (as one American ship was), or bombed by the Iraqi air force. When a ship is hit it burns furiously and casualties are high. Gareth Evans' Department of Foreign Affairs and Trade had written a position paper for him with the opening sentence, 'The worst possible outcome would be to find the international community drawn into a conflict in Kuwait.' White argued to him that this was the second-worst outcome: the worst would be for Saddam to end up owning Kuwait. Evans agreed, but remained ambivalent and anxious about the use of force. Being in the role of peacemaker in Cambodia, he was in an invidious position. Button was opposed, but agreed to keep his opposition to himself. Hawke, Ray and Keating—after an initial objection 'What has the United States done for us?' to which Hawke replied this was about the UN, not the United States—were in favour. White recalled,

The politics were *interesting* because the Keating challenge was already in the air—but once national security comes on the agenda, the prime minister becomes a king. That has to be noted. No matter how strong your Defence minister is, this is one issue that absolutely must be owned by the prime minister.

Ray wanted two more ships to be sent. Hawke overruled the idea. 'We had good reason to expect that Iraq's seemingly formidable air forces would pose a serious threat to our ships,' White said.

A tormenting period for Keating had begun. In June 1990, he had seemed to have a headlock on the Prime Minister. Now Hawke was the king and the undisputed centre of power in government. A whole new aspect of his leadership abilities emerged, and by early October he had reversed by 14 per cent Hewson's former lead over him and was once again preferred prime minister. The Coalition, however, led Labor by 10 per cent.

Paul Kelly noted, 'Keating was burning with frustration, fearful that Hawke would repudiate his Kirribilli pact, yet resentful that if he became prime minister he might inherit only the ashes of an era.'[14]

In October 1990, Hawke had told Keating he wanted to stay in his job until the South African issue was settled, at the CHOGM to be held in one year's time. Keating had said *he* needed time to change his image in the electorate, and October 1991 would allow him very little leeway. Hawke had been unmoved. Keating had then approached both Kelty and Abeles to ask them to pressure Hawke. Pressure is the least effective way of influencing Hawke, as it stimulates his formidable will power. He had begun to harden further against Keating and a cat-and-mouse game of leak and counter-leak from their offices began.

Meanwhile, the economy was sliding into recession.

On 29 November 1990, the national statistics revealed a second quarter of negative growth and Keating, in a moment of lamentable political judgment, issued a press statement announcing, 'this is a recession that Australia had to have'. Keating and Hawke had repeatedly promised there would be no recession. In one phrase the Treasurer and deputy Prime Minister presented himself to the voters as a heartless deceiver, uncaring for those who were losing their jobs and businesses. Hawke publicly apologised for the recession, repeatedly expressing remorse. Keating refused to do so, further entrenching the findings of Labor and other polling that, while brilliant and exciting, he was considered arrogant and nasty. Hawke had been spending a lot of time in public and at Labor branches, where he was constantly hearing complaints against Keating. There was a strong 'Keating has to go' sentiment in both the electorate and the party. Much of Keating's problem as a politician was that he was introverted; while with intimates he was warm, affectionate and funny, with strangers he was shy and even nervous. A journalist recalled walking through a crowd with him, Keating muttering, 'Don't make eye contact! Don't look at them. Just keep going.' Hawke, by contrast, was forever eager to meet people, to stop, shake hands, tell a joke, ruffle the hair of a child. He loved 'the mob' and exuded the disarming conviction that every stranger would like him. Many people who liked neither him nor his government found themselves apologising for not voting Labor and asking for a photograph with him. If encountering outright hostility Hawke would react with a tomcat's glare, and stalk off, lashing his tail.

To preserve his claim on The Lodge, Keating needed to reserve his position on the war carefully in case it turned out disastrously. He needed to be able to claim that he had been against it all along. Although he and his staffer, Don Russell, denied it later, White says 'Keating expressed significant reservations'.

White kept a daily diary of events; he was in the room when Keating spoke, as was Russell, and was 'paying careful attention, because this seemed pretty relevant to me', he said. Keating would later claim that Hawke was indecisive, and that he, Keating, had had to push Hawke into the war. White, who likes Keating, later spoke to him about these assertions, 'and what he had to say was quite profane'.

On 3 December 1990, Hawke consulted the Caucus leaders and 'received solid support', he wrote in his memoirs. He had spent hours, from night into the morning, reassuring them that this war would in no way be a rerun of Vietnam, explaining that 144 nations supported Resolution 678, that forty of them had agreed to provide, or to help sustain, military forces deployed in the Gulf, that these included NATO countries, former Soviet-bloc countries, Arab states, Muslim nations, Pacific nations—indeed people from every inhabited continent. He pointed out that the centrepiece of the United Nations Charter was the collective use of force in extreme cases where no other way was left to punish and defeat aggression. The Left, and more especially the Centre Left, Hayden stalwarts who had never really forgiven Hawke and were now solidly behind Keating's leadership ambitions, remained deeply troubled at the prospect of war.

That afternoon Cabinet agreed Australia must support Resolution 678 and the next day Hawke made a second statement to parliament on the Gulf crisis, noting:

> For much of its one hundred years the ALP has struggled to ensure that Australia's armed forces are not used to fight other peoples' wars. In the 1930s that led Labor to turn its back on aggression ... But Labor learned the lessons of that mistake.

Parliamentary debate went on for days.

White said, 'I was struck that right from the beginning Hawke had a framework for thinking about these things that was very clear.' That framework was sophisticated, and included the possibility that the United States, having worked through the UN, might peel off and rush into Iraq. 'That was a huge concern for Bob,' White said. The United States was already on oil life support, and had been for more than a decade. Saddam's flashing of a blade near the superpower's carotid artery made the American response unpredictable.

By December enormous numbers of armed forces from all over the world were gathering on Kuwait's borders. The terrible days of waiting began.

For Keating, too, they were days of waiting that became unbearable. On 6 December his head of department, Chris Higgins, a man of whom he was very fond, and who was just a few months older than Keating, suddenly died. The following evening Keating was to address the annual Press Club dinner. He arrived in an emotional state, a Hamlet mood, and after a few jokes, launched into a rambling but fascinating *tour d'horizon* of how he saw the world, Australia, leadership and Australia's leaders. 'Leadership is not about being popular, it's about being right ... The trouble with Australia is that we've never had [a great leader]. We've never had one leader, not one, and it shows.' Curtin, he said, was a 'trier'; Chifley 'a plodder'. He ended with a lightly masked appeal to the 120 journalists, spellbound at what a great story they had, to support *him* against Hawke. He had raised to an art the management of economics and politics, he said. His economics was a pure, consummate form devoid of personal content, to be admired for its astounding intelligence and the beauty of its craftsmanship. He was, he said, the Placido Domingo of Australian politics. Everyone knew he considered the Spaniard far superior to Hawke's favourite tenor, the lovable fat Italian, Luciano Pavarotti.

Keating's speech was off the record. Next morning Hawke received a full report of it. He had believed for many years that Keating not only did not love the Australian people, as he, Hawke, did, but actually rather despised them. The Treasurer's speech demonstrated that. It condescended to Australia as a second-rate country.

Keating's timing could scarcely have been worse. Hawke was himself nursing a private grief: his greatest love, his father Clem, who had suffered a minor stroke earlier in the year, was fading towards death, while Hawke was emotionally keyed up to shoulder the burden of sending scores of young Australians into harm's way with the distinct possibility of some returning in coffins. Curtin, who drove himself to death with worry over the men he sent to be slaughtered, was in Hawke's mind constantly. Keating had been dodging and weaving in his commitment to the war; his gratuitous scorn for Curtin (which he had absorbed from Jack Lang, who hated Curtin and was expelled from the party by Curtin) drove Hawke to fury. By implication Keating also scorned the ALP. As Hawke interpreted it, not only did Keating lust for his job, he was also attempting to destroy Hawke's place in history by rewriting it, inserting his own name into reforms that had been Hawke's. There was plenty of evidence for Hawke to point to about Keating's rewriting of history. He had been busily doing so with the press gallery for years. *And he didn't even love and respect Australia*, it now appeared. He had virtually said so himself: if he could not become prime minister, he would decamp and live in Paris.

The Sunday newspapers carried versions of the speech. All the professionals—politicians and gallery journalists—recognised that the Hawke–Keating team was now a façade.

On Monday morning Keating publicly performed a mea culpa, saying he had intended no disrespect to past or present Labor leaders. Headlines read, 'Keating Speech Puts New Strain on Ties with Hawke', 'Can They Last?' and 'Labor's Love Lost'. On the afternoon of 10 December, Hawke called Keating in for a long discussion, during which he hammered Keating on Curtin's greatness. It was left unspoken, but Keating knew Hawke now had no intention of abiding by the still-secret Kirribilli agreement. The next day Hawke made this clear to Keating when, in a press conference, he said he would stay on until the next election, and were he to win, would lead the party through that term: that is, he would be staying for another five years if the party wanted him.

It was Richardson, now fully rehearsed to the role he had chosen—a wolf in sheep's clothing—who had advised Hawke to make this statement, hoping, as he was to write in his autobiography, that it would be regarded as ridiculous by the media and bring discredit on the Prime Minister. He was not disappointed. The gallery, having accepted Keating's invitation to become participants in the question of leadership of the Labor Party, greeted Hawke's statement with supercilious smiles. By the end of the week the *Financial Review* carried a page-one story by Geoff Kitney that said,

> An important, unstated motivation for the Prime Minister's decision to commit himself to another five years as Labor leader appears to be a decision... that he now does not want... Mr Keating to be his successor. Senior Labor figures believe Mr Hawke has had a decisive change of mind... and that he no longer believes Mr Keating has the qualities of leadership that would make him a successful inheritor of his job.

Other headlines spoke of 'Richardson bid to heal rift'.

On 21 December, Clem Hawke said, 'I can't go yet. Bobby needs me.' But two days later he died. 'He just ran out of breath,'

Hawke said. He had flown as frequently as he could to Adelaide in the last weeks of Clem's life. On their final meeting, Clem had drawn from his old hand a gold signet ring and pressed it into his son's palm. Hawke slipped it on his little finger. He found the ring brought Clem's presence to him, and was a comfort in the harsh times that lay ahead.

The year 1990 had been a year of triumphs and setbacks: Labor had won an election against the odds and the ALP national conference had been a huge success, thanks largely to the efforts of Kim Beazley, who was as excellent in Transport and Communications as he had been in Defence. Against the gnashing teeth of his friend, Keating, for whom telecommunications had become a new passion, Beazley developed policies for opening the Australian telecommunications industry to competition—Keating wanted a much more dramatic scheme—and for the sale of Australian Airlines and 49 per cent of Qantas. In the Prime Minister's office, Beazley debated his telecommunications policy against the one Keating had designed, with Hawke adjudicating. Having won Hawke's endorsement, Beazley won Cabinet approval, then had both policies accepted by the national conference and steered them through the House and the Senate. The sale of a new telecommunications licence (and of the airlines) added $5 billion to the government's coffers and took place without a single day lost from industrial action by the telecommunications unions. But for each silver lining there was a cloud. There had been a dreadful brawl in Cabinet about telecommunications—Keating flung his pencil on the table, swore at his colleagues and stalked out, Robert Ray jeering after him, 'Spit the dummy' (Jack Lang had always said if you couldn't win a debate, then wreck it)—and the Treasurer's behaviour in Cabinet was so widely reported it overshadowed the reform itself. The Liberal Party was now united. And the government won scant plaudits for airline privatisation, although this had entailed the Herculean task of overturning a venerable plank in the party platform and would save taxpayers hundreds of millions of dollars.

Above all, the economic downturn now darkened everything: the vaunted 1.6 million new jobs of one year earlier had evaporated and unemployment was approaching 10 per cent. Businesses were going bankrupt; families were losing their houses. The doyen of the gallery, Laurie Oakes, had an article in the Christmas issue of the *Bulletin* with the double-entendre headline, 'Wanted: a new tenor'.

Meanwhile 100 000 armed men and women had already arrived in the Persian Gulf, ready to fight the first great conventional desert war since Rommel and El Alamein.

10

AS THE NEW YEAR BEGAN, Saddam released all his hostages. He was still plundering Kuwait.

Frantic international diplomacy in the first two weeks of January 1991 came to nothing and at 4 p.m. on 16 January, Australian eastern daylight-saving time, the UN deadline expired. War was expected at any moment. The government's popularity sank to 32 per cent, its lowest point ever. People were frightened of a war and about the economy. Melbourne, where the Left was strongest, held a huge 'Save Australia' rally, evocative of the rallies against the Vietnam War. Hawke called a Cabinet meeting to tell his colleagues that hostilities would begin within twenty-four hours. Early next morning the head of Australian forces in the Gulf rang to alert the Prime Minister that the attack would start that day. At 9.50 a.m. President Bush rang Hawke to say that within an hour action would be underway. Hawke then authorised the Australian chief of the defence force, General Gration, to signal to the Australian ships that they were to join operations against Iraq in accordance with Resolution 678. An hour later he called a press conference to remind the nation why, for the first time since 1972, Australian forces were fighting in a foreign land. He finished by saying,

'War is full of terrible uncertainty.' Having praised the serving men and women, he concluded, 'We know they will serve bravely and well, and we hope, above all, that they will return safely home.'

Within hours demonstrators were on the streets and by the weekend there were protest rallies in all the capital cities and many provincial centres. The Anglican and Catholic churches were moderate in their response, but Sir Ronald Wilson, President of the National Assembly of the Uniting Church, declared, 'This is a senseless war. History will condemn us for having allowed national pride and self-interest—although hidden behind fine words about right and wrong—to dictate the course of events.' The general secretary of the Australian Council of Churches, the Reverend Mr David Gill, said the war was 'pure madness with no moral justification ... the most monumental stupidity'.

Failure goes with the job of politics and all great politicians must be unafraid of it. They hold to their own judgment with intransigence, convinced that in the end history will vindicate them. The balance to this is humility, their regret for terrible actions. Hawke had no second thoughts about going to war. He was deeply worried about the possible loss of young lives.

The CNN version of what was happening in the Gulf was full of hype about the destruction of Saddam's weaponry, but Hawke had intelligence that the television reports were incorrect and Iraq's Scud missiles were still intact. Saddam had let it be known they were equipped with chemical warheads. The next day Iraq launched eight scuds at Israel, none chemically armed. The world held its breath, awaiting the Israeli response—which might, Hawke wrote, 'rupture the coalition by alienating the Arab and Muslim members'. When it was clear that Israel had stalled—temporarily, at least, its policy of massive retaliation—and that the coalition would hold, Hawke recalled parliament in the third week of January.

Ten

In half a century of parliamentary debates, those of 21 and 22 January 1991 were among the finest. The parliamentarians spoke with sincerity, thoughtfulness and deep feeling about the violence and turmoil that again confronted a world so recently liberated from the tensions of the Cold War. For once Hawke did not detest the House as a game of charades. He gave his best parliamentary performance, speaking at length, his conviction untainted by point-scoring or rodomontade, unfazed by a group of demonstrators who screamed at him from the Visitors' Gallery. Hugh White recalled, 'The parliamentary atmospherics were remarkable. We in the office were watching the debate *to see how our side voted.*'

Despite Hawke's hours of reassurance to Caucus, there was still no certainty that the Left would support Resolution 678 for Australia to continue in the war. Left and Centre Left support almost collapsed when the Americans asked for twenty-five skin divers to clear mines. White said, 'The Americans were planning a massive amphibious assault by marines on the Kuwaiti coast and there were a lot of mines around. The US doesn't have very good mine countermeasure capacity, but we do.' A few years earlier Saddam had mined the Gulf, endangering ships carrying oil from Iran. Australian divers had cleared the mines with an expertise the American navy noted well.

White said,

> I remember getting a request from the Americans and talking to Robert [Ray], saying, 'Look—they are not just trying this on. This is a serious operational request. They really need our guys.' Robert was persuaded and he took it to Bob who said, 'Yep. OK. We'll send them.' They had to be based on American ships. Just twenty-five divers—but it almost undid the whole deal with the Caucus.

Throughout his speech to parliament, Hawke had stressed the importance of the UN members acting in unison. Hewson, the leader of the Opposition (whom Hawke had invited to accompany him to Gallipoli nine months earlier), strongly supported the Prime Minister's motion, saying,

> that Gallipoli pilgrimage was one of the most moving experiences of my life ... and taught me a lot about my country. Throughout our history we have been a genuinely peaceful people, but we have never been a pacifist people. We have been a proudly independent country, but never a neutral one.

Hewson's response was an enormous relief to the government, which had been concerned that, once again, the Opposition might seek a way to attack Labor as not tough enough on national security.

More than 100 parliamentarians spoke over two days. The most poignant moment came when Gerry Hand, leader of the Left, announced in a shaking voice, 'I support the resolution,' and began to weep.

No vote was needed and only one man, Ted Mack, the Independent member for North Sydney, demanded that Hansard record him as opposed.

The air war in the Gulf concluded quickly and by mid-February the land war was about to begin. There were no Australian casualties. White recalled,

> A bizarre situation arose in which it appeared there might be a peace deal on the table, brokered by the Russians, which the Americans weren't prepared to accept. Now this was a fascinating and marvellous study of confusion in policy making: Brent Scowcroft,

the President's national security adviser, rang Bob at The Lodge in the middle of the night. They had a conversation which, when Bob recounted it to us half an hour later—at 4 a.m.—just didn't make any sense. I phoned Michael Cook, head of the Office of National Assessment, and told him what Scowcroft had said to the PM. He said, 'What!' So he rang the [United States] National Security Council to say, 'Your boss has just said to my boss . . .' and they said, 'What!' And this went round and round in international phone calls—there were no emails in those days—and we all spoke elliptically, because we didn't know who was listening in. It got very confusing. For a while it seemed that the US was putting to us the proposition that they were not going to pay any attention to the possibility of a peace deal, and that even if Saddam said he was now prepared to withdraw, the Americans would expel Iraq from Kuwait anyway. It seemed to us, on good grounds, they were saying, 'Bugger Saddam: whatever he promises, we're going ahead with the land war.' And what was interesting to me was that Bob was *absolutely* prepared to walk up to these blokes and say: 'No. In that circumstance, you will lose our support.'

Another idea to which Hawke was opposed was 'going on to Baghdad'. First, such an attack would destroy the UN foundation for the war, which in turn would destroy the objective of strengthening the UN. Second, Hawke and his office had made the judgment that invading Iraq would be simply stupid.

'In the end,' White said,

> that was a view shared by Bush, Colin Powell [chairman of the American joint chiefs of staff] and, interestingly,

Dick Cheney [American Secretary for Defense]. We discussed in the office the possibility of the US going off on a hay-making expedition to Baghdad and Bob was absolutely clear that we would say, 'We're not with you on that.' For us, the UN concern was more important than the alliance. It's hard to imagine now, because those hopes have been washed away into history.

In the *Bulletin* edition at the end of January, Laurie Oakes, who had been a leader of the press gallery's chorus for a change to Keating, wrote,

> Since hostilities began, Hawke has given some strong media performances. Particularly in his first news conference ... the Prime Minister struck exactly the right note—authoritative, determined, but suitably grave, and obviously affected by the decision ... Gone was the sense of drift which had fed the speculation about a leadership change.

Hawke's speech to parliament, Oakes said,

> was one of the most carefully crafted and persuasively argued of his career ... It was strong, uncompromising—the speech of a leader ... Keating in contrast, did not bother to break his holiday to attend the final Cabinet briefing before Australians were officially committed to the war—strange, some Caucus members thought, for a man who is deputy Prime Minister and who has leadership ambitions.

The headline of Oakes' piece was 'Keating: our first Gulf casualty?'

Ten

On the last day of January, Hawke called Keating in for a further discussion of the leadership, during which they argued over which of them would be able to revive the party's chances at the next election. Hawke's popularity had shot up. He asserted he had a better chance than Keating, who was very unpopular. He pointed out that Hewson was a greenhorn, with little idea of how intense the heat of a national election campaign could be, while he, Hawke, bore the scars from campaigns going back to 1963. Keating asserted Hawke had no chance, whereas he, Keating, might have a chance. Hawke dismissed his argument as delusion. By this stage Hawke considered Keating's desperation for the leadership had made him slightly mad. Keating held a similar view of the protagonist.

The stalemate made one thing certain: Hawke believed his promise to the people to stay on and fight the next election was a matter of honour of a higher order than his promise to Keating made two years earlier in Kirribilli. He could not keep both promises, therefore he would keep the more important one.

Keating was furious. Believing himself to be the energy source that drove the government, the anodic electrode that is gradually devoured, Keating's sense of being used up by the dynamic of the relationship was revealed soon afterwards when he lamented his fate to Paul Kelly, who wrote:

> Keating never recovered from the war. He complained later that his support had peaked before Christmas 1990 ... 'The war changed the thinking about my leadership from being an expectation to an act of sedition,' Keating bemoaned. As 1991 advanced Keating drew his own deadline—a challenge before the winter recess ... [he] was hellbent upon a showdown in the current term.[1]

The trauma for the Labor Party was that it had two leaders in one government. Keating, like Hawke, was convinced in every cell of his body that he was meant to be prime minister, impregnated with the idea of something within himself that he must bring into the light. Like a woman in childbirth, he had no choice in the matter: the man had to give birth to The Man. Or die in the attempt.

Keating's political mentor, Jack Lang, had wired into his protégé the idea that he had to move fast. It seems Keating had developed an image of himself as prime minister by the age of forty-five; his emotions, his intellect, his physical stamina focused on that ideal. When it was denied him in 1988, as with an athlete denied the race for which he has trained for a lifetime, a sense of debilitation began to engulf him. But in 1991, as distinct from 1988, there was a significant difference. Keating had a skilled and eager new coach. He had Graham Richardson. It was Richardson who would tell Keating and his team when to rush forward, when to pause, when to strive again. Many months, perhaps years earlier, Keating had told Richardson about the Kirribilli agreement, one of a number of people Keating told. It was something Richardson was keeping in reserve, to be used at the right moment.

Keating had to act before winter 1991, otherwise he would have to frame and sell the next Budget, be Treasurer for another year with an economy in deep recession for which he was much to blame.

The war in the Gulf meanwhile was moving swiftly to a UN victory. By 28 February it was over, but not before Saddam had ordered all Kuwait's oil wells set on fire. Huge, pungent black clouds billowed for weeks from the well heads as millions of tonnes of oil burned. All of Kuwait and some neighbouring countries became covered in oily black dust, as if hell had opened its terrible mouth and roared from beneath the earth. With his air force vanished and his army in tatters, President Saddam Hussein announced a week of jubilation to celebrate his amazing and blessed victory over the United States and the rest of the world. Truly, he declared, Almighty God, The Beneficent, The Merciful, had shone His face upon him.

Hawke remarked that God must be very confused, since He was known to be fighting on the UN side as well.

With the war over, the Prime Minister refocused his attention on the economic reforms with which he hoped to crown his fourth term in office.

In July 1990, in a speech to the Press Club, Hawke had launched a concept titled 'New Federalism'. He wanted to establish in the public's mind how inefficient and conflicted Australia was in its duplication of services and regulations. He told the gathered journalists,

> Schools in different states have different minimum starting ages, and different patterns of [primary and secondary] schooling ... different curricula and different ways of assessing Year 12 students ... Lawyers and doctors and other professionals may have qualifications from the best universities ... skilled tradesmen may have the finest on-the-job experience—but to work outside their home state they need a licence from a state licensing board.

The rail system was not integrated, there were six different sizes of loading gauge, ten different engineering standards for basic rail trade, products in one state needed relabelling to be sold in another, daylight saving started on one date in one state and another elsewhere, and so on and on in knots of red tape. In some states, margarine could only be sold in round tubs; in others, only in rectangular. There was not even a national electricity grid. There was no national water plan, or even a plan for managing the waters of the Murray–Darling basin, which Hawke had proposed before the 1990 election. He described much of the economy as 'Balkanised', but because of the federal system there was little his government could change without the agreement of the states.

The idea for reform had been presented to him by Mike Codd, the head of the Prime Minister and Cabinet Department, who had mulled over Commonwealth–state relations for more than twenty years (as had Hawke who, in his 1979 Boyer Lectures, had proposed abolishing the states).

Codd had been unable to snag the interest of John Gorton, Bill McMahon, Gough Whitlam or Malcolm Fraser in a reform that to those outside politics appears both necessary and virtuous. But good public policy and good politics do not necessarily mate, especially when good public policy may cause the government to lose the next election. The kilometres of red tape created jobs and power, some in the Commonwealth, most in the states. The Commonwealth would have to give up a portion of its power to win the states' agreement to change. This meant that federal parliamentarians—backbenchers, mostly—would be deprived of the privilege of announcing new playgrounds or swimming pools in their electorates and having their photographs in the local newspapers. In this lay danger for Hawke: the government was unpopular, unemployment was rising, and the backbenchers were nervous. Any move that would weaken their local appeal and thus reduce their chances for re-election could panic them.

Codd first put the proposition of Commonwealth–state reform to Hawke in 1987, on the Sunday after the election.

> Bob was attracted to it, and so was the political side of his office [but] he got back to me a week or two later to

say that having talked it through with his colleagues it was not a possibility in this term of government. There was too much else going on that would be difficult for the Labor Party to come to terms with—uranium mining was one of the problems—and I should bring it back to him at a more appropriate time.

Codd believed that Keating and Button had opposed the idea. His paper sat in a drawer for three more years, until the Sunday after the 1990 election. 'And this time Bob said, "Right. We're going to do this!" And away we went.'

A Commonwealth–state steering committee was set up to write proposals for an initial Special Premiers' Conference to be held at the end of October 1990 in Brisbane.

Nick Greiner, Premier of New South Wales, recalled his first Premiers' Conference, in 1988, as 'old nonsense'. He said,

> We—premiers and our Treasurers—all stayed at the Hyatt Hotel in Canberra and in the middle of the night someone from the Commonwealth would put a letter under your door, telling you what you were being offered. And I remember [Premier] Robin Gray from Tasmania, who was a stirrer, saying to me next morning, 'Why don't you threaten to walk out? That will get Hawkey going.' So I made the first statement and said, 'Well, if this is all we get, Prime Minister, we may as well go home now.' Bob had a look on his face that said, *Who is this kid?* He's only just arrived and he's carrying on.' Anyway, we had the usual toing and froing—but the reality was that Commonwealth–state relations were a joke. There was no single direction, no notion of what was good for the nation. We'd argue over money and at the end we'd come out and say, 'Well, the

Commonwealth won't give us enough, so we're going to have to put up taxes.' We could tax cigarettes and stuff. Whichever party you were in there was a standard state response: *blame Canberra*. It was completely dysfunctional, both financially, and in health and education. To this day [late 2009] the Commonwealth has 300 people in Canberra playing around with education, but they run no schools at all. There was duplication—even triplication, when local councils got involved.

Since World War II the Commonwealth had collected all major taxes—personal income tax and business tax—and had the money. It called the tune. But the conditions it imposed on the states in 'tied grants' made it difficult, even impossible, for the states to manage themselves financially.

By 1990 Greiner was the only non-Labor premier and unusual in that he was not a knee-jerk decentralist. 'I was actually interested in getting national outcomes,' he said. 'And Bob was not the normal, centralist Labor prime minister, but interested in getting a workable compromise. Most of the Labor premiers would go along with Bob, if I did. So there was a unique opportunity for reform.' The electoral cycle was also benevolent, for aside from some local councils, there was no election due anywhere in Australia for at least eighteen months. Greiner said, 'I thought, and I'm sure Bob thought, "The bloody Federation is going to be 100 years old in 2000 and the notion that you don't change the way we manage ourselves is bizarre."'

Hawke established a secretariat of federal public servants, each with a state counterpart, led by Helen Williams from his department. Williams is one of Australia's most outstanding bureaucrats. An economist, she was the first woman, aside from typists, to be employed in Treasury and the first to break the glass ceiling and become a departmental head (Education, in 1985). She is slender and softly spoken, with an aura of gentle, civilised wisdom. Greiner recalled,

> There was a group of public servants that developed a very unusual camaraderie. They all felt, 'Gee—we're driving some real reform.' They thought it was fantastic that they were being given a chance to do something new and different, rather than just incrementally changing things, the way things normally change.

The group called themselves the Piglets, because they were the offspring of the HOGs, the heads of government: Prime Minister, premiers and Treasurers. Williams recalled that before the Brisbane conference, 'There was a buzz in the air, there was excitement. We really felt there was a different way of working together, a different partnership, a real window of opportunity that we all felt we could grab.'

Codd said,

> What was to be put at the conference was quite wide-ranging and the scope for the premiers to get bogged down in one issue or another was significant. How to manage the meeting was a huge challenge. Kevin Rudd was advising Wayne Goss [Queensland's Premier] and Gary Sturgess was Nick Greiner's adviser.

Sturgess was another outstandingly effective state-level public servant, known for his forceful personality, verve and drive. Some of the premiers disliked what they saw as his arrogance, condescending airs and self-appointed role as policy savant. Codd said,

I knew Rudd and Sturgess, and I knew they would want to put their own views forward. They were keen and enthusiastic for something to be done, but they wanted their own model. I could see it would end up in turgid debate. So I actually drafted a press release before the meeting and suggested to Bob that he have a private dinner with just the premiers, at which he would give them each a copy of the press release and try to get their agreement to it before the meeting even started. And that's what happened. The advisers were furious.

Another person who was at least miffed was Paul Keating, who had not been included in the dinner the night before. His discomfit at the press conference when the joint communiqué was announced was not reported by the media. Codd said, 'But you could see it in his body language.'

The conference was a huge success. There was progress on a wide front, from uniform vehicle regulation to an intergovernmental agreement on the environment. At the press conference, Greiner said it was 'the most constructive thing that I've done in two and three-quarter years as premier'.

The Victorian premier, Joan Kirner, a Centre Left politician who did not much care for Hawke, said, 'May I ... Prime Minister, again thank you for having the vision and the leadership and the patience to enable this conference to happen.'

The states were delighted that, almost immediately, they would be getting a new income stream, thanks to a correction of 'vertical fiscal imbalance'. This is the gap between the money raised by the states and what they spend. In his initial announcement of his New Federalism in July 1990, Hawke had announced that the Commonwealth, as a gesture of good faith towards his New Federalism, would forgo bank account debits tax to the states. The Brisbane conference confirmed it, adding $385 million to state revenues. Keating had worked with Hawke on the vertical fiscal imbalance proposal, but by the time of the Brisbane conference, Codd noticed, especially at the press conference, 'Keating was a reluctant participant.'

Like all heads of the Prime Minister and Cabinet Department, Codd had a good political eye. He recognised then or soon afterwards that Keating could engineer from these proposals a battle favourable to himself in his struggle against Hawke.

In the same press conference, Nick Greiner warned, 'The Empire will strike back.' He was referring to the various state authorities that controlled utilities: water and electricity, for example. 'I was trying to make the point that all the people whose power was going to be affected if you moved to a national approach were not going to just roll over to have their tummies tickled,' he said.

Nevertheless the mood was almost euphoric and two further special conferences were scheduled for mid-1991 and late 1991 to consolidate progress. New Federalism had a new name and status: the Council of Australian Governments, COAG.

Besides his planned reforms of Commonwealth–state relations, which—as events were to show—became, mostly, casualties in the war of succession, Hawke had a second major reform for his fourth term. More than two years earlier, in October 1989, Ross Garnaut, by then a professor at the Australian National University, had completed a report Hawke had commissioned from him. The full title was *A Report for the Prime Minister and the Minister for Foreign Affairs and Trade: Australia and the North-east Asian Ascendancy.* Garnaut had prepared it with the assistance of another very highly respected Australian National University economist, Dr Peter Drysdale. Their research was a prescient analysis of where the countries of north-east Asia, China in particular, would be in the future, and how their arousal after centuries of economic slumber would affect Australia. But because the economy was 'a bloody runaway beast' in 1989, because an election would be held in 1990 and because there was a war in 1991, Hawke kept the report, and policy recommendations based on it, under wraps until he had some clear air. He chaired the Structural Adjustment Committee (SAC) that, taking the report as its premise, worked out policy options for the nation. The report established Garnaut as the *éminence grise* of Australia's economic reform.

On 12 March 1991, as soon as Saddam was off the front pages, Hawke made an economic statement, based on Garnaut's and the SAC's work, that was, arguably, the most important of his term in office. Called 'Building a Competitive Australia', it recommended further dismantling of Australian protectionism to ready the country for the challenge of north-east Asia rising. Back in 1984, after conferring with Hawke and Treasury, John Button had put an end to protectionism in the motor vehicle industry and since then quotas on steel imports, white goods and some heavy engineering products had been removed. Hawke's March statement announced a brave new Australia of free trade. John Hyde, the Liberal intellectual, described it as 'an impeccable statement of economic principle'.[2]

Hawke, reaffirming his government's intention to open the Australian economy to the world, told parliament:

> The most powerful spur to greater competitiveness is further tariff reduction. Tariffs have been one of the abiding features of the Australian economy. Since Federation ... the supposed virtues of this protection became deeply embedded in the psyche of the nation. But what was the result? Inefficient industries that could not compete overseas. And higher prices for consumers, and higher costs.

Ten

Hawke believed the new policy would give body to his announcement a few months earlier, at the launch of the 1990 election campaign, that Australia should become 'the clever country', a phrase that John Dawkins had coined.

Next day Ross Gittins, a respected economic commentator, wrote in the *Sydney Morning Herald*,

> In the depths of this recession, Bob Hawke has not only resisted the temptation to reverse the phased tariff reductions he began in 1988, he has extended and hastened them. Rightly or wrongly—I think rightly—the government is sticking to its guns.

Hewson, who agreed with the policy, tried to deflect interest in it and stir up trouble by asserting on 14 March that there was a 'leadership vacuum' in the federal government. It was known that Richardson had opposed Hawke in Cabinet over the statement.

On 15 March, Peter Hartcher, political commentator for the *Sydney Morning Herald*, wrote,

> the [decision] to cut industry protection in a single, breathtaking sweep ... was the most dramatic cut in protection that any Australian government has made ... Standard political theory would dictate that a government in the grips of a self-made recession, lagging in the opinion polls, and periodically unsettled by the prospect of a leadership challenge, should not take such profoundly controversial and potentially divisive decisions. But it is. Is this evidence of a wimpy government? Does it expose a weak-kneed Prime Minister? Does it demonstrate a leadership vacuum? No. It suggests a government which, despite eight tiring years in office,

is well able to make fundamental and hugely controversial decisions about the restructuring of the economy, even at the potential expense of a large loss of Labor's electoral support.

Paul Kelly, at this time a Keating supporter, later described the statement as 'an historic milestone ... [Hawke] demolished the edifice of Protection, the cornerstone of the post-federation Settlement. It is this decision, providing it sticks, which will guarantee that the direction of the 1990s maintains the course launched in the 1980s.' Kelly added, 'Hawke's announcement effectively terminated Australia's century of Protection ... [it] confirms the transformation in politics and economics which his government launched in the 1980s.'[3]

The March 1991 policy statement did stick. It is difficult to overstate its importance, for it transformed Australia's identity: as the country saw itself, as it was seen in the region, as it behaved in the world. Garnaut had recommended, and Hawke foreshadowed, among other things: faster cuts in protection, more Asian investment, new foreign-financed ports, foreign competition on shipping routes, complete aviation deregulation, more emphasis on age, skill and education in the immigration program, and compulsory Asian languages and history courses in schools. Garnaut's thesis was that closer economic integration between Australia and the Asian region would pay huge export dividends in primary products, secondary processing, and in services. Time has proved him correct. Hawke's acceptance of Garnaut's work and the 'Building a Competitive Australia' statement of March 1991 became granite in the foundation of a national prosperity that has stretched into the twenty-first century. Garnaut had no part in drawing up the statement and by now was outside the policy-making loop; he remarked with pleasure that the changes were bigger than the end of the British Corn Laws that had earned Peel and Cobden a dozen pages in high school history books. Hawke said, 'The Keating camp and the press gallery were saying I'd run out of puff for a fourth term. The March statement ['Building a Competitive Australia'] proves that is crap.'

In 2010 John Bowan remarked,

> Hawke is really the unsung hero of Australia's strong economy today, of how well we've come through the global financial crisis. It was his idea to establish a China trade, and to dismantle protectionism so that trade with Asia could flourish.

Meanwhile Hawke had another idea for increasing national wealth—but politically it was radioactive. He took seriously the environmentalist argument that humanity has only one home, which must be husbanded. He was aware that the storage of nuclear waste from power plants, weapons and medicinal manufacture, especially in Europe and the former Soviet Union, potentially endangered the planet. At the 1990 election he had announced that as part of being 'the clever country' Australia would establish a network of Co-operative Research Centres. This idea had come from Professor Ralph Slatyer, the chief scientist, a friend from Hawke's school days at Perth Modern. Hawke knew he could trust Slatyer with a delicate undertaking: the Prime Minister believed that Australia had the safest geological areas in the world for the long-term storage of nuclear waste. He asked Slatyer to confirm their existence, and that they were far from centres of population. Hawke's idea was that Australia could become the world's guardian of nuclear waste—for a price. Nations storing waste in Australia would have to pay rent and this rent could be an abundant national income. His estimate, confirmed by Slatyer's figures on the quantity of waste in storage and its annual increase, was hundreds of millions of dollars annually.

It would be hypothecated for education and health in Aboriginal communities, and for environmental protection. Slatyer reported back in 1991 that large areas of northern Western Australia and the Northern Territory were indeed so geologically stable and far from human habitation they would be ideally suited. Thanks to geology, remoteness and the political stability of Australia, these areas offered the safest planetary option for storing nuclear waste. The problem was emotional: the very people who proclaimed the importance of 'one world', when discretely sounded out, reverted to 'my backyard'. Environmental movement leaders warned Hawke that activists would instantly respond to his suggestion as an immoral outrage. From then until the present day he has quietly proposed it to ministers, shadow ministers and business groups, but no government, state or federal, has been willing to face the cannonade of hysteria that discussion of the idea will attract. Nuclear waste increases internationally year by year while the problem of long-term safe storage remains. But in February 2010, at a meeting of the American Association for the Advancement of Science in California, Finland announced that in 2020 it would open a deep geological repository for the disposal of spent nuclear fuel. Sweden announced it would do the same in 2023. European experts at the conference said, 'A growing consensus both in Europe and in other parts of the world is that deep geological disposal is the most appropriate solution for long-term management of spent fuel, high level waste, and other long-lived radioactive wastes.'

With the foreign war over and the sailors safely home, the civil war, which had been abandoned for the duration of hostilities in the Gulf, began heating up again.

Keating's generals, especially John Dawkins and Gary Punch from the New South Wales Right, had been working both the ministry and the backbench as hard as they could, but had been unable to gain enough numbers for a successful Keating challenge. Richardson was playing a duplicitous game. Anger and resentment had destroyed his affection for Hawke but he pretended to the Prime Minister to have recovered from his shock over the Communications and Defence jobs and was still Hawke's admirer. To others he presented himself as a man with only the welfare of the government at heart. Meanwhile, master tactician that he was, he bided his time on how to use the Kirribilli agreement against Hawke. Richardson had chosen for himself and would successfully fill the role of Judas.

In itself, he saw the political agreement reached at Kirribilli House in November 1988 as a piece of straw. But he recognised that in skilful hands it could be fashioned into a length of iron. It could become a bar with which to beat the Prime Minister over the head, and a lever to raise Keating to the moral high ground.

Having talked itself into the belief that the Prime Minister was lacking courage, the Keating camp still hoped to scare Hawke out of office. Peter Walsh, who had often found Hawke annoying for one reason or another, although he considered him the best prime minister of his political lifetime, had nicknamed him in a fit of pique, 'Old Jellyback'. This estimation of Hawke's strength of character was the one to which his enemies clung. Few understood that Hawke's emotional softness, his tendency to tears, his habit—maddening to staff and colleagues—of wanting to listen to the stories of ordinary Australians, was the saving balance in his character, a humility without which his alpha-male swagger would have made him unbearable. The electorate had come to admire him for being a leader unafraid of showing tender feelings. As Hazel said publicly several times, people respected a man who had the strength to cry.

While in Canberra internal Labor affairs were bad, in the west they were atrocious. A Royal Commission was underway to investigate the doings of WA Inc., the nexus between the state government and New Capitalists. Scandalous behaviour was being reported on a weekly, sometimes daily, basis. Respect for Labor in Western Australia plummeted, while the behaviour of its former leader, Brian Burke, once premier, now ambassador to Ireland and the Holy See, cast a garish light east, north and south onto the whole of the ALP and especially the Prime Minister, who had given him the job and continued to stand by him. In the midst of the WA Inc. drama, Hawke blundered. On Thursday, 11 April 1991, he gave a woeful performance in parliament when questioned about allegations made by a corrupt businessman, Laurie Connell. Some years earlier Hawke had met and instantly disliked Connell, his sentiment confirmed when a racehorse trainer told him of Connell's cunning illegalities in the racing industry. Hawke was annoyed and embarrassed when Connell unexpectedly joined a West Australian fishing trip and was photographed in a dinghy with him. Hawke warned Premier Brian Burke to keep away from Connell.

While the Prime Minister had judged Connell accurately, he showed lamentable judgment about Burke, whose charm with his Labor colleagues and even non-Labor people had the potency of an opiate. There was something ineffably beguiling about Burke. Kim Beazley, a man incapable of dishonesty himself, maintained affection for him decades after he was proven crooked and sent to prison. In the early 1980s Hawke wanted Burke to transfer to federal politics, believing he would be a fine future minister. On Burke's advice, and against his own wishes and instinct, in 1984 Hawke ditched legislation that would benefit Aboriginal people in Western Australia. This action caused a bitter rupture with his son, Stephen, who was devoting his life to improving the lives of Indigenous people. When in 1987 Burke asked for a grace and favour appointment as ambassador to Ireland and the Holy See, Hawke obliged him, asking Hayden, who was still Foreign minister, to arrange it.

Burke was a conman and a thief. Burke told Connell what the Prime Minister thought of him, confirming what Connell already guessed. In the Royal Commission, Connell found his moment for revenge: he claimed Hawke had promised to remove the gold tax in exchange for a $250 000 donation to the Labor Party. Hawke had made no such promise. In fact, the government's decision on the tax was made weeks in advance of a lunch with Connell. Hawke's answer about the dates of meetings and decisions was based on misinformation provided by his new chief of staff, Dennis Richardson. Hawke had to return to the Chamber to correct himself. This was the most embarrassing moment of his parliamentary career. It became excruciating when Keating, fully versed in the issue, in which he had taken an interest for more than a decade, leapt to the Prime Minister's defence with dazzling acumen. 'Who taxed the gold industry?' Keating demanded.

> Who removed the exemption [from tax]? The Government! Who did not? The Opposition! The question is: why? Why did those opposite not remove the exemption? We know, but we are waiting for their answer. Who was contributing to them? Who was so successful in their contribution as to keep them loyal to their cause ... It is very interesting to get this question [from the leader of the National Party]. The most proven corrupt party in this country is the National Party of Australia ... The proven corrupt party. Half of the former Queensland Cabinet is in gaol. And we have the Leader of the National Party up asking questions about issues of propriety. Do not make us laugh![4]

On the same day the unemployment figures were announced: 9.2 per cent. Caucus was reported to be feeling helpless, hopeless and guilty.

Then things got worse.

A short time later that day Hawke had to enter the Chamber a second time to explain that he had again given incorrect information about the gold tax dates. He apologised and asked the House's indulgence. Dennis Richardson offered his resignation. Hawke refused to accept it. Hewson launched a censure motion against Hawke, referring to 'a stench' about the government and accusing him of lack of leadership. The government made barely a token of defence and allowed Hewson's motion to be defeated on party lines. That weekend in a state by-election in Western Australia Labor's primary vote dropped 30 per cent.

The incident—short, sharp and humiliating—dramatically raised Keating's stocks in the ministry and the Caucus. Laurie Oakes wrote in the *Bulletin*,

> the admiration for Keating's brilliance in single-handedly turning the issue back on the coalition is just about universal. Without Keating's parliamentary skills, his toughness, his aggression, his cold gunfighter's nerve, the government would have been routed and every MP ... knows it.

John Howard, rather conveniently for Hawke, riposted that Keating was so unpopular 'you can't give him away'. It was an autumn of miseries for the government. By mid-May, Australia's big banks were forced to admit they were reaping the whirlwind of their profligacy. Westpac and the National Australia Bank announced a combined total of $10 billion in bad debts.

On 24 May 1991, Bob Hogg, the ALP national secretary, advised Hawke to organise a transition to Keating. He told Paul Kelly,

> You can't win if the party's divided. [Keating's] challenge, obviously, wasn't going away and would only get worse ... I think Hawke was beyond the point of electability. In terms of getting energy, drive and unity in government, I just don't think it was possible under Hawke.[5]

During their face-to-face conversation Hawke told Hogg his analysis and judgment were wrong. Hogg said in 2009, 'The one regret that I ever had was that I succumbed to the view that on balance it was better to go with Keating. But by that time, the party was in a mess.'

Ground down by the pressure from Keating's camp and disheartened by the recession, Hogg and many others in the party and the Caucus had reached a point of solipsism: they had forgotten that their enemy was the Opposition, and that it was the Opposition's actions, and the skills of its leader John Hewson (who had replaced Andrew Peacock after the 1990 election loss), which would be a determining factor in the next election. The election was two years away, time in which the economy would come out of recession and return to growth. Hawke believed that Hewson had no chance of connecting with the Australian electorate: he was too fast, too impatient for change, too much the blue-eyed hitman. He had been talking since his election as leader of the Liberal Party about a consumption tax and lower income taxes. But he was too inexperienced, Hawke believed, in how difficult it is to straighten the bent timber of humanity to accept the shape of a new idea. The Prime Minister believed that if Hewson went to the electorate with his consumption tax package, he would cause lots of excitement and praise in the media and be slaughtered in the electorate. Keating bore scars from 1985 to show how dangerous it was to handle a consumption tax.

Within days of Hogg's visit to Hawke, Keating decided he could wait no longer: to do so would saddle him with formulating the 1991/92 Budget—and as he had warned Hawke earlier, the job and his frustrations were driving him 'ga-ga'.

Trying to scare Hawke out of his job had proved ineffective, so by agreement with Keating and the other leaders of his camp, on 29 May 1991 Graham Richardson visited the Prime Minister to lie to him that he was *shocked. Shocked!* He had just learned of the Kirribilli agreement. Therefore, Keating would challenge for the leadership.

Keating, as he had promised he would if it ever came to this, personally called on Hawke on the evening of 30 May to tell him he was about to challenge.

Keating's supporters had already briefed Laurie Oakes on the Kirribilli pact and on the six o'clock news of 30 May, Oakes broke the story on Channel Nine. It was presented as a scandal: the fate of the nation decided in secret by the Prime Minister behind closed doors. The scandal was confected, but the crisis was real.

The press gallery and the general news media turned on the Prime Minister with hectic glee. There was a frenzy of indignation in the press, on television and in talkback radio. In parliament Andrew Peacock, harking back to the ads 'a vote for Hawke is a vote for Keating', shouted at the Prime Minister, 'I was the victim of your lie!' Hawke, actually, had not lied to the electorate; having promised the people he would stay on and fight the 1993 election, that is what he was committed to do. The media chose not to point this out but instead went into uproar over Sir Peter Abeles being Hawke's witness.

This was poker for the highest stakes, and there were no options but to raise or fold. Keating had tried 'call' in his earlier moves against Hawke. In big poker, calling is for wimps.

Unknown to everyone except a few of their staff, both men were preparing to fold. Keating was negotiating to buy a piggery. For a man who described himself, and is, at heart an aesthete, a piggery was a curious choice. Life was not imitating art, but rather the old north England saying, 'Where there's muck there's brass.' Keating had studied the international pork and bacon markets with the intensity he brought to all his hobbies and was confident his investment would provide a lucrative retirement income. His love of art, architecture, music and his family would sustain his soul. Meanwhile Hawke, with the help of Sir Peter Abeles' secretary, Joy Annan, was hunting for a house to buy in Sydney. The Hawke family home in Melbourne had long since been sold, the income used to help the three children buy their own houses. Hawke had no more than a hazy idea about what he would do after politics, but having spent forty years as an interviewee, he fancied turning the tables and being an interviewer himself. He was as unsuited to this as Keating was to pig farming, an indication that both men, after a lifetime in politics, really did not know what to do with themselves. The horrible anomie that overcomes old soldiers loomed at them. In politics, happiness comes from the knowledge that one has made the lives of others better than they were, but this is very difficult to achieve and to maintain. As the saying goes, most political careers end in tears.

From the end of the Gulf War to the end of the Hawke–Keating war, there were months of tears in the party.

In the Keating camp there was no political advantage or desire to resist the reforms of 'Building a Competitive Australia'. But Keating had much to gain in backbench support by rebuffing its close relative, Hawke's New Federalism (COAG) reforms.

By the beginning of June the government was 18 percentage points behind the Coalition in the polls and Keating's supporters were stressing to journalists 'the stability of Mr Keating's private life and his commitment to his family'. (There was a sad irony to this: whereas life in The Lodge had strengthened Hawke and Hazel's partnership, and brought Hazel the happiest years of her married life, the Keating marriage began to disintegrate from the time they moved in. A former staffer said, 'We knew there was something wrong at home, but we never knew what it was.')

Keating challenged Hawke on 3 June 1991. That morning Max Walsh predicted in the *Sydney Morning Herald* that Hawke would win, but the government's great problem would be in drawing up and selling a Budget without Keating. The Treasury bureaucracy was at its weakest in decades. Walsh wrote,

> Tony Cole would not be heading up the department at this stage of his career had he not served as a personal economic adviser to Paul Keating. The combination of a massive brain drain out of Treasury to the private sector [many of the best and brightest had gone to merchant banks] ... and the premature death of Dr Chris Higgins ... saw Cole installed by Keating. The intellectual firepower of Treasury may still be high but this is, without doubt the most inexperienced team it has ever fielded for a Budget ... Keating has demonstrated quite remarkable marketing skills, especially in enlisting the support of the Canberra press gallery, in selling his economic policies. His successor will not exert the same seductive charm ... there is simply nobody, within Labor ranks, who has Keating's chutzpah, who can tell an audience black is white and have half of them believing it.

Walsh's pronouncement was both shrewd and prophetic.

Hawke defeated Keating 66 votes to 44. Keating resigned as Treasurer and went to the backbench, declaring he had 'only one shot in the locker'. Many, including Hawke, believed Keating

Ten

had folded. But Richardson, when asked by journalists about Keating's vote, muttered it was 'enough'. This cryptic comment lay uninterpreted for what it was in the Hawke camp, certainly by Hawke, whose optimism bore him up to a cloud of belief that he had prevailed. But Keating had not folded. 'Enough' meant enough for a second challenge for which he would gamble his bottom dollar. It was: make the government unworkable.

As soon as the challenge was lost, the government and Hawke leapt in the polls. Hawke led Hewson by 9 percentage points, but the Opposition was still well ahead of Labor.

A fortnight later there was an excruciating Cabinet meeting over further mining at Coronation Hill in the Northern Territory. The Australian Mining Industry Council (AMIC) had been running a campaign of misinformation and intimidation about the value of mining at Coronation Hill and the worthlessness of the local Jawoyn people's beliefs about disturbing the earth spirit that ruled the area. John Hewson and the Opposition loudly embraced the AMIC's assertions. In Cabinet, Hawke, alone, opposed them, on the grounds it was discriminatory to Jawoyn beliefs about the spirit, Bula. To simply dismiss them was racist, he said. He accused his ministry of rank hypocrisy— able to accept, and some to believe, in Christian metaphysics (the virgin birth, the resurrection, the holy trinity)—but not to allow Aboriginal people credence for their metaphysics. 'There's no doubt,' he said, 'that calling them hypocrites upset quite a few. But I believed so profoundly in the principle I didn't give a bugger if they were embarrassed.' For five and a half hours the Cabinet argued, Hawke vehement from the outset. Richardson and the economic ministers were equally vehement in their opposition. The meeting ended in acrimonious fatigue, a sullen Cabinet falling in behind the leader. This was the first time an Australian government had rejected a mining venture through respect for Aboriginal belief.

Next day there was outrage in the mining community and news media. Richardson told anyone who would listen that he had talked to the Aboriginal elders at Coronation Hill and Bula was 'Bula-shit'. He intimated to selected journalists that Hawke's Cabinet performance was the 'worst'. Hawke was very proud of it. He had argued on principles he had held to throughout his life: tolerance for other beliefs and abhorrence for all forms of racism.

Richardson, Punch, Dawkins and others meanwhile kept themselves busy blackguarding the Prime Minister to the media, to the unconverted within the Caucus and party branches, and to business. The most favoured—Kerry Packer, for example—were quietly informed there would be a second Keating challenge.

By now the news media was fully engaged as a player in the leadership struggle. As Max Walsh had pointed out in the *Sydney Morning Herald* on the day of the challenge,

> Rupert [Murdoch] now controls, thanks to Paul Keating, most of the Australian newspaper market. So it was hardly surprising to see his paper enthusiastically endorsing Keating over the weekend. Should they continue to push the Keating cause over the next 18 months or so this will eat at the morale of the Government.

There was, perhaps, a personal element at play. Notwithstanding that Murdoch and Abeles were friends, Hawke had felt an aversion to Murdoch from their first meeting, in the 1960s. From time to time Abeles tried to form a bridge between them, without success. Keating and Murdoch enjoyed each other's company.

On the morning of the challenge, the *Age* began its editorial, 'We will say it at once, and say it clearly. Today's climactic Caucus meeting in Canberra ought to elect Paul Keating to replace Bob Hawke as Prime Minister of Australia.' But the *Age* did not say it once. It said it three times, for it also ran two pro-Keating articles, one by Michelle Grattan, its Canberra bureau chief, and one by its business and finance commentator, Glenda Korporaal. The next morning it pontificated that Caucus had been guilty of a 'tragic mistake'.

The *Australian* of 5 June ran an article by Richard Farmer, one of the few Hawke supporters, who wrote that the press campaign was similar to that by the press barons Lords Rothermere and Beaverbrook against British Prime Minister Stanley Baldwin in 1928. Baldwin described their methods, Farmer recorded,

> [as] direct falsehood, misrepresentation, half-truths, the alteration of the speaker's meaning by publishing a sentence apart from its context ... this contest is not a contest as to whom is to lead the party, but as to who is to appoint the leader of the party.

He remarked, 'The journalists in the era of Hawke are trying just as hard to be kingmakers as the proprietors in the age of Baldwin.'

On 18 June, Sam Lipski wrote in the *Bulletin*,

> the Press displayed naked triumphalism about its perceived role as would-be kingmakers before [Keating's challenge] and a quantum leap in fury afterwards when the majority of the caucus ignored its 'advice'. The rush to judgment undoubtedly affected the fairness of reporting—against Hawke, for Keating ... [journalists] have made it clear they will continue to promote [Keating's] candidacy until they have their way or until their hero chooses the Paris option.

The ALP National Conference was scheduled for the very end of June, in Hobart. Keating's supporters hoped, and were whispering to all and sundry, that Hawke would take this chance to fold.

Instead, Hawke raised.

Always at his most determined when under pressure, his address to the conference was among the great fighting speeches of his career. He spoke of his forty-five years of membership of the party and how he had been nourished throughout by 'steadfast commitment to its fundamental goal—the welfare of the Australian people'. He argued that the Opposition's proposed consumption tax would be 'the most concerted attack in the history of this nation on the living standards of the poor, the underprivileged, the aged and low- and middle-income families'. It would, he said, 'pay the rich by slugging the poor'. He concluded: 'That is why I am determined, delegates, to work to the limit of my capacity for a fifth Labor victory in 1993.'

But he was talking to a dispirited audience. Delegates from Western Australia, Victoria, South Australia and Tasmania knew their state governments were facing defeat at the polls. And privately, Hawke had to confront a deep sadness. Jean Sinclair had been his secretary and confidante since 1973—and she was also the one member of his staff whom Hazel had always disliked. The low pay at the ACTU had not been an issue, since Mrs Sinclair had private wealth. She and her husband, Professor Angus Sinclair, lived in a large house in East Melbourne, where Hawke would call in for a drink or dinner with them after work. She was an economics graduate, English-born, with English restraint and a merry sense of humour. By her late fifties she had changed little in appearance—still slim, with a pixie face and long, straight sherry-coloured hair that she wore up. She dressed in quietly expensive clothes. Earlier in the year she had told Hawke she had cancer and needed time off for treatment.

She was back at work for the conference, attired for the cold in long dark skirts. Hawke asked how her treatment was progressing. For answer she drew her skirt aside to reveal a hugely swollen limb. Her doctors had advised her, she said, that she had three months to live. Discreet to the end, she was not telling colleagues. Hawke was grief-stricken but respected her wish not to speak about her approaching death in the office. Nor could he share his grief at home, as Hazel's dislike had not softened. His emotional world was beginning to unravel.

Graham Freudenberg, who was Sinclair's closest friend in the office, recalled, 'Jean didn't talk about herself, but I remember she was very worried about a second Keating challenge. She thought it would happen, although Bob did not.'

In Adelaide in July 1991 there was a second Special Premiers' Conference. Greiner recalled,

> I wanted a big bang deal. I said I thought you could justify the Commonwealth getting out of education up to the end of high school, and get the states out of post-school education. My point was that you ought to be able to allocate responsibility, rather than having everything shared, which is where we still are today. I said, 'Can't we cut through this bullshit and do an allocation of what goes to the Commonwealth and what goes to the states?' I said, 'If you try to do it in detail, it won't work, because every little vested interest will defend its turf.' But that didn't fly. And it still [in 2009] hasn't.

Nevertheless, a further raft of reforms was agreed, involving devolution of power in some federal portfolios to the states. Hawke was immensely proud: here, in his fourth term, he had innovative reforms that could bring improvements for the next half-century, or more. He was not feeling worn out or politically disheartened. The prospect of new achievements invigorated him. The media, however, remained unimpressed. The Commonwealth–state reforms resisted snappy explanation; as their complexity was beyond the competence of many journalists, most of the media ignored them altogether. By this stage the press gallery was so sullen about Hawke that a majority was unwilling to report anything positive about him.

Hawke, meanwhile, continued his attack on Hewson's consumption tax proposal, which was yet to be fully revealed. He told a union conference in July that it would make 'every trip to the supermarket, every trip to McDonald's, a visit to the tax man'.

Hawke promoted John Kerin, his very successful Primary Industries minister, and a good economist, to the Treasury job.

On 20 August Kerin brought down his first Budget. It was, as Max Walsh had cannily predicted, a lemon: poorly expressed, poorly delivered and containing political poison in the form of Medicare co-payments. The new deputy Prime Minister, Brian Howe, leader of the Left, had proposed the Medicare payment, assuring Hawke and Kerin that the Left would accept it. But the Left promptly rebelled. Keating immediately promised Caucus to reverse the proposal were he prime minister. The timing of the Budget was also unfortunate for it coincided with the anti-Gorbachev coup in Moscow. Trying to sell the Budget, with a nervous new Treasurer, Hawke was distracted by questions about the violence in Russia. Kerin made numerous small mistakes, upon each of which the media seized, having had them pointed out by Keating. The Treasurer became more nervous. Dawkins was leaking from Cabinet so much that Brian Howe, who had been a Baptist minister before entering politics, felt moved to quote from the Book of Proverbs, declaring publicly, 'a house divided against itself simply cannot stand'. That may have worked with an unruly congregation; it was a faux pas for a divided government. The New South Wales Right was now in such a state of atavistic tribal anger that some were ready to cut off their noses to spite their faces, willing for their struggle against the Prime Minister to destroy the government. Gary Punch was warning, 'We will take this into Opposition if we need to.'[6]

The most vehement fights were between the staff of the competing camps, for many of whom personal careers were at stake. Once happy offices roiled with discontent and ill temper. A gloom settled over the government wing of Parliament House.

Graham Richardson, for all his determination to bring Hawke down, did not want to bring the government (and therefore himself) down in the process. In late August, after the Budget embarrassment, he called on Hawke at The Lodge to discuss the danger of destabilisation. He was friendly. He gave the Prime Minister a guarantee: provided Hawke made no mistakes, there would be no challenge. He was lying. Keating afterwards maintained that 'Richardson didn't get me a single vote', but the assertion is not credible. Richardson was as ruthless and skilful for Keating as he had been for Hawke; he could still influence preselections in New South Wales, still tell people they would be political corpses if they did not vote for Keating. And Richardson was the one person in Keating's camp with the tactical nous to plan a successful second challenge. But he was treading very carefully, and not prepared, like the hotheaded Punch, to wreck the government by keeping up the pressure for Keating indefinitely. A sidelight to this was that Keating and Richardson did not consistently like each other; 'Keating's lack of discipline was and is his biggest problem,' Richardson wrote of him in a tone of irritation.[7] Their friendship ran hot and cold—inevitable between two such contrasting characters. But Keating had offered Richardson the reward he craved: Richardson would be Minister for Transport and Communications in a Keating government.

After his talk with Richardson at The Lodge, Hawke immediately made a mistake. Wreathed in smiles, he told journalists he believed Cabinet leaks would now cease. They ferreted around for the background to the Prime Minister's confidence and good humour, discovered his private meeting with Richardson, and thus had another story to write on the woes of the government.

In September, Jean Sinclair died. Hawke sat through the funeral as though thunderstruck, too distressed to deliver her eulogy. Her death was the end of an era for him: 'It is difficult,' he said later,

> to overstate Jeanie's importance in my life and career— as a supremely efficient assistant, friend and stabilising counsellor. The deepest respect and affection I had for her was only enhanced by the courage with which she comported herself in those final months and days.

Graham Richardson meanwhile set out to cool press gallery expectations of a challenge. In the same month as Jean's death, in very matey tones, he interviewed Hawke on Sydney radio station 2KY, giving the Prime Minister another opportunity to attack the proposed consumption tax. Hawke did so, asserting dire social and economic consequences for ordinary people from such a tax, which would put up the price of their food, education and medical services at the same rate for the poor as for the rich, while income tax offsets for the rich would be far greater than for the poor. He added, 'That's why I want to lead us to victory in the '93 election, and that's what's driving me.' Still on air, Richardson again lied—as he later admitted[8]—saying he did not think there would be a second challenge. Hawke believed him, admitting later, 'I think my natural tendency to think the best of people has generally served me well though life—but I was a sucker not to make an exception for Richo.'

Ten

During October planning was underway for the third Special Premiers' Conference to be held in November. John Bannon of South Australia and Nick Greiner of New South Wales drafted a submission, with which all the other premiers agreed, asking the Commonwealth to surrender some taxing powers to the states. Greiner and Bannon called on Hawke at The Lodge to present it to him. But Keating heard of the plan's existence. According to Paul Kelly, 'he decided to destroy Hawke's New Federalism [COAG] initiative to the extent it undermined the revenue powers of the Commonwealth'. Keating had made 'the accurate assessment that the ALP caucus, forced to choose, would back [his] centralism against Hawke's devolution option'.[9]

Mike Codd recalled,

> COAG was rolling along and it was known that I was the key driver of it in the bureaucracy. On Monday mornings we had a regular meeting of heads of all departments, which I chaired. I was busy chairing when a message came in from my staff that Senator Richardson wanted to come and see me in the department, and was on his way, and would be there in ten minutes. It was the only time in my memory that any minister had ever come to a department to talk. So Richardson's visit was very unusual. We sat in my office and I offered him coffee, and he proceeded to tell me that I should find a way of slowing the COAG process down, and preferably of stopping it altogether, because he said, 'The PM is going to lose in the Caucus on this.' He said, 'I know the numbers' and he proceeded to rattle off names and numbers in Caucus. It was really quite extraordinary for a political leader to come in to a public servant's office and say, 'You don't do such-and-such. I know what the numbers are in the Caucus.' He basically gave me the

message [to kill the reforms]. I listened politely and thanked him for coming over, and he left. But his visit made no difference. Bob would not back off.

Helen Williams recalled,

Gary Sturgess wanted principles of federation: we needed to sort out clearly exactly which area of government was doing what. And that area should take *the whole* of the functional area ... We were trying to progress all these streams and parallels. And certainly there was a feeling that a very careful look at the taxing powers was necessary. My memory is that the premiers' Adelaide meeting actually recommended that the Commonwealth would reduce personal income tax by a particular percentage to leave way for the states to introduce their own tax, and that was going to be revenue neutral, tax neutral. The Commonwealth was collecting and not spending, the states were spending and not collecting—or at least, spending far more than they were collecting.

On 22 October, Keating launched his offensive against COAG in a speech to the National Press Club in which he argued against surrendering any Commonwealth revenue powers to the states. He was reasserting Labor's tradition of centralism. Hawke and Kerin had assured Caucus no taxing powers would be surrendered, but Kerin then circulated a Cabinet submission that left this option open. The death blow came when the premiers' submission was leaked in its entirety to Keating. The premiers asked for 6 per cent of national revenue to be handed to the states. Keating used their submission to white-ant the proposal through a whispering campaign in Caucus. This white-anting was sapping the collective will of the government. Hawke was now unable to deliver to the premiers the extra tax he had led them to believe he could. On hearing the rumblings from Canberra, the premiers conferred and, not realising how precarious the situation was inside the government, decided if they could not have the whole loaf, they would not settle for half. They pulled out of the November conference and the reform process collapsed.

The Prime Minister's COAG agenda for his fourth term was in ruins.

Keating's tactic had worked, but the correction of vertical fiscal imbalance *had to be* tackled somehow. And it was when in 2000 John Howard introduced a goods and services tax with all the revenue going to the states.

Williams remarked in 2009,

> In education, in welfare, in health, in disability services, there's still this pull between the Commonwealth and the states and we still haven't got much clarity as to who is doing what, everything complicated now [post-GST] by cost-shifting ... In essence, we're still fighting the same battles.

Greiner made a similar point when he commented,

> Basically, since Bob's left, no one has been willing to take it on. Keating wasn't interested because he used COAG against Bob. I tried to persuade Howard and Costello but they were never remotely interested. I think they had the view that the states were hopeless and couldn't organise a chook raffle in a pub, therefore any attempt to separate and clarify responsibility would fail because it would involve the states. Since then Victoria has come up with a reform agenda, a national program

for obesity, for Indigenous health, which is all useful, but they are motherhood issues on which everyone can agree. The hard questions are where the states disagree: like the allocation of water. We've lost eighteen years.

Keating did implement a few ideas from COAG, but Greiner's statement is broadly accurate. In the November 2007 election COAG was a centrepiece for Kevin Rudd's successful campaign. He promised to usher in a new era of co-operative federalism.

Hawke should have prepared the Caucus for an ideological shift on COAG, but by late 1991 his authority was fracturing through the fissures within the government. Only if he could end the Keating destabilisation would the ministry and Caucus reunite and focus on being a government. Like an army, a government needs *esprit de corps*. The military rule of thumb is that an army without bonding will break and run when 10 per cent of its soldiers are killed; an army well bonded will fight until only 10 per cent of its soldiers are still alive. The government's *esprit de corps* was steadily eroding.

In the first week of November there was some good economic news: interest rates were to be cut by 1 per cent. But Kerin was too rattled by the media to come out of his office to make the announcement. Instead, he put out a press release. At that moment Hawke realised that he would have to shift Kerin out of Treasury. He planned to do so over the Christmas break.

The *Age* editorial of 5 November was headlined 'Labor and the Pain of Decline'.

> The Labor Party is entering a state of advanced political decline as Mr Paul Keating continues his campaign to topple Mr Bob Hawke ... It is hard to see

how Labor can now prevent decline becoming fall. Part of the problem is Mr Hawke's obdurate insistence that he is Labor's best hope for another election victory. The other part is Mr Keating's transparent opportunism and obvious unpopularity ... He wants to be prime minister, and will do and say what he judges will achieve that end. The painful dilemma for the Caucus, which makes and unmakes Labor leaders, is the choice between a diminished Bob Hawke and an opportunist Paul Keating. Given Labor's parlous electoral outlook, the party ought urgently to consider putting the leadership to another Caucus vote. The alternative is to allow this debilitating struggle to continue thereby ensuring that decline becomes fall.

Hawke by now was determined to ignore all negative comments. He knew Keating did not yet have the numbers for a challenge.

On 8 November Keating told the ABC radio program *PM*, 'I will not be challenging the Prime Minister.' He had made the statement under duress from Richardson, knowing it was a lie. The press gallery recognised it as such. With Dr Hewson at last ready to launch his economic policy, Keating would be seen as a saboteur if he did not back down. Richardson intensified his media campaign to persuade the leaders of the press gallery that Keating had, indeed, folded. Michelle Grattan wrote, 'Hawke has won an important round.' Keating's popularity was stuck at 30 per cent, while Hawke's edged up 2 percentage points, to 54 per cent. Bruce Jones, reporting for the Sydney *Sun Herald* on 10 November remarked of Keating's statements of recent days, 'The current flurry of activity should be seen for what it is, a last desperate bid by Keating to crank up support for a final tilt at the leadership.'

By 14 November the economy was still stubbornly flat. That day Hawke unveiled a $300 million stimulus for education and training to help the unemployed, now numbering 800 000 people.

One week later Hewson detonated his tax bomb. It was called *'Fightback!'* and was a 600-page monster riddled with statistics. As expected, it proposed a 15 per cent goods and services tax on everything, with offsetting income-tax cuts. To the government's chagrin the media, especially economic journalists, embraced *Fightback!* with rapture. Not that they understood it. Neither did the government, yet. Hewson and some others in the Opposition did. Warwick Smith, a member of the shadow Cabinet, recalled the optimism and *esprit de corps* in Coalition ranks over Hewson and *Fightback!*.

> With Hewson we were looking at a fresh face, new ideas, modern man, an investment banker with a globalised feel of things, someone who could take Australia to the next level. People like me were saying, 'This breaks the nexus between the Hawke and Peacock thing. We've got a new horse.' We thought we might be able to run Hawke down ... I never thought [Keating] was going to take the gun out and try to shoot everyone. We thought we were going to be up against Hawke.

Cautious after his embarrassment over the gold tax, denied Keating's parliamentary demolition power, Hawke was determined not to appear on the field of battle against Hewson's policy without full armour. He wanted a thorough analysis of *Fightback!* by Treasury before launching into its dismantlement. He knew that the public did not understand the ramifications of a consumption tax, although he had been railing against it all year. He was also certain that the financial journalists who were so joyfully embracing it did not really understand it either. He (and Keating) understood economics and politics too well to want to rush in, half-baked, against a document prepared after more than a year's work by an expert and experienced professional economist and a team of assistants. Hawke said he wanted time to respond. Keating remained silent. For the Prime Minister, it was good policy but poor politics, for he seemed scared of Hewson. For Keating, it was good politics: as a backbencher, he had no obligation to speak up.

By 26 November the government had found the first of many weaknesses it would uncover in *Fightback!*. Dr Hewson had failed to take account of the cost of new road-user charges that would reduce the value of his promise to lower petrol prices, and would add to inflation. Hawke waded in to attack during Question Time. The result was bedlam. The Opposition, recognising Kerin's shaky nerve, set out to stop the Prime Minister by demanding that the Treasurer debate the whole package, which Kerin was not yet equipped to do. Nor was Hawke. His only weapon was the one flaw so far revealed. He and the government repeatedly dodged Opposition demands to debate the whole of *Fightback!*. The Speaker of the House, Leo McLeay from the New South Wales Right, allowed the Opposition to turn parliament into a madhouse. Instead of naming then having members of the Opposition expelled from the Chamber, as was the Westminster practice in such circumstances, he actively undermined the Prime Minister. As Hawke attempted to drive home his attack on the flaw in *Fightback!*, McLeay interrupted him 53 times in thirty minutes. Each call to order from the Speaker pulled Hawke up in mid-sentence. The message was clear: the Keating camp had decided to make parliament unworkable for the government.

'Leo: how the lion became a squeaker' was the headline to a story by Mike Seccombe in the *Sydney Morning Herald* the next day:

It was virtually impossible for Ministers to make themselves heard. Hawke looked particularly bad, because he stopped innumerable times to glare at the Speaker in the vain hope Leo would do something. Hawke even pointed out at one stage that the opposition was not heeding Leo's call to order, but Leo steadfastly did nothing. Question time was a disaster from beginning to end for the government, as a result.

The following day the House was a rumpus of baboons. McLeay called for order or warned parliamentarians they would be named 89 times in sixty minutes. But he named no one, expelled no one.

That week the Morgan poll had Hewson as preferred prime minister, 45 to 43 per cent, over Hawke. It was joyous news for Keating since it destroyed Hawke's major claim to the leadership: that he could win.

But by the first week of December the Treasury officials who had been analysing *Fightback!* for the government had struck gold. There was a $2.6 billion hole in Hewson's policy—and that was just the beginning of its problems. Parliament was to sit on Monday, 9 December: Hawke's birthday, a day when he always felt cheerful, although he was not as cheerful as usual leading up to this birthday, since Hazel had fallen ill for the second time in a few months and needed surgery.

Hawke had arranged that on 9 December the government's own fight back would begin. Ministers were briefed during the preceding week so the attack on the Opposition could be launched across a broad front. On the morning of 5 December, John Kerin announced the economy had turned around—but he was in error, and by lunchtime he had to contradict himself: for the fifth consecutive quarter, the economy had contracted. The recession was still in force. Hawke was in Sydney to address

Ten

a luncheon and listened to Kerin's press conference on his car radio. Kerin fell into a panic in front of the media, so flustered he could not remember what the initials GOS (Gross Operating Surplus) meant. Finally he turned to the assembled reporters to ask them. Hawke, who was travelling across the Harbour Bridge from Kirribilli House to the CBD, clasped his head in his hands and yelled, 'Fuck!'

Richardson, also listening to Kerin's press conference, recognised that the moment to attack once more had arrived. Within hours he had leaked a story to the *Sydney Morning Herald* that he, Robert Ray and Kim Beazley, the latter both known Hawke supporters, had already advised the Prime Minister to sack both Kerin and Button, and to make a major reshuffle of the ministry. Button, the Industry minister, always keen for attention and admiration as a free spirit, had in the past few years appointed himself devil's advocate, publicly criticising the government whenever he felt moved to do so. Privately he was inactive in his portfolio.

Saturday, 7 December, was an appalling day for the Prime Minister. That morning's press was almost universally opposed to him. Later that day he was due to address the New South Wales state ALP conference. The word had gone out to the Right 'to get Hawke'. Graham Freudenberg, who loves the party as if it were his child, recalled, 'I knew it would be very ugly. I refused to attend.' The delegates greeted their Prime Minister with cold silence at first, later with jeers and abuse. 'It was a disgrace,' Freudenberg lamented.

Next day, Hawke declared he would not be standing down.

He made the smallest reshuffle possible. He moved Willis to Treasury—the job he had promised Willis back in 1982 but had been unable to deliver—and put Kerin into Transport and Communications. He moved Beazley into Finance.

Years earlier Keating's adviser, Don Russell, had predicted, 'the caucus will only turn to Keating when it feels the government is completely demoralised'.[10] Now it was. Hawke's minor reshuffle was interpreted in the media as a condemnation of the government's handling of the recession. History's wheel was turning, and whatever Hawke did was destined, by this stage, for damnation.

Richardson, meanwhile, was working furiously to isolate the Prime Minister from the support of his inner-most circle of political allies: those in Cabinet, his backbench friends, even his friends in the business community. Peter Hartcher, who researched the final days of the Hawke government, wrote later, '[Richardson] wanted it to become utterly clear to Hawke that he was hopelessly, desperately, friendlessly finished.'[11] Richardson was still trying to pressure Hawke into resignation. On the night of 11 December, Kim Beazley, Robert Ray, Gareth Evans, Michael Duffy, Nick Bolkus and Gerry Hand, all Hawke supporters, arrived in a body to ask the Prime Minister to give up. He listened to their arguments, promised to consider them, and said he would meet them later with his answer.

Richardson wrote, '"That's enough", I thought. He has no choice now. He will resign.'

But Hawke's answer was 'No'.

Richardson said in his memoir, 'All of them were aware that the fatally wounded leadership that was Hawke's could not recover.' To Richardson it was incredible that Hawke would fight on. But then an awful fear entered his mind: the Prime Minister could 'get in his car and drive out to Yarralumla to advise the Governor-General to dissolve the Parliament and call an election'. He and the Keating camp became panicky. As Hawke stood firm, they began to feel their numbers waning.[12]

But Richardson, for all his earlier hero worship of Hawke, did not understand what a hero is, nor what a hero does.

Throughout history, and in every culture, the hero cannot surrender. He will fight and die for his beliefs. Hawke believed he was the only one at that stage who could successfully lead the party and the country. For this he would fight to his political death.

In droves, friends advised Hawke to stand down. Kim Beazley said,

> I always accepted the view that Bob was not burnt out—as I had a practical example [of his energy] from what he was making me do in Communications. He was far and a long way our most successful leader and if everybody was loyally in behind him, then we would win the next election. I always accepted that Paul was the legitimate successor to Bob, and I accepted that Paul would bring a sharper attack on the other side. But whereas Paul thought he was the only one who could exploit the consumption tax issue, I thought many could. *Fightback!* was a long political suicide note that Hewson had written. But before the second challenge I didn't think Bob had nearly enough supporters. I couldn't *bear* the idea of him being humiliated in Caucus. I tried very hard to get him to stand down.

Twelve out of sixteen Cabinet ministers tried to persuade the Prime Minister to resign. Gareth Evans told him, 'Pull out, digger. The dogs are pissing on your swag.' Hawke's reply to them was always the same: first, he was convinced Keating could not win against Hewson. Second, he had not devoted his life to the Labor Party to allow it to commit suicide.

By 18 December Ray and Beazley knew most of the Caucus numbers: Keating had about 60, Hawke about 50. By now Senator Evans had left Canberra for emergency talks in

Jakarta about a massacre in Dili some weeks earlier. Everyone knew there would be no chivalrous offer from the Keating side of a 'pair' for Senator Evans. Hawke had to decide between the national interest—leaving the Foreign minister in Jakarta—and giving himself an extra vote by recalling Evans. He chose the national interest. Ray and Beazley came to The Lodge to tell Hawke he was beaten and to make one last plea to him to step down. They stayed with him until 3 a.m. Hawke had decided to call on the challenge for the evening of 19 December. At around 4 a.m. Hawke and his press secretary, Grant Nihil, woke Hazel to tell her the challenge was on. She supported her husband in the determination to fight. Hawke had a few hours sleep, then set out, in the little time he had left, to gather his forces.

He was fighting virtually alone.

Hartcher wrote,

> Most of Hawke's numbers men had resigned themselves to defeat and did not work to maximise his vote. For the first time in his Federal political career, Hawke did most of the numbers work himself ... If his supporters had not despaired, if the Left had not freed its members to vote as they pleased, and if Hawke had decided to recall Gareth Evans ... the ballot would have been tied at 54 votes each.[13]

In Keating's camp the same nerve-racking process was in train, but Keating was not working on his own: he had his generals Richardson, Punch and Laurie Brereton working for him. Friendships of a lifetime broke during the struggle. Hearts broke. Richardson recalled,

> I prevailed on David Simmonds—without any threat of repercussions—but I said to him, 'You've got to vote for

Keating, because New South Wales can't be left alone on this. We can't have anyone going outside the tent. We'd already had Roger Price [New South Wales Right] going outside the tent and we can't afford anyone else.' I said, 'We have to make sure the numbers are respectable—and I need you.' So I asked him as a favour to me. And he did it. And he cried. He was very upset because he loved Hawke. He loved him. But he did the right thing.

Kim Beazley, who loved both Hawke and Keating, said,

I lost the joy of politics during that time. I [still] enjoyed it as a profession, but the sparkling joy that you got out of what you thought was the most important game in town receded as you confronted the misery. It was just appalling.

Richardson recorded,

At 5.30, an hour before the ballot was due to begin, a very worried Gary Punch entered my office. Without even bothering to sit down, he said, solemnly: 'We can actually lose this challenge.' I stood up, took a deep breath and told him that, yes, we could lose because it was very close.[14]

At the appointed hour, Hawke presented himself for what he expected would be his execution.

The vote was 56 to 51. Many were in tears as the numbers were read out, among them John Dawkins, who had fought relentlessly to defeat Hawke. Richardson, seeing Dawkins' tears, described a feeling of numbed disgust. The destruction of Hawke was, he said,

Very ugly. I was looking around at all these people crying and thinking, 'Jeeze! You know, if you're in it, you're in it.' I wasn't crying. I thought, 'I can't believe these people.' Everyone wants to salve their consciences all the time. But you can't do that. The truth is, if you're going to shaft someone, then you can't cry after you've shafted them. It's ridiculous. And Dawkins did a lot of the shafting. I've never forgotten him sobbing. There was no joy in any of it. No joy. It was just a job. Hayden had to go because Hayden wasn't going to win. And Hawke had to go because Hawke wasn't going to win.

Keating was almost trembling as he stood at the podium to accept victory. But the slightly nervous hand he laid upon the wheel of history was pleasing to it, and fifteen months later it rewarded the new Prime Minister with the 'sweetest victory of all': winning the 1993 election. Hawke would have won it too—*Fightback!* was indeed a long political suicide note—but history had judged it was time for Keating to have his turn at holding the reins of power.

11

Brian Toohey said later, 'Hawke would have won the 1993 election. *Fightback!* looked worse and worse the longer it was examined.' Many political observers shared this view. Hawke was certain it was true, and deeply angry that his colleagues had rejected him too soon.

For months after he left parliament, in January 1992, there were malicious stories about him in the media, some true, some fabricated, to suit the mood of triumph that, finally, the man journalists had once called 'The Messiah' had had his comeuppance.

It was a time of purgatory and bitterness, both for him and for some of his former staff who were also out in the cold, without jobs. Aged sixty-two, Hawke found himself beyond a comfort zone. His life had been spent within organisations: church, university, trade union movement, parliament. Suddenly he had no structure to shape and discipline his time. He was used to the advice and information of an army of professionals when in private, in public to protection by armed men; to a chauffeur and his own aeroplane. He had lost the small repertoire he once had of normal urban skills and when, for the first time in years, he did some shopping, did not recognise a fifty-cent piece. From two houses staffed with servants, he and Hazel were living in a hotel suite in Double Bay.

The hotel was comfortable and sumptuous enough for Lady Diana to stay there some years later but it was cramped by the standards to which the Hawkes were accustomed. The Sydney property they had bought needed demolition and their new house would take almost two years to complete. Aside from close political colleagues and old buddies from union days, Hawke was relatively friendless after defeat. There were some notable exceptions: among the well known, Sir Peter Abeles, Richard Pratt and John Singleton stood by him, but many others in the business world who had been delighted to brag of their friendship with the prime minister swiftly moved their allegiance to Paul Keating (and in due course dropped him for John Howard).

Hawke did not seek power once he had lost it, but he had occasional fugues of hollow bombast, speaking as if he were still a national leader with an army at his command. Whereas he had adjusted to the role of prime minister 'instantly' as Graham Freudenberg observed, it took several years to adjust to being the ex. His cherished self-image needed time to decay.

But when it had mouldered away, Hawke began to flower again, and from the death of his old persona a new, more autonomous man started to take form.

Freed from the constraints of power, at liberty to act without political tensions pulling this way and that, away from relentless media scrutiny, Hawke arose, liberated, from the grave of his ambition. He brought with him a gift whose value he did not himself recognise at first but others did: his altruism. From childhood his ideal had been to work for the welfare of others, while his entire career had been lived beneath the shadow of, and had been shaped by, the Cold War. His career died as the Soviet empire collapsed. Now a new world order was struggling uncertainly to its feet. It was in this not-yet-brave new world that he would take a stand and set out to advance, once more, his vision of reconciliation, recovery and reconstruction.

On a trip to Europe in 1992, Hawke met the secretary general of the International Federation of Free Teachers' Unions, Fred van Leeuwen. van Leeuwen was a physically slight, politically astute Dutchman of profound humanity. He lived on a farm outside Amsterdam with his partner, an Amerindian veteran of the Vietnam War, and a family of dogs, horses, goats and other creatures. On first meeting it was as if Hawke and 'Freddie', as he always called him, had known each other forever. The Dutchman, young enough to be Hawke's son, proposed he join in a socio-political adventure that would reach across the globe: he wanted the former prime minister and former president of the ACTU to involve himself once more in the trade union movement.

For the forty-three years of the Cold War, there had been two separate industrial blocs: on one side, genuine trade unions; on the other, organisations that called themselves unions but that were in fact arms of government. In 1989 van Leeuwen, observing the approaching death of European Communism, proposed that the world's teachers' unions try to amalgamate. He and a working party envisaged that through such an organisation teachers in rich countries could help those in poor nations; the status of teachers, their terms and conditions could be improved by pressure on governments; their training upgraded and international agreements negotiated on basic curriculum development and issues like the right to education for girls. It would be not only a professional but also a human rights organisation. 'For us it was very important in creating this new organisation that it would consist of genuine teachers' unions,' van Leeuwen said.

> During the Cold War many unions claimed to have millions of members but really many of these simply did not exist and were yellow unions, mailbox organisations. So the question arose: how do we determine genuine from false? There is not a universal answer to

what independence means for a union, and maybe also to what democratic means.

The planning group came up with the idea of an independent committee of experts, people with a trade union background and political nous, who could be called in to investigate and report on disputed unions. The idea was the final piece to the puzzle that empowered the new organisation to come into creation. 'Everybody thought Bob would be the best possible solution as the chairman of the committee of experts,' van Leeuwen said, 'because he would be acceptable across a broad political spectrum, but many of us thought he'd never accept. The organisation was still to be born.'

But Hawke did accept and in 1993 took up his role in chairing the committee of experts of Education International, which met annually in Brussels. By 2010 EI had 36 million members, represented more than 90 per cent of the teaching profession outside China and was one of the world's most important non-government organisations, internationally recognised as the voice of the world's teaching profession.

EI has helped and sometimes saved the lives of teachers in countries from Afghanistan to Zimbabwe. Teaching can be a dangerous job in the Third World: as the only literate people in illiterate communities, or in areas ruled by drug lords—Colombia, for example—teachers' influence riles the powerful. Thousands of teachers have been murdered in the past two decades. In the 1990s, Albanian teachers were under death threats from Serbs for teaching the Albanian language. EI managed to rescue some. In other countries EI provided funds to keep destitute teachers from starving. Hawke went to Mongolia, Moldova, Malaysia, Serbia and twice to Turkey (especially difficult because of the Kurdish issue) to investigate. In Belgrade and Ankara passions turned the meetings into shouting matches. In Ankara, a Turk with a walrus moustache and a wrestler's neck became so angry about Kurdish teachers he shouted at Hawke—and was stunned when Hawke roared back at him, louder, longer, stronger. Turks and Kurds were accusing each other of murder. In Belgrade, a two-metre-tall Montenegran kept interjecting. Hawke finally shouted at him too—whereupon the giant leapt to his feet, grinning, to shake the hand of a man more aggressive than himself. But in the collapsed economies of Soviet satellite states the meetings with teachers' unions were tragic affairs. Their members had been unpaid for months. In Mongolia, some teachers had become prostitutes to stay alive. In Moldova, old women and children could be seen on their knees in the snow, begging. Other members of EI's committee of experts, all former leaders of their unions, have travelled to inhospitable, dangerous, impoverished and difficult countries in Africa, South America and the Middle East to find out what can be done to help teachers. van Leeuwen, the secretary general, said, 'No international organisation, not the United Nations or UNESCO or the World Bank, would decide on plans involving education without asking our opinion.' Hawke said,

> I've always had a passionate commitment to the importance of education, so it's been not just a challenge, but a joy, to play a small but, I think, important role in the work of EI for improving the quality and the equity of global education.

By 2015, EI estimates that the world will have a shortage of 18 million teachers.

Hawke's most influential contribution to world development is closer to home. In 1993 the new Chinese leadership invited him to Beijing, his first contact with China since the rupture after Tiananmen. Despite his apprehension, President Jiang Zemin welcomed Hawke as 'an old friend'. On this trip he was waiting in the hotel lobby one day when a slender man with a refined, elfin face introduced himself, explaining he recognised Hawke from media photographs. He was Jiang Xiaosong, an entrepreneur who had prospered in television production and real estate development in Japan. Unknown to Hawke, Jiang was the son of the 1930s and 1940s movie star, Bai Yang, who counted among her fans Mao Zedong, Zhou En-lai and the new President of China, Jiang Zemin. After the Communist takeover, Bai Yang had had the unique honour, for an actress, of being appointed to the People's Congress. Her son was friendly and modest in his demeanour, giving no hint he was already a multimillionaire. (He is also a member of the People's Congress.) He did not speak English but, through an interpreter, pleasantries and cards were exchanged in the lobby, and that was it.

Except it wasn't. Five years later, in mid-1997 when Hawke was visiting Tokyo, Jiang Xiaosong again made contact. He wanted Hawke and the liberal, reformist former Japanese prime minister, Morihiro Hosokawa, to come as his guests to the island of Hainan to see the site on which he planned to build a resort. He thought it could include a conference centre for regional economic discussion. The Asian financial crisis of 1997, which began on 2 July when the Thai baht collapsed, was threatening to engulf not only the region but to become a worldwide economic meltdown. Jiang knew Hawke was 'an old friend of China's' and 'the father of APEC'. The need for more profound regional discussion was evident. Jiang's other guest, Hosokawa, had an impeccable humanitarian pedigree. He had been born a marquis, son of the lord of the Hosokawa samurai clan, and descendant of emperor Morihiro's grandfather, Prince Fumimaro Konoe, had tried to limit the power of the military in the 1940s and to keep Japan's war with China from spreading into a world conflagration. Hosokawa himself had resigned from his party, the Liberal Democrats, because of its corruption, but in his eight months as prime minister he did what no other Japanese leader would: he described Japan as having launched 'a war of aggression, a mistaken war' and expressed his country's responsibility and condolences. In 1994 Hosokawa had visited China and signed an environmental protection treaty between the two nations: a stride forward, given Chinese feelings about the Japanese.

On 28 July, after a long drive from Hainan's main airport, Jiang's guests arrived at a smaller island. It was contained within a pretty river that ran down to a yellow sandy beach and the South China Sea. Hainan is China's only tropical island and, apart from two cities, is largely uninhabited. Next to Jiang's resort site there was a traditional walled village entered through a moon gate. Every house had small pictures of the ancestors outside its front door. The landscape around it was an emerald stretch of rice fields and hills covered in tropical forest—except for a half-finished golf course and a small concrete building from which lunch appeared, to be served alfresco beneath beach umbrellas. The area was called Boao, after a monster, Ao, whom the goddess of mercy had conquered, turning his haunt into a place of tranquillity and beauty: thus Boao. Over this lunch in a rice field the seed of the Boao Forum for Asia was sown. Jiang asked Hosokawa and Hawke to use their contacts to gather a board of former leaders that he asked Hawke to chair. (A Japanese chairman at the time would have been too much for the Chinese to countenance and, English being the lingua franca of business in Asia, someone fluent in English was desirable.) Hawke objected that the chair would have to be Asian and nominated his friend, Fidel Ramos, former president of the Philippines, a hero of the war in the Pacific and a charming, playful dynamo who chomps constantly on an unlit cigar and wears spectacles with empty frames, occasionally alarming audiences by wriggling his fingers through what they thought was glass. Ramos had helped revive his country's economy and democracy after the misrule of Marcos. After more than a year of meetings between the Chinese, the Japanese, Hawke and Ramos, on 5 September 1998 in Manila they laid out the vision for the Boao Forum for Asia. Twenty-eight countries were foundation members—Australia, Bangladesh, Brunei, Cambodia, China, India, Indonesia, Iran, Israel, Japan, Kazakhstan, Kyrgyzstan, Laos, Malaysia, Mongolia, Myanmar, Nepal, New Zealand, Pakistan, the Philippines, Republic of Korea, Singapore, Sri Lanka, Tajikistan, Thailand, Turkmenistan, Uzbekistan and Vietnam—and the first annual conference was in April 2002. By then rice fields had vanished beneath a five-star hotel, a conference centre and landscaped gardens. The golf course was manicured and a towering white statue of the goddess of mercy blessed the enterprise from another small island in the river.

While Jiang spent millions on infrastructure, Ramos as chairman and Hawke as deputy spent thousands of hours over eight years in nurturing BFA's life and growth. It was exceptionally difficult. They and their associates had to create a new culture in China, which at the time was familiar only with government-to-government meetings. China still had a long way to go in introducing herself to the world and to understanding other cultures. The inclusion of non-government participants was neither understood nor greatly appreciated, and the whole enterprise almost collapsed several times in its early days. Ramos and Hawke had to go to Beijing to make representations to the leadership, asking for continued support. But with the appointment of a new and very astute secretary general, Long Yongtu (the main negotiator for China's entry to the World Trade Organization), the forum's original intent of being the pre-eminent intellectual resource centre in Asia began to shape up.

Chinese leaders had been used to a command-and-obey system and, as Long said, were unused to speaking to foreign audiences: they read speeches to bored delegates. Unfortunately, this was taken to be correct form, and copied. But gradually the culture changed. Set-piece speeches were abandoned; in their place came lively panel discussions with media personalities from the BBC, CNN and the *Financial Times* as moderators. There were questions from the floor that, a few years earlier, would have been considered 'rude'. By April 2010, Boao was the foremost meeting place in the Asia–Pacific region for leaders in government, business, academia and the media. Only the World Economic Forum in Davos, which began in 1971, outdid it as a venue for the planet's movers and shakers. 'Chinese people felt uncomfortable at Davos,' Long said.

> But we learned from Davos. We have famous people, like Old Bush and Young Bush, Colin Powell and outstanding statesmen from Asia, and these famous people have an impact. Others want to come. Boao has given Chinese businesses a world perspective, and for foreign business leaders it has great networking value: if they go to Beijing, it will taken them ten days to meet ten government or business people. In Boao in one day they can meet twenty people. Hawke is very sensitive and has a deep understanding. His greatest contribution has been to bring the West and the East together. He has been a bridge, because both sides have confidence in him.

In 2010 Ramos, Hawke and Long all stepped down from the leadership, the former national leaders being immediately appointed to a Boao advisory board. Hawke said,

> I find it difficult to describe the satisfaction—and the pride—I feel in the evolution of the BFA. The rise of world-class conference facilities from an expanse of paddy fields that we contemplated in 1997 is the

physical manifestation of something much more important. My goal was the creation of a Davos, but better, in Asia, and I think we have—certainly by the comments of many European participants—already achieved that. At the annual April conference political, business and academic leaders meet formally and informally to discuss and co-operate on issues of significance to the welfare of the Asian region and beyond. In particular, the continuing strong support of the Chinese government means that attendees can hear and get a real sense of the thinking of the Chinese leadership in government, business and intellectual circles.

One of Hawke's most unusual Education International meetings was held in a herdsman's yurt on the Mongolian steppe, where the refreshment was fermented mare's milk. But his most dramatic experience in pursuing his ideal of reconciliation was a journey from Jerusalem to Ramallah to see Yasser Arafat in September 2003. The second intifada was raging and Hawke travelled in an armoured four-wheel drive. His self-appointed mission—to which Australian businessmen Dick Pratt, a Jew, Fred Shahin, an Arab Palestinian, and John Symond, 'Aussie John', whose family was Lebanese, gave financial support—was to present Arafat with a plan to bring peace and prosperity to Palestine. Hawke had developed it during 2002, alarmed at the warmongering that was beginning to engulf the West. He considered a war in Iraq would be a disaster, and wrote and gave speeches against Australian participation. He had long held the belief that there could be no peace in the Middle East until the Israel–Palestine issue was settled, and that the United States and the West would only continue to make themselves more hated the longer the fighting between Israel and the Palestinians continued. He also believed that Israel was destroying its own future through endless war. He thought that seeking a political solution as the first step on the so-called 'Roadmap to Peace' was putting the cart before the horse. He was convinced that the Palestinian economy had to be revived before Palestinians would have any good reason for wanting peace: with 55 per cent unemployment, shattered infrastructure and houses, why not fight the Israelis? There was nothing much else to do.

By December Hawke had developed an idea that he named after the American Secretary of State, Colin Powell, 'The Powell Plan for Palestine' (see Appendix). It envisaged that the world community, led by the United States, would rebuild the economy and social infrastructure of Palestine, in return for a guaranteed halt to attacks on Israel. He sent the plan to, or talked it through with, Powell himself; George Bush Senior; John Major, the former UK prime minister; President Musharaff of Pakistan; Prince Hassan of Jordan; Alexander Downer, the Australian Foreign minister; UK Prime Minister, Tony Blair; the *éminence grise* of Egyptian politics, Osama el Baz; the Egyptian Prime Minister, Dr Atef Ebeid; Shimon Peres and Ehud Barak, leaders of the Israeli Labor Party, both former prime ministers; Ehud Olmert, the Israeli deputy Prime Minister, of the Likud Party; Ahmed Qurei, the Palestinian Prime Minister ('the smartest man in the world' Peres called him); James Wolfensohn, head of the World Bank; and George Soros, the billionaire financier and philanthropist. Wolfensohn and all the politicians thought the plan was worth trying. Soros alone dismissed the idea as futile.

By the time Hawke had garnered the interest of world leaders, the war in Iraq had begun—and was, the American administration announced, a triumph.

A pall of misery and despair hung over the towns and villages of the West Bank in the autumn of 2003. The few food shops that were open had scant supplies: limp carrots, tinned milk, some apples, bags of rice. Israel was already building the Separation Wall. It ran through the middle of the village of Abu Dis, where Qurei had his office, and was made of concrete. Hawke had to get down from the armoured vehicle and climb over a sort of stile to call on Qurei. The new Palestinian Prime Minister thought the plan was a good idea, but he was clearly distracted by a myriad of worries that he found more pressing.

Hawke was driven on to Ramallah, which seemed a ghost town. There was a high wall around Arafat's compound and Israeli soldiers on the top of all the buildings that overlooked it. Inside the compound a number of buildings had been bombed and lay in ruins, as did the entrance to Arafat's house. Hawke was ushered through khaki canvas flaps, which now served as a door, up a flight of stairs where a wardrobe and sandbags covered a bomb-hole in the wall. Hawke had detested Arafat for decades as the embodiment of violence. It was only his conviction that the international situation was increasingly dangerous that had brought him this far.

The chairman of the Palestinian Authority had been the world's foremost political trickster for more than thirty years, its Great Survivor, the Br'er Rabbit of international affairs: smart, cunning, funny, charming, lucky. And a killer. But when he entered dressed in military uniform, surrounded by aides, he was a pitiful figure, a warlord defeated, depressed and enervated. The dream he had pursued for decades lay in rubble. Whatever his other illnesses, the visible one was vitiligo. It had bleached his face chalk white but left the skin on the backs of his small hands brown, with pale mottles. He immediately launched into a lament, reciting the horrors of what had occurred in the past forty-eight hours—a church bombed in Gaza, a statue of Mary destroyed, 'Our Mary! Our Mary!' he wailed, as if speaking of his own mother. But he had the strange, charismatic power of narcissism. Vanquished and half-dead—he would die fifteen months later—he was still mesmerising.

Arafat liked the plan when Hawke explained it to him. They talked at length, 'between four eyes'. Hawke stressed that the World Bank would be in charge of distributing funds, that the process would be transparent. Arafat knew the head of the bank, James Wolfensohn (Hawke's friend, who had helped break apartheid). 'I trust him,' the chairman said. He was genuinely enthusiastic. Hawke questioned him repeatedly about attacks on Israel. Arafat told Hawke he believed he could persuade the most extreme elements to stop attacks in exchange for the implementation of the proposal. Over lunch he cheered up, declaring, 'Why not? We'll be getting the money.'

Lunch was served on the conference table, and turned out to be a feast of grilled chicken, barbecued prawns, rice, lamb, sweet corn and vegetable dishes. As a host, Arafat could not have been more gracious. The conference room, with its noisy air conditioner and bricked-up windows, became an enchanted place far from bloodshed and violence. The defeated warlord turned into an indulgent father, choosing from the serving dishes delicacies that he placed on the plates of his guests, and passing to them sections of sweet corn delicately held in the tips of his fingers.

After lunch Hawke and the chairman withdrew for another serious talk. Hawke left believing at least one step forward had been taken.

Wherever and whenever he met senior members of the American government, at conferences around the world, in universities, in Washington itself, he continued to sound them out. But the Bush administration had psychologically shifted into a parallel universe, and from that curious unreality was dragging the nation and the world ever more deeply into the quicksands of Mesopotamia. There was no one in the White House who would listen. Years later, after he had left office, Powell told Hawke,

'Bob, I thought your plan was great, but I couldn't get it up on my watch because all they wanted to talk about was Iraq.'

Despite the relentless ethos of hatred between Israel and Palestine and the lack of interest in the United States in doing anything that could offend the Israeli or Christian lobbies, Hawke did not give up his ideal of fostering peace. But in a slow, relentless tide, hatred was spreading.

One avenue blocked, he sought another.

In 1998 the University of South Australia had established the Bob Hawke Prime Ministerial Centre, an institution modelled on the presidential libraries in the United States. Hawke is the only prime minister to have been born in South Australia and the university wanted both to honour him and to extend its range of courses. The centre's motto is 'Strengthening democracy, valuing diversity, building the future'. The Hawke Lecture, given annually in the Adelaide town hall by speakers from Australia and around the world, has become a fixture in the city's intellectual calendar. Under the umbrella of the centre, Hawke has set out to establish another centre, for Muslim–non-Muslim understanding. As of 2010 he had raised $10 million dollars for it, and the search for an appropriate Islamic scholar to lead it was beginning.

Sixteen years earlier his relationship with Hazel had broken down; they lived together less than a year in their new house. The marriage had been unstable for decades, but The Lodge had brought them happiness. It had been the fulfilment of a long-shared dream, for the achievement of which both had been willing to make sacrifices. Once the dream was behind them, their relationship began to deteriorate, a process that hastened when Hazel wrote her autobiography, published in 1992. The manuscript contained passages of deep resentment about Hawke. Some sections were deleted, but old wounds reopened and the situation became acute when the friend who launched the book for Hazel took the opportunity to attack Hawke publicly, in the presence of media, as a bad husband, even a bad man. He was furious. As a matter of honour he had never either publicly or privately voiced dissatisfaction about his marriage and would have stayed in it had he not fallen in love. Hawke had been in love several times in earlier decades, but he and Hazel were now in their sixty-fifth year, and the prospect of enduring the death of a thousand nicks inflicted each on the other in unhappy domestic circumstances, for the rest of their lives, focused his mind. Divorce was not a zero–sum game, he decided, and a clean cut could benefit all parties. During 1994 he and Hazel separated and in 1995 Hawke married a woman he had first met in 1970, who had been his lover on and off for almost twenty years: this author. Hazel seemed relieved the sham was over and on the day Hawke remarried she threw a 'Liberation Party'.

For Hawke, a life of new adventures opened, but the first effect was that he forgave Paul Keating. It took him many years to tell Keating to his face that he was actually indebted to him, but he often remarked to others, 'Paul is my best friend. If I'd stayed PM I couldn't have remarried.' (His second wife would have married someone else.) He began to take annual holidays, often adventurous: to remote tropical islands, on a small ship to the Antarctic. In 2009 the Labor Party honoured him with life membership. Gough and Margaret Whitlam were the only others so rewarded for their decades of devotion to the party. In his eightieth year Hawke hit his third hole-in-one, snorkelled for the first time, went swimming with dolphins in the North Pacific, conducted the Sydney Philharmonic Orchestra and Choir at the Sydney Opera House, and learned to waltz. A year later he began tango lessons and was planning a trip to the Galapagos and Easter Island where he hoped to see stone replicas—if not of himself and Paul Keating—certainly of Malcolm Fraser, circa 1983.

Appendix: A Powell Plan for Palestine

The fall of the Berlin Wall and the collapse of the Soviet Union gave birth to heroic assumptions about a New World Order. Those assumptions were strengthened with the emergence of the Oslo process and what seemed to be substantive developments based on that apparent accord. But now, a decade on, the world is more apprehensive about the possibility of a stable future than at any stage, probably, since the Cuban missile crisis.

The elements of instability have changed dramatically. In the Cold War the threat was constituted by a hegemonistic, atheistic nation-state—the Soviet Union. States and forces of differing political persuasions were united against a threat which was equally offensive to the Judaeo-Christian and Islamic religious traditions. The menace of Soviet Communism made allies of Bin Ladens and Bushes.

But with the dissolution of the cement of anti-Sovietism, restrained hatreds have been released and violently manifested, from September 11 2001 in New York to 12 October 2002 in Bali. This is not the occasion to attempt to analyse all the strands that go to make up the totality of the threat of international terrorism from fundamental Islamic extremists and their supporters. But, for present purposes, two points are relevant.

First, America, the world superpower, and those deemed to be its supporters, are designated as the 'enemy' for having no respect, understanding or sympathy for Islamic people and their aspirations, and indeed for contemptuously acting against those interests.

Second, whatever may be said or done to attempt to correct this extremist representation, which resonates in many quarters of the globe, nothing effective can be done in this direction while the festering sore of the Palestinian problem continues. This issue is used to encapsulate and dramatise the 'enemy' syndrome, with America and its deemed supporters cast as the villains.

It is imperative, therefore, that an entirely new approach be formulated to the Palestinian question, an issue which, in any case, cries out for resolution in terms of the aspirations of the Palestinians themselves, and the security of Israel and the region. It is not argued that resolving this issue resolves the challenge of international terrorism but that it is a sine qua non for meeting that challenge.

The only proposition concerning the Israeli–Palestinian crisis that can be advanced with any certainty is that everything that has been tried to this point has not worked and that, if anything, the situation is now, in many respects, worse than it has ever been. The hurdy-gurdy of hatred has ground on remorselessly with increasing casualties and diminishing hope. The cycle of hatred and violence, I repeat, can only be broken and a positive outcome achieved by radically new thinking.

In looking for historical support for such an approach we can do no better than look to immediate postwar Europe and the Marshall Plan, named after the then Secretary of State, George Marshall. In an act displaying a generosity of spirit and enlightened self-interest unequalled in the twentieth century, the Truman administration poured billions of dollars into creating viable economic entities in the war-torn countries of Western

Europe. In addressing, practically, the needs and aspirations of the peoples of those countries it did as much to meet the threat of Soviet hegemony as any military outlays.

There is a general recognition, including among the majority of Israelis, that the Palestinians are entitled to their own independent state, an outcome that was envisioned by the 1947 United Nations Resolution enabling the creation of the state of Israel. But the political shell of a state lacking a viable and vibrant economy is a recipe for even greater disaster.

Palestinians, particularly young Palestinians, exist in a dysfunctional economic environment with virtually no hope of employment or maintenance, let alone improvement, of their living standards. This is a breeding ground for despair and worse—while there is no hope among the young for jobs and the constructive development of their talents there will be no shortage of recruits for the martyrdom of the suicide bomber.

What is required now is the 'Powell Plan'. The United States should take the lead, with the support of Europe, the moderate Arab states and Israel in making an unequivocal commitment to a massive supply of capital, technical and educational expertise and equipment dedicated to the creation of an education system and an economic structure that will give the reality of hope to the Palestinian people.

The World Bank should provide the delivery mechanism and technical assistance for the implementation of this program and there should be co-operation through the World Trade Organization to provide a period of most favoured access to export markets for the products from the new economy. The genuine commitment of the United States and other donors should be communicated and detailed to the Palestinian Authority, the leaders of the militant groups and, through television and other media, to the people of Palestine and the region.

The financial and technical capacity of the donor states to meet the requirements of this initiative is not in question. What is required is the will and the imagination. It is easy enough to list the difficulties that may lie in the path of carrying through with the initiative, but that is the counsel of despair and hopelessness. If genuinely embraced, I believe this concept can mark the beginning of a sea change in the poisonous atmosphere of hatreds and misconceptions that threaten the very stability and existence of the world as we know it.

R. J. L. Hawke
17 December 2002

NOTES

CHAPTER 1

1. Edna Carew and Patrick Cook, *Keating: Shut Up and Listen and You Might Learn Something!* New Endeavour Press, Sydney, 1990.
2. Bob Hawke, *The Hawke Memoirs*, William Heinemann Australia, Melbourne, 1994, pp. 178–86.
3. Hansard, 3 March 1983, p. 94.
4. John le Carré, *A Small Town in Germany*, Heinemann, London, 1968, p. 303.
5. Meena Blesing, *'Was Your Dad a Russian Spy?': The Personal Story of the Combe/Ivanov Affair by David Combe's Wife*, Meena Blesing, Sun Books, South Melbourne, 1986, pp. 48–9.
6. Ibid., p. 49.
7. David Marr, *The Ivanov Trail*, Nelson, Melbourne, 1984, p. 285.
8. Blesing, *'Was Your Dad a Russian Spy?'*, p. 103.
9. Marr, *The Ivanov Trail*, pp. 295, 301.

CHAPTER 2

1. Max Weber, *Politik als Beruf* (Politics as Vocation), delivered in January 1919 to the Free Students Society, Munich University, and published in October 1919.

CHAPTER 3

1. Paul Kelly, *The End of Certainty: The Story of the 1980s*, Allen & Unwin, Sydney, 1992, p. 157.
2. Ibid., p. 160.

3   Ibid., p. 156.
4   Ibid., p. 157.
5   Ibid., p. 158.
6   Ibid., p. 161.
7   John Hyde, *Dry: In Defence of Economic Freedom: The Saga of How the Dries Changed the Australian Economy for the Better*, Institute of Public Affairs, Melbourne, 2002, p. 226.
8   Kelly, *The End of Certainty*, p. 170.
9   Ibid.
10 Ibid., p. 173.

Chapter 4

1   Foreign Affairs cable, 19 May 1986.

Chapter 5

1   John Edwards, *Keating: The Inside Story*, Viking, Melbourne, 1996; Don Watson, *Recollections of a Bleeding Heart: A Portrait of Paul Keating PM*, Knopf, Sydney, 2002.
2   Stephen Mills, *The Hawke Years: The Story from the Inside*, Viking, Melbourne, 1993, pp. 91–2.
3   Graham Richardson, *Whatever It Takes*, Bantam Books, Sydney, 1994, p. 189.
4   Mills, *The Hawke Years*, p. 93.
5   Richardson, *Whatever It Takes*, p. 214.
6   Ibid., p. 205.
7   Hansard, 3 June 1987, p. 3880–1.
8   Ibid., 3 June 1987, p. 3890.
9   Richardson, *Whatever It Takes*, p. 249.
10 Ibid., p. 247.

Chapter 6

1   Bill Hayden, *Hayden: An Autobiography*, Angus & Robertson, Sydney, 1996, p. 380.
2   Ibid., p. 381.
3   Secret cable, Department of Foreign Affairs, 21 May 1986.

4 Quoted in an address by Prof. Kader Ismal, Minister for Education for South Africa, at the symposium organised by the Anti-apartheid Movement Archives Committee to mark the 40th anniversary of the establishment of the anti-apartheid movement, South Africa House, London, 26 June 1999.

Chapter 7

1 Mills, *The Hawke Years*, p. 168.
2 Ibid., pp. 168–9.
3 Kelly, *The End of Certainty*, pp. 440–1.

Chapter 8

1 Kelly, *The End of Certainty*, p. 492.
2 Richardson, *Whatever It Takes*, p. 257.
3 Kelly, *The End of Certainty*, p. 533.

Chapter 9

1 Richardson, *Whatever It Takes*, p. 264.
2 Ibid., p. 271.
3 Mills, *The Hawke Years*, p. 129.
4 Ibid., p. 130.
5 Richardson, *Whatever It Takes*, p. 278.
6 Marian Wilkinson, *The Fixer: The Untold Story of Graham Richardson*, William Heinemann Australia, Melbourne, p. 51.
7 Richardson, *Whatever It Takes*, p. 281.
8 Wilkinson, *The Fixer*, p. 328.
9 Richardson, *Whatever It Takes*.
10 Ibid., pp. 279–82.
11 Ibid., p. 282.
12 Ibid.
13 Ibid., pp. 283–4.
14 Kelly, *The End of Certainty*, p. 618.

Chapter 10

1 Kelly, *The End of Certainty*, p. 627.

2 Hyde, *Dry*, p. 234.
3 Kelly, *The End of Certainty*, pp. 665–7.
4 Hansard, 11 April 1991, p. 2447.
5 Kelly, *The End of Certainty*, p. 629.
6 Mills, *The Hawke Years*, pp. 255–6.
7 Richardson, *Whatever It Takes*, p. 302.
8 Ibid., p. 328.
9 Kelly, *The End of Certainty*, p. 641.
10 Ibid., p. 639.
11 Peter Hartcher, 'The Execution of Brother Bob: The Inside Story', *Good Weekend*, supplement to the *Sydney Morning Herald* and the *Age*, 2 May 1992.
12 Richardson, *Whatever It Takes*, pp. 335–6.
13 Hartcher, 'The Execution of Brother Bob'.
14 Richardson, *Whatever It Takes*, p. 337.

BIBLIOGRAPHY

Barnett, Harvey. *Tale of the Scorpion*. Allen & Unwin, Sydney, 1988.
Barry, Paul. *The Rise and Rise of Kerry Packer*. Bantam, Sydney, 1993.
Beazley, Kim. *National Security: A Report to the Constituents of Brand: A Collection of Speeches by Kim Beazley*. Glide, Perth, 2007.
Blesing, Meena. *'Was Your Dad a Russian Spy?': The Personal Story of the Combe/Ivanov Affair by David Combe's Wife, Meena Blesing*. Sun Books, Melbourne, 1986.
Carew, Edna. *Keating: A Biography*. Allen & Unwin, Sydney, 1988.
—— and Patrick Cook. *Keating: Shut Up and Listen and You Might Learn Something!* New Endeavour Press, Sydney, 1990.
Edwards, John. *Keating: The Inside Story*. Viking, Melbourne, 1996.
FitzSimons, Peter. *Beazley: A Biography*. HarperCollins, Sydney, 1998.
Freudenberg, Graham. *A Figure of Speech: A Political Memoir*. John Wiley & Sons, Brisbane, 2005.
Grattan, Michelle (ed.). *Australian Prime Ministers*. New Holland, Sydney, 2000.
Hartcher, Peter. 'The Execution of Brother Bob: The Inside Story', *Good Weekend*, supplement to the *Sydney Morning Herald* and the *Age*, 2 May 1992.
Hawke, Bob. *The Hawke Memoirs*. William Heinemann Australia, Melbourne, 1994.
Hayden, Bill. *Hayden: An Autobiography*. Angus & Robertson, Sydney, 1996.
Hyde, John. *Dry: In Defence of Economic Freedom: The Saga of How the Dries Changed the Australian Economy for the Better*. Institute of Public Affairs, Melbourne, 2002.

Kelly, Paul. *The End of Certainty: The Story of the 1980s*. Allen & Unwin, Sydney, 1992.
le Carré, John. *A Small Town in Germany*. Heinemann, London, 1968.
Lloyd, C. J. *Parliament and the Press*. Melbourne University Press, Melbourne, 1988.
Marr, David. *The Ivanov Trail*. Nelson, Melbourne, 1984.
Mills, Stephen. *The Hawke Years: The Story from the Inside*. Viking, Melbourne, 1993.
Oxley, Alan. *The Challenge of Free Trade*. St Martin's Press, New York, 1990.
Richardson, Graham. *Whatever It Takes*. Bantam Books, Sydney, 1994.
Ryan, Susan and Troy Bramston (eds). *The Hawke Government: A Critical Retrospective*. Pluto Press, Melbourne, 2003.
Thatcher, Margaret. *The Downing Street Years*. HarperCollins, London, 1993.
Watson, Don. *Recollections of a Bleeding Heart: A Portrait of Paul Keating PM*. Knopf, Sydney, 2002.
Weber, Max. *Politik als Beruf* (Politics as Vocation), delivered in January 1919 to the Free Students Society, Munich University, and published in October 1919.
Wilkinson, Marian. *The Fixer: The Untold Story of Graham Richardson*. William Heinemann Australia, Melbourne, 1996.
Zhao Ziyang (trs. Bao Pu, Renee Chiang and Adi Ignatius). *Prisoner of the State: The Secret Journal of Premier Zhao Ziyang*. Simon & Schuster, New York, 2009.

INDEX

Abeles, Sir Peter, 68–9, 84, 85, 231, 240, 244, 246, 247, 264, 265–6, 281–2, 299, 332, 333, 336, 358
Accord, 13, 81; brainchild of Willis, 23; and domestic pilots strike, 244, 245, 247; Hawke enthusiasm for, 24–5; Hayden unwilling, 24; Keating initially sceptical, 26, 30–1; negotiating team, 25; union movement input, 25
ACTU *see* Australian Council of Trade Unions (ACTU)
Adams, Phillip, 272
Advisory Council on Prices and Incomes, 143
Afghanistan, 15, 175, 179
Age of Anxiety, 263–4
airlines: duopoly, 43; pilots strike, 243, 244–7, 263, 264; privatisation, 242–3, 305–6
America's Cup win, 54–5
American alliance (ANZUS); American bases in Australia, 99–100, 110; Hawke and Shultz, 102, 106–7, 109–10;

Hayden educates electorate and party, 103–4; MX missile tests, 100–1, 102–11
Annan, Joy, 333
Antarctic Minerals Convention, 254–8
Antarctic Treaty, 176
anti-Vietnam War campaigns, 34
ANZUS *see* American alliance (ANZUS)
apartheid: Eminent Persons negotiations fail, 201, 202; Hawke's role in fight against, 200; international financial boycotting, 204–7; sanctions, 201, 202; Springbok tour 1970, 200
APEC *see* Asia–Pacific Economic Cooperation (APEC)
Arafat, Yasser, 214, 366, 368–9
ASEAN *see* Australia and South East Asian Nations (ASEAN)
Ash Wednesday bushfires, 7
Asia–Pacific Economic Cooperation (APEC): China and, 196, 197–8, 199, 200;

effectiveness, 200; first meeting, Canberra 1989, 199; Hawke and, 192–4, 199–200; hurdles to formation, 194–5; inclusion of Hong Kong and Taiwan, 196; Keating raises to leaders' meeting, 200; membership in 2009, 200; US and formation, 194–6, 198–9; Woolcott's negotiation, 196–9
ASIO *see* Australian Security and Intelligence Organisation (ASIO)
ASIS *see* Australian Secret Intelligence Service (ASIS)
Australia of South East Asian Nations (ASEAN), 179, 181, 185, 186, 188, 195, 196, 197, 198–9
Australia II, 54–5
Australia–USSR Friendship Society, 17
Australian Conservation Foundation, 250, 252
Australian Council of Trade Unions (ACTU): opposes Tax Summit, 115–16, 119, 139; and wage restraint, 119, 242
Australian Democrats, 247
Australian Federation of Air Pilots, 243, 244–7
Australian Labor Party (ALP): and American alliance, 100, 103–4; anti-Vietnam War campaigns, 34; under Chifley and Curtin, 11; Communist infiltration allegations, 34; and foreign banks, 83; Hawke most successful prime minister, 169; in Hawke's youth, 11; history on security matters, 33–4; hostility to ASIO, 16, 17–18, 22, 32, 38, 39; learning of economic crisis, 148–50; life membership for Hawke, 371; loses electoral base in Hawke's second term, 158–9; National Conference (1991), 338; NSW Left, 279; NSW Right, 64, 279, 280–1, 341; party of natural conflict, 66–7; Split in mid-1950s, 16, 280; and John Stone, 55–6; uranium issue, 71–2, 83; Victorian Right, 280
Australian Labor Party Caucus: and American alliance, 100, 103–4; Caucus elects ministry, PM allots portfolios, 230; and destabilising effect of Keating, 346–7; and Gulf War, 301; and Hawke's emotional outbursts, 92; and Ivanov Affair, 41–2; and MX missile tests, 103, 104–6; selection of ministers, 67–8, 230; and Young's resignation over security breach, 49
Australian Mining Industry Council, 335
Australian Secret Intelligence Service (ASIS), 16
Australian Security and Intelligence Organisation

(ASIO): ALP hostility to, 16, 17–18, 22, 32, 38, 39; and Combe–Ivanov affair, 21–2, 32–3, 38, 39, 45–7; Hawke and, 32

Baker, Jim, 193, 195–6, 199, 234
Balderstone, Simon, 252
'banana republic', 138, 140–3, 144–5, 146, 155
banks: bad debts, 330; financial deregulation, 262–3; foreign, 83
Bannon, John, 130, 343
Barak, Ehud, 367
Barnes, Alan, 260
Barnett, Harvey, 22, 32–7, 38, 45
Barron, Peter, 62, 68–9, 70, 73, 74–5, 77, 92, 114, 120, 139, 144–5, 156, 157, 276, 283
Barton, John, 6
Beazley, Kim, 71, 95, 226, 230, 279, 280, 328, 351, 352, 353, 354, 355; Defence, 67, 100–3, 104, 106, 107–8, 283–4; on economy under Hawke, 78; on Hawke as a politician, 259; as Hawke's successor, 284; and proposed MX test, 102–3, 104, 106, 107–8; and Tax Summit, 116; Transport and Communications, 281, 305; turns 'American bases' into 'joint facilities', 110
Berlin Wall, 290, 291
Bjelke-Petersen, Sir Joh, 31, 119; and fall of Whitlam government, 154; Hawke humiliates over flat tax proposal, 167; 'Joh for Canberra', 155, 162–8; and road through Daintree, 250
Blair, Tony, 367
Blandy, Richard, 245
Blesing, Meena, 17–18, 20, 39, 49, 51, 53
Blewett, Neal, 5
Boao Forum for Asia, 362–6
Bob Hawke Prime Ministerial Centre, 208, 370
Bolkus, Nick, 352
Bond, Alan, 276
'bottom of the harbour scheme', 86
Bowan, John, 65, 157, 187, 278–9, 325; Foreign Affairs adviser, 64, 67–8, 101, 194, 211–12, 217; on Hawke, 210; and MX tests, 101, 173
Bowen, Lionel, 5, 38, 79, 143–4
Bowers, Peter, 265
Brereton, Laurie, 354
Brown, Bob, 160, 161–2
Builders Labourers' Federation, 29
'Building a Competitive Australia', 322–5, 333
Burke, Brian, 328–9
Bush, George H., 10, 133, 234, 240, 241, 256, 291, 292, 293, 294, 307, 311, 367, 369
Business Council of Australia, 29, 116, 117–18
Butler, David, 41

Button, John, 2–3, 8–9, 10, 41, 76, 93, 149, 227, 286, 296–7, 317, 322, 351

Cain, John, 105, 267
Cairns, Jim, 71–2
Caldicott, Dr Helen, 105
Calwell, Arthur, 74
Cambodia, 176–91
Cameron, Clyde, 27
Cameron, Rod, 38, 39, 43, 165
Canberra, 37
capital gains tax, 93, 112
Carleton, Richard, 5–6, 45, 163–4
Carmichael, Laurie, 25
Carroll, Bishop James, 280
Caucus *see* Australian Labor Party Caucus
Ceauşescu, Nicolae, 220
Chaney, Fred, 93
Charles, Stephen, 46
Cheney, Dick, 110–11, 311–12
Chifley, Ben, 11, 170, 302
China: and APEC formation, 196, 197–8, 199, 200; Australia a gateway to the West, 123, 125; Australia's relations with after Tiananmen, 239–40; corruption problems, 135–6; cultural exchanges, 130; Cultural Revolution, 122–3, 124, 129–30; death of Hu Yaobang, 235; Deng moving to market economy, 122, 123; destabilising Cambodian government, 179; early obstacles to diplomatic relations, 123; economy in recession, 240; Gang of Four, 124; Gorbachev visit, 238; Hawke and Hu, 128–9, 131, 132–5, 184–5; Hawke popular in China, 124, 235–7; Hawke and Zhao, 122, 125, 126–8, 131, 135; Hu disgraced, 136–7; iron and steel the foundation of friendship, 125, 126–9, 135; and Japan, 123, 134–5; protocol for leaders, 132; recognising Hong Kong, 194; and Soviet Union, 125, 134; students in Australia, 131, 239–40; supports Khmer Rouge, 179; and Taiwan, 133–4, 194, 195, 199; Tiananmen Square, 137, 189, 190, 197–8, 199, 237–9, 240; and US, 125, 132–4, 240–1; Whitlam and Fraser well regarded, 122
Chipp, Don, 219
CHOGM *see* Commonwealth Heads of Government meetings
Civil Aviation Authority, 246
Clark, Professor Manning, 296
'clever country', 269, 323, 325
Clinton, Bill, 30, 107
COAG *see* Council of Australian Governments (COAG)
Codd, Mike, 157, 161, 193–4, 196, 198, 202–7, 316, 319–20, 343–4

Cohen, Barry, 161
Cold War, 14–15, 16, 263, 291, 293, 359
Cole, Tony, 120, 206, 334
Combe, David, 165; accepts overseas post, 53; ASIO concern about, 21–2, 32–3, 38, 39, 45–7; background, 18–19; blackballed as lobbyist, 42, 45, 52; and Dunstan, 18–19; friendship with Hawke, 19–20; Hope Royal Commission, 47, 50–2, 53; and Iraqi Loans Affair, 20; and Ivanov, 16–18, 20–1, 32–53
Commonwealth Heads of Government meetings: 1985 anti-apartheid negotiations, 201–2; 1987 financial lever against apartheid, 202–3
Commonwealth–state relations *see* Council of Australian Governments (COAG)
Conciliation and Arbitration Commission, 31
Connell, Laurie, 328, 329
consumption tax, 111–12, 115, 116, 118, 119, 139, 331, 338, 340, 342
Cook, Michael, 35–6, 311
Cook, Peter, 230
Coronation Hill mining, 335–6
Costello, Michael, 174, 176–91, 210, 214
Costigan, Frank, 85, 86
Costigan Royal Commission, 85–7, 89, 153, 264

Council of Australian Governments (COAG): established, 321; Greiner sees as a 'joke', 317–18; Hawke on (1979), 316; initiative, 333, 343–5; Keating and, 333, 343–6; need for economic reform, 315–16; Piglets, 319; premiers' advisers, 319–20; Special Premiers' Conference on (1990), 317, 319–20; tied grants a problem, 318; 'vertical fiscal imbalance' corrected, 320–1
Cousteau, Jacques, 255
Crawford, John, 57
Crawford Study Group for Structural Adjustment, 57
Crean, Simon, 119
Crimes Act, 47–8
Curtin, John, 11, 22, 28, 97, 141, 159, 170, 219, 302, 303

Dawkins, John, 5, 8, 76, 149, 150, 159, 170, 219, 252, 323, 336, 355, 356; Expenditure Review Committee, 79, 80; Finance, 40; Hawke sees as replacement for Keating, 227–30; Keating promises Treasury, 230; leaking from Cabinet, 340; supports Keating succession, 221–2, 229–30, 326–7; Trade, 53
death duties, 93, 111
defence *see* American alliance (ANZUS)

Deng Xiaoping, 122, 123, 127, 135–6, 137, 197–8, 220, 237, 238, 239, 240
Department of Foreign Affairs and Trade, 191–2
Department of Trade and Industry, 79
Deputy Prime Minister: Howe replaces Keating, 340; Keating, 296
Dibb, Paul, 17
Downer, Alexander, 367
drought, 7, 14
Drysdale, Dr Peter, 321–2
Duffy, Michael, 2–3, 70–1, 352
Dunstan, Don, 18–19

East Timor, 15
Ebeid, Dr Atef, 367
Economic Planning and Advisory Council (EPAC), 29–30
Economic Summit, 22–3, 81; cements Accord, 29; final communiqué, 31; Hawke's idea, 23; an international model, 30; Keating embraces, 30–1; Peacock on, 31; reactions to, 26–7; scepticism about, 26–7; spinoffs, 29–30; success, 27–9, 31; Willis on, 26–7
economy: 'Building a Competitive Australia', 322–5, 333; Hawke asks unions to cut wages, 148; when Hawke elected, 7, 12; Hawke's response to 'banana republic', 140; long-term perspectives, 82; macroeconomic policy, 80–1; microeconomic reform, 81, 287; Moody's downgrades AAA rating, 146; recession emerging 1990, 289–90, 300; reforms in New Federalism speech, 315–16; restructuring, 77–83; after stock market crash, 220–1, 241–2, 289–90; *see also* Expenditure Review Committee (ERC)
education: Chinese students at Australian universities, 131; proportion of children completing high school, 81; state differences, 315
Education International, 359–61, 366
Edwards, John, 228
el Baz, Osama, 367
election 1983: Hawke's campaign and vision, 5–7, 13; Liberals run a fear campaign, 12; political judgment untested, 8–9; popularity Hawke's strength, 2, 10; voters wary of Hawke's public demeanour, 4–5
election 1984: early election, 92; 8-week campaign, 92–3; electorate irritated at, 94; Hawke's eye injury debilitating, 94, 98; Hawke's performance, 95–7; Keating campaigns well, 96–7; Labor assumes an easy victory, 95–6;

Labor win less than hoped for, 97; Peacock wins debate, 96; pensions a major issue, 96
election 1987: announced, 167; Family Allowance Supplement, 172–3; Hawke's 'no child will live in poverty' slip, 172–3, 267–8; 'Joh for Canberra' a gift to Labor, 162–4, 167–8, 169; Singleton runs Labor's ad campaign, 165–6, 168–9; tax reform platform, 112; win a highpoint for Hawke and party, 169
election 1990: campaign driven by polling, 266; choice between lesser of two evils, 264; electioneering unexciting, 270; green preferences the votes to win, 249, 250, 252–3, 272–3; Hawke–Peacock debate a turning point, 269–70; Hawke promises to stay on till 1993, 266; Hawke's temper a source of anxiety, 270; Hawke win linked with Keating, 266; Hazel campaigning, 271; importance of win, 261–2; Labor launch, 267–9; Opposition expected to win, 259; Peacock's disastrous start, 269; Singleton runs ad campaign, 274; spontaneity a problem, 272; state Labor governments in trouble, 266–7; traditional Labor voters desert, 273–4

Elizabeth II, Queen, 282–3
Elliott, John, 226
Emerson, Dr Craig, 161–2, 249, 251, 252, 253, 254, 255–6, 257–8, 268, 274–5, 290
Eminent Persons' Group, 201, 202
environment: access to uranium through Daintree, 250, 251; Antarctic Minerals Convention, 254–8; Bob Brown talks to Hawke, 161–2; Emerson becomes environmental adviser, 161–2; greenhouse effect, 252; Hawke a green convert, 249–53; LandCare Australia, 252; logging and Tasmanian wilderness, 161–2, 250, 251; persuading Cabinet, 248–9; protecting Great Barrier Reef, 251; Richardson embraces cause, 160–1; Richardson sees future in preferences, 247–8, 252–3, 272–3; Shelburne Bay project, 251; unionists traditionally oppose issues, 249; World Heritage listings, 251
EPAC *see* Economic Planning and Advisory Council (EPAC)
ERC *see* Expenditure Review Committee (ERC)
Evans, Gareth, 116, 352, 353–4; Attorney-General and Combe–Ivanov affair, 32, 36, 39–40, 43, 45–6, 52; Foreign

Affairs, 186–7, 189, 190, 193, 195–6, 254, 298; and Gulf War, 294, 296–7
Evans, Graham, 32, 33, 35–6, 40–1, 48, 59, 62, 63, 67, 91, 94, 155–6, 173
exchange rate reform, 58–9, 61–3
Expenditure Review Committee (ERC): cuts to 1986 Budget, 148–50; Dawkins on, 80; first expenditure review statement, 80; justifying all expenditure, 148; levying fees on tertiary students, 150–1; members, 79; 1983 Budget preparation, 80; purpose, 79

Fairfax media empire, 276
Family Allowance Supplement, 172–3
Farmer, Richard, 41, 95, 337
Fightback!, 348, 349, 350, 356, 357
financial deregulation, 262–3
Fitchett, Ian, 260
floating the dollar, 61–3, 76–7
foreign affairs: Australia 'deputy sheriff' to US, 195; Australia's image abroad in 1980, 12; Cambodia, 176–91; Cold War threat to Australia, 15–16; 'enmeshment with Asia', 125, 193; under Fraser, 15; Gulf War, 296–302; Hawke accused of being 'lickspittle of the US', 175; Hawke's first visit overseas as PM, 174; Hawke intermediary role between USSR and US, 214; South Africa (apartheid), 200–7; *see also* American alliance (ANZUS); APEC; China; Gulf War; United Nations Security Council; Soviet Union
France: atomic testing on Mururoa Atoll, 255; and *Rainbow Warrior*, 255, 258
Franklin Dam, 160
Fraser, Malcolm: anti-apartheid, 200–1; appointed to Eminent Persons' Group, 201
Fraser, Malcolm, prime minister: campaign against Hawke, 12; and China, 122; a divisive leader, 13; faces Hawke not Hayden, 3; leadership qualities, 9–10; minor achievements, 1; and racial issues, 58
Fraser government: Costigan Royal Commission into the Ship Painters and Dockers, 85–7, 89, 153, 264; economic issues, 58; and Medicare, 25
free trade, 322–5
Freudenberg, Graham, 74, 159, 169, 268, 339, 351, 358
Fukuyama, Professor Francis, 290–1

Gallagher, Norm, 29
Gandhi, Rajiv, 201, 203, 206
Garnaut, Ross, 139, 156, 209; Ambassador to China, 129,

130, 132, 135, 137, 237–8, 240; at Australian National University, 321–2; chief economic adviser, 59–63, 67, 75–6, 80, 82; and economic reform, 82, 321–2, 324; and engagement with Asia, 57; and Hawke, 57, 73, 76, 157; on Hawke, 90–1, 265; on Hawke's advisers, 69–70; on Hawke's joint venture proposal to China, 126, 127; on Keating, 65–6, 75–6; on rise of north-east Asian economies, 321–2, 324; and Tax Summit, 94, 111, 114, 115
Garrett, Peter, 250–1
Gawenda, Michael, 97
Gaylor, John, 250
Gill, Reverend Mr David, 308
Gilroy, Cardinal, 280
Gittins, Ross, 323
gold tax, 329, 330
goods and services tax, 345, 348–9
Gorbachev, Mikhail, 210, 214–15, 216, 237, 238, 340
Gore, Al, 257–8
Gore, Mike, 154, 155
Gorton, John, 78, 157
Goss, Wayne, 319
Gration, General, 307–8
Grattan, Michelle, 241, 260, 337, 347
Gray, Robin, 317
Great Barrier Reef, 251
greenhouse effect, 252

Greiner, Nick, 317–18, 319, 320, 321, 343, 344–5
Grenada, US invasion of, 174–5
Grey Power, 93
Griffiths, Alan, 105–6
Gulf War, 304, 306; Australian deployment, 296, 297–8, 303, 307–8, 309; parliamentary debates, 309–10, 312; protest rallies, 307, 308; Saddam burns oil wells, 314–15; Saddam invades Kuwait, 291–3; war over, 314

Hand, Gerry, 230, 310, 352
Harris, Max, 289
Hartcher, Peter, 323–4, 352, 354
Hassan of Jordan, Prince, 294–5, 367
Hawke (TV docu-drama), 146
Hawke, Bert, 11
Hawke, Bob: admired as unafraid to show feelings, 327; anomaly in Labor politics, 66–7; Australian of the Year, 67; Christian principles, 11; depression, 90, 119; drugs issue close to home, 87–9, 91; enjoying job as prime minister, 169–70; 'enmeshment' with Asia, 193; eye injury before 1984 election, 94; frankness with electorate, 77; friendship with Abeles, 264–5; Gallipoli visit, 287–8, 310; and Garnaut, 76; a green convert, 249;

and Hayden, 183; health and stamina, 141; involving senior public servants, 194; and Jean Sinclair, 338–9, 342; and Jewish community, 216; and Keating, 64–5, 119–21, 141, 145; Liberals see as a trade unionist, 259; loses aura after 1984 election, 97; and mother, 8; nicknames, 229, 327; outstanding leader of Cabinet, 248; personality, 222; philandering, 10, 84, 232, 271; and press gallery, 260–1; record three election wins, 169; relaxing with crosswords, 142; religion, 11; seeks intellectual companionship, 265; teetotal, 4, 10; temper, 6–7, 70–1, 270; and Thatcher, 201; trusting of others, 266; vulnerable to praise, 71; weeping over family problems, 88, 89–90, 119; work habits, 141; World Jewish Congress honours, 216

Hawke, Bob, prime minister: advisers, 67–76; ambitions in role, 10–11; Australia's 23rd Prime Minister, 7–8; authority fracturing in government, 346; blunders after 1990 election win, 274–82; consensus approach to Cabinet, 116; embarrassed over misinformation on WA Inc., 329–30; evidence at Hope Royal Commission, 49–50; first budget, 60–1; at Gallipoli, 287–8; goal of historic fourth term, 232–3; government losing its edge, 287; importance of winning in 1990, 261–2; Keating camp make parliament unworkable, 349–50; Kirribilli pact, 231–2, 266, 299, 304, 313, 314, 327, 332; losing electoral base, 158–9; mishandles Richardson and Ray portfolios, 284–5; 'no child will live in poverty' slip, 172–3, 267–8; office staff, 74–6, 155–7; as parliamentary speaker, 52; political judgment untested, 8–9; popularity, 2, 10, 67, 83, 158, 159, 263; power in 1983, 55; refuses advice to stand down, 351, 352–3; role in economy, 77–83, 322–5; surgery affects public standing, 288–9

Hawke, Bob, retired from politics: Centre for Muslim-non-Muslim Understanding, 370; coping with no job, 357–8; and Education International, 359–61, 366; forgives Keating, 371; holidays and relaxation, 371; invited to China, 361–2; life membership of Labor Party, 371; meets Arafat, 368–9; Powell Plan for Palestine, 366–9, 372–5; pride in Boao

Forum for Asia, 362–6; relationship with Hazel breaks down, 370–1; remarries, 371; staunch friends, 358
Hawke, Clem, 7, 8, 202–3, 303, 304–5
Hawke, Ellie, 8
Hawke, Hazel: ambition to live in Lodge, 83–4; and Barbara Bush, 234; campaigning in 1990, 271; grandsons living at Lodge, 98; and Hawke's philandering, 83, 84; health problems, 350; and Jean Sinclair, 338, 339; protective of Hawke, 87; proud of Hawke, 83; relationship with Hawke, 334, 370–2; speaks about daughter's drug problem, 91; staying in the background, 83; supports Hawke's determination to fight, 354
Hawke, Rosslyn, 84–5, 88, 91, 92, 98, 120, 145–6
Hawke, Stephen, 84, 89, 328
Hawke, Susan, 64, 84, 85, 87, 88, 217
Hayden, Bill, 19–20, 167; and Combe–Ivanov affair, 36, 38; comment on Hawke's first win, 8; distrust of unions, 24; educates party and electorate about US alliance, 103–4; Foreign Minister, 5, 180–3, 189, 191; Governor-General, 186; leadership battle with Hawke, 2–3; on Keating, 63, 77, 118; on MX missile tests, 104–5, 106; rebuilds Labor Party, 1–2; on relationship with Hawke, 183; resigns as leader, 3, 356; and Shultz, 107, 181–2; on Whitlam, 9
Hawke Lecture, 370
Herzog, Chaim, 213
Hewson, John, 244, 261; consumption tax proposal, 331, 340; *Fightback!*, 348, 349, 350, 356, 357; to Gallipoli with Hawke, 310; Liberal leader, 274, 287, 323, 331, 335; polls show preferred PM, 288, 350; supports Hawke on Iraq War, 310
Higgins, Dr Chris, 302, 334
Hogg, Bob, 6, 39, 44, 68, 71, 72–3, 75, 77, 114, 144, 156, 158, 166, 242, 330–1
'holding paddock', 252, 272
Hollway, Sandy, 144–5, 173, 192–3, 194, 196–7, 208, 209, 210, 214, 217, 219, 220, 237, 268, 278–9
Hong Kong, 194, 196, 198, 199
Hope Royal Commission, 44–7; exonerates government, 53; Hawke in witness box, 49–50
Hornery, Stuart, 20
Hosokawa, Mirohiro, 362–3
Howard, John, 26, 89–90, 107, 330, 345; and 'Joh for Canberra' campaign, 168–9; leader of the Opposition, 121, 154–5, 215, 226; sacks

Peacock from shadow ministry, 167; Treasurer, 58, 86; Tuckey coup against, 244
Howe, Brian, 340
Hu Qili, 121
Hu Yaobang, 128–9, 130, 131, 132–5, 136, 137, 184–5, 235, 237
Hun Sen, 177, 182–4, 186, 187–91
Hussein, Saddam, 291–7
Hyde, John, 117–18, 322

Ignatieff, Michael, 267
Industries Assistance Commission, 157
inflation, 115, 148
International Federation of Free Teachers' Unions, 359–60
International Labour Organization, 228
Iraq *see* Gulf War
Iraqi Loans Affair, 20
IT revolution, 263
Ivanov, Valeriy, 16–18, 20–1, 32–53

Japan, 263
Jiang Xiaosong, 361–4
'Joh for Canberra' campaign, 155, 162–8
Jones, Barry, 148
Jones, Bruce, 347
Journalists' Club, 45

Kakadu National Park, 251
Keating, Annita, 113, 145
Keating, Paul, 15, 85; ambition for Australia, 113; and Asia, 65; background, 76; carried away with rhetoric, 143; a crusader, 113–14; describes PM's office as Manchu Court, 156–7; disrespectful of Curtin, 141, 303; escaping work pressures, 142; and Garnaut, 65–6, 75–6; health, 141–2, 171, 222–3, 228–9; image as friend of the rich, 151–2; Lang's influence, 96–7, 117, 224, 303, 314; marriage failing, 334; as orator, 52–3, 90; on Peacock, 52–3; Paris option, 223, 225, 226, 232, 284, 303, 337; personality, 64, 65, 76, 112–13, 117, 222, 300; piggery purchase, 333; Placido Domingo of Australian politics, 302–4; political skills, 112; protective of family, 140, 141; and press gallery, 260; relationship with Hawke, 64–5, 119–21, 141, 145–6, 170; respect for old people, 96; 'rewriting history', 120, 258, 303; as a salesman, 77; tax return omitted, 156; tendency to get side-tracked, 144; work ethic, 222
Keating, Paul, leadership challenges: aims at 1988 transition, 221, 223, 224, 226; convinced of his destiny, 314; destabilising government,

346–7; early ambitions, 65–6; game of leak and counter-leak, 299–300; Hawke advised to organise transition, 330–1; Hawke forgives, 371; heir apparent to Hawke, 141; impatience in 1990, 262, 286, 299; Kirribilli pact, 231–2, 266, 299, 304, 313, 314, 327, 332; loses first challenge, 332, 334; 1988 budget a stepping stone, 224–5; position on Gulf War, 300–1; prepares alternative options, 333; promises Dawkins Treasury, 230; to resign as treasurer if unsuccessful, 223, 225; Richardson's role, 225–6, 314, 327, 332, 341–2; second challenge, 336, 341, 342, 346–7; stalemate January 1991, 313; stamina questionable, 222–3, 228–9; stocks high after WA Inc. performance, 329, 330; support for, 221–2, 326–7; unpopular with electorate, 152, 225, 266, 313; wants a showdown, 313; wins leadership, 355–6

Keating, Paul, treasurer: angered at rejection of consumption tax, 139; attacks critics of his handling of economy, 286–7; 'banana republic' remark, 138, 140–3, 144–5, 146, 156; behaviour in Cabinet, 305; believes he is running the country, 139, 144; 'bringing home the bacon' budget, 224, 231; and COAG, 333, 343, 344–5, 346; denigration of Hawke, 117, 139; economic management problems 1989, 242; embraces Accord, 30; floats the dollar, 61–3, 66–7; on Hawke and Tax Summit, 26, 114, 117; Hawke hints Keating not irreplaceable, 225, 226–7; Hawke threatens to replace with Dawkins, 227; Hayden on, 118; inexperience, 30–1; and Kelty and ACTU, 31; member Expenditure Review Committee, 79; 'mini-summit' announced without reference to Hawke, 143–5; monetary mismanagement apology, 289–90; and MX missile tests, 104; 1989/90 Budget, 243; presents himself as real man in charge, 143; 'the recession Australia had to have', 300; reservations about Iraq war, 298–9; resigns after first leadership challenge, 334–5; sceptical about Summit and Accord, 26; shadow treasurer under Hayden, 26; staff, 156; struggling as Treasurer, 64; and tax reform, 111, 112; and telecommunications policy, 305; Tuckey's personal attack in House, 139–40

Keegan, Des, 163, 245
Kelly, Paul, 64, 76–7, 112, 114, 116, 118, 120, 138, 170, 223–4, 229, 246, 258, 260, 299, 313, 323–4, 343
Kelman, Bryan, 30
Kelty, Bill, 24, 25, 31, 119, 231, 242, 244, 299
Kerin, John, 248, 252, 340, 346, 350–1
Khmer Rouge, 176–80, 190
Khomeini, Ayatollah, 220
Kirner, Joan, 320
Kirribilli pact, 231–2, 266, 299, 304, 313, 314, 327, 332
Kissinger, Henry, 107
Kitney, Geoff, 304
Klenbort, Josh, 235–6
Knight, Michael, 279
Korea, 30
Korporaal, Glenda, 337
Kyoto Protocol, 249

Labor in Power television documentary, 146
LandCare Australia, 252
Lane, Bill, 210–11
Lang, Jack, 96–7, 117, 224, 303, 305, 314
Laws, John, 91, 138, 142
Lee Kuan Yew, 12, 179, 198, 211
Leibler, Isi, 216–17, 218
Lewis, Austin, 269
Li Peng, 197–8, 239, 240
Liberal Party: and Hawke's family secrets, 87–8, 89–90; leader able to choose own ministry, 230; *see also* Fraser; Hewson; Howard; Peacock
Lipski, Sam, 337–8
local officers' wage case (PNG), 57
logging and Tasmanian wilderness, 161–2, 250, 251
Long Yongtu, 364, 365

McAuley, James, 280
McCarthy, Captain Brian, 244–5, 247
McClelland, Doug, 282–3
McGuinness, Paddy, 273–4
McHugh, Jeanette, 44–5
McHugh, Michael, 44–7, 49–51
Mack, Ted, 310
McLeay, Leo, 349, 350
McMahon, Billy, 157
Madrid Protocol, 258
Mahathir, Mohamad, 89, 195, 198–9
Major, John, 367
Mandela, Nelson, 202, 207, 208
Marr, David, 47, 50
Marsh, Jan, 24, 25
Medicare, 25, 80, 269, 340
Menzies, Robert, 16, 232–3, 262, 271
Metal Workers' Union, 25
Middle East: Hawke's doctorate from Hebrew University, 212–13; Hawke sees a role in Arab–Israeli dispute, 211–12; Hawke's views on Israel change, 212–13, 214, 217;

West Bank, 367–9; *see also* Gulf War
Mills, Stephen, 156–7, 213, 253, 268, 271, 295
Milne, Glenn, 241–2, 288
Mitterand, François, 255–6, 258
Molotov, Vyacheslav Mikhailovich, 33–4
Mount Channar Sino–Australian joint mining venture, 128
Mugabe, Robert, 203
Mulroney, Brian, 30, 201, 203, 293
Murdoch, Rupert, 276, 336
Murphy, Lionel, 16
Musharaff, President, 367
MX missile tests, 100–1, 102–11

Narrunga, 100
National and International Security Committee, 36, 38, 42–3, 45
National Crime Authority, 86
National Economic Summit Conference *see* Economic Summit
National Farmers' Federation, 252
National Party: 'Joh for Canberra' campaign, 155, 162–8; Sinclair leader, 155
New Caledonia, independence, 176
New Federalism, 315–17, 321, 333, 343; Brisbane conference, 319–20; correcting 'vertical fiscal imbalance', 320–1, 345; secretariat of public servants, 318–19; *see also* Council of Australian Governments (COAG)
Nihil, Grant, 354
Nixon, Richard, 125, 177
North West Cape, 100
Nuclear Disarmament Party, 99
nuclear waste storage, 325–6

O'Reilly, David, 286–7
Oakes, Laurie, 88–9, 260, 288, 306, 312, 330, 332
Olmert, Ehud, 367

Packer, Sir Frank, 54
Packer, Kerry, 68, 86, 87, 153, 276, 336
Palestine, 217–18
Papua New Guinea, 57
Parliament House, new, 218
Parliament House, old, 219
Peacock, Andrew, 332; attacks Hawke over Mick Young, 52; on Bjelke-Petersen, 166; Foreign Minister, 180; Grey Power ammunition for 1984 election, 93; Howard sacks from shadow ministry, 167; last chance to win in 1990, 262; 1990 election lost in debate with Hawke, 269–70; Opposition leader, 12, 38–9, 87, 89–90, 107, 117, 121, 155, 244, 261; on Summit, 31
Peres, Shimon, 213, 367
Petrov Affair, 16, 33–4

pilots' strike, 243, 244–7, 263, 264
Pine Gap, 99, 110–11
Pol Pot, 184
Poland, 228
Powell, Colin, 311–12, 365, 367, 369
Powell Plan for Palestine, 366–9, 372–5
Pratt, Richard, 358, 366
Premiers' Conferences, 317; 1987 Bjelke-Petersen humiliated over flat tax proposal, 167; 1991 devolution of some powers to states, 339–40; 1991 premiers want some taxing powers, 343, 344–5
Prescott, John, 29
press gallery, 37, 304; bored and cynical about the government by 1990, 287; and Hawke, 260–1, 340; and Keating, 260; and Keating's second challenge, 336–7; *see also* particular journalists
Price, Roger, 355
Prime Minister's XI cricket team, 67–8
Pritchett, Bill, 102
privatisation of airlines, 242–3, 305–6
protectionism, dismantling, 58, 322–5
public service: and Accord, 26–7; creating DFAT, 191–2; Hawke involves senior representatives, 193–4; Hawke's relationship with, 35; restructure, 191; Whitlam's relationship with, 35
Punch, Gary, 326–7, 336, 341, 354, 355

Qantas, 242–3
Qurei, Ahmed, 367, 368

radioactive waste storage, 325–6
Rainbow Warrior, 255, 258
Ramallah, 368
Ramos, Fidel, 363, 364, 365
Ramsay, Alan, 260
Ray, Brian, 153–4, 166
Ray, Robert, 72–3, 230, 284, 285, 294, 296, 351, 352, 354
Reagan, Ronald, 15, 99, 133, 147, 175, 178, 199, 210, 215–16, 234
recession, 82–3, 300
refuseniks (Soviet Jews), 17, 209–10, 215, 216
register of lobbyists, 40–1
Reid, Alan, 260
Reith, Peter, 287
Richardson, Dennis, 329, 330
Richardson, Graham, 90, 91, 104, 109, 158, 224, 225, 227, 247, 264, 267, 304; and Abeles, 281; background, 277–8; claims offered UK High Commissioner post, 282–3; and COAG initiatives, 343–4; and Dawkins, 227; Defence portfolio offered

and withdrawn, 283–6;
and environmental cause,
160–1; expects Transport and
Communications, 275–7,
280–1, 341; fund-raising his
source of power, 278; and
green preferences, 247–8,
250, 252, 272–3; and Hawke,
4, 73, 95–6, 275–6, 277, 278,
281–2, 283, 285–6, 355–6; and
Keating's ambitions, 170–1,
224, 285, 314, 327, 332, 335,
336, 341, 342, 347, 351, 352,
354–5; Minister for Health,
161; offered Social Security,
285; personality, 73, 277–8,
280; shadow of scandal, 161;
underworld associations,
277–8; *Whatever It Takes*, 280
Rigby, Richard, 132, 135
Robertson, Clive, 91
Robinson, Peter, 66–7
Roh Tae-woo, 194, 195
Roosevelt, Franklin D., 8
Royal Commissions: Ship
Painters and Dockers Union,
85–7, 89, 153; WA Inc., 327–8
Rudd, Kevin, 230–1, 319, 320,
346
Russell, Don, 300, 301, 352
Russia *see* Soviet Union
Ryan, Susan, 76, 90–1, 131

Scowcroft, Brent, 310–11
Seccombe, Mike, 349–50
Separation Wall, West Bank, 368
Shahin, Fred, 366

Shamir, Itzak, 211
Shelburne Bay project, 251
Ship Painters and Dockers
Union, 85–7, 89, 153, 264
Shultz, George, 101–2, 106–7,
110, 133, 181–2, 234
Simmonds, David, 354–5
Sinclair, Ian, 42, 154–5, 166, 229
Sinclair, Jean, 71, 74, 85, 223,
338–9, 342
Singapore, 179
Singleton, John, 165–6, 168–9,
274, 358
Slatyer, Professor Ralph, 325–6
Smark, Peter, 275
Smith, Dick, 246
Smith, Warwick, 259, 272–3,
348
Solidarity (Poland), 228
Sorby, Bob, 165, 217, 224
Soros, George, 367
South Africa: economic
assistance for future black
governments, 209; Springbok
tour 1970, 200; *see also*
apartheid
Soviet Jews (refuseniks), 17,
209–10, 215, 216
Soviet Union: Gorbachev
perceives a 'pre-crisis
situation', 215, 237; Hawke
foresees 'constructive
involvement' with, 214,
215; Hawke humiliated over
'refuseniks', 209–10; Hawke
meets PM Ryzhkov, 210;
invades Afghanistan, 175,

179; ramifications of collapse, 290–1
Springbok tour, 1971, 200
states; joint communiqué on national economic policy, 30; revenue from goods and services tax, 345; seek taxing powers, 343; tied grants, 318; *see also* COAG
Sterkey, Doug, 209
stock market crash 1987, 173, 220–1, 289–90
Stone, John, 13–14, 31, 55–6, 61, 63, 96, 119
Stoyles, Megan, 78–9
Structural Adjustment Committee, 30, 322
Sturgess, Gary, 319, 320, 344
Suharto, President, 198–9
summits *see* Economic Summit; Tax Summit
Symond, John, 366

Taiwan, 133–4, 194, 195, 196, 199
tariff reduction, 58, 322–5
Tasmanian Wilderness Society, 160, 162
tax evasion, 86–7
Tax Summit: broad-based consumption tax, 111–12, 115, 116; Business Council rejects, 117–18; election promise, 93–4, 111; Garnaut works on, 94, 111; Hawke wants in place before 1987 election, 115; Hawke and Keating, 116–17, 118, 119–20; Keating confident of 'tax cart', 114, 116–17, 120; opened, 117; opposition groups, 119; White Paper, 114, 116
Taylor, John, 205
Thatcher, Margaret, 201, 202, 203, 206, 210, 256
Tiananmen Square, 137, 189, 190, 197–8, 199, 237–9, 240
tied grants, 318
Toohey, Brian, 42, 87, 104, 151, 264, 357
tourism and pilots strike, 244, 246–7
Toyne, Philip, 250–1
trade union movement: deregistration of Builders Labourers' Federation, 29; distrusted by Hayden, 24; Hawke asks to accept wage cuts, 148; opposition to environmental issues, 249; Royal Commission into the Ship Painters and Dockers, 85–6; *see also* Accord
Trans-Australian Airlines, 242
Tricontinental collapse, 267
Tuckey, Wilson, 90, 117, 139–40, 244

unemployment, 7, 22, 83
Union of Friendship Societies, 17
United Nations Security Council: Australia condemns US invasion of Grenada,

174–5; Australia's role in ending Iran–Iraq war, 175–6; global trade embargo on Iraq, 294; and Hussein's invasion of Kuwait, 292–3, 296, 301, 307; resurrected after Cold War, 293

United States: considers protectionism, 147; economy flagging, 291; and formation of APEC, 195–6, 198–9; Hawke's relationship with, 175; Hayden's relationship with, 175; invades Grenada, 174–5; and MX missile tests, 100–1, 102–11; Reagan's Farm Bill, 147; relations with China, 240–1; supports measures against South Africa, 202; withdrawal from Vietnam, 177–8; *see also* American alliance (ANZUS)

uranium issue, 71, 83, 89, 150, 250

Uruguay Round, 192

Valder, John, 166
value-added tax, 111–12
van Leeuwen, Fred, 359–60
Vietnam: alliance with Soviet Union, 178–9, 186; invasion of Cambodia, 177, 178, 179, 186
Vietnam War, 15, 34, 295
Visbord, Ed, 60, 114

WA Inc., 267, 276, 327–8
wage cuts, 148

wage restraint, 29, 115, 242
Walsh, Eric, 38, 48, 92
Walsh, Geoff, 6, 72, 74, 76, 77, 81–2, 88, 91, 94, 96, 223, 274–5, 279–80
Walsh, Max, 334, 336, 340
Walsh, Peter, 5, 63, 78–9, 92, 149, 227, 248–9, 252, 268, 286, 327
Weber, Max, 8, 34, 260
welfare payment abuse, 93
West Bank, 367–9
White, Bob, 117
White, Dr Hugh, 99, 101–2, 103, 107, 110–11, 291, 292, 293, 294, 295, 297, 298–9, 300–1, 302, 309, 310–12
white shoe brigade, 153, 154, 162, 166, 167, 267
Whitlam, Gough, 157; and China, 122; leader of the Opposition, 1, 9, 10, 35, 74; life membership of Labor Party, 371; Prime Minister, 9, 122, 157
Whitlam, Margaret, 371
Whitlam government, 9; Big Spender tag, 24; 'free university education', 31, 150–1; economic management, 58; foreign policy, 58; and Iraqi Loans Affair, 20; legacy of social and cultural reform, 1
Wilderness Society, 162
Wilkinson, Marian, 275, 277–8, 281

Williams, Helen, 318–19, 344, 345
Willis, Ralph, 22–3, 116, 221, 149, 276, 289, 351; and Accord, 23, 25, 26; and ERC, 79, 148; expectations of Treasury, 25–6, 64; considered as High Commissioner to UK, 282; Industrial Relations Minister, 29; shadow treasurer under Hayden, 23–4, 25
Wilson, Sir Ronald, 308
Wolfensohn, James, 204–5, 206, 367, 369
women's movement, 164
Woolcott, Richard, 174–5, 176, 186–7, 191–2, 193, 196–9

World Heritage listings, 251
World Jewish Congress, 216
World Trade Organization, 191–2, 364
Wran, Neville, 13, 68, 74

Yeend, Sir Geoffrey, 35–6, 45–6, 47, 73, 74–5, 157
Young, Mick, 36, 42–3, 45–6, 47–8, 49, 52, 168
Young, Neil, 45, 47, 48

Zhao Ziang, 122, 125, 126–8, 131, 135, 136–7, 197–8, 237, 238, 239
Zhou-En-Lai, 197, 234